LONGMAN
INTERNATIONAL
TECHNICAL
TEXTS

Mechanical Engineering Craft Theory and related subjects Volume 2

R.L. Timings and O. Alabi

 LONGMAN

Pearson Education Limited
Edinburgh Gate, Harlow
Essex CM20 2JE, England
and Associated Companies throughout
the world

First published 1984
Thirteenth impression 2010

ISBN 978-0-582-65802-8

Printed in Malaysia, VP

**British Library Cataloguing in
Publication Data**

Timings, R.L.
    Mechanical engineering craft theory. –
(Longman international technical texts)
Vol. 2
1. Mechanical engineering
I. Title   II. Alabi, O.
621   TJ145
ISBN 0-582-65802-0

**Library of Congress Cataloging in
Publication Data**

Timings, R.L. (Roger Leslie)
    Mechanical engineering craft theory.
(Longman international technical texts)
Includes indexes.
    1. Mechanical engineering.   I. Alabi, O.
II. Title.   III. Series.
TJ146. T54   1983   621   82-14909
ISBN 0-582-65801-2 (v. 1)
ISBN 0-582-65802-0 (v. 2)

Acknowledgements

The publishers are grateful to the
following for permission to use
photographs in the text:
Association of British Machine Tool
Makers for figs. 7.20 and 7.21;
Cassell Ltd for fig. 9.1; Colchester
Lathe Co. for figs. 6.3, 6.4 and 6.16;
Coventry Gauge Ltd for fig. 4.24;
Duplex Electrical Machines for figs.
5.23 and 5.24; Firth Brown Tools Ltd
for fig. 8.5; Galtona Ltd for fig. 8.10;
Ghana Information Services for   .
fig. 2.1a; Jones and Shipman Ltd for
figs. 4.30, 6.21, 6.25, 9.5, 9.13 and
10.6; J. Langdon and Sons Ltd for
fig. 5.25a; Davy Loewy Ltd for
fig. 12.5; Machinery for fig. 7.19; B &
S Massey Ltd for figs. 12.3, 12.4,
12.6 and 12.8; Photowork Ltd for
figs. 7.16 and 7.18b; Rabone
Chesterman for figs. 4.9 and 4.10;
R.L. Timings for figs. 4.40, 5.14, 5.19,
5.22, 5.25b, 5.26, 6.14, 7.4, 7.17,
7.18a, 8.1, 9.7, 12.9 and 13.8;
Transafrica Pix for fig. 2.1b; UAC for
fig. 11.18; Windley Bros Ltd for
fig. 4.29; Zambia Information
Services for fig. 2.1c.
Permission to use tables 4.2, 4.3, 4.4,
4.5 and 4.6 was kindly granted by
British Standards Institute.

Contents

milling, Angle milling cutters, Form-relieved milling cutters, Inserted tooth cutters, Speeds and feeds for milling, Work-holding on the milling machine, Simple indexing, The universal dividing head, Sector arms, Helical milling, Cam milling, Miscellaneous indexing devices, Gear cutting

Fundamental principles, Grinding wheel specification, Wheel selection, Grinding defects, Wheel dressing and turning, Balancing the grinding wheel, Grinding wheel applications, Safety in the use of grinding wheels

Introduction to planning, Turning operations, Typical shaping operations, Milling, Combined operations

The need for maintenance, Installation, Preventative maintenance, Corrective maintenance, Unplanned maintenance

The forging process, Forging large components, Closed die forging, Upset forging, Cooling curves, The iron-carbon equilibrium diagram

(steel section), Annealing processes, Normalising, Hardening, Quenching, Tempering, Case-hardening

Thermal joining processes, Hard-soldering or brazing, Braze (bronze) welding, Full fusion welding

1. Calculations

Speed and feed rates

The calculation of speeds and feeds for a range of machine tools was introduced in *Mechanical Engineering Craft Theory and Related Studies: Part 1.* The basic cutting speed formula is:

$$S = \frac{\pi D N}{1000}$$

where: S = cutting speed m/min,
D = diameter in mm,
N = spindle speed in rev/min.
The spindle speed for a given application is most important to the craftsman and the formula can be rearranged as:

$$N = \frac{1000\,S}{\pi D}$$

When using grinding wheels it is sometimes necessary to calculate the maximum safe diameter for a given wheel, knowing the spindle speed and the safe surface or cutting speed for the wheel. The formula would then be written as:

$$D = \frac{1000\,S}{\pi N}$$

The speed and feed rates used throughout this book (and in *Part 1*) are

Table 1.1   High Speed Steel Twist Drills

Material being drilled	Cutting speed m/min	Drill diameter mm	Rate of feed mm/rev
Aluminium	70–100	1·0– 2·5	0·040–0·060
Brass	35–50	2·6– 4·5	0·050–0·100
Bronze (phosphor)	20–35	4·6– 6·0	0·075–0·150
Cast iron (grey)	25–40	6·1– 9·0	0·100–0·200
Copper	35–45	9·1–12·0	0·150–0·250
Steel (mild)	30–40	12·1–15·0	0·200–0·300
Steel (medium carbon)	20–30	15·1–18·0	0·230–0·330
Steel (Alloy – high tensile)	5–8	18·1–21·0	0·260–0·360
Thermo-setting plastic	20–30	21·1–25·0	0·280–0·380
(Low speed due to abrasive properties)			

summarised in Tables 1.1 to 1.5 inclusive for use in examples and exercises.

Example 1.1   Calculate the spindle speed for a high-speed steel twist drill 2·5 mm diameter, cutting brass.

Solution

$$N = \frac{1000\,S}{\pi D}$$

where: S = 45 m/min (from Table 1.1),
D = 2·5 mm diameter, π = 3·142.

$$N = \frac{1000 \times 45}{3·142 \times 2·5}$$
$$= \underline{5729 \text{ rev/min (to nearest}}$$
$$\underline{\text{whole number)}}$$

Note: Some drilling machines do not have such a high spindle speed as this so care has to be taken in feeding the drill into the work. One of the main causes of failure in small-diameter drills is running them too slowly so that the feed per revolution is excessive.

Example 1.2   Calculate the time taken for a 5 mm diameter high-speed steel twist drill to penetrate a mild steel plate 10 mm thick.

Solution

$$N = \frac{1000\,S}{\pi D}$$

where: S = 35 m/min (from Table 1.1),
D = 5 mm diameter, π = 3·142.

Table 1.2 Turning, Shaping and Planing Tools

Material to be cut	Cutting speed in m/min					
	High-speed steel	Super high-speed steel	Stellite	Tungsten carbide	'Mixed' carbide	Diamond
Aluminium and aluminium alloys	70–100	90–120	over 200	over 350		Up to 700
Brass (alpha)	50–80	70–100	120–200	250–350		
Brass (free-cutting)	70–100	90–120	170–250	350–500		
Bronze (ordinary)	35–70	50–85	75–150	150–250		Up to 700
Bronze (high tensile)	25–35	30–45	60–75	125–150		
Cast iron (soft)	35–50	45–60	60–90	90–125		
Cast iron (medium)	25–30	30–40	45–70	60–100		
Cast iron (hard)	15–20	18–25	35–55	50–80		
Cast iron (chilled)	8–12	10–15	18–25	25–40		
Copper	35–70	50–90	75–150	100–300		Up to 500
Magnesium and 'electron' alloys	85–135	110–150				
Malleable cast iron	25–30	30–40	45–70	60–100		
Mazak (zinc-based, die-casting alloy)	70–100	90–120				
Monel metal	15–20	18–25	25–45	50–80		
Nimonic alloys	7–10	9–12	17–25		25–50	
Steel (free-cutting, mild)	35–50	45–60	70–120		100–200	
Steel (up to 600 MN/m² tensile)	30–35	40–45	60–100		80–150	
Steel (600–900 MN/m² tensile)	15–25	20–30	40–70		60–100	
Steel (900–1200 MN/m² tensile)	10–15	12–17	30–50		50–80	
Steel (over 1200 MN/m² tensile)	5–10	7–12	20–35		40–60	
Steel, manganese	5–10	7–12	20–35		40–60	
Steel, stainless, martensitic and ferritic	10–15	12–17	30–50		50–80	
Steel, stainless, austenitic and heat-resistant	7–12	9–15	22–40		35–70	
Thermosetting plastics	35–50	45–60	70–120	100–200	—	

$$N = \frac{1000 \times 35}{3 \cdot 142 \times 5}$$
$$= \underline{2228 \text{ rev/min (to nearest}}$$
$$\underline{\text{whole number)}}$$

Feed/rev for a 5 mm diameter drill is 0·1 mm/rev for a medium-strength material (Table 1.1).

now:

$$t = \frac{60\,P}{NF}$$

where: t = time (s), P = depth of penetration (mm), N = spindle speed (rev/min), F = feed (mm/rev).

therefore:

$$t = \frac{60 \times 10}{2228 \times 0 \cdot 1}$$
$$= \underline{2 \cdot 7 \text{ s}}$$

Table 1.3 Centre Lathe Turning

Material being turned	Feed in millimetres per revolution		
	High-speed	Stellite	Carbide
Aluminium alloys	0·2 –1·0	0·15–0·8	
Brass (ductile)	0·2 –1·0	0·15 0·8	
Brass (free-cutting)	0·2 –1·5	0·15–1·0	
Bronze (ordinary)	0·2 –1·0	0·15–0·8	
Bronze (high tensile)	0·1 –0·5	0·08–0·3	
Cast iron (soft)	0·2 –1·0	0·15–0·8	
Cast iron (medium)	0·15–0·7	0·10–0·5	0·05 to 0·4
Cast iron (hard)	0·08–0·3	0·05–0·2	
Copper	0·2 –1·0	0·15–0·8	
Steel (free cutting)	0·2 –1·0	0·15–0·8	
Steel (medium carbon)	0·15–0·7	0·10–0·5	
Steel (high carbon)	0·1 –0·5	0·08–0·3	
Steel (alloy, high-tensile)	0·08–0·3	0·05–0·2	
Thermo-setting plastics	0·2 –1·0	0·1 –0·8	

Table 1.4 High Speed Steel Milling Cutters

Material Being Milled	Cutting Speed m/min	Feed Per Tooth (mm)			
		Face Mill	Slab Mill	Side & Face	End Mill
Aluminium	70–100	0·2 –0·8	0·2 –0·6	0·15 –0·4	0·1 –0·4
Brass (ductile)	35–50	0·15–0·6	0·15–0·5	0·1 –0·3	0·07 –0·3
Brass (free-cutting)	50–70	0·2 –0·8	0·2 –0·6	0·15 –0·4	0·1 –0·4
Bronze (Phosphor)	20–35	0·07–0·3	0·07–0·25	0·05 –0·15	0·04 –0·15
Cast Iron (Grey)	25–40	0·1 –0·4	0·1 –0·3	0·07 –0·2	0·05 –0·2
Copper	35–45	0·1 –0·4	0·1 –0·3	0·07 –0·2	0·05 –0·2
Steel (mild)	30–40	0·1 –0·4	0·1 –0·3	0·07 –0·2	0·05 –0·2
Steel (medium carbon)	20–30	0·07–0·3	0·07–0·25	0·05 –0·15	0·04 –0·15
Steel (alloy)	5–8	0·05–0·2	0·05–0·15	0·035 –0·1	0·025 –0·1
Thermo-setting plastic	20–30	0·15–0·6	0·15–0·5	0·1 –0·3	0·07 –0·3

Table 1.5 Abrasive Wheels

Application	Surface Speed (m/min)	Notes
Cylindrical grinding	1675–2000	(i) Except where specified it is assumed that vitrified bonds are used.
Internal grinding	600–1200	
Surface grinding	1200–1520	
Off-hand (Dry)	1200–1620	(ii) The maximum speed stated by the abrasive wheel maker must NOT be exceeded.
(with coolant)	1520–1820	
Cutting off (rubber, shellac and bakelite bands)	2750–3650	

Notes
Although the rate of feed may seem low for the softer materials, the problem is one of 'clogging' which may cause tool failure if too high a feed rate is used.

The lower rate of feed associated with carbide tooling is due to the brittle nature of this material. However the overall rate of material removal is very much higher than for high speed steel because of the higher cutting speeds employed.

Feeds for *planing and shaping* are the same as for turning except that instead of being measured in mm/revolution they are *measured in mm/cutting stroke*.

Where a heavily interrupted cut occurs as in the 'chain' planing of a number of castings, the feed rate should be reduced.

Example 1.3 Calculate the time taken to turn a grey (soft) cast iron component 100 mm long by 70 mm diameter using a carbide-tipped tool. Cutting speed from Table 1.2 is 100 m/min. Feed rate from Table 1.3 is 0·4 mm/rev.

Solution

$$N = \frac{1000\,S}{\pi D}$$

where: $S = 100$ m/min, $D = 70$ mm diameter, $\pi = 3·142$.

$$N = \frac{1000 \times 100}{3·142 \times 70}$$
$$= 455 \text{ rev/min /to nearest whole number)}$$

Rate of feed = 0·4 mm/rev
$$= 0·4 \times 455 \text{ mm/min}$$
$$= 182 \text{ mm/min}$$

3

Thus, time taken to traverse 100 mm

$$= \frac{100}{182} \text{ min}$$

$$= \frac{100 \times 60}{182} \text{ s}$$

$$= \underline{33 \text{ s}.}$$

Example 1.4 A high-speed steel milling cutter, 125 mm diameter, is set to run at 90 rev/min whilst cutting mild steel. Calculate whether or not this is a suitable spindle speed.
Solution

$$S = \frac{\pi D N}{1000}$$

where: $\pi = 3$, $D = 125$ mm diameter, $N = 90$ rev/min.

$$S = \frac{3 \times 125 \times 90}{1000}$$

$$= 33 \cdot 75 \text{ m/min.}$$

Reference to Table 1.4 shows that for mild steel, a cutting speed between 30 and 40 m/ min is suitable when using high speed steel milling cutters. Therefore, the spindle speed selected in this example (90 rev/min) is satisfactory.

Example 1.5 Using the following data, calculate the time taken to complete a 300 mm long cut using a slab mill. Diameter of cutter = 100 mm; number of teeth = 8; feed/tooth = 0·05 mm; cutting speed = 30 m/min.
Solution

$$N = \frac{1000 \, S}{\pi D}$$

where: $S = 30$ m/min,

$D = 100$ mm diameter $\pi = 3$.

$$N = \frac{1000 \times 30}{3 \times 100}$$

$$= 100 \text{ rev/min} \dots\dots\dots\dots(1)$$

Feed/rev = feed/tooth × number of teeth
  = 0·05 × 8
  = 0·4 mm/rev

Table feed = feed/rev × rev/min
per minute (from (1))
  = 0·4 × 100
  = 40 mm/min ....(2)

Time to complete 300 mm long cut

$$= \frac{\text{length of cut}}{\text{table feed/min}}$$
  (from (2))

$$= \frac{300}{40}$$

$$= \underline{7 \cdot 5 \text{ min}}$$

Example 1.6 Calculate the maximum diameter grinding wheel that can be used on a surface grinding machine with a spindle speed of 2300 rev/min.
Solution From Table 1.5 it will be seen that for a vitrified grinding wheel (the type normally used for surface grinding) the maximum surface speed recommended when surface grinding is 1520 m/min.

$$D = \frac{1000 \, S}{\pi N}$$

where: $S = 1520$ m/min, $\pi = 3 \cdot 142$, $N = 2300$ rev/min.

$$D = \frac{1000 \times 1520}{3 \cdot 142 \times 2300}$$

$$= \underline{210 \text{ mm to nearest whole number}}$$

For several popular makes of small surface grinders used in toolrooms, the recommended wheel size is 200 mm which falls within the range of this calculation. *Always* check that the manufacturer's recommended wheel speed is the same or less than the spindle speed of the machine. Over-speeding a wheel can cause it to burst with serious (sometimes fatal) results.

Example 1.7 An external, cylindrical grinding machine is fitted with a 350 mm diameter by 25 mm wide grinding wheel rotating at 1350 rev/min. Calculate:
a) The surface speed of the grinding wheel.
b) The work speed and feed for a medium-carbon steel component 75 mm diameter.
Solution

a) $$S = \frac{\pi D N}{1000}$$

where: $\pi = 3 \cdot 142$, $D = 350$ mm diameter, $N = 1350$ rev/min.

$$S = \frac{3 \cdot 142 \times 350 \times 1350}{1000}$$

$$= \underline{1485 \text{ m/min (to nearest whole number)}}$$

b) The work speed for cylindrical grinding is normally taken to be the same as for a finishing cut when turning. From Table 1.2, 25 m/min is suitable for a medium-carbon steel component.

$$N = \frac{1000 \, S}{\pi D}$$

where: S = 25 m/min, D = 75 mm
diameter, π = 3:142

$$N = \frac{1000 \times 25}{3 \cdot 142 \times 75}$$
$$= \underline{106 \text{ rev/min}}$$

The feed when cylindrically grinding is normally taken as $\frac{2}{3}$ the width of the grinding wheel per revolution of the work piece (see Chapter 9).

Feed per revolution of workpiece
$$= \frac{2}{3} \times 25 \text{ mm}$$

Thus, feed per minute
= feed/rev × rev/min (work)
$$= \frac{2}{3} \times 25 \times 106$$
= 1767 mm/min
Table feed (work)
= $\underline{1 \cdot 8 \text{ m/min}}$ (to 1 decimal place)

Example 1.8 Calculate the number of cycles (double strokes)/min for shaping aluminium if the stroke length is 250 mm. From Table 1.2, 100 m/min is a suitable cutting speed for a HSS tool.
Solution

$$\text{Cycles/min} = \frac{1000 \, S}{2 \, L}$$

where: S = 100 m/min, L = stroke length (mm).

$$\text{cycles/min} = \frac{1000 \times 100}{2 \times 250}$$
$$= \underline{200}$$

Example 1.9 Calculate the traverse rate for a shaping machine equipped with a 6 mm lead traverse screw and a 30-tooth ratchet wheel, when set to an increment of 3 teeth per double stroke (cycle). If the machine is set to run at 50 double strokes/min calculate the time to traverse 24 mm.
Solution

$$\text{Traverse rate} = \frac{6 \text{ mm}}{30 \text{ teeth}} \times 3 \text{ teeth}$$
$$= 0 \cdot 6 \text{ mm/double stroke}$$

Time to traverse 24 mm at 50 double strokes/min

$$\text{Time taken} = \frac{\text{width of component}}{\text{traverse rate} \times \text{double strokes/min}}$$
$$= \frac{24}{0 \cdot 6 \times 50}$$
$$= \frac{4}{5} \text{ min or 48 s}$$

Introduction to trigonometry

Figure 1.1(a) shows two triangles – their angles are the same but the lengths of their sides vary. To keep the angles equal, the lengths of the corresponding sides must vary in the ratios shown. Thus, the size of the acute angles in any right-angled triangle can be stated as the ratio of any two of the sides.

Figure 1.1(b) shows how the sides of a right-angled triangle are named. The ratios of these sides for a given angle have the special names shown in Fig. 1.1(c). They are called the *trigonometrical ratios*. Only the right-angled triangle will be considered in this chapter, and for most workshop purposes this is sufficient. At a more advanced level, trigonometry can be applied to any sort of triangle and angles of any magnitude.

Trigonometrical tables

These are used to solve problems involving the sides and angles of triangles (trigonometry). Tables of natural tangents, natural sines, and natural cosines can be found in sets of mathematical tables and many engineers reference and pocket books. In the following explanations, the figures in this book should be compared with standard trigonometrical tables.

Natural tangents

The tangents of angles are used to solve problems related to right-angled triangles when the length of the hypotenuse is not known (Fig. 1.1(c)).

Figure 1.2(a) shows how to read tables of natural tangents. The tangent of the angle 14° 39′ is 0·2614. For any right-angled triangle in which the ratio of the length of the opposite side to the adjacent side is 0·2614 the angle will be 14° 39′. Examples of triangles of different sizes in which the ratios of the opposite and adjacent sides are the same are shown in Fig. 1.2(b). As you will see they all have the same angles.

Natural sines

The sines of angles are used when the length of the hypotenuse and the length of the side opposite the angle is known (Fig. 1.1(c)). Figure 1.3(a) shows how to read tables of natural sines. The sine of

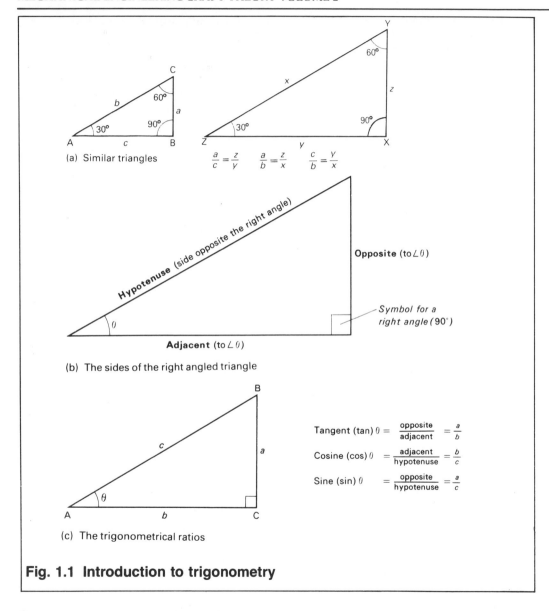

(a) Similar triangles

$$\frac{a}{c} = \frac{z}{y} \qquad \frac{a}{b} = \frac{z}{x} \qquad \frac{c}{b} = \frac{y}{x}$$

Hypotenuse (side opposite the right angle)

Opposite (to $\angle\theta$)

Symbol for a right angle (90°)

Adjacent (to $\angle\theta$)

(b) The sides of the right angled triangle

Tangent (tan) $\theta = \dfrac{\text{opposite}}{\text{adjacent}} = \dfrac{a}{b}$

Cosine (cos) $\theta = \dfrac{\text{adjacent}}{\text{hypotenuse}} = \dfrac{b}{c}$

Sine (sin) $\theta = \dfrac{\text{opposite}}{\text{hypotenuse}} = \dfrac{a}{c}$

(c) The trigonometrical ratios

Fig. 1.1 Introduction to trigonometry

the angle 34° 17′ is 0·5633. Figure 1.3(b) shows three triangles with the angle 34° 17′ and for each one the ratio of the lengths of the opposite sides to the hypotenuse is 0·5633 for this angle.

Natural sines are used for setting the *sine-bar* when measuring angles accurately (see Chapter 4).

Natural cosines

The cosines of angles are used when the length of the hypotenuse and the length of the side adjacent to the angle is known. Figure 1.4(a) shows how to read tables of natural cosines.
Note: the numbers in the mean difference columns are *subtracted* when using cosines.

Figure 1.4(b) shows three triangles with the angle 49° 34′ and for each one the ratio of the lengths of the adjacent sides to the lengths of the hypotenuses is 0·6485.

Further examples of the use of trigonometry are given by Figs. 1.5 to 1.7 inclusive.

Angles and tapers

Tapers may be stated as shown in Fig. 1.8 as:
1 the included angle,
2 the half angle,
3 the gradient.

When turning or grinding cylindrical components the taper is symmetrical about the centre line. Under these circumstances it is usual to give the *included angle* as shown in Fig. 1.8(a). To machine this angle the machine is set to the *half angle* as shown in Fig. 1.8(b).

Alternatively the taper may be given as a gradient (e.g. 1 in 16) as shown in Fig. 1.8(c). Again, the machine is set to half the gradient for cylindrical components.

For simple rectangular wedges the actual angle of taper or the gradient may be given as shown in Fig. 1.8(d). In this instance the machine is set to the full angle.

Helix angle

The helix is defined as the path of a point around an imaginary cylinder such that the circumferential and axial velocities of the point maintain a constant ratio.

Figure 1.9(a) shows a helix plotted around a cylinder. The lead of the helix is the distance the point moves parallel to the axis of the cylinder for each complete revolution. A helix may be made by cutting out a paper triangle and wrapping it round a tube or cylinder, therefore, a helix is an inclined plane. The helix angle ($\theta°$) is shown in Fig. 1.9(b). The helix angle can be calculated if the diameter and lead of the helix is known:

$$\tan \theta = \frac{\text{lead}}{\text{circumference}}$$
$$= \frac{\text{lead}}{\pi \times \text{diameter}}$$

A screw thread is a practical example of a helix.

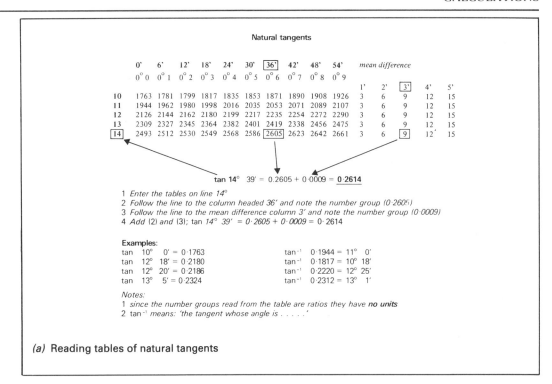

(a) Reading tables of natural tangents

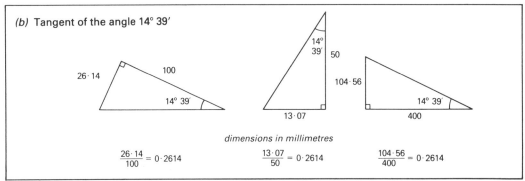

(b) Tangent of the angle 14° 39′

dimensions in millimetres

Fig. 1.2 Natural tangents

Natural sines

	0'	6'	12'	18'	24'	30'	36'	42'	48'	54'	mean difference				
	0°0	0°1	0°2	0°3	0°4	0°5	0°6	0°7	0°8	0°9					
											1'	2'	3'	4'	5'
30	5000	5015	5030	5045	5060	5075	5090	5105	5120	5135	3	5	8	10	13
31	5150	5165	5180	5195	5210	5225	5240	5255	5270	5284	2	5	7	10	12
32	5299	5314	5329	5344	5358	5373	5388	5402	5417	5432	2	5	7	10	12
33	5446	5461	5476	5490	5505	5519	5534	5548	5563	5577	2	5	7	10	12
34	5592	5606	5621	5635	5650	5664	5678	5693	5707	5721	2	5	7	10	12

sin 34° 17' = 0·5621 + 0·0012 = **0·5633**

1 *Enter the tables on line 34°*
2 *Follow the line to the column headed 12' and note the number group (0·5621)*
3 *Follow the line to the mean difference column 5' and note the number group (0·0012)*
4 *Add (2) and (3): sin 34° 17' = 0·5621 + 0·0012 = 0·5633*

(a) Reading tables of natural sines

Examples:

sin 30° 0' = 0·5000	sin⁻¹ 0·5150 = 31° 0'
sin 31° 30' = 0·5225	sin⁻¹ 0·5388 = 32° 36'
sin 32° 45' = 0·5409	sin⁻¹ 0·5558 = 33° 46'
sin 33° 1' = 0·5448	sin⁻¹ 0·5594 = 34° 1'

Notes:
1 *Since the number groups read from the table are ratios they have* **no units**
2 *sin⁻¹ means: 'the sine whose angle is . . . . .*

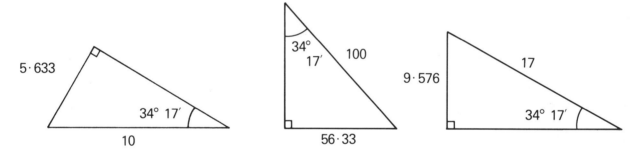

dimensions in millimetres

$$\frac{5\cdot633}{10} = 0\cdot5633 \qquad \frac{56\cdot33}{100} = 0\cdot5633 \qquad \frac{9\cdot576}{17} = 0\cdot5633$$

(b) Sine of the angle 34° 17'

Fig. 1.3 Natural sines

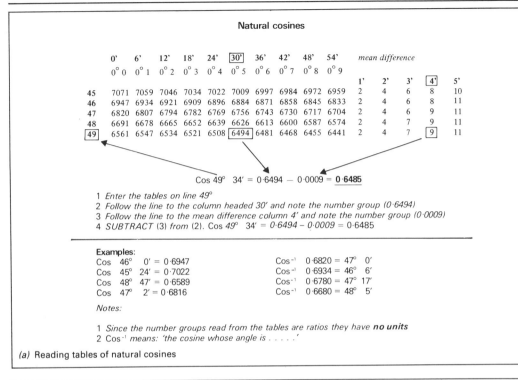

Natural cosines

	0'	6'	12'	18'	24'	30'	36'	42'	48'	54'	mean difference				
	0°0	0°1	0°2	0°3	0°4	0°5	0°6	0°7	0°8	0°9					
											1'	2'	3'	4'	5'
45	7071	7059	7046	7034	7022	7009	6997	6984	6972	6959	2	4	6	8	10
46	6947	6934	6921	6909	6896	6884	6871	6858	6845	6833	2	4	6	8	11
47	6820	6807	6794	6782	6769	6756	6743	6730	6717	6704	2	4	6	9	11
48	6691	6678	6665	6652	6639	6626	6613	6600	6587	6574	2	4	7	9	11
49	6561	6547	6534	6521	6508	6494	6481	6468	6455	6441	2	4	7	9	11

$$\text{Cos } 49° \; 34' = 0·6494 - 0·0009 = \mathbf{0·6485}$$

1 *Enter the tables on line 49°*
2 *Follow the line to the column headed 30' and note the number group (0·6494)*
3 *Follow the line to the mean difference column 4' and note the number group (0·0009)*
4 *SUBTRACT (3) from (2). Cos 49° 34' = 0·6494 – 0·0009 = 0·6485*

Examples:

Cos 46° 0' = 0·6947	Cos⁻¹ 0·6820 = 47° 0'
Cos 45° 24' = 0·7022	Cos⁻¹ 0·6934 = 46° 6'
Cos 48° 47' = 0·6589	Cos⁻¹ 0·6780 = 47° 17'
Cos 47° 2' = 0·6816	Cos⁻¹ 0·6680 = 48° 5'

Cos 46° 0' = 0·6947   Cos⁻¹ 0·6820 = 47° 0'
Cos 45° 24' = 0·7022   Cos⁻¹ 0·6934 = 46° 6'
Cos 48° 47' = 0·6589   Cos⁻¹ 0·6780 = 47° 17'
Cos 47° 2' = 0·6816   Cos⁻¹ 0·6680 = 48° 5'

Notes:

1 *Since the number groups read from the tables are ratios they have* **no units**
2 *Cos⁻¹ means: 'the cosine whose angle is . . . . .'*

(a) Reading tables of natural cosines

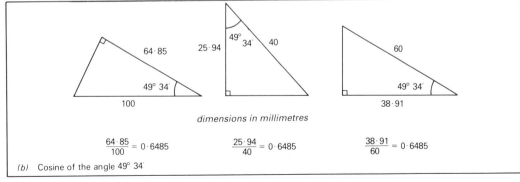

dimensions in millimetres

$$\frac{64·85}{100} = 0·6485 \qquad \frac{25·94}{40} = 0·6485 \qquad \frac{38·91}{60} = 0·6485$$

(b) Cosine of the angle 49° 34'

Fig. 1.4 Natural cosines

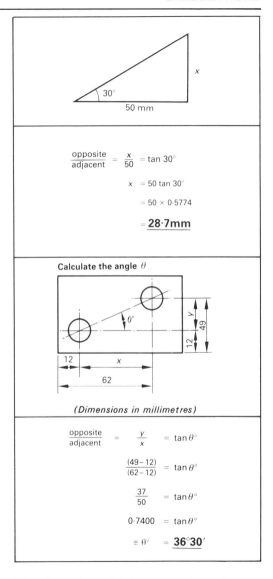

$$\frac{\text{opposite}}{\text{adjacent}} = \frac{x}{50} = \tan 30°$$

$$x = 50 \tan 30°$$

$$= 50 \times 0·5774$$

$$= \mathbf{\underline{28·7mm}}$$

Calculate the angle θ

(Dimensions in millimetres)

$$\frac{\text{opposite}}{\text{adjacent}} = \frac{y}{x} = \tan\theta°$$

$$\frac{(49-12)}{(62-12)} = \tan\theta°$$

$$\frac{37}{50} = \tan\theta°$$

$$0·7400 = \tan\theta°$$

$$\equiv \theta° = \mathbf{36°30'}$$

Fig. 1.5 Use of trigonometry – tangents

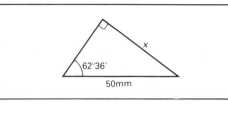

$$\frac{opposite}{hypotenuse} = \frac{x}{50} = \text{Sin } 36° 36'$$

$$x = 50 \sin 36° 36'$$

$$= 50 \times 0.8878$$

$$= \underline{44.99\text{mm}}$$

Calculate the checking dimension x

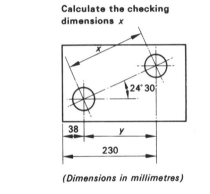

(Dimensions in millimetres)

$$\frac{opposite}{hypotenuse} = \frac{x}{y} = \sin 35°$$

$$\frac{(40 - 11.32)}{x} = \sin 35°$$

$$\frac{28.68}{x} = 0.5736$$

$$x = \frac{28.68}{0.5736}$$

$$= \underline{50\text{mm}}$$

Fig. 1.6
Use of trigonometry – sines

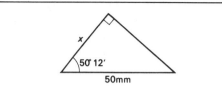

$$\frac{adjacent}{hypotenuse} = \frac{x}{50} = \cos 50° 12'$$

$$x = 50 \cos 50° 12'$$

$$= 50 \times 0.6401$$

$$= \underline{32.005\text{mm}}$$

Calculate the checking dimensions x

(Dimensions in millimetres)

$$\frac{adjacent}{hypotenuse} = \frac{y}{x} = \cos 24° 30'$$

$$\frac{(230 - 38)}{x} = \cos 24° 30'$$

$$\frac{182}{x} = 0.9100$$

$$x = \frac{182}{0.9100}$$

$$\underline{200\text{mm}}$$

Fig. 1.7
Use of trigonometry – cosines

Example 1.10 Calculate the helix angle for a lead of 5 mm and a diameter of 50 mm ($\pi = 3.142$).
Solution

$$\tan \theta = \frac{lead}{circumference}$$

$$= \frac{lead}{\pi \times diameter}$$

$$= \frac{5}{50 \, \pi}$$

$$= \frac{1}{31.42}$$

$$= 0.0318$$

$$\therefore \theta = \underline{1° 49' \text{ (from tables)}}$$

Screw-cutting calculations

Although most modern lathes are fitted with quick-change gear boxes which are very convenient when setting up to cut a screw thread, some older machines and most special-purpose machines have to be set by physically changing the gears that couple the lead screw to the machine spindle. These gears are variously referred to as the *change wheels* or the *end-train gears*. The calculation of suitable trains of gears for screw cutting will now be explained for cutting:
1 inch threads with an inch lead screw;
2 metric threads with an inch lead screw;
3 metric threads with a metric lead screw;
4 inch threads with a metric lead screw.

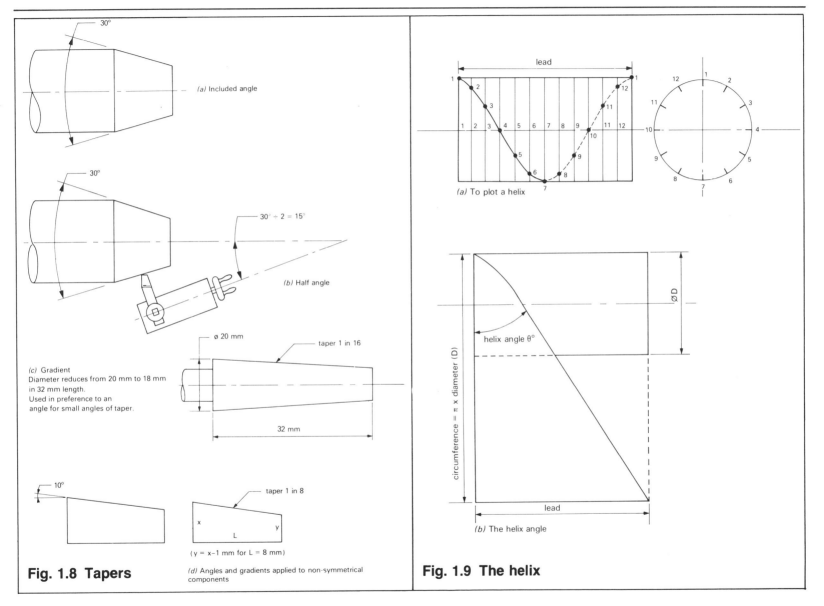

30°

(a) Included angle

30°

30° ÷ 2 = 15°

(b) Half angle

(c) Gradient
Diameter reduces from 20 mm to 18 mm
in 32 mm length.
Used in preference to an
angle for small angles of taper.

ø 20 mm

taper 1 in 16

32 mm

10°

taper 1 in 8

x

L

y

(y = x–1 mm for L = 8 mm)

Fig. 1.8 Tapers

(d) Angles and gradients applied to non-symmetrical components

lead

1 2 3 4 5 6 7 8 9 10 11 12

(a) To plot a helix

12 1 2 3 4 5 6 7 8 9 10 11

ø D

helix angle θ°

circumference = π × diameter (D)

lead

(b) The helix angle

Fig. 1.9 The helix

Inch to inch

The general formula can be stated as follows where tpi = threads per inch:

$$\frac{\text{driver gear}}{\text{driven gear}} = \frac{\text{pitch to be cut}}{\text{pitch of lead screw}}$$
$$= \frac{\text{tpi of lead screw}}{\text{tpi to be cut}}$$

Example 1.11 Given a set of change wheels from 20 teeth to 120 teeth inclusive in steps of 5 teeth, calculate the gear trains for the following screw threads on a lathe fitted with a 4 tpi lead screw.
a) 9 tpi   b) 0·2 inch pitch c) 27 tpi
Solution

a) $\dfrac{\text{Driver}}{\text{Driven}} = \dfrac{\text{tpi of lead screw}}{\text{tpi to be cut}}$

$$= \frac{4}{9}$$

$$= \frac{4 \times 5}{9 \times 5}$$ (multiply top and bottom × 5 as gears have multiples of 5 teeth)

$$= \frac{20}{45}$$

Thus the gear train would use a 20-tooth gear driving a 45-tooth gear through an intermediate or idler gear as shown in Fig. 1.10(a). The intermediate or idler gear does not influence the overall ratio, it ensures that the lead screw and work rotate in the same direction so that a *right-hand* thread will be cut. Two idler gears will reverse the direction of rotation of the lead screw as shown in

Fig. 1.10(b) and a *left-hand* thread will be cut.

b) $\dfrac{\text{Driver}}{\text{Driven}} = \dfrac{\text{pitch to be cut}}{\text{pitch of lead screw}}$

$$= \frac{0 \cdot 2}{0 \cdot 25}\,(4\text{ tpi lead screw} = \tfrac{1}{4}\text{ in pitch})$$

$$= \frac{0 \cdot 2 \times 10}{0 \cdot 25 \times 10}$$

$$= \frac{20}{25}$$

Thus the gear train would use a 20-tooth gear driving a 25-tooth gear through an intermediate or idler gear. To reduce wear and help to build up the centre distance between the driving shaft and the lead screw it would be more likely that a 40-tooth gear driving a 50-tooth gear would be used.

c) $\dfrac{\text{Driver}}{\text{Driven}} = \dfrac{\text{tpi lead screw}}{\text{tpi to be cut}}$

$$= \frac{4}{27}$$

$$= \frac{4 \times 5}{27 \times 5}$$

$$= \frac{20}{135}$$

However, the standard set of gears does not exceed 120 teeth, so in this instance a simple train cannot be used. The compound train shown in Fig. 1.10(c) has to be used and the gears are calculated as follows.

First, factorise the ratio from c).

$$\frac{20}{135} = \frac{5 \times 4}{15 \times 9}$$

Second, multiply up the new ratios to suit the available gears:

$$\frac{5 \times 6}{15 \times 6} = \frac{30}{90}$$

and:

$$\frac{4 \times 5}{9 \times 5} = \frac{20}{45}$$

Therefore, the compound train becomes:
a 30-tooth gear driving an intermediate 90-tooth gear keyed to the intermediate shaft and driving a 20-tooth gear which in turn drives a 45-tooth gear on the lead screw as shown in Fig. 1.10(c). In this instance the intermediate gears do influence the overall ratio. This is referred to as a *compound gear train*.

Metric to inch

Example 1.12 Calculate the change wheels to cut a 1·5 mm pitch using a 4 tpi lead screw.
Solution

$$\frac{\text{Driver}}{\text{Driven}} = \frac{5\,NP}{127}$$

where: N = tpi lead screw, P = pitch to be cut (mm).

$$= \frac{5 \times 4 \times 1 \cdot 5}{127}$$

$$= \frac{30}{127}$$

This would be a gear train using a 30-tooth gear to drive a 127 metric conversion gear (standard) through an intermediate gear in a simple train (Fig. 1.10(a)).

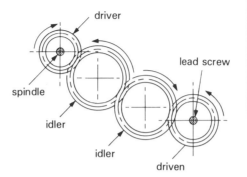

(a) Simple train – single idler (driver and driven gears rotate in the same direction)

driver (20-tooth, Example 1.11)
intermediate or idler (any convenient size)
driven (45-tooth, Example 1.11)
spindle
lead screw

(b) Simple train – two idlers – reverse drive

driver
spindle
idler
idler
lead screw
driven

first driver (30-tooth, Example 1.11)
first driven, intermediate (90-tooth, Example 1.11)
spindle
second driven (45-tooth, Example 1.11)
second driver, intermediate (20-tooth, Example 1.11)
lead screw

(c) Compound train

Fig. 1.10 Gear trains

Metric to metric

Example 1.13 Calculate the change wheels to cut a 1·75 mm pitch thread on a lathe fitted with a 6 mm pitch lead screw.
Solution

$$\frac{\text{Driver}}{\text{Driven}} = \frac{\text{pitch to be cut}}{\text{pitch of lead screw}}$$

$$= \frac{1·75}{6}$$

$$= \frac{175}{600}$$

$$= \frac{35}{120}$$ (after cancelling top and bottom by 5 to bring the gears within the standard range)

This would give a 35-tooth gear driving a 120-tooth gear in a simple train. (Fig. 1.10(a))

Inch to metric

Example 1.14 Calculate the change wheels to cut a 0·125 inch pitch screw thread on a lathe fitted with a 6 mm pitch lead screw (25·4 mm = 1 inch)
Solution

$$\frac{\text{Driver}}{\text{Driven}} = \frac{\text{pitch to be cut}}{\text{pitch of lead screw}}$$

$$= \frac{0·125 \times 25·4}{6}$$

$$= \frac{0·125 \times 127}{6 \times 5}$$ (note use of 127-tooth metric conversion gear)

$$= \frac{127}{240}$$

Since a 240-tooth gear is not available a compound train must be used.

$$\frac{127}{240} = \frac{1 \times 127}{3 \times 80}$$

$$= \frac{20}{60} \times \frac{127}{80} \text{ (multiply } \tfrac{1}{3} \text{ by 20 top and bottom)}$$

Thus a 20-tooth gear would drive a 60-tooth intermediate gear keyed to a 127-tooth gear driving an 80-tooth gear in a compound train (see Fig. 1.10(c)).

Approximate gear trains (continued fractions)

Consider Example 1.12 in which a 1·5 mm pitch thread is to be cut on a lathe fitted with a 4 tpi lead screw. The ratio arrived at was:

$$\frac{\text{driver}}{\text{driven}} = \frac{30}{127}$$

Had the 127-tooth gear not been available, a close approximation could be obtained using a compound train. To do so the following method must be used.

A series of alternative gear ratios is calculated using a *continued fraction*. The denominators are obtained as follows.

The fraction is inverted so that the numerator becomes the denominator and the division is carried out. The remainder is divided into each previous denominator. This process is continued until there is no remainder.

```
30)127 (4
   120
      7 )30 (4
        28
          2 )7 (3
            6
             1 )2 (2
               2
```

The continued fraction is built up as follows:

$$\cfrac{1}{4 + \cfrac{1}{4 + \cfrac{1}{3 + \cfrac{1}{2}}}}$$

The next step is to calculate the convergent series of ratios as follows:

1   $= \dfrac{1}{4}$

2   $= \dfrac{1}{4 + \frac{1}{4}} = \dfrac{1}{4\frac{1}{4}} = \dfrac{1}{\frac{17}{4}} = \dfrac{4}{17}$

3   $= \dfrac{1}{4 + \cfrac{1}{4 + \frac{1}{3}}} = \dfrac{1}{4 + \frac{1}{4\frac{1}{3}}} = \dfrac{1}{4\frac{3}{13}} = \dfrac{13}{55}$

4   $= \dfrac{1}{4 + \cfrac{1}{4 + \cfrac{1}{3 + \frac{1}{2}}}} \quad \dots \quad = \dfrac{30}{127}$

Convergent gear ratios are:

$\frac{1}{4}$	$\frac{4}{17}$	$\frac{13}{55}$	$\frac{30}{127}$
least accurate approximation		most accurate approximation	ideal ratio

The most accurate approximation that can be built up from the available gears is then selected:

$$\frac{\text{drivers}}{\text{driven}} = \frac{13}{55} = \frac{13 \times 1}{11 \times 5} = \frac{65}{55} \times \frac{20}{100}$$

Thus a compound gear train would be used with a 65-tooth gear driving a 55-tooth gear on the intermediate shaft keyed to a 20-tooth gear driving a 100-tooth gear on the lead screw.

The accuracy of this approximation can be calculated as follows.

$$\frac{\text{Driver}}{\text{Driven}} = \frac{5PN}{127}$$

$$\frac{13}{55} = \frac{5P \times 4}{127}$$

$$P = \frac{13}{55} \times \frac{127}{5 \times 4}$$

$$= 1{\cdot}5009 \text{ mm compared with the 1·5 mm required.}$$

For all practical purposes this error can be ignored.

Continued fractions are also used for working out the gear trains used when differential indexing with the dividing head on the milling machine.

Multi-start screw threads

With a single start thread, any increase in lead results in a corresponding increase in the depth of the thread and a corresponding weakening of the component as the cross-sectional area of the core of the thread is decreased.

One way to avoid this effect is to use a multi-start thread. This results in an increase in lead with no increase in pitch or reduction in component strength. Figure 1.11 compares the pitch and lead of a single-start, two-start and a three-start helix. The techniques for cutting such threads are discussed in Chapter 6. The relationship between lead and pitch is given by the following expression:

$$L = NP$$

where: L = lead, N = number of starts, P = pitch.

Example 1.15 Calculate the lead for a three-start thread having a pitch of 2·5 mm.

Solution

$$L = NP$$

where: N = 3, P = 2·5 mm.

$$L = 3 \times 2\cdot5$$
$$= \underline{7\cdot5 \text{ mm}}$$

The main difference between single-start and multi-start threads is in the magnitude of the helix angle, particularly when cutting square threads. It may become necessary to incline the tool at the helix angle, this will prevent the tool interfering with the flanks of the screw thread. This is further considered in Chapter 6.

Example 1.16 Calculate the helix angle for a) a single-start square thread of 5 mm pitch
and b) a four-start square thread of 6 mm pitch. In each case the top diameter of the component is 40 mm (π = 3·142).

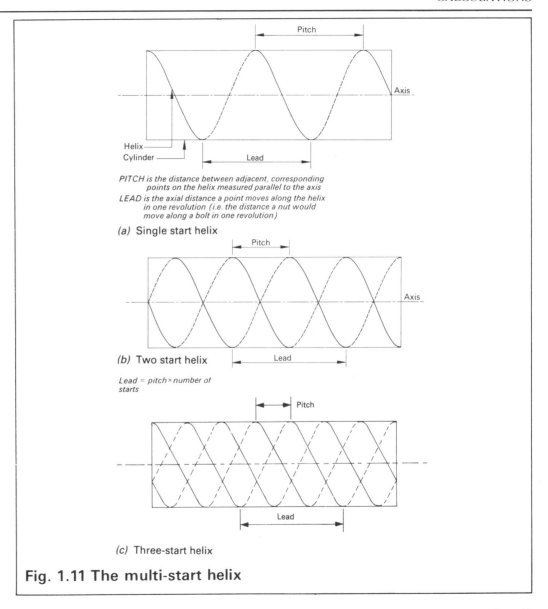

PITCH is the distance between adjacent, corresponding points on the helix measured parallel to the axis

LEAD is the axial distance a point moves along the helix in one revolution (i.e. the distance a nut would move along a bolt in one revolution)

(a) Single start helix

(b) Two start helix

Lead = pitch × number of starts

(c) Three-start helix

Fig. 1.11 The multi-start helix

Solution

a) Pitch = lead = 6 mm
Mean diameter = 40 – 3 = 37 mm (see Fig. 1.12)
Let θ = helix angle, then

$\tan \theta = \dfrac{\text{lead}}{\text{mean circumference}}$ (see p. 7).

$\tan \theta = \dfrac{6}{37}\pi$

$= 0.0516$

$\therefore \theta = \underline{2° 57'}$

b) Lead = $\overline{4 \times \text{pitch}} = 4 \times 6 = 24$ mm

$\tan \theta = \dfrac{\text{lead}}{\text{mean circumference}}$

$= \dfrac{24}{37}\pi$

$= 0.2064$

$\therefore \theta = \underline{11° 40'}$

Such a 'quick' thread as this would put a considerable strain on the lathe whilst being cut. A very heavy-duty machine would be required, and except for a one-off thread for maintenance purposes it would be better to thread mill this component.

Simple indexing

Direct and universal dividing heads are used on milling machines and are described with the aid of illustrations in Chapter 8. Indexing is the rotation of the workpiece so that slots, grooves, teeth, etc., can be cut in the face or periphery of the workpiece.

The direct dividing head is very simple and is used mainly for batch work with simple components where a small number of cuts are to be made.

For example, milling the hexagon head on a special bolt.

More widely used is the universal dividing head which has a 40:1 reduction drive between the crank and the workpiece as shown in Fig. 8.21. Different makes have different hole arrangements in the index plate. For example, a typical index plate has the following hole circles:

side 1: 24, 25, 28, 30, 34, 37, 38, 39, 41, 42 and 43 holes
     2: 46, 47, 49, 51, 53, 54, 57, 58, 59, 62 and 66 holes

This index plate will be used as the basis of all the following examples in this chapter.

Since the gear ratio between the crank (plunger arm) and the spindle of the dividing head is 40:1, it follows that for 1 revolution of the plunger arm the spindle and the work will rotate $\frac{1}{40}$ revolution. Therefore:

Revolutions of the work	Revolutions of the crank
1	40
1	40
$\dfrac{1}{2}$	$\dfrac{40}{2}$
$\dfrac{1}{4}$	$\dfrac{40}{4}$
$\dfrac{1}{n}$	$\dfrac{40}{n}$

Thus for n divisions of the workpiece the crank will rotate $\dfrac{40}{n}$ revolutions.

Example 1.17   To index the following divisions using the index plate above.
a) 12 b) 17 c) 25 d) 36 e) 52 f) 86

Solution

a) Indexing $= \dfrac{40}{n} = \dfrac{40}{12} = 3\dfrac{4}{12} = 3\dfrac{8}{24}$
i.e. 3 complete turns of the plunger arm and 8 holes in a 24-hole circle.

b) Indexing $= \dfrac{40}{n} = \dfrac{40}{17} = 2\dfrac{6}{17} = 2\dfrac{12}{34}$
i.e. 2 complete turns of the plunger arm and 12 holes in a 34-hole circle.

c) Indexing $= \dfrac{40}{n} = \dfrac{40}{25} = 1\dfrac{15}{25}$
i.e. 1 complete turn of the plunger arm and 15 holes in a 25-hole circle.

d) Indexing $= \dfrac{40}{n} = \dfrac{40}{36} = 1\dfrac{4}{36} = 1\dfrac{6}{54}$
i.e. 1 complete turn of the plunger arm and 6 holes in a 54-hole circle.

e) Indexing $= \dfrac{40}{n} = \dfrac{40}{52} = \dfrac{30}{39}$
i.e. no complete turn, only 30 holes in a 39-hole circle.

f) Indexing $= \dfrac{40}{n} = \dfrac{40}{86} = \dfrac{20}{43}$
i.e. 20 holes in a 43-hole circle.

Angular indexing

Sometimes the angle between flats or grooves is given instead of the number of flats or grooves required. Since there are 360° in a complete revolution of the work, then one revolution of the crank will index the work through $\dfrac{360}{40} = 9°$

$$\text{Indexing} = \frac{\text{angle required (degrees)}}{9}$$

$$= \frac{\text{angle required (minutes)}}{540}$$

Example 1.18 To index the following angles using the index plate given above.
a) 38° b) 50° 30′ c) 62° 20′
Solution

a) Indexing $= \dfrac{38}{9} = 4\dfrac{2}{9} = 4\dfrac{12}{54}$

i.e. 4 turns of the plunger arm and 12 holes in a 54-hole circle.

b) Indexing $= \dfrac{50°\ 30′}{9} = \dfrac{3030′}{540}$

$= 5\dfrac{330}{540} = 5\dfrac{33}{54}$

i.e. 5 turns of the plunger arm and 33 holes in a 54-hole circle.

c) Indexing $= \dfrac{62°\ 20′}{9°} = \dfrac{3720′}{540}$

$= 6\dfrac{500}{540} = 6\dfrac{50}{54}$

i.e. 6 turns of the plunger arm and 50 holes in a 54-hole circle.

Differential indexing

Divisions outside the range of a standard index plate can be obtained by *differential indexing*.

Instead of the index plate being clamped to the body of the dividing head, it is coupled to the work spindle by a gear train (see Chapter 8). It will be seen that as the plunger arm is rotated through the required number of turns,

the index plate is advanced or retarded through a small amount automatically. The calculation of the gear train will now be considered. The same index plate will be used as previously and the gears available are: 24(2), 28, 32, 40, 48, 56, 64, 72, 86, 100 teeth. The expression used is difficult to prove, but easy to use, it is:

$$\frac{\text{driver}}{\text{driven}} = \frac{N_1 - N_2}{N_2} \times 40$$

where: N_1 = required divisions,
N_2 = actual divisions available on the index plate.

Example 1.19 Using the index plate and gears already given, calculate the gear train for 119 divisions.
Solution

Indexing required $= \dfrac{40}{n}$

$= \dfrac{40}{119}$

but this is not available with the index plate selected, therefore, the near approximation of $\frac{40}{120}$ will be used as a basis for calculation.

Indexing available $= \dfrac{40}{120}$

$= \dfrac{1}{3}$

$= \dfrac{10}{30}$

i.e. 10 holes of the plunger arm in a 30-hole circle.
To calculate the gears:

$$\frac{\text{driver}}{\text{driven}} = \frac{N_1 - N_2}{N_2} \times 40$$

where: N_1 = 119, N_2 = 120.

$$\frac{\text{driver}}{\text{driven}} = \frac{119 - 120}{120} \times 40$$

$= -\dfrac{1}{3}$ (the minus sign can be disregarded as it only indicates the direction of rotation)

$= \dfrac{24}{72}$

Note: The *negative* sign indicates that the index plate rotates in the same direction as the plunger arm, i.e. one idler gear between the driver and the driven gears.

A *positive* sign indicates that the index plate rotates in the opposite direction to the plunger arm, i.e. two idler gears. Sometimes a compound train will be required, and for very awkward divisions – usually angular – an approximate train using the continued fraction (p. 14) will have to be used.

Compound indexing

This is an older technique than differential indexing and is no longer much used. Instead of moving the index plate automatically through a gear train it is moved manually. That is, the plunger arm is located by the holes on the front of the plate and the plate is located by a plunger on the dividing head body engaging the holes on the back of the plate.

This method has the following disadvantages. A double-sided plate is required but most dividing heads have a

number of single-sided plates.
It is an inconvenient and tedious technique since two indexing operations have to be made on the same plate for each division.

Suppose the plunger arm is indexed 15 holes in a 28-hole circle, on side 1 of the index plate introduced previously, and then the index plate together with the plunger arm is indexed 1 hole in a 54-hole circle on side 2 of the plate.

If both movements are made in the same direction the total indexing will have been:

$$\frac{15}{28} + \frac{1}{54} = \frac{405}{756} + \frac{14}{756}$$

$$= \frac{419}{756} \text{ on the work.}$$

Therefore, the movement of the workpiece will have been:

$$\frac{419}{756} \times \frac{1}{40} = 0\cdot014 \text{ revolutions}$$

If the plate had been turned in the opposite direction to the crank the indexing would have been:

$$\frac{15}{28} - \frac{1}{54} = \frac{405}{756} - \frac{14}{756} = \frac{391}{756}$$

Therefore, the movement of the workpiece would have been:

$$\frac{391}{756} \times \frac{1}{40} = 0\cdot013 \text{ revolutions}$$

By compounding in this way a large range of divisions may be obtained.

If n is the number of divisions required on the work, and $\frac{40}{n}$ is the indexing (see p. 16), then the fractions representing the two movements must give $\frac{40}{n}$ when adding or subtracting. Further, the denominators of the fractions must be numbers available as hole circles on the index plate. Their determination is largely trial and error. Further applications of the use of the dividing head together with worked examples are given in Chapter 8.

Exercises

1. (a) Calculate the spindle speed for a high speed steel twist drill 6 mm diameter if the cutting speed is 33 rev/min.
   (b) Calculate the time taken for the drill to travel 18 mm through the workpiece if the feed rate is 0·5 mm/rev. ($\pi = {}^{22}/_{7}$).
2. Calculate the maximum diameter of grinding wheel that can be used on a grinding machine having a spindle speed of 2500 rev/min, if the safe working speed for the grinding wheel is 1500 rev/min. ($\pi = 3\cdot1416$).
3. (a) Use tables to find the following trigonometrical values:
   sin 47°, sin 36° 11′, cos 36°, cos 76° 33′, tan 50°, tan 7° 57′.
   (b) Use tables to find the following angles:
   $\sin^{-1} 0\cdot1736$, $\sin^{-1} 0\cdot9100$, $\cos^{-1} 0\cdot6401$, $\cos^{-1} 0\cdot3368$, $\tan^{-1} 2\cdot1543$, $\tan^{-1} 3\cdot5857$.
4. Complete Table 1.6 with reference to the triangle shown in Fig. 1.12.

a	b	c	$\angle\theta°$
10·2	30·5		
		100	30°
	76·1		42° 11′
25·4			62° 37′

Dimensions in millimetres.

Table 1.6

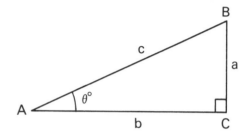

Fig. 1.12

5. Calculate the helix angle for a thread having a lead of 150 mm and a mean diameter of 50 mm ($\pi = 3\cdot142$).
6. Calculate the gear trains for cutting the following screw threads on a centre lathe fitted with a 4 TPI lead screw. The gears available are 25t to 120t inclusive in steps of 5t plus 2 × 20t and a 127t conversion gear.
   (a) 12 TPI, (b) 22 TPI, (c) 0·15 inch pitch, (d) 2·75 mm pitch, (e) 3·4 mm pitch.
7. Calculate the gear trains for cutting the following screw threads on a centre lathe fitted with a 6 mm pitch lead screw. The gears available are 25t to 120t inclusive in

steps of 5t plus 2 × 20t and a 127t conversion gear.
(a) 1·75 mm pitch, (b) 0·8 mm pitch,
(c) 6·25 mm pitch, (d) 19 TPI,
(e) 0·125 inch pitch.

8. The index plate for a universal dividing head (40:1 drive) has the following hole circles available:
Side (1) 24, 25, 28, 30, 34, 37, 38, 39, 41, 42 and 43 holes;
Side (2) 46, 47, 49, 51, 53, 54, 57, 58, 59, 62 and 66 holes.
(a) Calculate the indexing for each of the following number of divisions: 14, 19, 30, 48, 56, 106.
(b) Calculate the indexing for each of the following angular divisions: 49° 30′, 61° 20′, 8° 15′, 25° 36′.

9. A dividing head (40:1 drive) is fitted with the index plate previously used in question 8. The gears available are: 24 (2), 28, 32, 40, 48, 56, 64, 72, 86, 100 teeth. Calculate the gear train for the differential indexing of (a) 93 divisions, (b) 153 divisions.

10. Calculate the helix angle for a three-start square thread of 8 mm pitch. The top diameter is 50 mm for this component.

2. Engineering science

Friction

Figure 2.1(a) shows a small boat being pulled out of the water. It requires many men using a lot of strength to pull it up a ramp. However Fig. 2.1 (b and c) show how a laden boat and even a very big raft can easily be moved in water using long sticks and very little effort.

The boat was difficult to handle on dry land because of the *friction* between the wooden hull of the boat and the sand and stones. But the boats on the water had their hulls separated from the sand and stones by a layer of water. The water acted as a *lubricant* and reduced

Fig. 2.1 Friction and lubrication

the friction, thus making the boats easier to move.

Friction is defined as the resistance which opposes the motion of one surface across another.

Figure 2.2 shows a magnified section through two mating surfaces from which any form of lubricant has been removed. The entire weight of the sliding block is supported on the high spots only. Thus the stresses at these points will be very large and interlocking will take place.

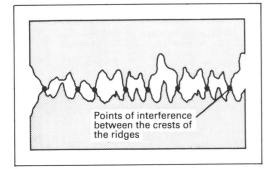

Fig. 2.2 Unlubricated surfaces

Friction

When seen under a microscope a smooth, machined surface is made up of ridges and craters (Fig. 2.2). All the weight is supported at the tips of the ridges which tend to bite into each other and become interlocked as shown in the enlarged diagram. Before movement can take place the interlocked ridges have to shear along the planes AA or BB or both. The resisting (friction) force is the sum of these shear forces. The

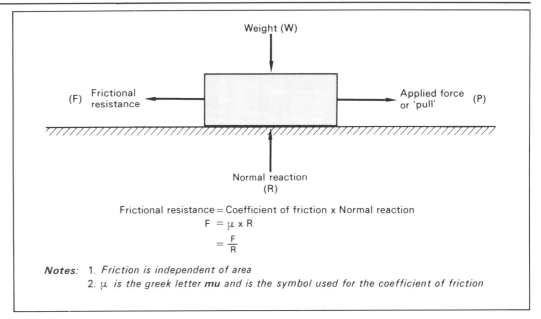

Frictional resistance = Coefficient of friction x Normal reaction

$$F = \mu \times R$$

$$= \frac{F}{R}$$

Notes: 1. *Friction is independent of area*
2. *μ is the greek letter **mu** and is the symbol used for the coefficient of friction*

Fig. 2.3 Coefficient of friction

continual interlocking and shearing away of the ridges causes the wear that occurs between unlubricated (dry) moving surfaces.

Seizure

Certain metals have an affinity for each other and when subject to local heating and intense pressure they will weld together. This has happened in the dry bearing shown in Fig. 2.2. Two bearing surfaces that have become welded together in this way are said to have *seized*. The resisting force created and the wear that takes place under such conditions will be much greater than for

simple friction. In extreme cases of seizure the resisting force may be so great that the shaft is broken or the bearing is torn from its housing before slip occurs.

Movement requires the application of a suitable force to the sliding member of the bearing. This force must be great enough and applied in the right direction to shear apart the interlocked high spots.

This applied force is resisted by the friction force (Fig. 2.3). The friction force is a reaction force and never exceeds the applied force. However, there is a limit to the value it may reach.

If the magnitude of the applied force is increased beyond this limit slipping will take place.

It should also be noted that static friction is greater than moving (kinetic) friction. Table 2.1 gives typical values for the coefficient of limiting friction at the point of slipping.

Table 2.1   Typical Co-efficients of Limiting Friction

Materials in dry contact	μ
Cast iron on brass	0·15
Steel on brass	0·16
Steel on cast iron	0·20
Steel on steel	0·25
Cast iron on leather	0·55
Brake lining (Ferodo) on cast iron	0·60
Rubber on asphalt	0·65
Rubber on concrete	0·70

Some examples showing how problems involving friction can be calculated are given in Fig. 2.4.

Friction may be undesirable where it causes wear and waste of power or desirable as in a belt drive where friction prevents slipping (Fig. 2.5).

Lubrication

If dry surfaces can be kept apart the friction between them disappears and they do not weld together under pressure. The purpose of a lubricant (oil or grease) is to separate the surfaces slightly. The friction between the surfaces is replaced by the internal friction of the lubricant. This is of a

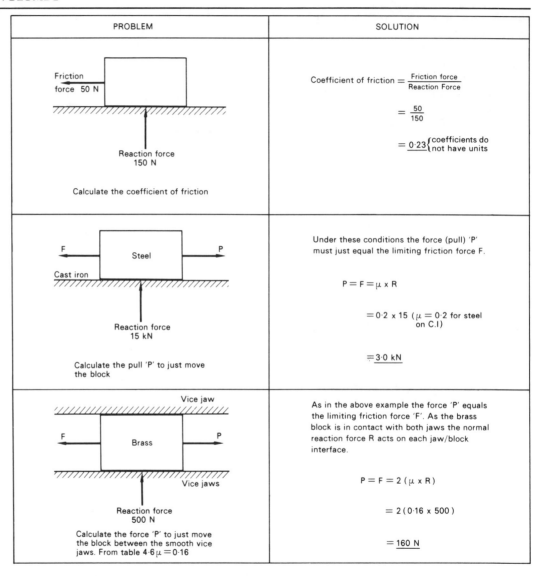

PROBLEM	SOLUTION
Friction force 50 N · Reaction force 150 N · Calculate the coefficient of friction	Coefficient of friction $= \dfrac{\text{Friction force}}{\text{Reaction Force}}$ $= \dfrac{50}{150}$ $= 0\cdot23$ {coefficients do not have units}
F · Steel · P · Cast iron · Reaction force 15 kN · Calculate the pull 'P' to just move the block	Under these conditions the force (pull) 'P' must just equal the limiting friction force F. $P = F = \mu \times R$ $= 0\cdot2 \times 15$ ($\mu = 0\cdot2$ for steel on C.I) $= 3\cdot0$ kN
Vice jaw · F · Brass · P · Vice jaws · Reaction force 500 N · Calculate the force 'P' to just move the block between the smooth vice jaws. From table 4·6 $\mu = 0\cdot16$	As in the above example the force 'P' equals the limiting friction force 'F'. As the brass block is in contact with both jaws the normal reaction force R acts on each jaw/block interface. $P = F = 2(\mu \times R)$ $= 2(0\cdot16 \times 500)$ $= 160$ N

Fig. 2.4 Examples involving friction

much lower value. Figure 2.6 shows a lubricated bearing.

The lubricant prevents metal-to-metal contact. The correct lubrication of the machines and equipment in a workshop:

1 prevents power-loss through friction;
2 minimises the amount of wear on the metal;
3 prevents overheating of the metal surfaces;
4 avoids breakdowns;
5 makes the equipment more pleasant to use.

Properties of a lubricant

Correct viscosity The lubricant must be the correct thickness (viscosity) for the bearing to which it is applied. Too thick and it will cause drag resulting in loss of power and overheating. Too thin and it may not be able to support the load on the bearing. Oils tend to become thinner as they warm up but modern technology has produced better oils where changes in viscosity due to temperature fluctuations are kept to a minimum.

Acidity The lubricant must be free from acids that could corrode the shaft and bearing.

High temperature If the oil has to work at high temperatures it must not form a sludge.

Non-abrasive The lubricant must be perfectly clean, so that no abrasive matter enters the bearings causing rapid wear.

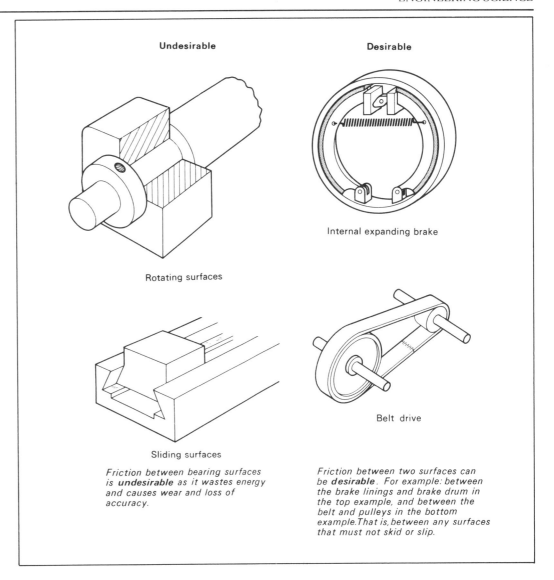

Undesirable

Desirable

Internal expanding brake

Rotating surfaces

Belt drive

Sliding surfaces

*Friction between bearing surfaces is **undesirable** as it wastes energy and causes wear and loss of accuracy.*

*Friction between two surfaces can be **desirable**. For example: between the brake linings and brake drum in the top example, and between the belt and pulleys in the bottom example. That is, between any surfaces that must not skid or slip.*

Fig. 2.5 Friction in practice

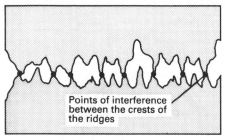

Unlubricated (dry) surfaces

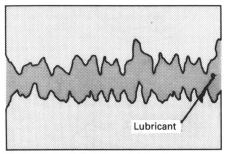

Surfaces separated by a lubricant

Fig. 2.6 Lubrication

Types of lubricant

Figure 2.7 shows three different types of bearing. Each one uses the oil in a different way and requires it to have different properties. It is essential that the right oil is used for each job.

Most bearing lubricants are based on *mineral oils*. These are the oils that are pumped up from oil wells and then refined. They are supplied to the user either as a liquid oil or as a grease which is a mixture of oil and a suitable soap.

Another sort of oil is the *fatty oil*

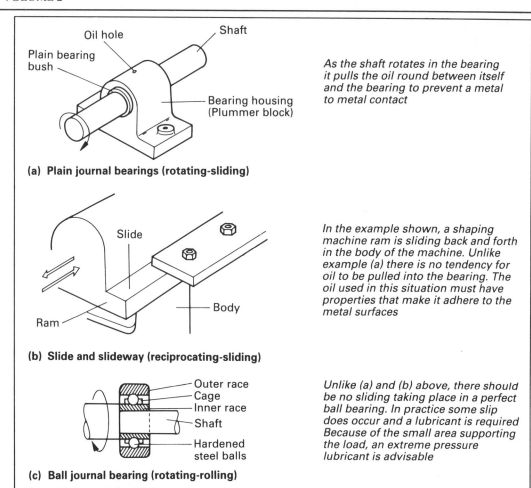

(a) Plain journal bearings (rotating-sliding)

As the shaft rotates in the bearing it pulls the oil round between itself and the bearing to prevent a metal to metal contact

(b) Slide and slideway (reciprocating-sliding)

In the example shown, a shaping machine ram is sliding back and forth in the body of the machine. Unlike example (a) there is no tendency for oil to be pulled into the bearing. The oil used in this situation must have properties that make it adhere to the metal surfaces

(c) Ball journal bearing (rotating-rolling)

Unlike (a) and (b) above, there should be no sliding taking place in a perfect ball bearing. In practice some slip does occur and a lubricant is required Because of the small area supporting the load, an extreme pressure lubricant is advisable

Fig. 2.7 Types of bearings

extracted from animal lards and vegetable seeds. These oils can withstand higher pressures than mineral oils. Unfortunately, they are expensive, sludge easily, and deteriorate by bacterial attack (go rancid). Generally, they are blended with mineral oils to lessen these defects.

'Hard' or dry lubricants are also used under certain difficult conditions. For example, stainless steel sheets are often treated by hot dipping in a phosphate solution before being formed in a power press. The dipped steel dries out before use and is left with its surface coated with phosphorus compounds. These compounds and compounds of sulphur and chlorine have excellent extreme pressure-lubricating properties. A surface so treated does not deteriorate in storage.

Between them the major oil companies market a bewildering number of oils and greases. These are compounded by specialists under closely controlled conditions. The selection of oils for a particular application is also best left to experts, and for this reason the manufacturers of machine tools and equipment always supply very full lubrication instructions in the operator handbooks supplied with their products. The information given includes:
1 type of lubricant and alternatives;
2 place of application;
3 method of application;
4 frequency of application.

This information must be obeyed most carefully, as any deviation can lead to breakdown, loss of guarantee rights, serious accidents, and a machine that is not working at maximum efficiency.

You may wonder how the wrong lubricant can cause a serious accident. The author once saw the flywheel of a large air compressor break free from its shaft when the shaft seized through lack of oil. This flywheel smashed through a brick wall and hurtled into a crowded machine shop!

When there are a large number of machines of varying types in a workshop it is not economical to stock all the various lubricants specified in the handbooks. Under these conditions, it is advisable to call in a reputable oil company to carry out a lubrication survey. They will draw up a chart standardising on the minimum number of suitable lubricants that will give effective service and they will give full instructions as to the application of these lubricants.

Storage, identification and handling

It should now be apparent that the oil stores of any workshop can contain a wide variety of oils and greases. To mix these oils, to use the wrong oil, or to allow water and dirt to contaminate the oil, will lead to serious trouble. Therefore, it is essential that the various lubricants are properly stored. The following points must be taken into consideration.
1 Fire prevention precautions.
2. Correct and easy identification.
3 Methods of dispensing the lubricants without having to manhandle the drums and barrels.
4 An adequate quantity of measuring cans to prevent contamination.
5 Light, dust-free surroundings.
6 Proper lifting tackle, as full barrels are very heavy.

Fire prevention All oils are flammable to some degree and some cutting fluids are very flammable. If large quantities of oil are to be stored, they should be kept in a fireproof building away from crowded workshops. In any case, an oil store should be well ventilated to get rid of any explosive vapours and to keep the lubricants cool. Electric light fittings should be fireproof to 'Buxton Specification', and the wiring should be fireproof and mineral insulated. The lights should be controlled from a switch *outside* the stores as sparking often occurs when the switch is operated. Adequate fire extinguishers should be provided adjacent to the entrance to the stores but outside it. Suitable types of extinguisher will be specified by the local fire brigade.

Identification Drums (45·5 litres) and barrels (204·5 litres) are identified by code numbers and names stencilled on by the suppliers. These often become partly obliterated in transit and it is essential that they are checked, and re-marked if necessary, upon receipt.

If a number of people are to use the stores a more positive method of identification is required. A colour code system is ideal. A chart is provided and displayed in the oil stores allocating a different colour to each type of lubricant. This colour can then be carried through by painting a flash on the barrel, its dispenser, measuring cans, oil-guns, and even to the machine tool where a ring of the same colour can be painted around the appropriate oil or grease nipple.

Dispensing the lubricant It is not easy to pour oil from full drums and, because of their weight, it is impossible to pour from barrels. However, there are two other methods by which oil can be dispensed easily from both drums and barrels.

1 The drums and barrels are racked up on a frame which has a ramp leading up to it and provided with taps as shown in Fig. 2.8. In all oil drums and barrels there is a bung with a standard thread which may be replaced by a tap. The drawback to this method is that the taps are inclined to drip as they are always under pressure. Proper drip trays must be provided to catch the oil and this oil must never be poured back into the drums.

2 The drums and barrels are up-ended on the floor and lift pumps are used. This saves handling and there is less chance of dripping since the pump is not under pressure.

Unfortunately, the pumps have a higher initial cost than the taps and the drums and barrels take up more room.

Mechanical advantage, velocity ratio and efficiency

The lever was introduced in *Mechanical Engineering Craft Theory and Related Studies: Part 1* as a simple machine. A lever can be used to magnify an effort in order to overcome a load.

The ability of a machine to magnify the effort (or reduce it) is called the *mechanical advantage* (MA).

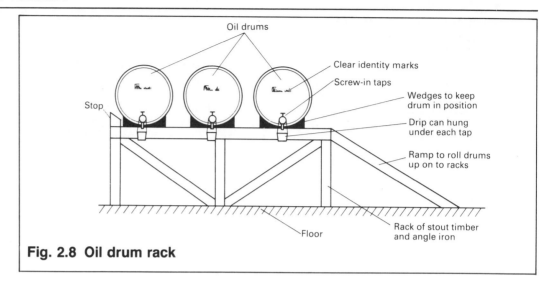

Fig. 2.8 Oil drum rack

$$\text{mechanical advantage} = \frac{\text{load}}{\text{effort}}$$

When the simple lever magnifies an effort, the effort has to move further than the load. This is referred to conventionally as the *velocity ratio* (VR) but, since the time taken by the effort is the same as the time taken by the load to move, the time factor cancels out and is usually ignored. Thus, in practice, velocity ratio is a distance ratio. The relationships between mechanical advantage, velocity ratio and efficiency are shown in Table 2.2 overleaf.

Mechanical advantage, velocity ratio and efficiency can be applied to all machines. Some examples of various types of machines will now be considered together with examples of calculations.

Rope and chain lifting gear

Snatch blocks

Figure 2.9(a) shows a typical set of pulley blocks used for raising loads by hand. The effort is applied to the 'tail' rope and the load to the lower hook. Since the velocity ratio of a set of rope pulley blocks is always equal to the total number of pulleys in the two blocks, the velocity ratio in this example is 4:1.

Table 2.3 gives some examples of velocity ratio for various combinations of pulley blocks.

Example 2.1 A set of rope blocks having three pulleys in the upper block and two pulleys in the lower block is used to lift a load of 150 kg mass. If the efficiency of the blocks is 80 per cent, calculate the effort required (g = 10).

Solution

a) Total number of pulleys = 3 + 2 = 5
   Therefore the velocity ratio = <u>5:1</u>

b) Efficiency $= \dfrac{MA}{VR} \times 100$

   $80 = \dfrac{MA}{5} \times 100$

Therefore:

   $MA = \dfrac{80 \times 5}{100}$

   $= \underline{4:1}$

c) Mechanical advantage $= \dfrac{load}{effort}$

   $= \dfrac{4}{1}$

   but, load = 150 kg or 150 × 10
   = 1500 *N*

   Thus substituting in c):

   effort $= \dfrac{load}{4}$

   $= \dfrac{1500}{4}$

   $= \underline{375\ N}$

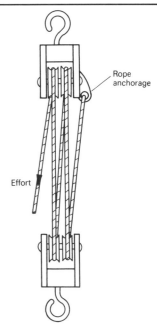

Fig. 2.9 Pulley blocks

Table 2.2

velocity ratio $= \dfrac{\text{distance moved by effort}}{\text{distance moved by load.}}$
(in the same time)

The *efficiency* of a machine is given by the expression:

efficiency $= \dfrac{\text{work done by machine}}{\text{work put into the machine}}$

but,   work done   = load × distance moved by load
and   work input = effort × distance moved by effort

thus the expression can be re-written:

efficiency $= \dfrac{\text{load} \times \text{distance moved by load}}{\text{effort} \times \text{distance moved by effort}}$

$= \dfrac{\text{mechanical advantage}}{\text{velocity ratio}}$

$= \dfrac{MA}{VR}$ (as a fraction)

or: $= \dfrac{MA \times 100}{VR}$ (as a percentage)

Table 2.3   Pulley Blocks – Velocity Ratio

Number of Pulleys Upper Sheave	Number of Pulleys Lower Sheave	Velocity Ratio
2	2	4·1
3	3	6·1
3	2	5·1
2	3	5·1
1	0	1·1
1	1	2·1
5	7	Would not work. Difference between sheaves can never exceed one pulley.

Weston pulley blocks

Figure 2.10 shows a set of differential or Weston pulley blocks. To ensure that there is no slip between the 'rope' and the pulleys, a chain is used and the pulleys are formed to engage with the chain links.

To raise the load, the effort is applied to the chain in the direction indicated. As the chain is wound in over the larger diameter pulley, it is unwound over the smaller pulley. The two pulleys are coupled together on the same shaft to form a differential pulley.

The velocity ratio of a Weston pulley block is calculated as follows.

Calculation The part of the chain supporting the load is shortened by:

circumference of pulley diameter D_1 minus circumference of pulley D_2
Thus, amount chain shortens
$= (\pi D_1 - \pi D_2)$

The load is raised by half this amount since it is supported by two falls of chain.

Thus, amount load is lifted
$= \dfrac{(\pi D_1 - \pi D_2)}{2}$

At the same time the effort moves through a distance equal to the circumference of the larger pulley.

Thus, distance moved by effort $= \pi D_1$

But, $VR = \dfrac{\text{distance moved by effort}}{\text{distance moved by load}}$

$= \dfrac{\pi D_1}{\frac{1}{2}(\pi D_1 - \pi D_2)}$

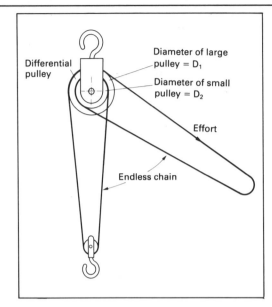

Fig. 2.10 Weston pulley blocks

$\therefore VR = \dfrac{2D_1}{D_1 - D_2}$

Example 2.2 Calculate the velocity ratio for a set of Weston differential chain blocks where the larger pulley has a diameter of 300 mm and the smaller pulley has a diameter of 250 mm.

Solution

$VR = \dfrac{2D_1}{D_1 - D_2}$

where: $D_1 = 300$ mm, ø $D_2 = 250$ mm.

$VR = \dfrac{2 \times 300}{300 - 250}$

$= \dfrac{600}{50}$

$= \underline{12:1}$

Winch

In the winch, the load is raised by winding in the rope around a drum as shown in Fig. 2.11.

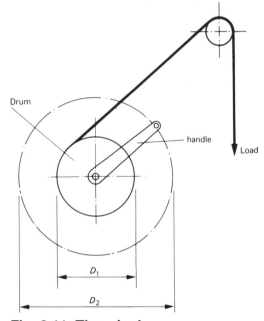

Fig. 2.11 The winch

In one revolution of the drum, the load is raised through a distance equal to the circumference of the drum. At the same time, the effort travels through a distance equal to the circumference of the circle swept out by the handle. Thus,

$VR = \dfrac{\pi D_2}{\pi D_1} = \dfrac{D_2}{D_1}$

where: $D_2 =$ diameter for the circle swept out by the handle,
$D_1 =$ diameter of the drum.

Example 2.3 Calculate the efficiency of a winch where an effort of 100 N raises a load of 60 kg. The handle is 600 mm in length and the drum is 150 mm diameter (g = 10).
Solution

$$VR = \frac{D_2}{D_1}$$

where: $D_2 = 2 \times 600$ mm = 1200 mm, $D_1 = 150$ mm.

$$VR = \frac{1200}{150}$$
$$= \underline{8:1}$$

$$MA = \frac{load}{effort}$$

where: load = 60 kg = 60 × 10 N = 600 N, effort = 100 N.

$$MA = \frac{600}{100}$$
$$= \underline{6:1}$$

$$efficiency = \frac{MA}{VR} \times 100$$

where: MA = 6:1, VR = 8:1.

$$efficiency = \frac{6}{8} \times 100$$
$$= \underline{75\%}$$

The screw-jack

The screw-jack uses a nut and screw to raise the load and to magnify the effort. A typical screw-jack is shown in Fig. 2.12.

It will be seen that the velocity ratio depends upon the radius at which the effort is applied and upon the lead of the screw.

$$VR = \frac{distance\ moved\ by\ effort}{distance\ moved\ by\ load}$$
$$VR = \frac{2\pi R}{L}$$

where: R = radius of application of effort, L = lead of screw.

Note: lead = pitch × number of starts to the thread.

Example 2.4 A screw-jack has a single start thread of 6 mm lead. The effort of 20 N is applied at a radius of 125 mm, and the load lifted is 600 N. What is the efficiency of this screw-jack?
Solution

$$Velocity\ ratio = \frac{2\pi R}{L}$$

Where R = 125 mm, L = 6 mm, π = 3·142.

$$\therefore VR = \frac{2 \times 3\cdot142 \times 125}{6}$$
$$= 131\cdot1$$
$$MA = \frac{load}{effort}$$
$$= \frac{600\ N}{20\ N}$$
$$= 30:1$$

$$Efficiency = \frac{MA}{VR} \times 100$$
$$= \frac{30 \times 100}{131}$$
$$= \underline{23\%}$$

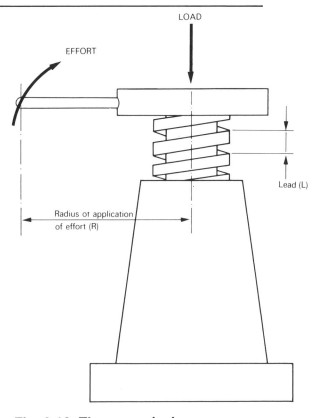

Fig. 2.12 The screw jack

Power transmission

Belt drives

Belt drives are widely used in machine tools and have the following advantages.
1 They do not transmit vibration.
2 They are cheap.

3 They can transmit power between shafts whose axes are widely spaced.
4 They can give an infinitely wide range of velocity ratios between the driving and driven members.
5 They do not require lubrication and will continue to function with a minimum of maintenance in relatively hostile environments since they are made of anti-corrosive materials.

Belt drives have the following limitations.
1 They are prone to slip and are, therefore, unsuitable for synchronised drives, for example, spindle and lead screw when screw cutting on the centre lathe.
2 They are bulky when transmitting high powers.
3 Some form of belt-tensioning device must be used.
4 They inflict a considerable radial load on the pulley bearings when they are tightened.
5 They are not very efficient when used at short centre distances and high velocity ratios due to the small angle of lap round the smaller pulley.

Figure 2.13 shows typical belt drives and how their velocity ratios are calculated. These drives are generally used between the electric motor (power source) and the transmission gear box as shown in Fig. 2.14(a). Two methods of belt tensioning to prevent slip are shown in Fig. 2.14(b).

In order to damp out the cutting vibrations in machine tools, some manufacturers use belts in the final drive to the spindle. To prevent slip, toothed belts are often used as shown in Fig. 2.14(c).

Worm and wheel

The worm and wheel provides a convenient means of obtaining a right-angle drive with extremely high velocity ratios. This is because a worm wheel acts as a gear with the number of teeth equal to the number of starts of the worm. Figure 2.15 shows the worm and wheel together with examples of calculating the velocity ratio.

Spur gears

Gears are a convenient method of transmitting power where the centre distance between the shafts is limited. They give a positive drive of a fixed velocity ratio and do not slip. Typical combinations of spur gears are shown in Fig. 2.16, together with the methods of calculating their velocity ratios.

Type of drive	Velocity ratio	Example
Open belt drive 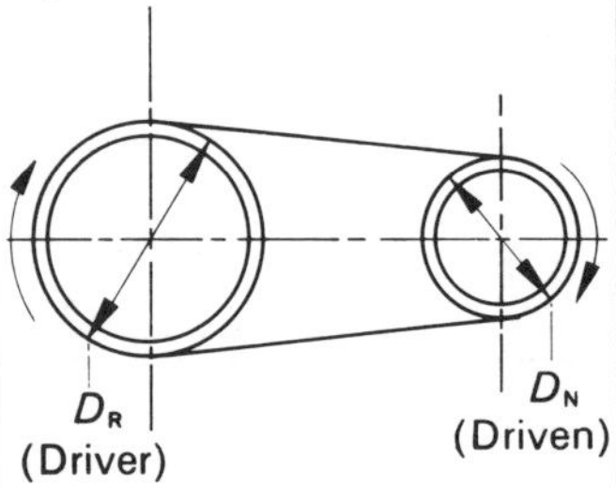 D_R (Driver) D_N (Driven)	$\dfrac{\text{Rev/min } D_R}{\text{Rev/min } D_N} = \dfrac{D_N}{D_R}$ D_R and D_N rotate in same direction	Calculate the speed in rev/min of D_N if D_R rotates at 100 rev/min. D_R is 500 mm and D_N is 200 mm $$\dfrac{100}{\text{Rev/min } D_N} = \dfrac{200}{500}$$ $$\text{Rev/min } D_N = \dfrac{100 \times 500}{200}$$ $$= 250 \text{ rev/min}$$
Crossed belt drive 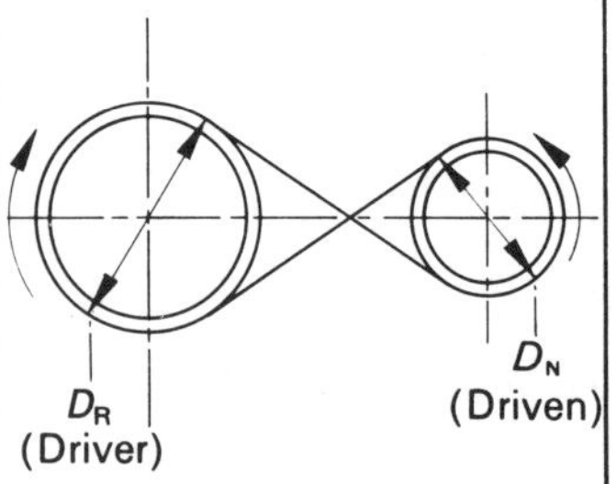 D_R (Driver) D_N (Driven)	$\dfrac{\text{Rev/min } D_R}{\text{Rev/min } D_N} = \dfrac{D_N}{D_R}$ D_R and D_N rotate in opposite directions	Calculate the speed in rev/min of D_N if D_R rotates at 20 rev/min. D_R is 700 mm and D_N is 350 mm $$\dfrac{20}{\text{Rev/min } D_N} = \dfrac{350}{700}$$ $$\text{Rev/min } D_N = \dfrac{20 \times 700}{350}$$ $$= 40 \text{ rev/min}$$

Fig. 2.13 Types of belt drive

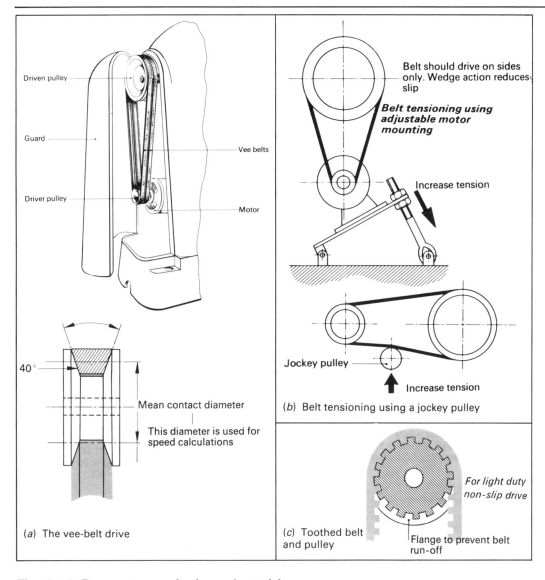

Driven pulley

Guard

Vee belts

Driver pulley

Motor

40°

Mean contact diameter

This diameter is used for speed calculations

(a) The vee-belt drive

Belt should drive on sides only. Wedge action reduces slip

Belt tensioning using adjustable motor mounting

Increase tension

Jockey pulley

Increase tension

(b) Belt tensioning using a jockey pulley

For light duty non-slip drive

(c) Toothed belt and pulley

Flange to prevent belt run-off

Fig. 2.14 Power transmission – belt drives

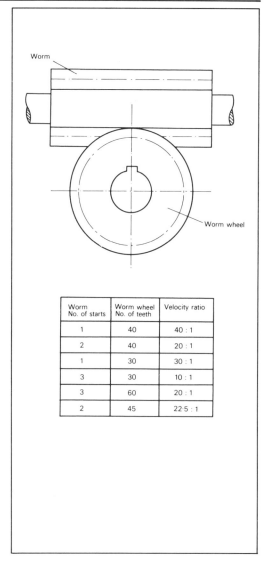

Worm

Worm wheel

Worm No. of starts	Worm wheel No. of teeth	Velocity ratio
1	40	40 : 1
2	40	20 : 1
1	30	30 : 1
3	30	10 : 1
3	60	20 : 1
2	45	22·5 : 1

Fig. 2.15 Worm and worm wheel

Type of train	Velocity ratio	Example
Simple train Pitch circle D_R D_N *Opposite rotation*	$\dfrac{\text{Rev/min } D_R}{\text{Rev/min } D_N} = \dfrac{\text{Pitch circle diam } (D_N)}{\text{Pitch circle diam } (D_R)}$ *But*, For a given pitch the number of teeth on each gear is proportional to the pitch circle diameter Since it is easier to count the teeth than to measure the pitch circle diameter, the following method of calculation is used in practice $\dfrac{\text{Rev/min } D_R}{\text{Rev/min } D_N} = \dfrac{\text{No. of teeth Driven}}{\text{No. of teeth Driver}}$	(i) Calculate the speed of the driven gear in rev/min if the driving gear is rotating at 150 rev/min. Number of teeth on Driver is 30, number of teeth on Driven is 50 $\dfrac{150}{\text{Rev/min Driven}} = \dfrac{50}{30}$ $\text{Rev/min Driven} = \dfrac{150 \times 30}{50}$ $\underline{= 90 \text{ rev/min}}$ (ii) As (i) but insert idler gear of 100 teeth $\text{Rev/min Driven} = 150 \times \dfrac{30}{100} \times \dfrac{100}{50}$ $\underline{= 90 \text{ rev/min}}$ The idler does not alter the overall velocity ratio
Simple train with idler Driver Idler Driven *Same direction of rotation*		
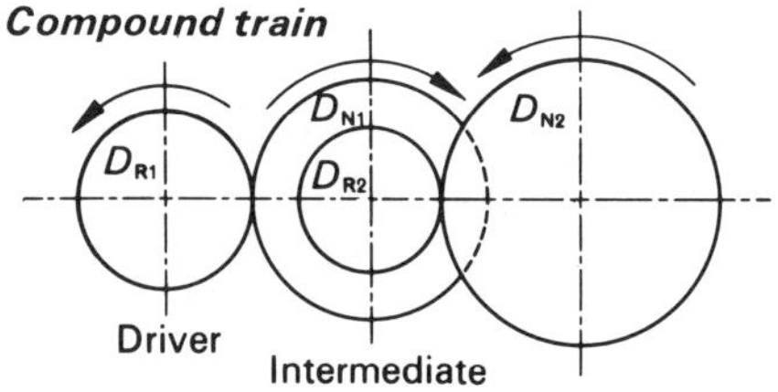 **Compound train** D_{R1} D_{N1} D_{R2} D_{N2} Driver Intermediate	Intermediate gears influence overall velocity ratio as well as the direction of rotation $\dfrac{\text{Rev/min Driver } (D_{R1})}{\text{Rev/min Driven } (D_{N2})} =$ $\dfrac{\text{Teeth } D_{N1}}{\text{Teeth } D_{R1}} \times \dfrac{\text{Teeth } D_{N2}}{\text{Teeth } D_{R2}}$	Calculate the speed of the driven gear (D_{N2}) in a compound train if the driver gear D_{R1} is rotating at 1 000 rev/min. Teeth on $D_{R1} = 20$; $D_{R2} = 30$; $D_{N1} = 40$; $D_{N2} = 50$ $\dfrac{1\,000}{\text{Rev/min } D_{N2}} = \dfrac{40}{20} \times \dfrac{50}{30}$ $\text{Rev/min } D_{N2} = 1\,000 \times \dfrac{20}{40} \times \dfrac{30}{50}$ $\underline{= 300 \text{ rev/min}}$

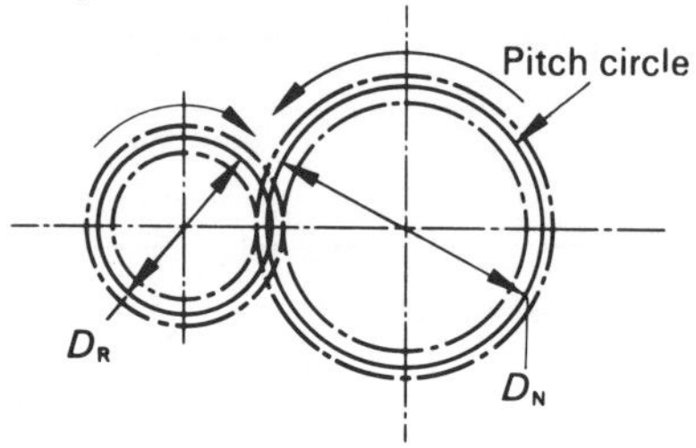

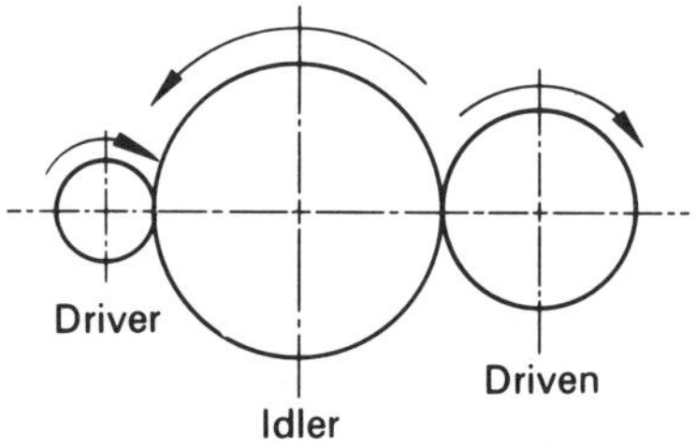

Fig. 2.16 Types of gear trains

Application of gearing

Figure 2.17 shows a typical machine tool gear box based upon a well-known milling machine. Note the following details.

1 The use of bevel gears for the reverse drive.

2 The use of a multi-plate clutch for the initial drive as the power source will be running when it is engaged; by partial engagement the cutter can be 'inched' round.

3 The use of positive dog clutches for picking up the drive from the individual gears. These require to be 'felt in' with the machine stationary (see 2).

4 The gear selections are interlocked so that only one train at a time can be engaged to prevent a jam up.

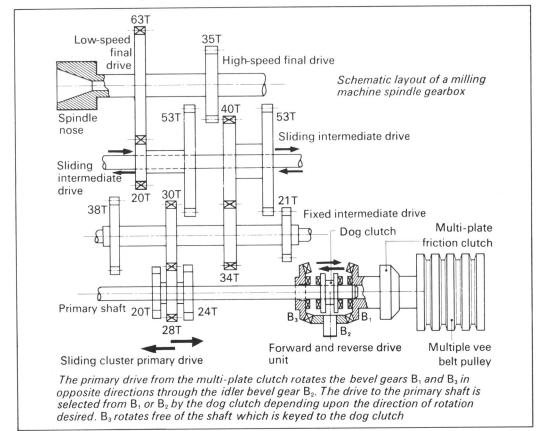

Schematic layout of a milling machine spindle gearbox

63T
Low-speed final drive
35T
High-speed final drive
Spindle nose
53T   40T   53T
Sliding intermediate drive
Sliding intermediate drive
20T   30T   21T
38T
Fixed intermediate drive
Dog clutch
Multi-plate friction clutch
34T
Primary shaft   20T   24T
28T
B₃   B₁
B₂
Sliding cluster primary drive
Forward and reverse drive unit
Multiple vee belt pulley

The primary drive from the multi-plate clutch rotates the bevel gears B₁ *and* B₃ *in opposite directions through the idler bevel gear* B₂. *The drive to the primary shaft is selected from* B₁ *or* B₂ *by the dog clutch depending upon the direction of rotation desired.* B₃ *rotates free of the shaft which is keyed to the dog clutch*

Fig. 2.17 Power transmission – gear drives

Exercises

1. Explain how a lubricant reduces the friction between sliding surfaces.

2. Explain what is meant by the following properties of a lubricant: (a) viscosity, (b) acidity, (c) lubricity.

3. Describe the basic precautions that should be taken in the storage, identification and handling of oils and grease.

4. (a) Define: (i) Mechanical advantage, (ii) Velocity ratio.
    (b) A set of rope blocks is 75% efficient. There are three pulleys in both the upper and lower blocks. Calculate the effort to raise a load of 180 kg mass (g = 10).

5. A screw-jack has a two start thread of 6 mm pitch. An effort of 40 N is applied at a radius of 200 mm and the load lifted is 1000 N. Calculate the efficiency of this screw-jack ($\pi = 3 \cdot 142$).

6. (a) Tabulate the advantages and limitations of belt drives as a means of transmitting energy in a machine tool.
    (b) A motor pulley has a diameter of 150 mm and rotates at 1500 rev/min. The driven pulley is 900 mm diameter.

(i) Calculate the speed of the driven pulley in rev/min.

(ii) Calculate the belt speed in m/min.

7. (a) Tabulate the advantages and limitations of gear drives as a means of transmitting energy in machine tools.

(b) A gear having 25 teeth and rotating at 1000 rev/min drives a gear having 150 teeth. Calculate the speed of this latter gear in rev/min. What will be the effect of the speed, and direction of rotation, of the driven gear if an idler gear of 50t is introduced between the driver and driven gears?

8. Calculate the velocity ratios for a worm and wheel gear train in the following examples:

(a) single start worm, 56t worm wheel;

(b) two start worm, 96t worm wheel;

(c) three start worm, 57t worm wheel.

State two advantages of this type of drive and one disadvantage.

9. Explain, with the aid of a sketch, the principle of a Weston

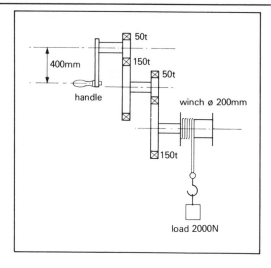

Fig. 2.18

differential chain block. Calculate the velocity ratio if the larger pulley has a diameter of 200 mm and the smaller pulley 180 mm.

10. Calculate the effort to raise the load for the system shown in Fig. 2.18. The handle drives the winch drum through a compound gear train. The overall efficiency is 0·6. ($\pi = 3$).

3. Engineering drawing

General arrangement and detail drawing

Figure 3.1 shows a pictorial view of a simple press-tool for piercing holes in sheet metal. It consists of a number of components, some of which are 'bought in' as ready made stock items; others have to be made specially. Figure 3.2 shows the *general arrangement* drawing of this press-tool. In this drawing the tool is shown assembled ready for use. It provides the craftsman with the information he needs to assemble all the parts together. It also carries the parts list so that the workshop supervisor knows which parts are to be made and which parts are to be bought in. The general assembly drawing also lists the serial numbers of the *detail drawings* for the parts that have to be manufactured specially.

The detail drawing (working drawing) is so called because it provides all the details necessary to manufacture the component represented on it. Detail drawings are fully dimensioned and also give details of material to be used, standard of finish required and heat treatment where applicable.

Figures 3.3 and 3.4 are two of the six detail drawings necessary for the manufacture of the press-tool shown in

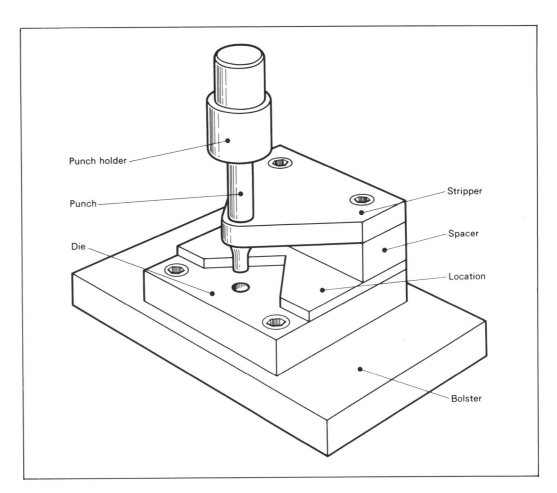

Fig. 3.1 Piercing tool for use in a fly press

Punch holder

Punch

Die

Stripper

Spacer

Location

Bolster

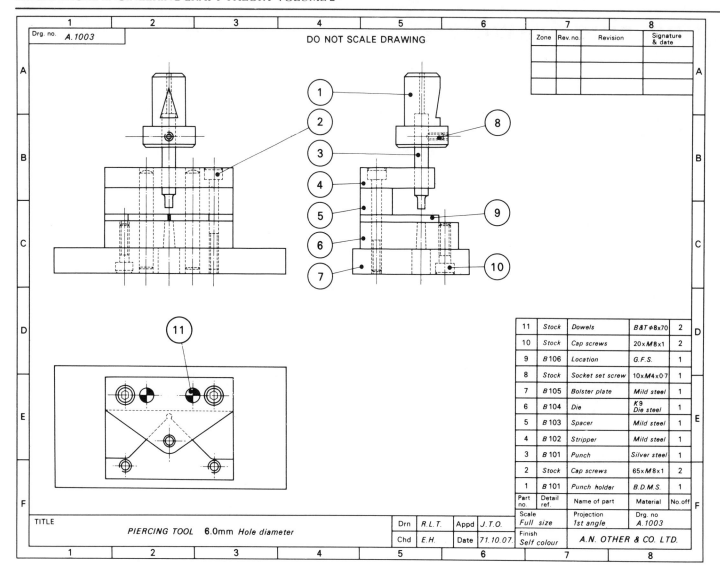

1	Stock	Dowels	B&T ⌀8x70	2
10	Stock	Cap screws	20xM8x1	2
9	B106	Location	G.F.S.	1
8	Stock	Socket set screw	10xM4x0·7	1
7	B105	Bolster plate	Mild steel	1
6	B104	Die	K9 Die steel	1
5	B103	Spacer	Mild steel	1
4	B102	Stripper	Mild steel	1
3	B101	Punch	Silver steel	1
2	Stock	Cap screws	65xM8x1	2
1	B101	Punch holder	B.D.M.S.	1
Part no.	Detail ref.	Name of part	Material	No.off

TITLE						
PIERCING TOOL 6.0mm Hole diameter	Drn	R.L.T.	Appd	J.T.O.	Scale Full size	Projection 1st angle	Drg. no A.1003
	Chd	E.H.	Date	71.10.07.	Finish Self colour	A.N. OTHER & CO. LTD.

Drg. no. A.1003   DO NOT SCALE DRAWING

Zone	Rev. no.	Revision	Signature & date

Fig. 3.2 General arrangement drawing

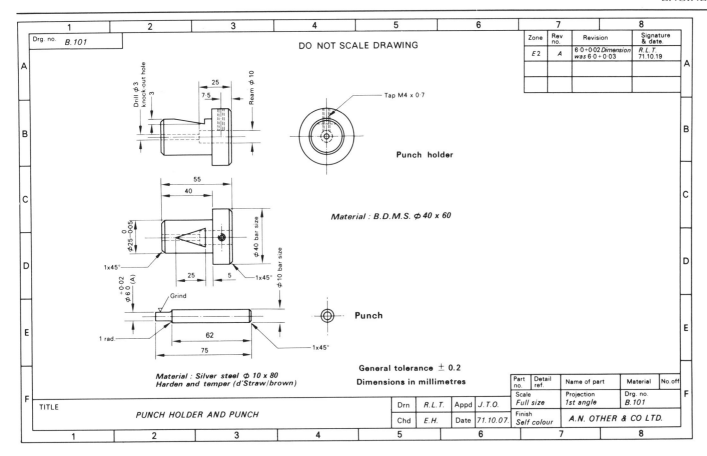

DO NOT SCALE DRAWING

Punch holder

Tap M4 x 0.7

Drill ⌀3 knock-out hole

Ream ⌀10

25

7.5

Material : B.D.M.S. ⌀40 x 60

55

40

⌀25−0.05 / 0

⌀40 bar size

⌀10 bar size

1x45°

25

5

1x45°

⌀6.0 +0.02 (A)

Grind

1 rad.

62

75

1x45°

Punch

Material : Silver steel ⌀ 10 x 80
Harden and temper (d'Straw/brown)

General tolerance ± 0.2

Dimensions in millimetres

Drg. no.	B.101

Zone	Rev no.	Revision	Signature & date.
E2	A	6·0 + 0·02 *Dimension was* 6·0 + 0·03	R.L.T. 71.10.19

Part no.	Detail ref.	Name of part	Material	No.off
Scale Full size		Projection 1st angle	Drg. no. B.101	
Finish Self colour		A.N. OTHER & CO LTD.		

TITLE	PUNCH HOLDER AND PUNCH	Drn	R.L.T.	Appd	J.T.O.
		Chd	E.H.	Date	71.10.07.

Fig. 3.3 Detail drawing – punch holder and punch

37

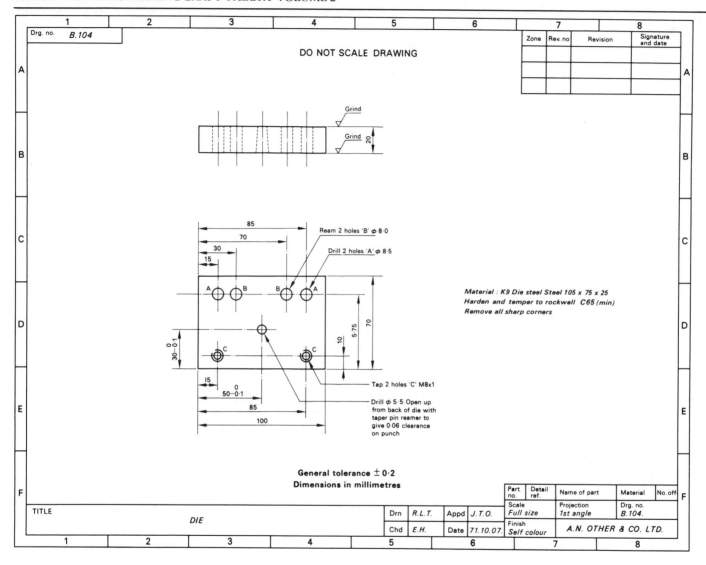

Fig. 3.4 Detail drawing – die

Fig. 3.1. These drawings show many of the techniques of drawing and dimensioning introduced in *Part 1* of this course.

Machining symbols

Machining symbols and instructions are used to:
1 specify a particular surface finish,
2 determine a manufacturing process,
3 define which surfaces are to be machined.

Figure 3.5(a) shows the standard machining symbol (BS 308) and the proportions to which it should be drawn.

When applied to the views of a drawing as shown in Fig. 3.5(b) the symbol should be drawn as follows. (Normal means at right angles to.)
1 Normal to a surface.
2 Normal to a projection line.
3 Normal to an extension line.
4 As a general note.

Because a machining symbol is interpreted as a precise instruction, its form should be drawn carefully. Figure 3.5(c) shows three fundamental variations of the symbol which, in turn, instruct the craftsman to:
1 machine,
2 machine if necessary,
3 do not machine.

These symbols must be used carefully, one incorrect symbol or incorrect application can result in unnecessary manufacturing costs or even the scrapping of a component.

Finally, the symbol can be used as

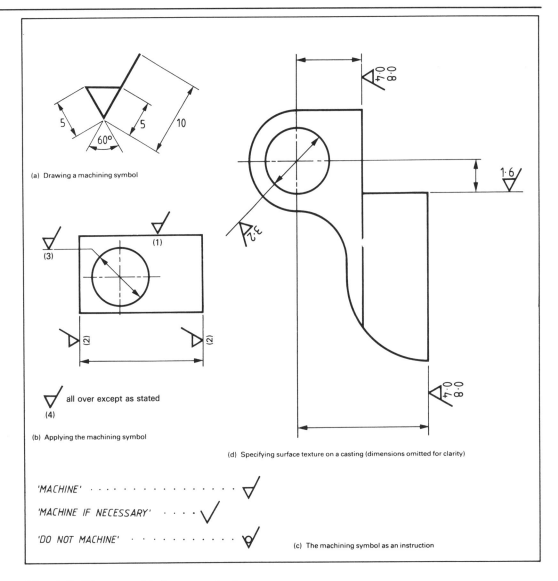

(a) Drawing a machining symbol

(b) Applying the machining symbol

all over except as stated (4)

(d) Specifying surface texture on a casting (dimensions omitted for clarity)

'MACHINE' · · · · · · · · · · · · · · ·

'MACHINE IF NECESSARY' · · · ·

'DO NOT MACHINE' · · · · · · · · ·

(c) The machining symbol as an instruction

Fig. 3.5 The machining symbol

shown in Fig. 3.5(d) to indicate the quality of surface finish (acceptable roughness) and/or the production process to be used.

Surface finish is usually specified as a roughness value in micrometres (microns) and the figure is printed above the machining symbol as shown in Fig. 3.5(d). One micrometre = 0·000 001 m, or 0·001 mm. The symbol for micrometre is μm. Like tolerances, roughness values can be related to manufacturing processes and a guide to average values and processes is given in Fig. 3.6.

The roughness value itself represents the average roughness of a surface. Even a surface that appears smooth to the naked eye, if magnified, would reveal hundreds of minute humps and hollows. For more exacting manufacturing requirements, it is more usual to specify upper and lower limits for roughness values.

Production processes related to a given surface finish are specified by extending the form of the symbol as shown in Fig. 3.7, and stating the exact process to be used on the extension as shown. Figure 3.8 shows a single view of an alloy steel breech cover. It illustrates the use of toleranced dimensions and machining symbols to specify precise manufacturing requirements.

Welding symbols

Welding is a permanent fastening technique which involves fusing

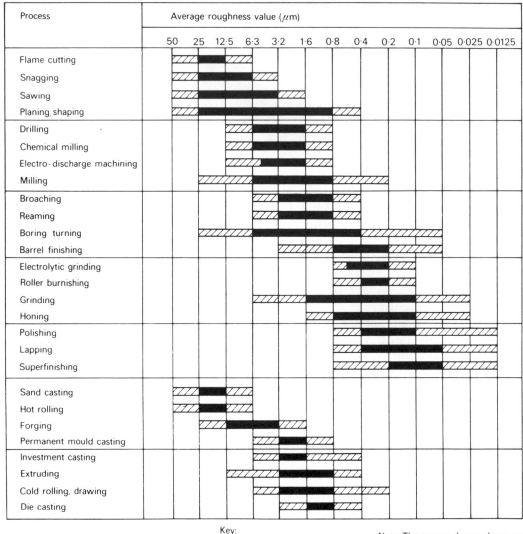

Fig. 3.6 Roughness values

Key:

▨▨▨ Less frequent application

▬▬▬ Average application

Note: The ranges shown above are typical of the processes listed. Higher or lower values may be obtained under special conditions

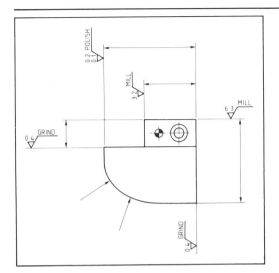

Fig. 3.7 Process specification

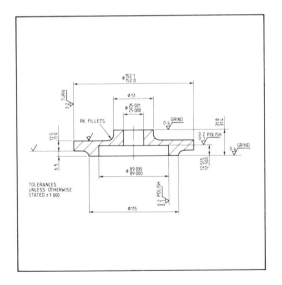

Fig. 3.8 Applying limits and machining symbols

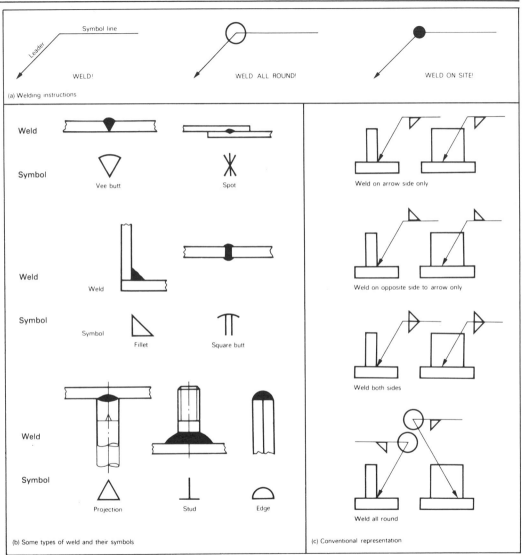

(a) Welding instructions

Symbol line

Leader

WELD!

WELD ALL ROUND!

WELD ON SITE!

| Weld | Symbol | | Weld | Symbol |

Vee butt

Spot

Weld

Symbol

Weld

Symbol

Fillet

Square butt

Weld

Symbol

Projection

Stud

Edge

(b) Some types of weld and their symbols

Weld on arrow side only

Weld on opposite side to arrow only

Weld both sides

Weld all round

(c) Conventional representation

Fig. 3.9 Welding symbols

(melting) together components made of similar material (usually steel). As with any other form of fastening, the component drawing must give the craftsman full instructions as to the type of weld to be used, its position and its quality. Symbols are used to give these instructions and full details can be found in BS 499.

Figure 3.9(a) shows the basic instruction symbol together with the variations to indicate that welding is to take place all round the component, or that the components are to be delivered separately and welded together on site.

Figure 3.9(b) shows some typical types of weld and the symbols which represent those welds. These symbols are added to the symbol line shown in Fig. 3.9(a).

Figure 3.9(c) shows the complete conventional representation for a number of welding possibilities. Figure 3.10 shows the applications of conventional symbols to typical working drawings indicating a variety of welds.

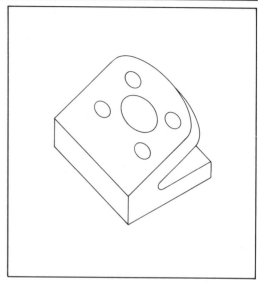

Fig. 3.11   Bracket with inclined face

Auxiliary views

Figure 3.11 shows a simple component in which one of the faces is neither parallel nor perpendicular to the projection planes. In order to provide the craftsman with a drawing of the true profile of the surface together with its dimensions an auxiliary view is used. Figure 3.12 shows how this surface is distorted in the conventional views and is only correct in the auxiliary view. Some of the construction lines have been left in for clarity. In Figs 3.9–12 the dimensions have been largely omitted for clarity.

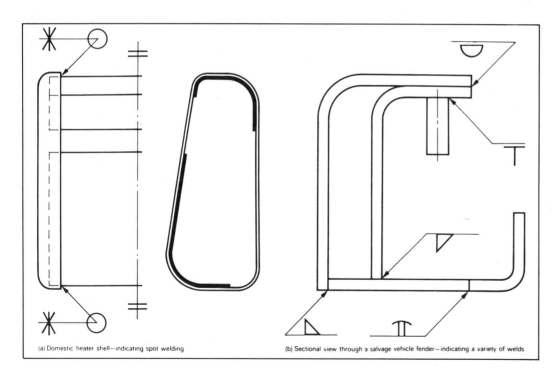

(a) Domestic heater shell—indicating spot welding

(b) Sectional view through a salvage vehicle fender—indicating a variety of welds

Fig. 3.10 Applications of welding symbols

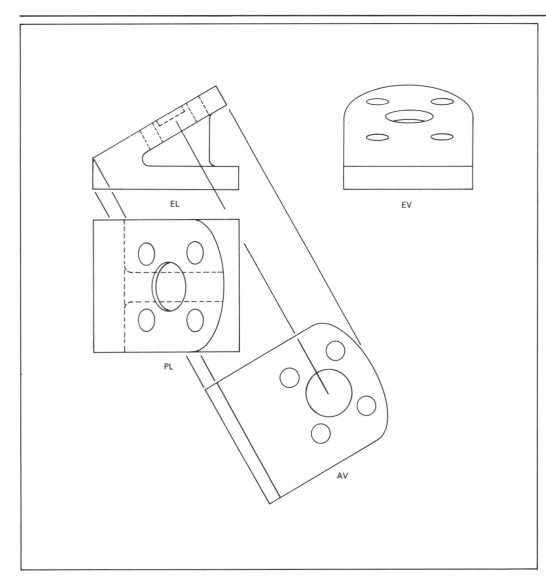

Fig. 3.12 Auxiliary view of inclined face

Third-angle projection

In *Part 1* of this course the technique of producing orthographic drawings in *first-angle* projection was introduced. All the subsequent examples and those used so far in this chapter have also been drawn in first-angle projection. However, some drawing offices use *third-angle* or American projection. Figure 3.13(a) shows a component drawn in first-angle projection whilst Fig. 3.13(b) shows the same component drawn in third-angle projection.

It will be seen that a drawing in third-angle projection has exactly the same views as in first-angle projection but that the views are positioned in a different relationship to each other. Figure 3.14(a) shows how the views are arranged in third-angle projection. The end view can be at either end or both ends at the same time if this improves the ease of reading the drawing. Figure 3.14(b) shows the geometrical construction used to arrive at the views given in Fig. 3.14(a). To avoid confusion the *projection used must always be clearly stated on the drawing*.

Thread forms

Figure 3.15 shows the more common thread forms found on machine tools and other engineering equipment. The advantages of each of the types illustrated are given below.

Vee-form This thread form has many advantages which is why it is so widely used.

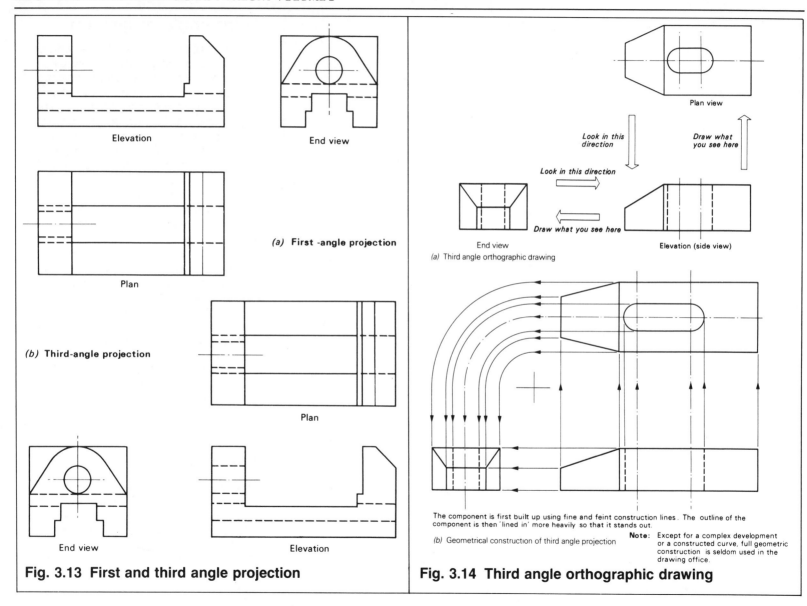

Elevation

End view

(a) First -angle projection

Plan

(b) Third-angle projection

Plan

End view

Elevation

Fig. 3.13 First and third angle projection

Plan view

Look in this direction

Draw what you see here

Look in this direction

Draw what you see here

End view

Elevation (side view)

(a) Third angle orthographic drawing

The component is first built up using fine and feint construction lines. The outline of the component is then 'lined in' more heavily so that it stands out.

(b) Geometrical construction of third angle projection

Note: Except for a complex development or a constructed curve, full geometric construction is seldom used in the drawing office.

Fig. 3.14 Third angle orthographic drawing

1 It is the easiest and cheapest to manufacture.
2 It is easily cut with taps and dies.
3 It is the strongest form.
4 It is self-locking and only works loose when subject to extreme vibration.

Square form   This thread form is used where rotary motion is to be transformed into linear motion. For example, a machine lead screw.
1 It has less friction as there is no locking action.
2 It is weaker than a vee-thread.
3 It is more difficult to cut than a vee-thread.

Knuckle form   This is a modified square thread used where rough usage and heavy wear would damage the corners of a true square form.
1 It is used for railway couplings and fire hydrants.
2 It is easier to cut than a square thread.

Acme form   This is a modified square thread and is used for lead screws operating in conjunction with a split nut.
1 There is less friction when the cut is being engaged and disengaged.
2 The taper gives the nut a lead when the nut is being engaged.
3 Wear can be compensated for by moving the nut deeper into engagement.

Buttress form   This form is used where the axial force operates in one direction only.
1 It is twice as strong as the square form.
2 It is used for quick-release vices and gun breach mechanisms.

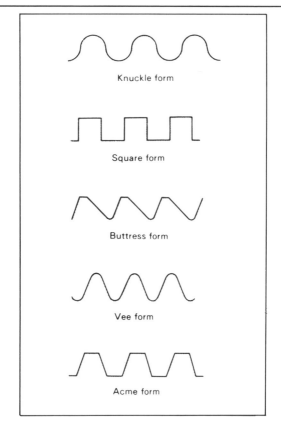

Fig. 3.15 Types of screw thread

Multi-start screw threads

Figure 3.16(a) shows a single-start screw thread of square form. Because it is a single-start thread the pitch and the lead are equal. It will also be seen that any attempt to increase the lead will also increase the pitch. Since the core diameter is equal to the major diameter

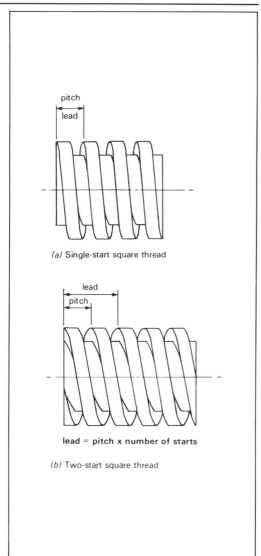

Fig. 3.16 Multi-start square thread

45

minus the pitch, any increase in pitch results in a reduction of the core diameter and a weakening of the screw.

One way of avoiding this problem is to use a multi-start thread. The screw of a fly-press has a multi-start thread of square section. Examine one in your workshop. This allows an increase in lead without any increase in pitch and depth of thread. Figure 3.16(b) shows a two-start, square thread. It has the same thread proportions as the single-start thread shown in (a) but twice the lead. Further examples of multi-start threads are given in Chapters 1 and 6.

Geometrical constructions

Some geometrical constructions were introduced in *Part 1* of this course. They showed how lines and angles could be bisected, how lines could be constructed perpendicular to each other, and how some plain figures could be constructed. Some further constructions that are useful when marking out will now be considered.

The circle   Figure 3.17(a) shows the parts of the circle together with their names, whilst Fig. 3.17(b) shows some useful relationships between angles and the circle.

The tangent   A tangent is a straight line which touches but does not cut a circle. Figure 3.18(a) shows a tangent and the normal at 90° to it. The normal is a radius of the circle. Where the normal joins the tangent is a *tangent point*. To construct a tangent at a given point to a

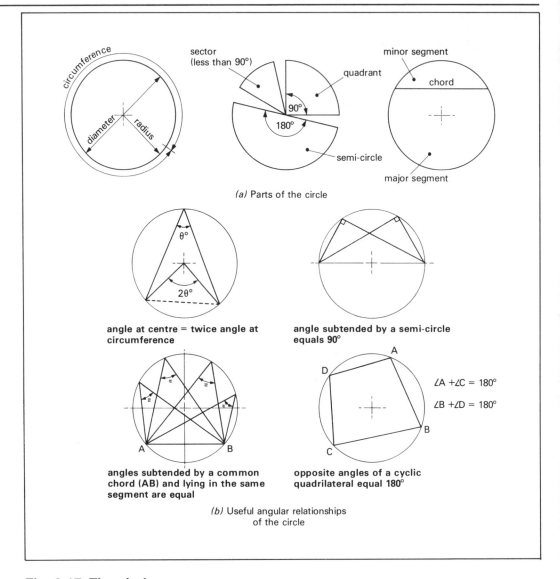

(a) Parts of the circle

angle at centre = twice angle at circumference

angle subtended by a semi-circle equals 90°

angles subtended by a common chord (AB) and lying in the same segment are equal

opposite angles of a cyclic quadrilateral equal 180°

$\angle A + \angle C = 180°$

$\angle B + \angle D = 180°$

(b) Useful angular relationships of the circle

Fig. 3.17 The circle

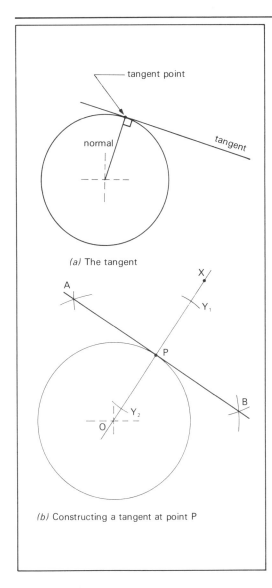

(a) The tangent

(b) Constructing a tangent at point P

Fig. 3.18 Tangency

circle is quite easy. Figure 3.18(b) shows a tangent drawn at the point *P* on the circumference of the circle centre O.

Construction

1 Join OP with a radial line and produce it to any convenient point X.
2 With centre P, strike two arcs equidistant from P on the line OPX.
3 With centre Y_1 strike arcs at A and B.
4 With centre Y_2 and the same radius as in (3) strike arcs to intersect those previously drawn at A and B.
5 Join A and B with a straight line which should pass through the point P. The line APB is the tangent to the circle at the point P and normal to (at 90°) the radial line joining OP.

Note: this is the construction given in *Part 1* for drawing lines perpendicular to each other at a given point.

Blending radii into a straight line This is a practical application of the above construction often required when marking out. Figure 3.19 shows the three alternative possibilities that can occur.

Where the arcs being joined by the straight line have the same radii as in Fig. 3.19(a) the normals CE and DF can be drawn in with a set square.

Where the radii are different as in Fig. 3.19(b) the problem is a little more difficult as the points of tangency are not known. The procedure is as follows.

Construction

1 Draw a circle centre C with radius X where $X = R-r$.
2 Bisect the line CD at Y, with centre Y and radius CY draw a semi-circle from C

to D so that it cuts the circle (radius X) at Z. (CZD is a right angle (angle in a semi-circle)).
3 Draw a line through CZ to cut the larger circle at E. This line is the normal to the tangent and (E) is the point of tangency.
4 Draw DF parallel to CE and join EF.
Note: with practice it is only necessary to plot the points of tangency (EF) and join them with a straight line. It is not necessary always to construct the tangent when two points of tangency are known.

The procedure for Fig. 3.19(c) is similar except that $X = R + r$ and the construction circle lies outside the given circle. In this case the normal is CEZ not CZE.

Blending external and internal arcs

1 Draw the centre line ABC.
2 Mark centre A and B at a distance $R + r$ apart as shown in Fig. 3.20(a) or $R - r$ apart as shown in Fig. 3.20(b).
3 From centres A and B draw radii R and r respectively. Point C is the common point of tangency.

Finding the centre of a circle Figure 3.21(a) shows how to find the centre of a circle.

1 Draw the chords AB and BC.
2 Bisect AB and BC so that the bisectors cut at O. Then O is the centre of the circle.

Similarly this same construction can be used to draw a circle through the three points of a triangle. In this case the chords AB and BC form any two adjacent sides of the given triangle as shown in Fig. 3.21(b).

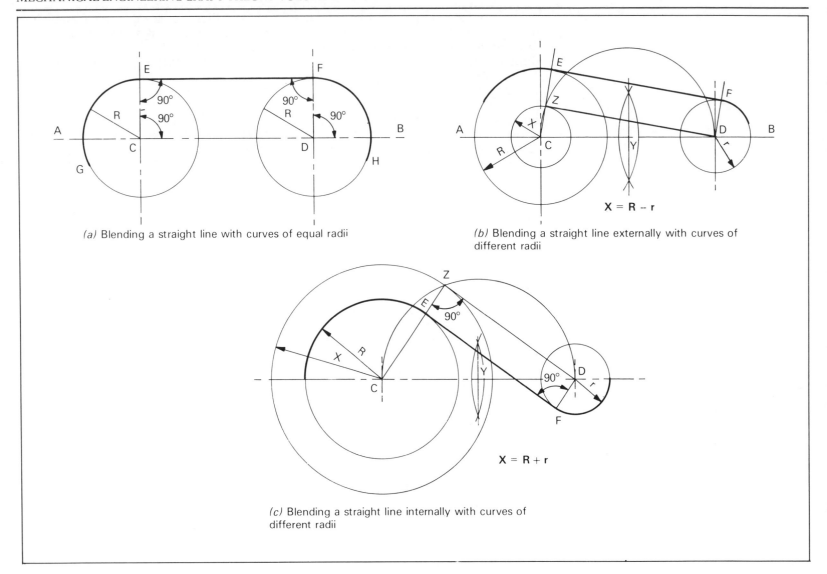

(a) Blending a straight line with curves of equal radii

(b) Blending a straight line externally with curves of different radii

$$X = R - r$$

(c) Blending a straight line internally with curves of different radii

$$X = R + r$$

Fig. 3.19 Blending curves and straight lines

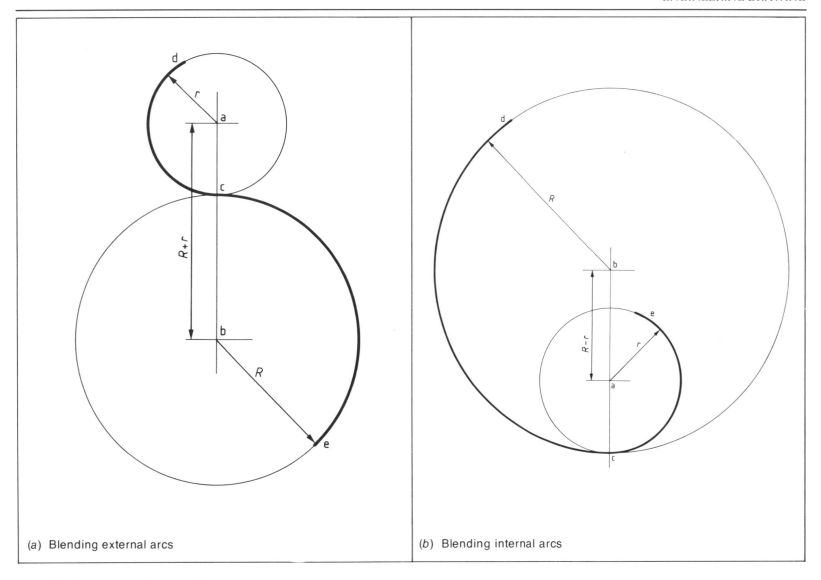

(a) Blending external arcs

(b) Blending internal arcs

Fig. 3.20 Blending tangential arcs

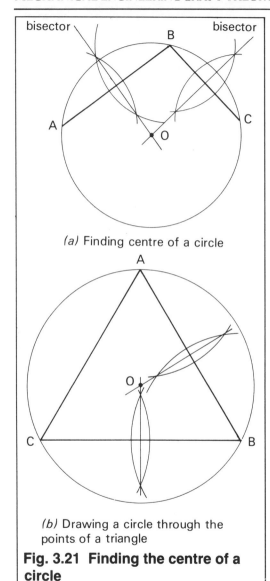

(a) Finding centre of a circle

(b) Drawing a circle through the points of a triangle

Fig. 3.21 Finding the centre of a circle

Exercises

1. Explain the difference between an assembly drawing and a detail drawing. State **three** items of information to be found on the assembly drawing and **three** items of information to be found on a detail drawing in addition to the drawing itself.
2. With the aid of sketches show what is meant by the welding symbols shown in Fig. 3.22.
3. With reference to BS499: Part 2C: 1980: Welding symbols,
    (a) explain what is meant by
        (i) the arrow line,
        (ii) the reference line,
        (iii) the symbol,
        (iv) the symbol being above or below the reference line;
    (b) sketch the symbols for the following types of weld:
        (i) square butt weld,
        (ii) single vee with broad root face,
        (iii) backing or sealing run,
        (iv) fillet weld, 'weld all round',
        (v) single-U butt weld, 'weld on site'.
4. BS308 states that machining symbols should be,
    (i) normal to a surface,
    (ii) normal to a projection line,
    (iii) normal to an extension line. Show, with the aid of sketches, what is meant by the above statements.
5. (a) Show how the machining symbol (BS308) can be used to indicate
        (i) machine,
        (ii) machine if necessary,
        (iii) do not machine.
    (b) Explain what is meant by the example of a machining symbol shown in Fig. 3.23.

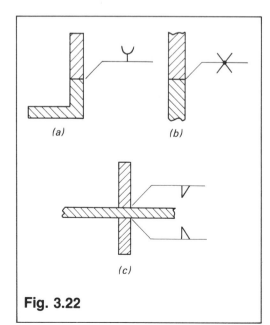

(a)   *(b)*

(c)

Fig. 3.22

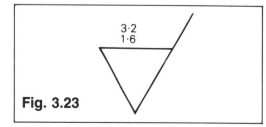

3·2
1·6

Fig. 3.23

6. Sketch an auxiliary view, of the component shown in Fig. 3.24 in the direction of arrow A so as to show the true shape of the boss. Scale the drawing given: dimensions omitted for clarity.

7. Sketch the drawing shown in Fig. 3.25 in *third angle* orthographic projection.
Sketch the BS308 symbol for third angle projection.

8. Sketch the following thread forms and state where each of them would be used and why.
  (i) Vee form
  (ii) Acme form
  (iii) Buttress form
  (iv) Square form

9. Sketch a two start square thread of 40 mm lead, and 60 mm major diameter by 80 mm long.

10. (a) Use a geometrical construction to find the centre of a 50 mm diameter circle.
  (b) Draw a circle 50 mm diameter and a second circle 40 mm diameter so that their centres are 60 mm apart. Connect the circles with a 70 mm radius arc tangential to the circles. The circles should be inside the arc. Use a geometrical construction to find the centre of the 70 mm arc.

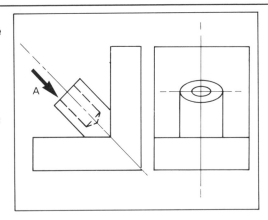

Fig. 3.24

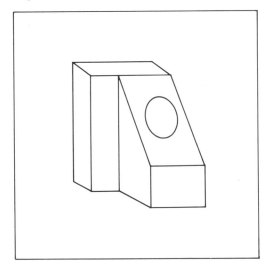

Fig. 3.25

51

4. Measurement

The micrometer

The operation of a micrometer depends upon the principle that the distance moved by a nut along a screw is proportional to the number of revolutions made by the nut. Therefore, by controlling the number of revolutions and fractions of a revolution made by the nut, the distance it moves along the screw can be predicted accurately. This principle forms the basis of a number of measuring devices. The principle applies whether the nut is fixed and the screw rotates or the screw is fixed and the nut rotates.

In application of the principle the following devices are needed.
1 A precision screw.
2 A means of counting one revolution of the screw.
3 A means of measuring parts of a revolution.

Examination of any micrometer measuring instrument will show how these devices are incorporated. The screw thread is rotated by the thimble which indicates the partial revolution. The whole revolutions are counted on the barrel of the instrument.

The micrometer caliper has already been introduced in *Part 1* of this course,

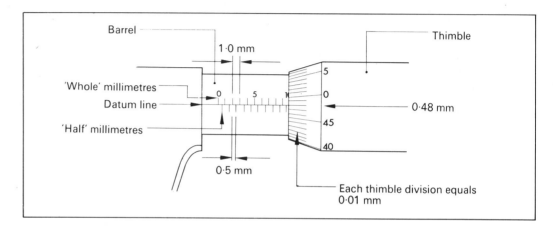

Fig. 4.1 Micrometer scales (metric)

but the application of the basic principles will again be considered. The micrometer screw has a lead of 0·5 mm and the thimble and barrel are graduated as shown in Fig. 4.1.

Since the lead of the screw is 0·5 mm for a standard metric micrometer, and the barrel divisions are 0·5 mm apart, one revolution of the thimble and the screw moves the thimble along a distance of one barrel division. The barrel divisions are placed on alternate sides of the datum line for clarity. Since the thimble has 50 equal divisions, and one revolution of the thimble equals 0·5 mm, then a movement of one

thimble division equals:

$$\frac{0·5}{50} = 0·01 \text{ mm}$$

Thus the micrometer reading equals: the largest visible whole millimetre + the largest visible half millimetre + the thimble division coincident with the datum line.
The reading for Fig. 4.1 is as follows:

9 whole millimetres	= 9·00 mm
1 half millimetre	= 0·50 mm
48 hundredths of a millimetre	= 0·48 mm
reading	= 9·98 mm

The construction, care and adjustment of the micrometer caliper was described in *Part 1* of this course.

The internal micrometer

The internal micrometer is shown in Fig. 4.2(a). Its range is 50–210 mm and for any one extension rod its range is 20 mm. This micrometer has the following limitations.

1 It cannot be used to measure small diameter holes.

2 It cannot be adjusted readily once it is in the hole and this affects the 'feel' that can be obtained.

An alternative and more satisfactory instrument is the *cylinder gauge* which employs a micrometer-controlled wedge to expand three equi-spaced anvils that touch the walls of the bore. This instrument is shown diagrammatically in Fig. 4.2(b).

The depth micrometer

The depth micrometer is shown in Fig. 4.3. It will be seen that it consists of a micrometer measuring head together with a number of extension rods. The desired rod can be inserted easily by removing the thimble cap. When the cap is replaced the rod is held firmly against a positive datum face. The rods are marked with their respective ranges and are square to the base at any reading. The measuring faces of the base and rods are hardened. Note that the scales of a depth micrometer give *reverse readings* as compared to the micrometer caliper.

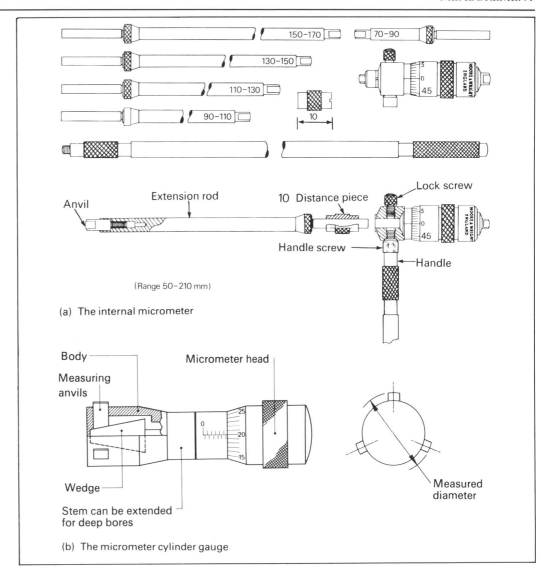

(a) The internal micrometer

(Range 50–210 mm)

(b) The micrometer cylinder gauge

Fig. 4.2 Bore diameter measurement

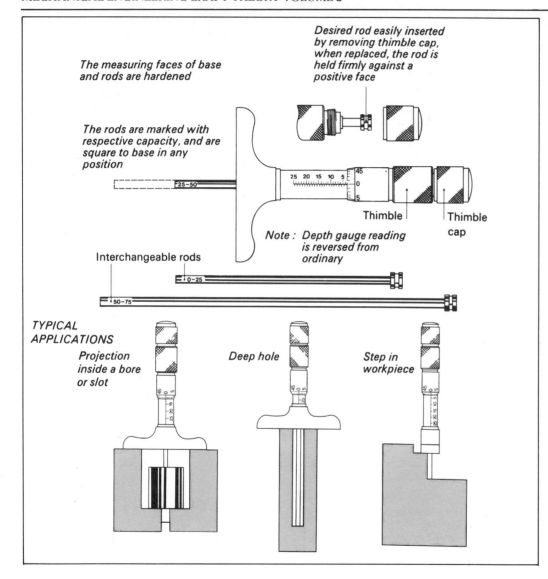

The measuring faces of base and rods are hardened

Desired rod easily inserted by removing thimble cap, when replaced, the rod is held firmly against a positive face

The rods are marked with respective capacity, and are square to base in any position

25–50

25 20 15 10 5

45
0
5

Thimble

Thimble cap

Note : Depth gauge reading is reversed from ordinary

Interchangeable rods

0–25

50–75

TYPICAL APPLICATIONS

Projection inside a bore or slot

Deep hole

Step in workpiece

Fig. 4.3 The depth micrometer

The bench micrometer

The simple hand-held micrometer caliper is capable of surprisingly accurate results when used by an experienced craftsman. It is unsuitable for high precision measurements. Figure 4.4 shows a typical bench micrometer which overcomes some of the limitations of the hand-held instrument.

1 The heavy cast body is less likely to deflect than the frame of a micrometer caliper.
2 The bench-mounted cast body will keep a steady temperature and will not expand and contract in use.
3 The *fiducial indicator* removes errors of 'feel'. The micrometer is 'zeroed' with the pointer of the fiducial indicator in line with its datum mark. All subsequent measurements are made with the pointer in this position. This ensures constant measuring pressures and deflections.
4 The anvil and spindle only slide, they do not rotate. This prevents their measuring faces from wear. In a hand-held micrometer the measuring face of the spindle rotates with the thimble and 'scrubs' against the component being measured.

The control of machine slides

Figure 4.5 shows a simplified machine slide operated by a lead screw and nut. A micrometer dial is built into the operating hand-wheel. This system differs from the measuring micrometer

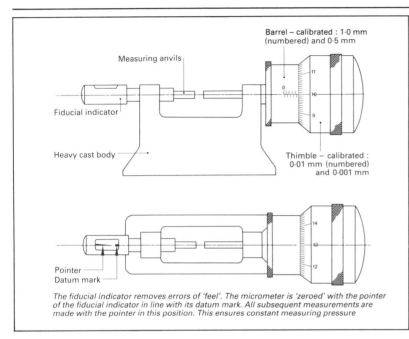

The fiducial indicator removes errors of 'feel'. The micrometer is 'zeroed' with the pointer of the fiducial indicator in line with its datum mark. All subsequent measurements are made with the pointer in this position. This ensures constant measuring pressure

Fig. 4.4 The bench micrometer

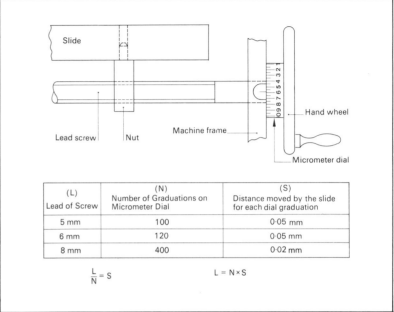

(L) Lead of Screw	(N) Number of Graduations on Micrometer Dial	(S) Distance moved by the slide for each dial graduation
5 mm	100	0·05 mm
6 mm	120	0·05 mm
8 mm	400	0·02 mm

$$\frac{L}{N} = S \qquad\qquad L = N \times S$$

Fig. 4.5 Machine slide control

in that the dial only indicates the partial revolutions of the screw. The complete revolutions have to be counted up in the head of the operator.

The use of a single screw both for measurement and for the movement of the machine slides is not good practice. The inevitable wear of the screw and nut soon reduces the accuracy of the measuring device.

Good modern practice has the screw moving the machine element. The positioning is performed by a separate measuring system which may be

mechanical, optical, electronic, pneumatic or a combination of these.

The vernier principle

In Fig. 4.6(a) it will be seen that the datum mark has been displaced from zero on the scale by one and a bit divisions. The problem is to determine accurately the magnitude of the bit. In engineering it is not good enough to say that it looks as if the datum is roughly halfway between divisions one and two

Therefore, in Fig. 4.6(b) an additional

scale has been added. This scale is referred to as a *vernier scale* and its purpose is to determine the intermediate readings more accurately.

Figure 4.6(c) shows how the scale is read in practice. To read the vernier, the first graduation of the vernier to be in line (coincident) with a main scale division is added to the main scale division immediately to the left of the vernier zero. In Fig. 4.6(c):
1 the zero reading of the vernier scale lies between 0·2 and 0·3 on the main scale;

2 the point of coincidence is 2 on the vernier scale and 0·4 on the main scale. Thus the reading is 0·2 + (2 × 0·01) = 0·22 units.

Note that 10 divisions on the vernier scale occupy 0·9 divisions on the main scale, that is a difference of 10 − 0·9 = 0·1 units. Therefore, each division of this particular vernier scale is 0·1 ÷ 10 = 0·01 units.

Figure 4.7 shows a typical 50-division vernier scale as used on modern metric measuring instruments. The 50-division vernier scale occupies 49 divisions on the main scale, that is a difference of 50 − 49 = 1 mm. Since there are 50 divisions on the vernier scale, each vernier division is 1 ÷ 50 = 0·02 mm.

The reading for the scales in Fig. 4.7 is:

$$\begin{array}{ll} 32 \text{ whole millimetres} & = 32\cdot00 \\ + \ 11 \times 0\cdot02 & = \ \underline{\ 0\cdot22} \\ \text{reading} & = \overline{32\cdot22 \text{ mm}} \end{array}$$

The vernier caliper

Figure 4.8 shows a vernier caliper. It will be seen that, unlike the micrometer caliper, the vernier caliper can make inside and outside measurements on the one instrument. The vernier caliper reads from zero to the full length of its beam scale, whereas the micrometer only reads over a range of 0·25 mm. *Note*: For inside readings the thickness of the jaws must be added to the scale readings.

Unfortunately the vernier caliper does not give such accurate readings as the

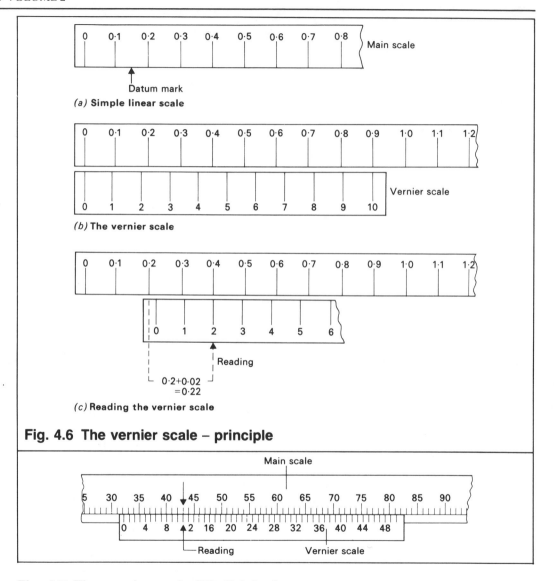

Fig. 4.6 The vernier scale – principle

Fig. 4.7 The vernier scale (50 division)

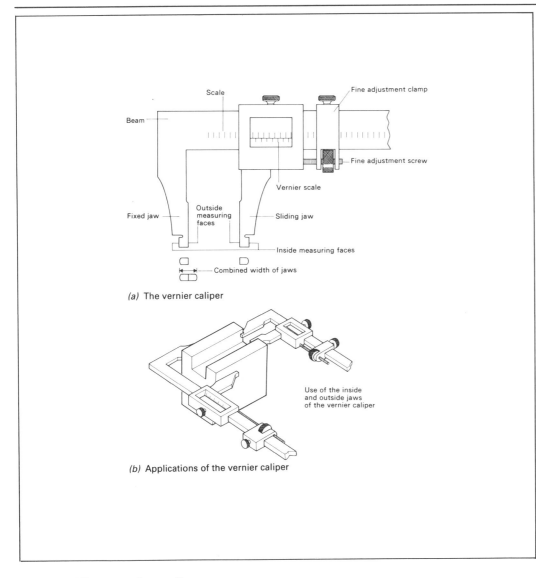

(a) The vernier caliper

Use of the inside
and outside jaws
of the vernier caliper

(b) Applications of the vernier caliper

Fig. 4.8 The vernier caliper

micrometer caliper for the following reasons:

1 It is difficult to obtain a correct 'feel' due to its size and weight.

2 The scales are difficult to read even with a magnifying glass.

3 The reading accuracy is only 0·02 mm (micrometer is 0·01 mm).

The vernier height gauge

Figure 4.9(a) shows a vernier height gauge. It will be seen that the fixed jaw has become the base of the instrument. This base is the datum from which the measurements and settings can be made. The reading obtained from the main and vernier scales represents the distance from the underside of the base (measuring datum) to the upper side of the moving jaw (lower surface of scribing point). The height gauge can be used for a number of applications in the workshop and inspection department. Figure 4.9(b) shows the height gauge being used for marking out. It is particularly useful for 'boxing' holes as described in Chapter 5. Figure 4.9(c) shows how it can be used to check the height of a surface. The accuracy of this latter application is limited by the skill of the operator in obtaining a 'feel' when the scribing blade is in contact with the work. To overcome this difficulty a dial test indicator is used (p. 61) as a fiducial indicator as shown in Fig. 4.9(c). That is, it removes errors due to 'feel' and ensures a constant measuring pressure providing its reading is the same for H_1, H_2 and H_3. In this case the readings obtained from the main and vernier

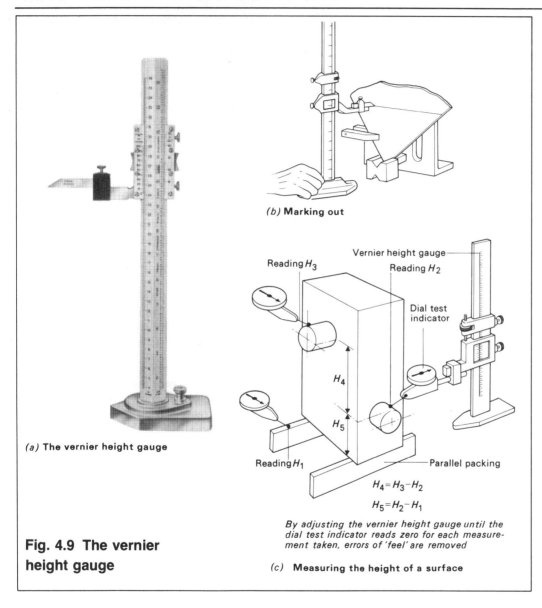

(b) **Marking out**

Vernier height gauge

Reading H_3

Reading H_2

Dial test indicator

H_4

H_5

Reading H_1

Parallel packing

$H_4 = H_3 - H_2$

$H_5 = H_2 - H_1$

By adjusting the vernier height gauge until the dial test indicator reads zero for each measurement taken, errors of 'feel' are removed

(c) **Measuring the height of a surface**

(a) **The vernier height gauge**

Fig. 4.9 The vernier height gauge

scales are no longer absolute (correct distances from the datum surface) but are difference readings as shown in the figure.

The vernier depth gauge

The vernier principle can also be applied to the depth gauge and an example is shown in Fig. 4.10(a). As with the micrometer depth gauge care has to be used when reading the scales as these are the reverse of those normally found on vernier calipers and vernier height gauges. Again it is difficult to obtain a satisfactory feel with this instrument as it is easily lifted off the datum surface by the adjusting screw. Figure 4.10(b) shows a typical application.

The vernier micrometer

The vernier scale can also be applied to the micrometer as shown in Fig. 4.11(a) in order to increase the reading accuracy. It does not follow, however, that the micrometer will measure to this accuracy. The measuring accuracy will largely depend upon the skill of the operator. For direct measurement to an accuracy of 0·001 mm the bench micrometer (Fig. 4.4 on p. 55) is preferable.

The vernier micrometer can be used for making comparative measurements by first reading the required size from a stack of slip gauges equal to the dimension required, and then checking the actual size of the component. This technique is shown in Fig. 4.11(b). With

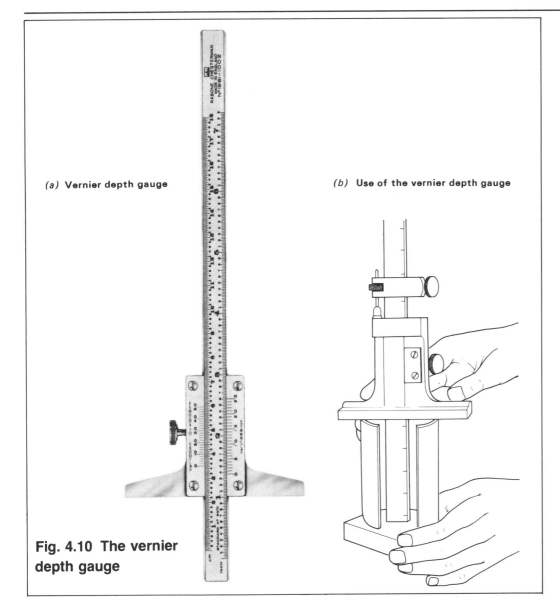

(a) **Vernier depth gauge**

(b) **Use of the vernier depth gauge**

Fig. 4.10 The vernier depth gauge

practice it is possible to work to an accuracy of 0·001 mm.

To take a reading on a vernier micrometer, the following procedure is recommended.

1 Read the micrometer to an accuracy of 0·01 mm in the normal way.

2 Read the vernier line which coincides with the graduated line of the thimble as shown in Fig. 4.11(a). This gives the number of thousandths of a millimetre that must be added to the initial reading.

Reading example shown in Fig. 4.11(a).

1 Normal reading	20·560 mm
2 Add reading indicated by the vernier line coincident with thimble graduation.	0·006 mm
3 Total reading	20·566 mm

One advantage of the vernier system of measurement is that it employs a full-length scale (unlike the micrometer whose range is limited to 25 mm). Therefore, the vernier can be applied directly to machine tool slides. The scale is laid parallel to the slide and the vernier scale is fixed to the moving element. The advantages of this arrangement are as follows.

1 The measuring equipment is divorced from the traverse mechanism and thus does not lose its accuracy through wear.

2 The operator does not have to count and remember the number of turns of the lead screw dial he has made. The vernier scales considered so far are linear scales.

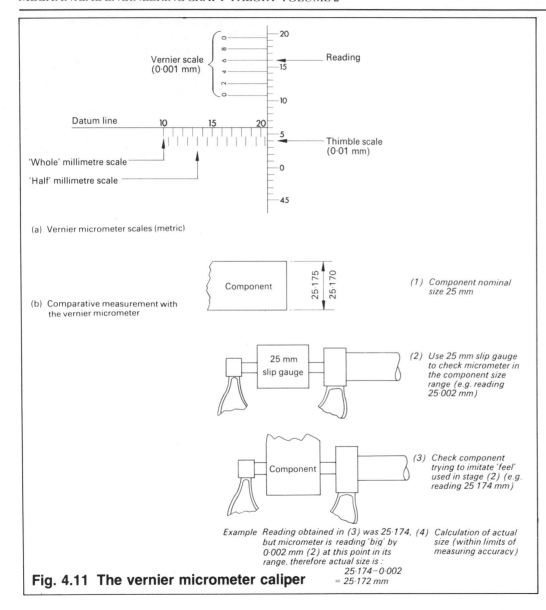

(a) Vernier micrometer scales (metric)

Vernier scale (0·001 mm)

Reading

Datum line

Thimble scale (0·01 mm)

'Whole' millimetre scale

'Half' millimetre scale

(b) Comparative measurement with the vernier micrometer

Component

25·175
25·170

(1) Component nominal size 25 mm

25 mm slip gauge

(2) Use 25 mm slip gauge to check micrometer in the component size range (e.g. reading 25·002 mm)

Component

(3) Check component trying to imitate 'feel' used in stage (2) (e.g. reading 25·174 mm)

Example Reading obtained in (3) was 25·174, but micrometer is reading 'big' by 0·002 mm (2) at this point in its range, therefore actual size is :
25·174 − 0·002
= 25·172 mm

(4) Calculation of actual size (within limits of measuring accuracy)

Fig. 4.11 The vernier micrometer caliper

However, the same principle can be applied to circular scales for angular measurements.

Vernier protractor

The simple or plain protractor was introduced in *Part 1* of this course, and its accuracy can be extended by the application of a circular vernier scale as shown in Fig. 4.12. It will be seen that the main scale is graduated in degrees of arc, and that the vernier scale has twelve divisions each side of the centre zero. These are marked 0–60 minutes of arc, so that each division equals $\frac{1}{12}$ of 60, which is 5 minutes of arc.

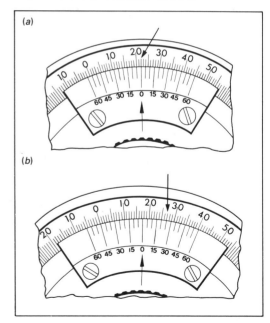

Fig. 4.12 Vernier protractor scales

The twelve divisions occupy the same space as 23 degrees on the main scale. Therefore, each division of the vernier is equal to $\frac{1}{12}$ of 23° or $1\frac{11}{12}°$.

Since two divisions on the main scale equal 2° of arc, the difference between two divisions on the main scale and one division on the vernier scale is:

$$2° - 1\frac{11}{12}° = \frac{1}{12}° \text{ or 5 minutes of arc.}$$

Thus the reading of the vernier protractor scale shown in Fig. 4.12(b) equals:
1 the largest whole degree on the main scale as indicated by the vernier zero division, *plus*
2 the reading on the vernier scale in line with the main scale division. Thus:

17 whole degrees	= 17°
+ vernier 25 mark in line with main scale	= 00° 25′
	17° 25′

Providing the vernier protractor has been manufactured to the specifications of BS 1685, it will have an accuracy of 5′ of arc. However, as with all measuring instruments, its performance will depend upon the skill of the user.

The dial test indicator

The *dial test indicator* (DTI) measures the displacement of its plunger or stylus on a circular dial by means of a rotating pointer. It is from the appearance of this dial that the DTI is familiarly known in

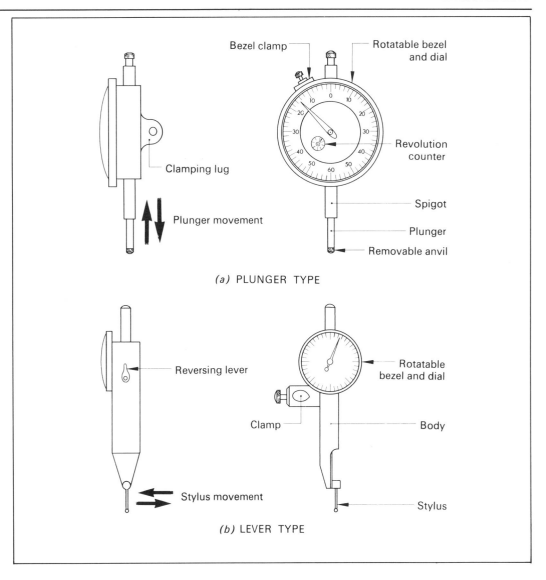

(a) PLUNGER TYPE

(b) LEVER TYPE

Fig. 4.13 Types of dial test indicator

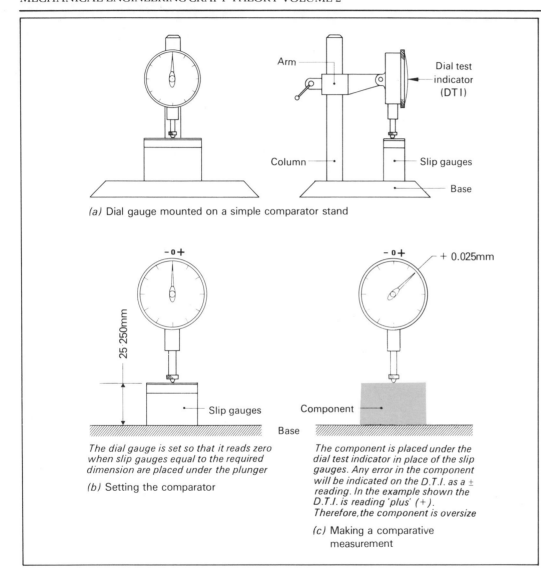

(a) Dial gauge mounted on a simple comparator stand

25·250mm

Slip gauges

Base

The dial gauge is set so that it reads zero when slip gauges equal to the required dimension are placed under the plunger

(b) Setting the comparator

+ 0.025mm

Component

The component is placed under the dial test indicator in place of the slip gauges. Any error in the component will be indicated on the D.T.I. as a ± reading. In the example shown the D.T.I. is reading 'plus' (+). Therefore, the component is oversize

(c) Making a comparative measurement

Fig. 4.14 Comparative measurement

the workshop as a clock. Figure 4.13 shows the two most popular types of this instrument normally used.

Figure 4.13(a) shows a plunger-type DTI. This relies upon a rack and pinion followed by a gear train to magnify the movement of the plunger to the main pointer. This type of instrument has a long plunger movement and is fitted with a secondary scale and a pointer for indicating the number of complete revolutions made by the main pointer. Various magnifications and dial markings are available.

Figure 4.13(b) shows a lever-type DTI. This type relies upon a lever and scroll system of magnification. It has only a limited range of stylus movement – little more than one revolution of the pointer. It is more compact than the plunger type and is very popular for both inspection and machine setting.

In both instances the movement of the measuring stylus is magnified mechanically. The magnified movement is indicated on a circular scale by a pointer.

Magnification
$$= \frac{\text{distance moved by pointer}}{\text{distance moved by stylus}}$$

Comparative measurement

In the strictest sense of the word, all measurement is comparative, that is, the component is compared with some measuring device such as a rule or a micrometer. However, in engineering, such techniques are referred to as *direct measurement*, and *comparative measurement* is the name given to the technique shown in Fig. 4.14. Here it is seen that the DTI is used to determine the difference between the component dimension and a standard of length. Since the accuracy of a DTI decreases as the amplitude of the plunger or stylus movement increases, it is advisable to arrange for the standard to be as near to the required component dimension as possible.

The dial test indicator in Fig. 4.14(b) has been set to read zero when slip gauges (p. 68) totalling 25·250 mm are placed under the plunger.

The component is then exchanged for the slip gauge setting standard. Any deviation in the component from the standard dimension will be indicated on the DTI as a ± reading. In Fig. 4.14(c) the reading is + 0·025 mm. Therefore, the actual size of the component is:

$$2·250 + 0·025 = 2·275 \text{ mm.}$$

Cosine error

The dial gauge only indicates the deflection of the measuring stylus. Whether or not this will be the same as the error in the workpiece will depend upon how the dial gauge is used. The most common error is *cosine error* resulting from the axis of the plunger being inclined to the datum surface from which the measurement is made. This is shown in Fig. 4.15. The following trigonometrical ratio applies to the triangle formed by the inclined DTI.

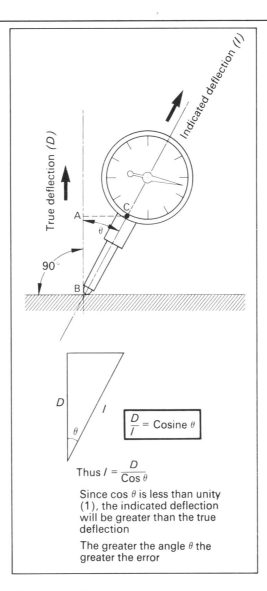

$$\frac{D}{l} = \text{Cosine } \theta$$

Thus $l = \dfrac{D}{\text{Cos } \theta}$

Since cos θ is less than unity (1), the indicated deflection will be greater than the true deflection

The greater the angle θ the greater the error

Fig. 4.15 Cosine error

$$\frac{D}{l} = \text{cosine } \theta$$

where: D = true deflection, *l* = indicated deflection.

$$\therefore \ l = \frac{D}{\text{cosine } \theta}$$

Since cos θ will be less than one, the indicated deflection will be greater than the true deflection. The greater the angle θ, the greater will be the error.

Testing out-of-roundness with a DTI

Out-of-roundness in some components is difficult to detect. The simplest out-of-round or lobed figure is shown in Fig. 4.16(a). It is based on an equilateral triangle and the tangential radii R and r are struck from the corners of the triangle. The dimension R + r appears to be the diameter of the figure which will behave as though it were truly cylindrical when tested between the anvils of a micrometer or the jaws of a vernier caliper as shown in Fig. 4.16(b). When measured by a comparator with a flat anvil as shown in Fig. 4.17(a) the same problem arises.

However, if a vee-block is substituted for the plain anvil, as shown in Fig. 4.17(b), then the out-of-round component will ride up and down as it is rotated and this movement will show up on the dial indicator.

Testing for concentricity with a DTI

Figure 4.18(a) shows a simple bush in

which the bore and the outside diameter have to be concentric. Any deviation from true concentricity will result in an uneven wall thickness as shown in Fig. 4.18(b). To test for this condition, the bush is supported on any rigid, round bar (clearance in the bore) as shown in Fig. 4.18(c). If the bore and outside diameter are concentric, the DTI reading will be constant. However, since lack of concentricity results in variations in wall thickness, an eccentric component will cause the needle of the DTI to swing back and forth as the bush is rotated.

Figure 4.19(a) shows how a solid component with two diameters may be checked if it does not possess centre holes. One diameter is supported in a vee-block, whilst the DTI rests upon the other diameter. If the diameters are concentric, the DTI reading will remain constant. If the diameters are eccentric, the DTI reading will vary cyclically.

Figure 4.19(c) shows a component supported between bench centres and being checked for concentricity by means of a DTI. The concentricity of each diameter is checked relatively to the common axis of the centres and not directly between each other.

Machine setting with a DTI

Figure 4.20 shows a few of the numerous applications of the DTI to machine setting. In Fig. 4.20(a) it is being used to set a workpiece concentric with the spindle axis of a lathe. The independent jaws of the chuck are adjusted until a constant

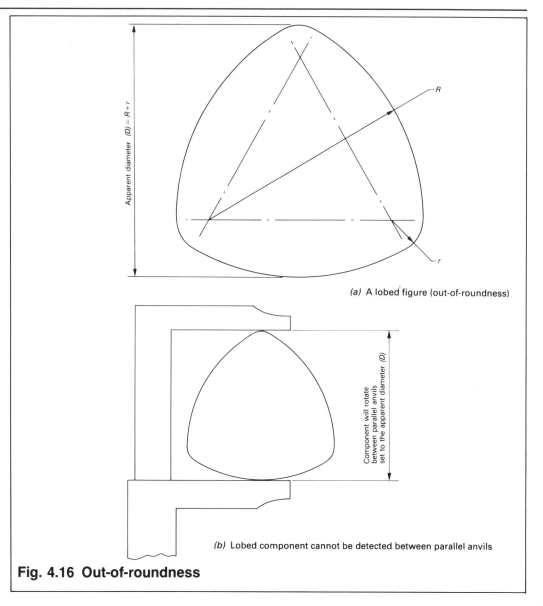

(a) A lobed figure (out-of-roundness)

(b) Lobed component cannot be detected between parallel anvils

Fig. 4.16 Out-of-roundness

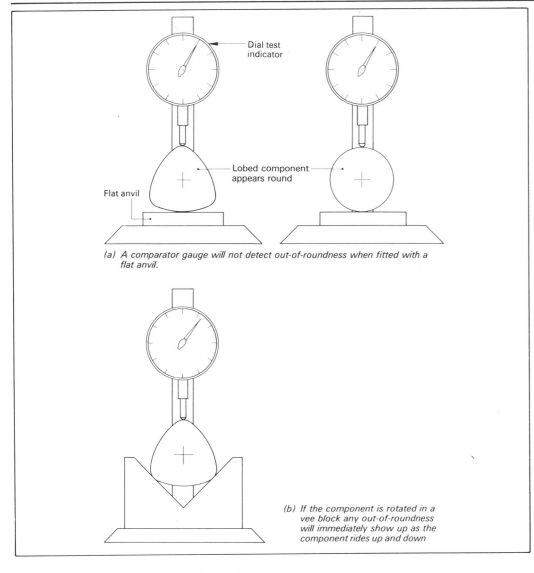

(a) A comparator gauge will not detect out-of-roundness when fitted with a flat anvil.

(b) If the component is rotated in a vee block any out-of-roundness will immediately show up as the component rides up and down

Fig. 4.17 Testing for out-of-roundness

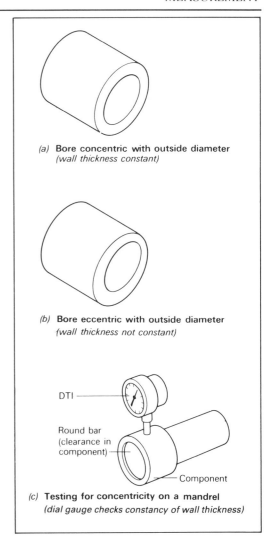

(a) **Bore concentric with outside diameter** (wall thickness constant)

(b) **Bore eccentric with outside diameter** (wall thickness not constant)

(c) **Testing for concentricity on a mandrel** (dial gauge checks constancy of wall thickness)

Fig. 4.18 Testing for concentricity (bored component)

65

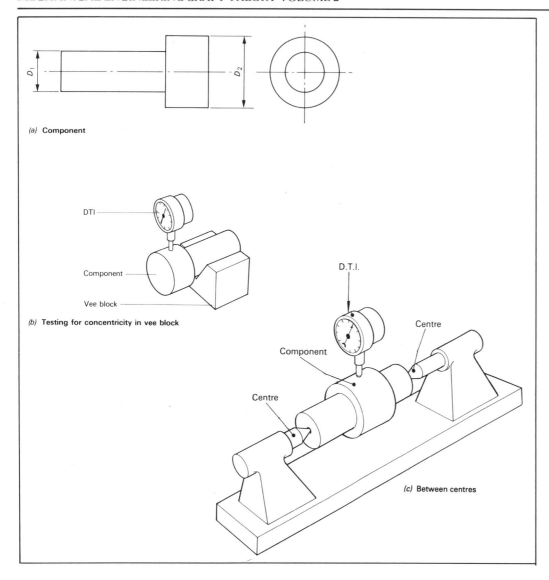

(a) **Component**

DTI

Component

Vee block

(b) **Testing for concentricity in vee block**

D.T.I.

Component

Centre

Centre

(c) **Between centres**

Fig. 4.19 Testing for concentricity (solid components)

reading is shown on the DTI. Thus, a comparative measurement is made between the alignment of the workpiece axis and the spindle axis of the lathe.

In Fig. 4.20(b) the fixed jaw of a milling machine vice is being set parallel to the spindle axis of a milling machine.

In Fig. 4.20(c) a component is being set concentric with a rotary machine table, whilst Fig. 4.20(d) shows a surface being checked for parallelism. In this instance a lever-type gauge mounted on a scribing block is being used so that the operator can look down on the dial at a more convenient angle than if a plunger type of DTI was used. In all the latter three examples the dial test indicator is being used to make a comparative reading, that is, the surface being checked is compared with the datum upon which the DTI stand is supported.

Squareness testing with a DTI

Figure 4.21 shows how a dial test indicator may be used to test for squareness. First the DTI is zeroed against a square of known accuracy as shown in Fig. 4.21(a). Then any error of squareness in the component will be shown as a + or − reading on the DTI as shown in Fig. 4.21(b). As the centre distance from the fixed contact to the DTI plunger is known, the angular error may be calculated as shown in Fig. 4.21.

$$\frac{x}{L} = \tan \theta°$$

where: $x =$ dial gauge reading, $L =$ centre distance, $\theta° =$ angular error.

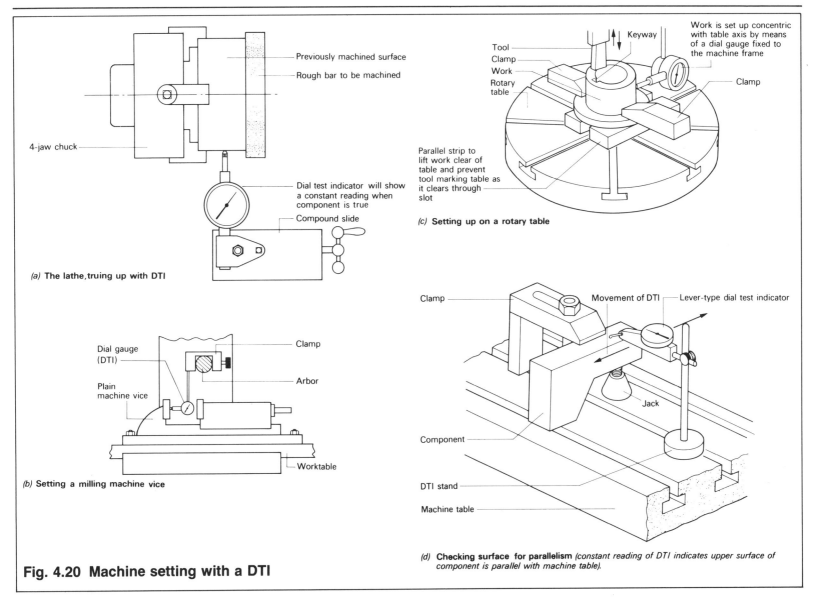

(a) **The lathe, truing up with DTI**

Previously machined surface

Rough bar to be machined

4-jaw chuck

Dial test indicator will show a constant reading when component is true

Compound slide

(b) **Setting a milling machine vice**

Dial gauge (DTI)

Plain machine vice

Clamp

Arbor

Worktable

(c) **Setting up on a rotary table**

Tool

Clamp

Work

Rotary table

Keyway

Work is set up concentric with table axis by means of a dial gauge fixed to the machine frame

Clamp

Parallel strip to lift work clear of table and prevent tool marking table as it clears through slot

(d) **Checking surface for parallelism** *(constant reading of DTI indicates upper surface of component is parallel with machine table).*

Clamp

Movement of DTI

Lever-type dial test indicator

Jack

Component

DTI stand

Machine table

Fig. 4.20 Machine setting with a DTI

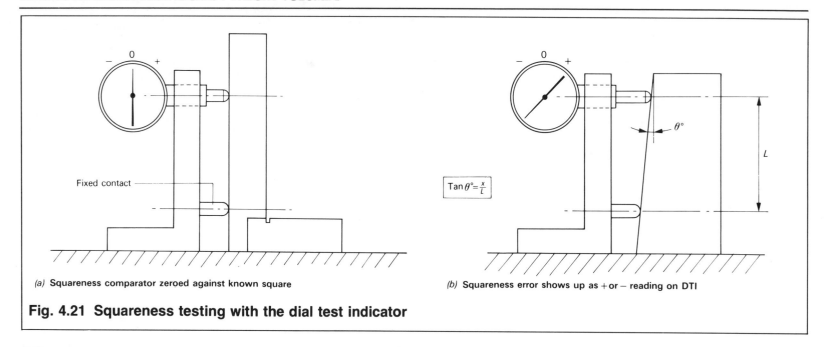

$$\text{Tan } \theta° = \frac{x}{L}$$

(a) **Squareness comparator zeroed against known square**

(b) **Squareness error shows up as + or − reading on DTI**

Fig. 4.21 Squareness testing with the dial test indicator

Slip gauges

Slip gauges are blocks of high-carbon steel that have been hardened and stabilised by heat treatment. They are then ground and lapped to size to very high standards of accuracy and finish as indicated in Table 4.1, based upon BS 888:1950. The essential requirements of the lapped, measuring surfaces of slip gauges are that:

1 the faces are parallel;
2 the faces are flat;
3 the faces are accurately the stated distance apart;
4 the finish is sufficiently high that two slip gauges may be wrung together.

The method of wringing individual slip gauges together is shown in Fig. 4.22. When correctly cleaned and wrung together the individual slip gauges adhere to each other by inter-molecular attraction and, if left like this too long, a partial cold weld will take place damaging the gauging faces irreparably. Therefore, immediately after use, the gauges should be separated carefully (Fig. 4.22), wiped clean, smeared with protective grease such as Vaseline, and returned to their case. BS 4311 recommends four metric sets of slip gauges; a medium-sized set comprising 78 blocks is listed in Set No. 78.

Set No. 78

Range (mm)	Steps (mm)	Pieces
1·01 to 1·49	0·01	49
0·50 to 9·50	0·50	19
10·00 to 50·00	10·00	5
75·00 and 100·00		2
1·0025		1
1·005		1
1·0075		1

In addition, some sets also contain protector slips which are 2·50 mm thick and are made from wear-resistant steel or tungsten carbide. They are added to the ends of the assembled stack to

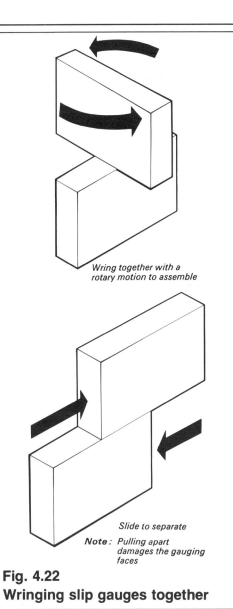

Wring together with a rotary motion to assemble

Slide to separate

Note : *Pulling apart damages the gauging faces*

Fig. 4.22
Wringing slip gauges together

Table 4.1   Accuracy of Slip or Block Gauges (Maximum Permissible Errors: 1 μ m (Micrometre))

Size of gauge (mm)		Grade 2			Grade 1			Grade 0		
Over	Up to and including	Flatness	Parallel-ism	Gauge length	Flatness	Parallel-ism	Gauge length	Flatness	Parallel-ism	Gauge length
–	20	2·5	3·5	+ 5·0 – 2·5	1·5	2·0	+2·0 –1·5	1·0	1·0	±1·0
20	60	2·5	3·5	+ 8·0 – 5·0	1·5	2·0	+3·0 –2·0	1·0	1·0	±1·5
60	80	2·5	3·5	+12·0 – 7·5	1·5	2·5	+5·0 –2·5	1·0	1·5	±2·0
80	100	2·5	3·5	+14·0 –10·0	1·5	2·5	+6·0 –3·0	1·0	1·5	±2·5

Grade 2: General workshop applications.
Grade 1: Precision workshop (toolroom) applications.
Grade 0: Inspection.

Not listed in table:
Grade 'calibration': A reference standard for testing grades 2, 1, 0.
Grade 00: A reference standard used only by slip gauge manufacturers to test all other grades.

protect the other gauge blocks from wear. Allowance must be made for their thickness when they are used.

Slip gauges are stacked together to give the required dimension. In order that the stack preserves the accuracy of the individual slip gauges, certain precautions must be observed in its assembly.
1 Use the minimum number of blocks.
2 Wipe the measuring faces clean.
3 Wring the individual blocks together. Figure 4.23 shows an example of a stack of slip gauges building up to the dimension of 39·9725 mm. It will be seen that the minimum number of four blocks

are used. The first slip selected is always the one giving the right-hand digit of the required dimension. The remainder are then selected in sequence. If protector slips were to be used in this example (2 × 2·5 mm), then block number three would be reduced to 2·50 mm.

As with any standard of length or angle. slip gauges may be sent to the National Physical Laboratory (UK) for calibration. (They may also be purchased ready calibrated.) The National Physical Laboratory will measure each slip in the set and issue a certificate of accuracy stating the exact amount the slip varies from the ideal size within the limits of the measuring process. Where a calibration certificate is available the stack of slip gauges is built up as described previously to give the required dimension. The algebraic sum of the errors for the slips used (as obtained from the calibration certificate) is added to the nominal size of the stack to give the actual size – as far as it is possible to measure it.

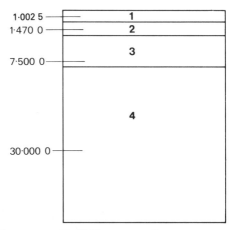

1·002 5	1
1·470 0	2
7·500 0	3
	4
30·000 0	

Fig. 4.23 Building up slip gauges

Slip gauge accessories

Sets of slip gauge accessories such as those shown in Fig. 4.24(a) are available for building up precision measuring devices. Some examples of these devices are shown in Fig. 4.24: (b) base, cage and type B jaw assembled to form an extremely accurate height gauge; (c) small cage and pair of A jaws assembled to form an internal caliper gauge of high

(a) Set of slip gauge accessories

(b) Basic cage and type 'B' jaw

(c) Small cage and pair of 'A' jaws

(d) Large cage and pair of 'A' jaws

(e) Small cage and pair of scribing joints

Fig. 4.24 Slip gauge accessories

accuracy; (d) large cage and pair of A jaws assembled to form an external caliper gauge of high accuracy; (e), small cage, and pair of scribing points assembled to form trammels for the accurate marking out of circles.

The examples shown indicate the convenient manner in which slip gauges and slip gauge accessories can be used to build up special measuring and limit gauging devices. They are particularly useful for single components and small production batches where the number of components does not warrant the introduction of specially manufactured gauges, or where greater accuracy than normal is required.

The sine-bar

The sine-bar provides a simple means of measuring angles to a high degree of accuracy. Figure 4.25(a) shows a typical sine-bar, and for accurate results the following points are essential.
1 The contact rollers must be of equal diameter and true geometric cylinders.
2 The distance between the roller axes must be precise and known, and these axes must be mutually parallel.
3 The upper surface of the bar must be flat and parallel with the roller axes, and equidistant from each axis.

The principle of the sine-bar is shown in Fig. 4.25(b). The sine-bar, slip gauges and datum surface on which they stand form a right-angled triangle. The sine-bar itself forms the hypotenuse of that triangle and the slip gauges form the side opposite the required angle.

Since: $\text{sine } \theta = \dfrac{\text{opposite side}}{\text{hypotenuse}}$

then: $\text{sine } \theta = \dfrac{\text{height of slip gauges}}{\text{length of sine-bar}}$

$= \dfrac{H}{L}$

Example 4.1
Calculate the slip gauges required to give an angle of 25° when using a 200 mm sine-bar.

Solution

$\text{Sine } \theta = \dfrac{H}{L}$

where: $\theta = 25°$,
$L = 200$ mm.

$H = L \text{ sine } \theta$
$= 200 \times 0.4226$
$= \underline{84.52 \text{ mm}}$

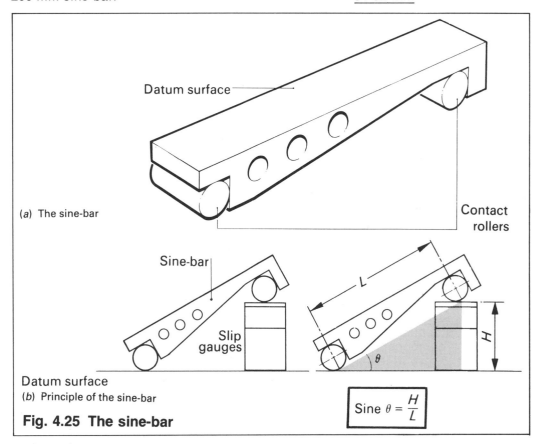

(a) The sine-bar

Contact rollers

Sine-bar

Slip gauges

Datum surface

(b) Principle of the sine-bar

$\text{Sine } \theta = \dfrac{H}{L}$

Fig. 4.25 The sine-bar

Note: The four-figure mathematical tables used by students are only of limited accuracy. Except when working examples for practice, always use more accurate tables of natural sines or the ready-worked sine-bar constants found in engineers' reference books.

Figure 4.26(a) shows how the sine-bar is used to check small components that may be mounted upon it. The dial test indicator (DTI) is mounted upon a suitable stand such as a universal surface gauge (scribing block) or a vernier height gauge (the latter is more rigid and gives more consistent readings). It is moved over the component into the first position as shown in Fig. 4.26(a) and zeroed. The stand and DTI is then slid along the datum surface to the second position as shown and the DTI reading is noted.

Method 1 The height of the slip gauges is adjusted until the DTI reads zero at both ends of the component. The actual angle is then calculated as explained in Example 4.1, and any deviation from the specified angle is the error.

Method 2 The sine-bar is set to the specified angle. The DTI will then indicate any error as a 'run' of so many hundredths of a millimetre along the length of the component. Providing the DTI was set to zero in the first position, the error will be shown as a plus or minus reading at the second position.

When a component is too large to be mounted on the sine-bar, the sine-bar can often be mounted on the

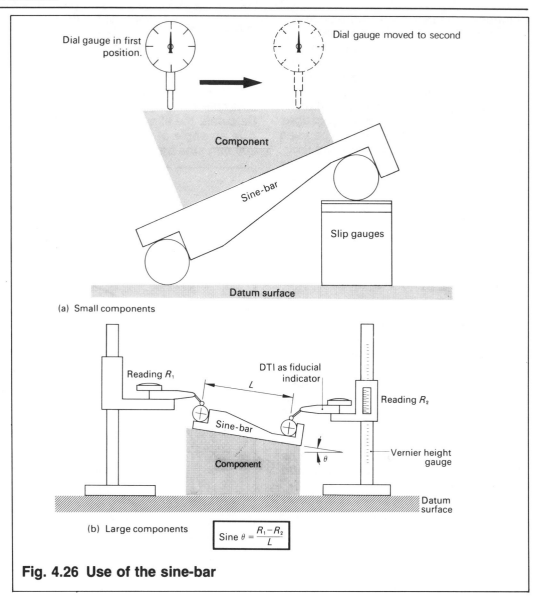

(a) Small components

(b) Large components

$$\text{Sine } \theta = \frac{R_1 - R_2}{L}$$

Fig. 4.26 Use of the sine-bar

component as shown in Fig. 4.26(b). In the example shown, the height over the rollers is measured by means of a vernier height gauge, using a DTI as a fiducial indicator to check the measuring pressure. This is achieved by adjusting the height gauge until the DTI shows the same zero reading each time. The difference of the two height gauge readings being the rise of the sine-bar as shown.

Where more accurate results are required slip gauges may be used as shown in Fig. 4.27. This example also introduces the concept of the secondary datum which is useful for checking tall components which are outside the convenient range of slip gauges built up from the primary datum surface.

1 Figure 4.27(a) shows that the DTI is set to zero as it touches the highest point of the lower sine-bar roller.
2 This setting is then transferred to a large vernier height gauge whose anvil is adjusted until the DTI again reads zero. The upper surface of the height gauge anvil is now aligned with the top of the sine-bar roller and the height gauge anvil becomes the secondary datum.
3 Figure 4.27(b) shows how the slips are built up on the height gauge anvil. The DTI is now set to zero over the slips.
4 The DTI is moved over the upper roller of the sine-bar and will indicate, by a reading plus or minus from zero, any error in the component angle.

Examination of natural sine tables will show that as the angle increases, the

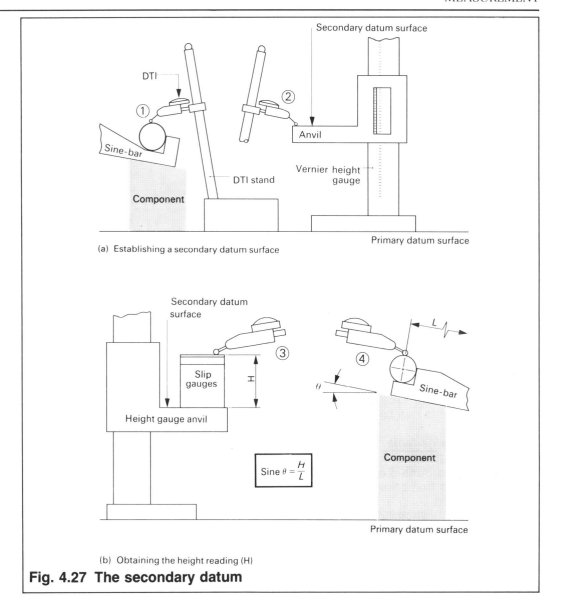

(a) Establishing a secondary datum surface

$$\text{Sine } \theta = \frac{H}{L}$$

(b) Obtaining the height reading (H)

Fig. 4.27 The secondary datum

accuracy of the tables decreases. Therefore, when measuring angles over 45° the component is turned over, if possible, so that the complementary angle can be used as illustrated in Fig. 4.28.

In Fig. 4.28(a) the angle θ° is considerably over 45° and it will not be possible to obtain sufficient accuracy from natural sine tables. In Fig. 4.28(b) the component is re-positioned and the sine-bar is set to the complementary angle of 90° – θ°. The sine of this smaller angle can be obtained more accurately from the tables and the angle θ° can be calculated.

The sine-table   This is shown in Fig. 4.29(a) and is, in fact, a wide sine-bar with a tee-slotted working surface and an integral datum surface upon which the slip gauges can be mounted. The work can be clamped directly to the working surface or mounted on a magnetic chuck which itself is clamped to the working surface. It is used exactly as the sine-bar previously described except that much larger components can be accommodated.

The compound sine-table   This is shown in Fig. 4.29(b), and consists of two sine-tables mounted at right angles to each other so that compound angles can be measured.

Sine-centres   These are derived from the sine-table by the addition of a pair of centres so that cylindrical components can be checked as shown in Fig. 4.30. Sine-centres are used exactly as the sine-bar.

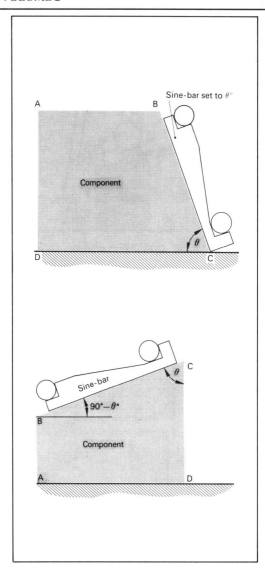

Fig. 4.28 The complementary angle

Limits and fits

Definitions

Before studying a standard limit system in detail, the following definitions should be understood.

Maximum and minimum metal conditions   The terms maximum metal condition and minimum metal condition are often met with in connection with limit systems and the gauging of work pieces. Figure 4.31 shows what is meant by these terms.

Hole and shaft basis systems   To obtain a given class of fit between two mating components, such as a shaft and bearing, the fit may be obtained in two ways.

1 By having a constant size of hole in the bearing and changing the shaft size to suit. **This is called a hole-basis system.**

2 By having a constant size of shaft and changing the hole size to suit. **This is called a shaft-basis system.**

The hole basis system is more usually employed since it is easier to maintain a standard hole size using standard drills and reamers. The shaft may be more easily adapted to size during the turning or grinding process. Figure 4.32 shows both systems.

The following definitions, which are amplified in Fig. 4.33 will also be helpful in understanding how limits and tolerances are applied to engineering components.

Nominal size   This is the size by which the component feature is known. For

(a) Sine-table

(b) Compound sine-table

Fig. 4.29 Types of sine-table

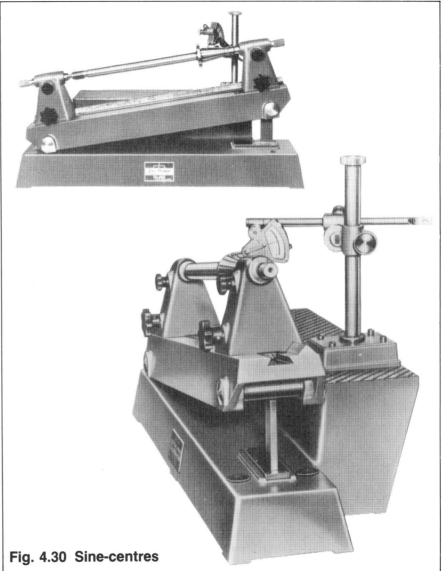

Fig. 4.30 Sine-centres

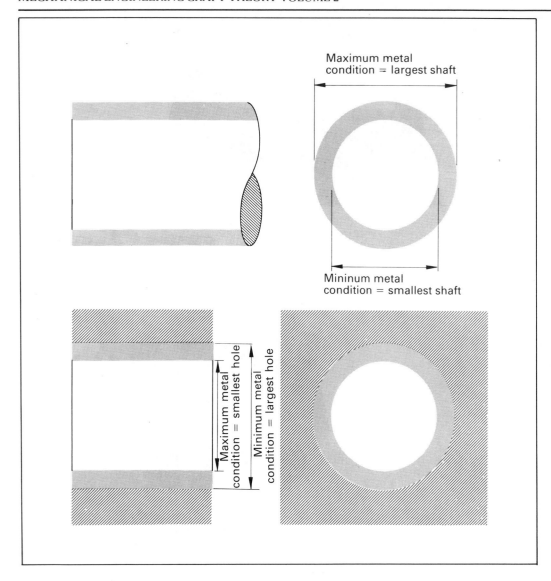

Fig. 4.31 Maximum and minimum metal conditions

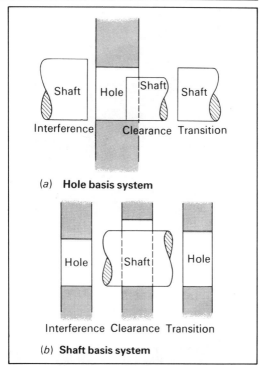

Fig. 4.32 Hole and shaft systems

example a 75·015 mm diameter hole would usually be referred to as 'the 75 mm hole'.

Basic size This is the exact functional size from which the limits are derived by the application of the necessary tolerances and clearance. The nominal size and the basic size are frequently the same.

Limits of size The limits of a dimension are the maximum and minimum sizes between which it is

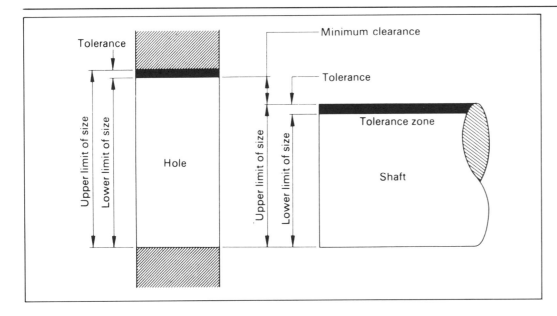

Fig. 4.33 Limit systems – definitions

permissible to manufacture a given workpiece if it is to function correctly.

Tolerance   This is the algebraic difference between the upper and lower limits of size. Its magnitude and disposition are determined by the functional needs of the component and the economics of production.

Minimum clearance   This used to be known as allowance and is the arithmetical difference between the maximum metal condition for a shaft and the maximum metal condition for the hole, i.e. the largest shaft and the smallest hole giving the 'tightest' fit that will function correctly.

Actual size   The measured size corrected to 20 °C.

Figure 4.34 shows how tolerances may be applied to a basic size together with alternative methods of dimensioning.

Unilateral tolerances are those where the tolerance zones lie to one side only of the basic size. *Bilateral tolerances* are those where the tolerance zones cross the basic size. In all the examples shown the basic size is 20·00 mm.

Figure 4.35 shows the various classes of fit that can exist between mating components.

Interference fit   This occurs when the shaft is larger than the hole, no matter

whether the largest shaft and the smallest hole is selected or the smallest shaft and the largest hole. This is shown in Fig. 4.35(a).

Transition fit   This is shown in Fig. 4.35(b), and occurs when:
1 the largest shaft and the smallest hole gives an *interference fit*;
2 the smallest shaft and the largest hole gives a *clearance* fit.

Clearance fit   This occurs when the shaft is smaller than the hole no matter what combination of shaft and hole is selected. This is shown in Fig. 4.35(c).

Standard systems

There are many standards of limits and fits used throughout the world, but the system used as an example in this section is BS 4500:1974 (part 1), Limits and Fits (metric units).

BS 4500 is based upon the work of the International Standards Organisation (ISO) and is suitable for application to all classes of work from the finest instruments to heavy engineering. BS 4500 allows for size and type of work; and provides for hole basis systems and shaft basis systems.

The tables provide for 28 types of shaft designated by lower case letters a,b,c,d, etc., and 28 types of hole designated by upper case letters A,B,C,D, etc. To each type of shaft or hole the grade of tolerance is designated by a number 01, 0, 1, 2.....16. Thus giving 18 grades of tolerance in all.

The letter indicates the position of the

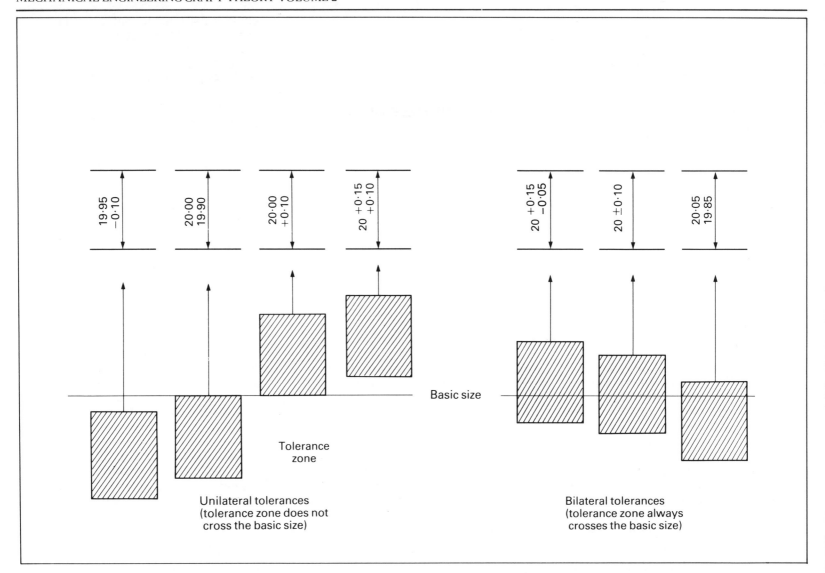

Fig. 4.34 Methods of tolerancing

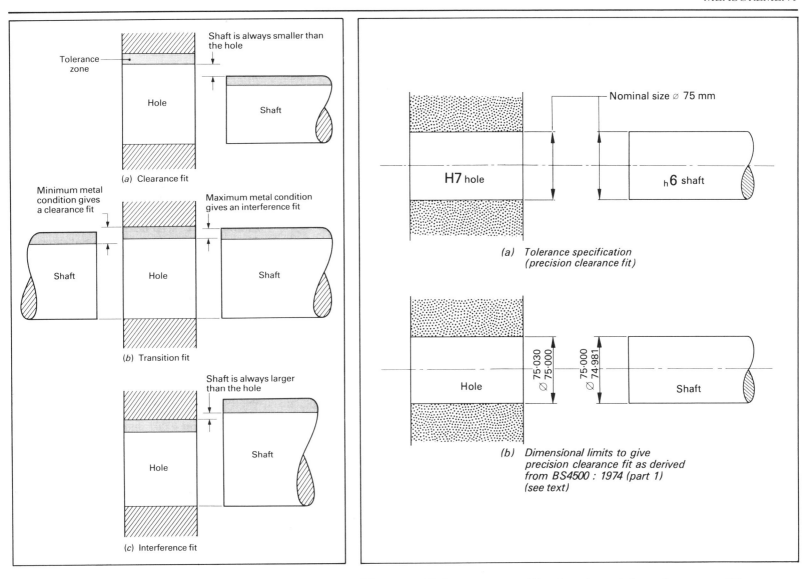

Fig. 4.35 Classes of fit

Fig. 4.36 Tolerance specification (precision clearance fit)

Table 4.2 Primary Selection of Fits. Abstract from BS 4500

Normal sizes (mm)		Loose clearance		Average clearance		Close clearance		Precision clearance		Transition		Interference	
Over	Up to	H9	e9	H8	f7	H7	g6	H7	h6	H7	k6	H7	p6
—	3	+25 +0	−14 −39	+14 +0	−6 −16	+10 +0	−2 −8	+10 +0	−0 −6	+10 +0	+6 +0	+10 +0	+12 +6
3	6	+30 +0	−20 −50	+18 +0	−10 −22	+12 +0	−4 −12	+12 +0	−0 −8	+12 +0	+9 +1	+12 +0	+20 +12
6	10	+36 +0	−25 −61	+22 +0	−13 −28	+15 +0	−5 −14	+15 +0	−0 −9	+15 +0	+10 +1	+15 +0	+24 +15
10	18	+43 +0	−32 −75	+27 +0	−16 −34	+18 +0	−6 −17	+18 +0	−0 −11	+18 +0	+12 +1	+18 +0	+29 +18
18	30	+52 +0	−40 −92	+33 +0	−20 −41	+21 +0	−7 −20	+21 +0	−0 −13	+21 +0	+15 +2	+21 +0	+35 +22
30	50	+62 +0	−50 −112	+39 +0	−25 −50	+25 +0	−9 −25	+25 +0	−0 −16	+25 +0	+18 +2	+25 +0	+42 +26
50	80	+74 +0	−60 −134	+46 +0	−30 −60	+30 +0	−10 −29	+30 +0	−0 −19	+30 +0	+21 +2	+30 +0	+51 +32
80	120	+87 +0	−72 −159	+54 +0	−36 −71	+35 +0	−12 −34	+35 +0	−0 −22	+35 +0	+25 +3	+35 +0	+59 +37
120	180	+100 +0	−85 −185	+63 +0	−43 −83	+40 +0	−14 −39	+40 +0	−0 −25	+40 +0	+28 +3	+40 +0	+68 +43
180	250	+115 +0	−100 −215	+72 +0	−50 −96	+46 +0	−15 −44	+46 +0	−0 −29	+46 +0	+33 +4	+46 +0	+79 +50
250	315	+130 +0	−110 −240	+81 +0	−56 −108	+52 +0	−17 −49	+52 +0	−0 −32	+52 +0	+36 +4	+52 +0	+88 +56
315	400	+140 +0	−125 −265	+89 +0	−62 −119	+57 +0	−18 −54	+57 +0	−0 −36	+57 +0	+40 +4	+57 +0	+98 +62
400	500	+155 +0	−135 −290	+97 +0	−68 −131	+63 +0	−20 −60	+63 +0	−0 −40	+63 +0	+45 +5	+63 +0	+108 +68

tolerance to the basic size and is called the *fundamental deviation* and the number indicates the magnitude of the tolerance and is called the *fundamental tolerance*. A shaft is completely defined by its basic size, letter and number, for example, 75 mm h6. Similarly, a hole is completely defined by its basic size, letter and number, for example, 75 mm H7. Figure 4.36 shows how a precision clearance fit is given by using a 75 mm H7/h6 hole and shaft combination. The sizes are based on Table 4.2.

Example 4.2 To derive the dimensions for a hole and shaft of nominal diameter 40 mm so that an average clearance fit is obtained.

Derivation Since the nominal size of the shaft/hole is 40 mm Table 4.2 is entered at the 30–50 mm band. The following conditions then apply.

Nominal size	H8	f7
30–50 mm	+ 39 + 0	− 25 − 50

tolerance unit 0·001 mm

Therefore,

hole diameter:
(upper limit) 40 + 0·039 = 40·039 mm
(lower limit) 40 + 0·000 = 40·000 mm
shaft diameter:
(upper limit) 40 − 0·025 = 39·975 mm
(lower limit) 40 − 0·050 = 39·950 mm

Since only an *average clearance fit* is required, there is no benefit in working to an accuracy of three decimal places.

The designer would use his experience and reduce the cost of manufacture by rounding off the limits to:

hole diameter:
(upper limit) = 40·04 mm
(lower limit) = 40·00 mm
shaft diameter:
(upper limit) = 39·98 mm
(lower limit) = 39·95 mm

Had a close or precision clearance been required, rounding off would not have been permissible and the increase in accuracy would have increased manufacturing costs and, therefore, unit component cost. There is no advantage in using greater precision than is required.

Other information that can be obtained from the above dimensions is as follows.

Hole tolerance   = 40·04 – 40·00
                   = 0·04 mm

Shaft tolerance   = 39·98 – 39·95
                   = 0·03 mm

Maximum clearance = 40·04 – 39·95
                   = 0·09 mm

(largest hole – smallest shaft)

Minimum clearance = 40·00 – 39·98
                   = 0·02 mm

(smallest hole – largest shaft)

Selection of tolerance grades

Obviously the closer the limits the more difficult it is to manufacture a component to a size that lies between

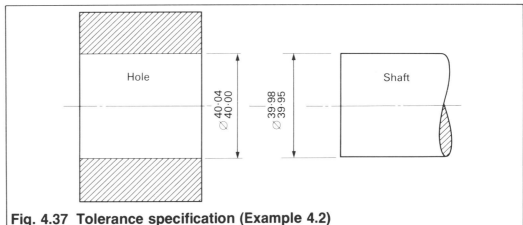

Fig. 4.37 Tolerance specification (Example 4.2)

them. It is no use specifying very close limits if the manufacturing process chosen cannot achieve such a high degree of precision.

Table 4.3 is taken from BS 4500:1974 (part 1) and shows the standard tolerances from which the tables of limits and fits are derived. It will be seen that as the IT number becomes larger the tolerance increases. The recommended relationship between process and standard tolerance is as follows.

IT	Class of work
16	Sand casting, flame cutting
15	Stamping
14	Die casting, plastic moulding
13	Presswork and extrusion
12	Light presswork, tube drawing
11	Drilling, rough turning, boring
10	Milling, slotting, planing, rolling
9	Low grade capstan and automatic lathe work
8	Centre lathe, capstan and automatic
7	High quality turning, broaching, honing
6	Grinding, fine honing
5	Machine lapping, fine grinding
4	Gauge making, precision lapping
3	High quality gap gauges
2	High quality plug gauges
1	Slip gauges, reference gauges

Example 4.3 Determine a process that is suitable for manufacturing the shaft dimensioned in Example 4.2.
The diameter of the shaft is 40 mm and the tolerance is 0·03 mm. From Table 4.3 it will be seen that the IT number that corresponds to these conditions lies between IT7 and IT8. Therefore, a good turned finish would be sufficiently accurate. However, to minimise wear, the shaft would probably receive some degree of heat treatment, in which case the tolerance would be easily achieved by commercial quality grinding.

Table 4.3 Standard tolerances Abstract from BS 4500

Tolerance unit 0·001 mm

Nominal sizes		Tolerance grades																		
Over	Up to and including	IT01	IT0	IT1	IT2	IT3	IT4	IT5	IT6†	IT7	IT8	IT9	IT10	IT11	IT12	IT13	IT14*	IT15*	IT16*
mm –	mm 3	0·3	0·5	0·8	1·2	2	3	4	6	10	14	25	40	60	100	140	250	400	600
3	6	0·4	0·6	1	1·5	2·5	4	5	8	12	18	30	48	75	120	180	300	480	750
6	10	0·4	0·6	1	1·5	2·5	4	6	9	15	22	36	58	90	150	220	360	580	900
10	18	0·5	0·8	1·2	2	3	5	8	11	18	27	43	70	110	180	270	430	700	1100
18	30	0·6	1	1·5	2·5	4	6	9	13	21	33	52	84	130	210	330	520	840	1300
30	50	0·6	1	1·5	2·5	4	7	11	16	25	39	62	100	160	250	390	620	1000	1600
50	80	0·8	1·2	2	3	5	8	13	19	30	46	74	120	190	300	460	740	1200	1900
80	120	1	1·5	2·5	4	6	10	15	22	35	54	87	140	220	350	540	870	1400	2200
120	180	1·2	2	3·5	5	8	12	18	25	40	63	100	160	250	400	630	1000	1600	2500
180	250	2	3	4·5	7	10	14	20	29	46	72	115	185	290	460	720	1150	1850	2900
250	315	2·5	4	6	8	12	16	23	32	52	81	130	210	320	520	810	1300	2100	3200
315	400	3	5	7	9	13	18	25	36	57	89	140	230	360	570	890	1400	2300	3600
400	500	4	6	8	10	15	20	27	40	63	97	155	250	400	630	970	1550	2500	4000
500	630	–	–	–	–	–	–	–	44	70	110	175	280	440	700	1100	1750	2800	4400
630	800	–	–	–	–	–	–	–	50	80	125	200	320	500	800	1250	2000	3200	5000
800	1000	–	–	–	–	–	–	–	56	90	140	230	360	560	900	1400	2300	3600	5600
1000	1250	–	–	–	–	–	–	–	66	105	165	260	420	660	1050	1650	2600	4200	6600
1250	1600	–	–	–	–	–	–	–	78	125	195	310	500	780	1250	1950	3100	5000	7800
1600	2000	–	–	–	–	–	–	–	92	150	230	370	600	920	1500	2300	3700	6000	9200
2000	2500	–	–	–	–	–	–	–	110	175	280	440	700	1100	1750	2800	4400	7000	11000
2500	3150	–	–	–	–	–	–	–	135	210	330	540	860	1350	2100	3300	5400	8600	13500

* Not applicable to sizes below 1 mm
† Not recommended for fits in sizes above 500 mm

Gauge tolerances

Like any other component, gauges cannot be manufactured to size but must have toleranced dimensions.

BS 4500:1974 (part 2) discusses the design and tolerancing of plug, ring and gap gauges for components which themselves have been toleranced in accordance with BS 4500:1974 (part 1). It also discusses the design and tolerancing of reference discs for checking gap gauges.

The tolerances, and their dispositions, for any gauge depend upon:

1 The nominal 'diameter' of the product feature being checked.

2 The tolerance grade (IT number) appropriate to the product feature being checked.

3 The type of gauge (e.g. plug, ring, gap, etc.).

Figure 4.38 shows how the tolerance zones are disposed for shafts and holes up to and including 180 mm nominal diameter. For larger sizes, and for reference discs of any size, tolerancing becomes more complex and BS 4500:1974 (part 2) should be referred to for further clarification.

Example 4.4 Calculate the dimensions for the GO and NOT GO elements of a plug gauge for checking a hole of nominal diameter 25 mm and tolerance grade IT6.

Solution From Table 4.5 it will be seen that for a nominal diameter 25 mm and tolerance grade IT6:

$$\text{product tolerance} = 0.013 \text{ mm}$$
$$Z = 0.002 \text{ mm}$$
$$Y = 0.0015 \text{ mm}$$

Product hole limits are:

$$\text{upper limit} = 25.013 \text{ mm}$$
$$\text{lower limit} = 25.000 \text{ mm}$$
$$\text{tolerance} = 0.013 \text{ mm}$$

From Table 4.4, a *plug gauge* for a component having a tolerance grade of IT6 will itself have:

plug gauge tolerance grade,
size = IT2
form = IT1

To obtain the gauge element tolerance (H), refer back to Table 4.5 using the nominal diameter 25 mm, but the gauge size tolerance grade or IT2.

Thus: H = 0.0025 mm.

Fig. 4.39(a) shows how these data are applied to the gauge elements.

NOT GO element

Upper limit	= hole U/L + H/2
	= 25.013 + 0.001 25
	= 25.014 25 mm
Lower limit	= hole U/L − H/2
	= 25.013 − 0.001 25
	= 25.011 75 mm

GO element

Upper limit	= hole L/L + Z + H/2
	= 25.000 + 0.002
	+ 0.001 25
	= 25.003 25 mm
Lower limit	= hole L/L + Z − H/2
	= 25.000 + 0.002
	− 0.001 25
	= 25.000 75 mm
Wear limit (Y)	= hole L/L − Y
	= 25.000 − 0.0015
	= 24.9985 mm

Table 4.4 Tolerance grades for gauges (from BS 4500: Part 2: 1974)

Workpiece tolerance grade (IT)*	6		7		8 to 10		11 and 12		13 to 16	
	Tolerance grade of gauge (IT)									
Type of gauge	Size	Form	Size	Form	Size	Form	Size	Form	Size	Form
Cylindrical plug gauge	2	1	3	2	3	2	5	4	7	5
Cylindrical bar gauge	2	1	3	2	3	2	5	4	7	5
Spherical plug or disc gauge	2	1	2	1	2	1	4	3	6	5
Spherically-ended rod gauge	2	1	2	1	2	1	4	3	6	5
Cylindrical ring gauge	3	2	3	2	4	3	5	4	7	5
Gap gauge	3	2	3	2	4	3	5	4	7	5
Reference disc for gap gauge	1	1	1	1	2	1	2	1	3	2
Reference cylindrical setting plug gauge	1	1	1	1	2	1	2	1	3	2
Reference cylindrical setting ring gauge	1	1	1	1	2	1	2	1	3	2

* See table of standard tolerances in BS 4500: Part 1.

Courtesy BSI.

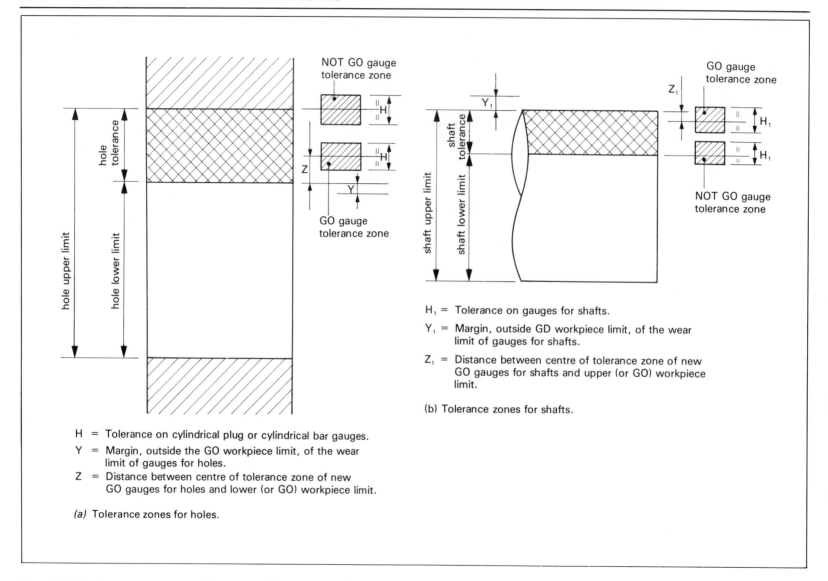

H = Tolerance on cylindrical plug or cylindrical bar gauges.

Y = Margin, outside the GO workpiece limit, of the wear limit of gauges for holes.

Z = Distance between centre of tolerance zone of new GO gauges for holes and lower (or GO) workpiece limit.

(a) Tolerance zones for holes.

H_1 = Tolerance on gauges for shafts.

Y_1 = Margin, outside GD workpiece limit, of the wear limit of gauges for shafts.

Z_1 = Distance between centre of tolerance zone of new GO gauges for shafts and upper (or GO) workpiece limit.

(b) Tolerance zones for shafts.

Fig. 4.38 Tolerance zones of limit gauges B.S. 4500: Part 2: 1974

For most practical purposes it is not necessary to derive the gauge element limits of size from first principles. Providing that some rounding off of sizes to avoid undersirable fractions of a micrometre is acceptable, then the gauge dimensions (plug gauge) may be taken direct from Table 4.6. For Example 4.4, the gauge element sizes would be obtained as follows.

For component diameter 25 mm and tolerance grade IT6 the table specifies:

NOT GO element

Upper limit + 0·0012 mm
Lower limit − 0·0012 mm

Thus the dimensions for the NOT GO element will be:

upper limit	= hole U/L + 0·0012
	= 25·013 + 0·0012
	= 25·0142 mm
lower limit	= hole U/L − 0·0012 mm
	= 25·013 − 0·0012 mm
	= 25·0118 mm

GO element

Upper limit + 0·0032 mm
Lower limit + 0·0008 mm
Limit of wear − 0·0015 mm

Thus the dimensions for the GO element will be:

upper limit	= hole L/L + 0·0032
	= 25·000 + 0·0032
	= 25·0032 mm
lower limit	= hole L/L + 0·0008
	= 25·000 + 0·0008
	= 25·0008 mm

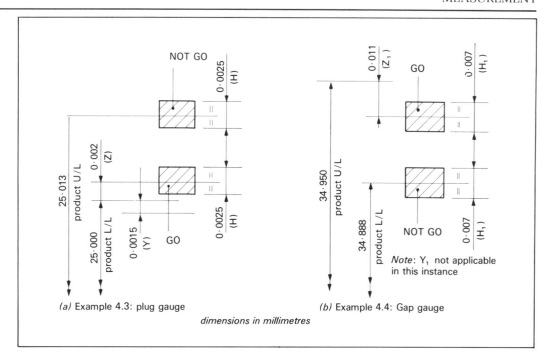

(a) Example 4.3: plug gauge

(b) Example 4.4: Gap gauge

Note: Y₁ not applicable in this instance

dimensions in millimetres

Fig. 4.39 Tolerances for plug gap gauge examples

Wear limit (Y)	= hole L/L − Y
	= 25·000 − 0·0015 mm
	= 24·9985 mm

Comparison with Example 4.4 shows that the dimensions have been rounded off to 4 decimal places in such a direction that the rounding is towards the *inside* of the gauge tolerance. This ensures that the deviations specified are always within the ISO deviations.

Example 4.5 Calculate the dimensions for the GO and NOT GO elements of a gap gauge for checking a turned shaft 35 mm e9.

Solution From Table 4.2 it will be seen that an e9 shaft will have the following dimensions:

upper limit	= 35·00 − 0·050
	= 34·950 mm
lower limit	= 35·00 − 0·112
	= 34·888 mm

That is, a deviation of −50 μm from the nominal size and a tolerance grade of 62 μ m.

Table 4.5 Location of the gauge tolerances and the limit of maximum permissible gauge wear in relation to the nominal limit of the workpiece, for grades 6 to 16 and sizes up to 500 mm

All values are in micrometres. (from BS 4500: Part 2: 1974)   *For grades 6N, 7N and 8N the values of y and y', y_1 and y'_1 are zero.   Courtesy BSI.

Location of the tolerances and the limit of maximum permissible gauge wear for workpiece tolerance grade

Diameter of product, D (mm) Over	To	IT 0	IT 1	IT 2	IT 3	IT 4	IT 5	IT 6	z	y	y'	α α_1	z_1	y_1	y'_1	IT 7	z_1	y_1	y'_1	α_1
	3	0·5	0·8	1·2	2	3	4	6	1	1	–	–	1·5	1·5	–	10	1·5	1·5	–	–
3	6	0·6	1	1·5	2·5	4	5	8	1·5	1	–	–	2	1·5	–	12	2	1·5	–	–
6	10	0·6	1	1·5	2·5	4	6	9	1·5	1	–	–	2	1·5	–	15	2	1·5	–	–
10	18	0·8	1·2	2	3	5	8	11	2	1·5	–	–	2·5	2	–	18	2·5	2	–	–
18	30	1	1·5	2·5	4	6	9	13	2	1·5	–	–	3	3	–	21	3	3	–	–
30	50	1	1·5	2·5	4	7	11	16	2·5	2	–	–	3·5	3	–	25	3·5	3	–	–
50	80	1·2	2	3	5	8	13	19	2·5	2	–	–	4	3	–	30	4	3	–	–
80	120	1·5	2·5	4	6	10	15	22	3	3	–	–	5	4	–	35	5	4	–	–
120	180	2	3·5	5	8	12	18	25	4	3	–	–	6	4	–	40	6	4	–	–
180	250	3	4·5	7	10	14	10	29	5	4	2	2	7	5	3	46	7	6	3	3
250	315	4	6	8	12	16	23	32	6	5	2	3	8	6	3	52	8	7	3	4
315	400	5	7	9	13	18	25	36	7	6	2	4	10	6	2	57	10	8	2	6
400	500	6	8	10	15	20	17	40	8	7	2	5	11	7	2	63	11	9	2	7

Over	To	IT 8	z_1	y_1	y'_1	α_1	IT 9	z_1	y_1	y'_1	α_1	IT 10	z_1	y_1	y'_1	α_1	IT 11	z_1	y_1	y'_1	α_1	IT 12	z_1	y_1	y'_1	α_1
	3	14	2	3	–	–	25	5	0	–	–	40	5	0	–	–	60	10	0	–	–	100	10	0	–	–
3	6	18	3	3	–	–	30	6	0	–	–	48	6	0	–	–	75	12	0	–	–	120	12	0	–	–
6	10	22	3	3	–	–	36	7	0	–	–	58	7	0	–	–	90	14	0	–	–	150	14	0	–	–
10	18	27	4	4	–	–	43	8	0	–	–	70	8	0	–	–	110	16	0	–	–	180	16	0	–	–
18	30	33	5	4	–	–	52	9	0	–	–	84	9	0	–	–	130	19	0	–	–	210	19	0	–	–
30	50	39	6	5	–	–	62	11	0	–	–	100	11	0	–	–	160	22	0	–	–	250	22	0	–	–
50	80	46	7	5	–	–	74	13	0	–	–	120	13	0	–	–	190	25	0	–	–	300	25	0	–	–
80	120	54	8	6	–	–	87	15	0	–	–	140	15	0	–	–	220	28	0	–	–	350	28	0	–	–
120	180	63	9	6	–	–	100	18	0	–	–	160	18	0	–	–	250	32	0	–	–	400	32	0	–	–
180	250	72	12	7	3	4	115	21	0	4	4	185	24	0	7	7	290	40	0	10	10	460	45	0	15	15
250	315	81	14	9	3	6	130	24	0	6	6	210	27	0	9	9	320	45	0	15	15	520	50	0	20	20
315	400	89	16	9	2	7	140	28	0	7	7	230	32	0	11	11	360	50	0	15	15	570	65	0	30	30
400	500	97	18	11	2	9	155	32	0	9	9	250	37	0	14	14	400	55	0	20	20	630	70	0	35	35

Table 4.6 Deviations for plug, ring and gap gauges in sizes up to 180 mm Tolerances are in micrometres.

Plug gauges — Diameter of product, D

Over (mm)	To (mm)	IT6 GO H limit of gauge tolerance from L limit of work	IT6 GO L limit of gauge tolerance from L limit of work	IT6 GO Limit of wear	IT6 NOT GO H limit of gauge tolerance from H limit of work	IT6 NOT GO L limit of gauge tolerance from H limit of work	IT7 GO H limit	IT7 GO L limit	IT7 GO wear	IT7 NOT GO H limit	IT7 NOT GO L limit	IT8 GO H limit	IT8 GO L limit	IT8 GO wear	IT8 NOT GO H limit	IT8 NOT GO L limit	IT9/10 GO H limit	IT9/10 GO L limit	IT9/10 GO wear	IT9/10 NOT GO H limit	IT9/10 NOT GO L limit
—	3	+1·6	+0·4	−1	+0·6	−0·6	+2·5	+0·5	−1·5	+1·0	−1·0	−0·5	−3·5	+3	+1·5	−1·5	−3·5	−6·5	+0	+1·5	−1·5
3	6	+2·2	+0·8	−1	+0·7	−0·7	+3·2	+0·8	−1·5	+1·2	−1·2	−1	−5	+3	+2	−2	−4	−8	+0	+2	−2
6	10	+2·2	+0·8	−1	+0·7	−0·7	+3·2	+0·8	−1·5	+1·2	−1·2	−1	−5	+3	+2	−2	−5	−9	+0	+2	−2
10	18	+3	+1·0	−1·5	+1·0	−1·0	+4	+1	−2	+1·5	−1·5	−1·5	−6·5	+4	+2·5	−2·5	−5·5	−10·5	+0	+2·5	−2·5
18	30	+3·2	+0·8	−1·5	+1·2	−1·2	+5	+1	−3	+2	−2	−2	−8	+4	+3	−3	−6	−12	+0	+3	−3
30	50	+3·7	+1·3	−2	+1·2	−1·2	+5·5	+1·5	−3	+2	−2	−2·5	−9·5	+5	+3·5	−3·5	−7·5	−14·5	+0	+3·5	−3·5
50	80	+4	+1	−2	+1·5	−1·5	+6·5	+1·5	−3	+2·5	−2·5	−3	−11	+5	+4	−4	−9	−17	+0	+4	−4
80	120	+5	+1	−3	+2	−2	+8	+2	−4	+3	−3	−3	−13	+6	+5	−5	−10	−20	+0	+5	−5
120	180	+6·5	+1·5	−3	+2·5	−2·5	+10	+2	−4	+4	−4	−3	−15	+6	+6	−6	−12	−24	+0	+6	−6

Ring and gap gauges — Diameter of product, D

Over (mm)	To (mm)	IT6 GO H limit of gauge tolerance from H limit of work	IT6 GO L limit of gauge tolerance from H limit of work	IT6 GO Limit of wear	IT6 NOT GO H limit of gauge tolerance from L limit of work	IT6 NOT GO L limit of gauge tolerance from L limit of work	IT7 GO H limit	IT7 GO L limit	IT7 GO wear	IT7 NOT GO H limit	IT7 NOT GO L limit	IT8 GO H limit	IT8 GO L limit	IT8 GO wear	IT8 NOT GO H limit	IT8 NOT GO L limit	IT9/10 GO H limit	IT9/10 GO L limit	IT9/10 GO wear	IT9/10 NOT GO H limit	IT9/10 NOT GO L limit
—	3	0	−2·0	+1	+1	−1	−0·5	−2·5	+1·5	+1	−1	+3·0	+1·0	−3	+1·0	−1·0	+6·0	+4·0	−0	+1·0	−1·0
3	6	−0·3	−2·7	+1	+1·2	−1·2	−0·8	−3·2	+1·5	+1·2	−1·2	+4·2	+1·8	−3	+1·2	−1·2	+7·2	+4·8	−0	+1·2	−1·2
6	10	−0·3	−2·7	+1	+1·2	−1·2	−0·8	−3·2	+1·5	+1·2	−1·2	+4·2	+1·8	−3	+1·2	−1·2	+7·2	+4·8	−0	+1·2	−1·2
10	18	−0·5	−3·5	+1·5	+1·5	−1·5	−1	−4	+2	+1·5	−1·5	+5·5	+2·5	−4	+2	−2	+9·5	+6·5	−0	+1·5	−1·5
18	30	0	−4	+1·5	+2	−2	−1	−5	+3	+2	−2	+7	+3	−4	+2	−2	+11	+7	−0	+2	−2
30	50	−0·5	−4·5	+2	+2	−2	−1·5	−5·5	+3	+2	−2	+8	+4	−5	+2	−2	+13	+9	−0	+2	−2
50	80	0	−5	+2	+2·5	−2·5	−1·5	−6·5	+3	+2·5	−2·5	+9·5	+4·5	−5	+2·5	−2·5	+15·5	+10·5	−0	+2·5	−2·5
80	120	0	−6	+3	+3	−3	−2	−8	+4	+3	−3	+11	+5	−6	+3	−3	+18	+12	−0	+3	−3
120	180	0	−8	+3	+4	−4	−2	−10	+4	+4	−4	+13	+5	−6	+4	−4	+22	+14	−0	+4	−4

Note Some of the values in the above table have been rounded to avoid specifying undesirable fractions of a micrometre but in all cases the rounding has been made in a direction towards the inside of the gauge tolerance so that the deviations specified are always within the ISO deviations.

Courtesy BSI.

From Table 4.5 it will be seen that for a nominal diameter of 35 mm and a tolerance grade IT9:

product tolerance $= 0 \cdot 062$ mm
(compare Table 4.1)
$Z = 0 \cdot 011$ mm

From Table 4.4 it will be seen that a gap gauge for a component having a tolerance grade of IT9 will itself have:

Gap gauge tolerance grade: size IT4 form IT3

To obtain the gauge element tolerance (H_1), refer back to Table 4.5 using the nominal diameter of 35 mm, but the gauge size tolerance grade of IT4.

Thus: $H_1 = 0 \cdot 007$ mm

Reference to Fig. 4.39(b) shows how these data are applied to the gauge elements.

NOT GO element

Upper limit
$$= \text{shaft L/L} + H_1/2$$
$$= 34 \cdot 888 + 0 \cdot 0035$$
$$= \underline{34 \cdot 8915 \text{ mm}}$$

Lower limit
$$= \text{shaft L/L} - H_1/2$$
$$= 34 \cdot 888 - 0 \cdot 0035$$
$$= \underline{34 \cdot 8845 \text{ mm}}$$

GO element

Upper limit
$$= \text{shaft U/L} - Z_1 + H_1/2$$
$$= 34 \cdot 950 - 0 \cdot 011 + 0 \cdot 0035$$
$$= \underline{34 \cdot 9425 \text{ mm}}$$

Lower limit
$$= \text{shaft U/L} - Z_1 - H_1/2$$
$$= 34 \cdot 950 - 0 \cdot 011 - 0 \cdot 0035$$
$$= \underline{34 \cdot 9355 \text{ mm}}$$

There is no wear limit (Y_1) in this instance.

For most practical purposes it is not necessary to derive the gauge element limits of size from first principles. As in Example 4.3 the gauge dimensions can be taken direct from the tables (in this case Table 4.6) and the sizes given are applied directly to product limits of size. In this instance the results are identical and there is no rounding off.

Screw thread gauges

As with the plain dimensions considered earlier, screw threads have to be toleranced so that they can be produced within the limits of accuracy of the threading equipment available. Therefore, limit gauges are made available for checking screwed components. They are more complex than the plain gauges previously considered as they have to check form as well as dimensional accuracy.

Figure 4.40(a) shows some typical solid thread gauges. The following points should be carefully noted.
1 The double-ended plug gauge has the

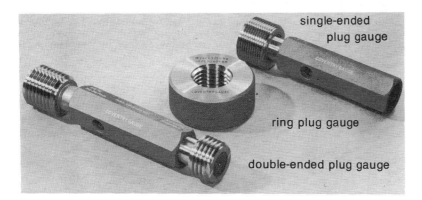

single-ended plug gauge

ring plug gauge

double-ended plug gauge

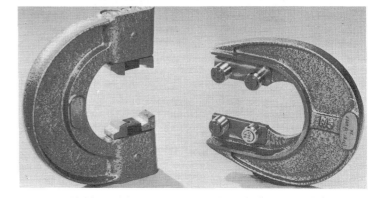

Fig. 4.40 Screw thread gauges

(a) Plug gauges

(b) Adjustable thread caliper gauges

NOT GO element *form relieved* and checks the effective diameter only. In addition, a plain plug gauge is required to check the minor diameter.

2 In general, the comments in 1 also apply to ring gauges (separate gauges being provided for the GO and NOT GO functions). A plain gap gauge or ring gauge is required to check, in this instance, the major diameter.

3 In the case of gauges for taper pipe threads, the component is the correct diameter when its end lies within the cut-away portion of the gauge. (This also applies to plain taper gauges, Fig. 4.44.)

Just as in plain gauges, adjustable caliper gauges are also available for checking screw threads. In this case they have to be set to special plug gauges. Figure 4.40(b) shows a typical adjustable thread caliper gauge.

From the illustration of the adjustable gauge it will be seen that the front anvils are a complete form GO gauge and no element of a screw which passes these anvils can be too large. The anvils are of sufficient width to test the required length of engagement of the screw. The work must pass freely through the full form anvils without undue pressure. Similarly, the NOT GO element is form relieved to check the effective diameter.

As with plain gauges the bulk and weight of adjustable thread gauges makes them less suitable for the smaller sizes of screwed components, for which solid gauges are preferable.

The main advantage of the screw

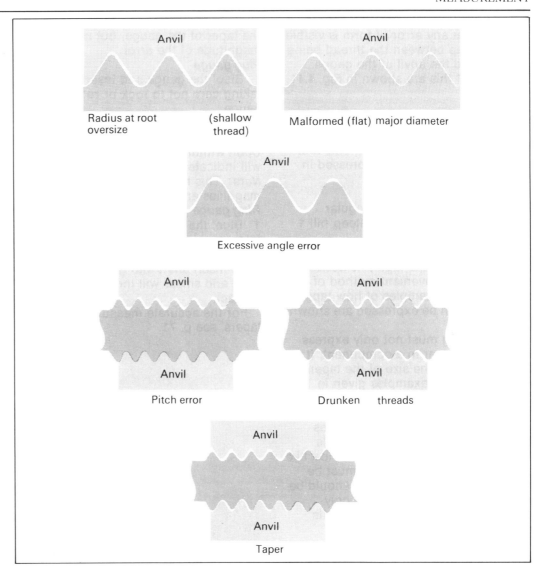

Fig. 4.41 Errors of thread form

thread caliper gauge over the solid ring gauge is that any error of form is visible as a light gap between the thread being checked and the anvil of the gauge. Examples of this are shown in Fig. 4.41.

Tapers

The slope of tapered components and angular surfaces can be expressed in two ways.
1 Degrees of arc.
2 As a gradient by its rectangular co-ordinates, for example, steep hill 1 in 4.

The method chosen will depend upon the steepness of the taper, its accuracy, and the most convenient method of measurement. Examples of how tapers and angles can be expressed are shown in Fig. 4.42.

The drawing must not only express the angle of taper in a component, it must also show the size of the tapered component. The examples given in Fig. 4.43 show the methods recommended in BS 308.

Figure 4.44 shows typical gauges used for checking male and female tapers. These are limit gauges since, like any other dimension, tapers must be given a tolerance. However, it should be noted that this type of gauge only checks the 'size' of the taper *not* its angle.

Considerable skill is required in checking angles with such a gauge and one technique is shown in Fig. 4.45. Unfortunately, it only shows whether the angle of taper is larger or smaller than the taper of the gauge, but not the magnitude of the error.

Plug gauge
1 'Blue' the gauge and insert into hole taking care not to rock or rotate the gauge.
2 Remove the gauge and wipe it clean.
3 Re-insert gauge carefully into hole. Upon withdrawing the gauge the 'smear' will indicate area of contact.
Note: This method of double insertion magnifies any error present.

Ring gauge
1 'Blue' the shaft and insert carefully into gauge.
2 Remove shaft and wipe it clean.
3 Re-insert shaft into gauge. Withdraw shaft and smear will indicate area of contact.

For the accurate measurement of tapers, see p. 71.

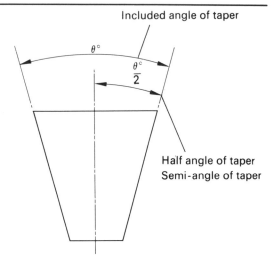

60 seconds (") = 1 minute (')

60 minutes (') = 1 degree of arc (°)

(A) AN ANGLE EXPRESSED IN DEGREES OF ARC

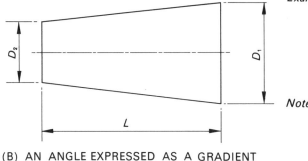

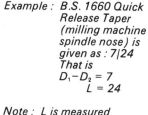

Example : B.S. 1660 Quick Release Taper (milling machine spindle nose) is given as : 7|24 That is
$D_1 - D_2 = 7$
$L = 24$

Note : L is measured **parallel** *to the* **axis**

$$\text{Taper} = \frac{D_1 - D_2}{L}$$

(B) AN ANGLE EXPRESSED AS A GRADIENT

Fig. 4.42 Specification of tapers

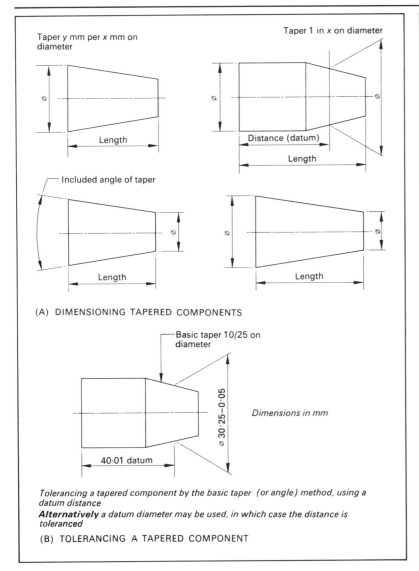

Fig. 4.43 Dimensioning tapered components

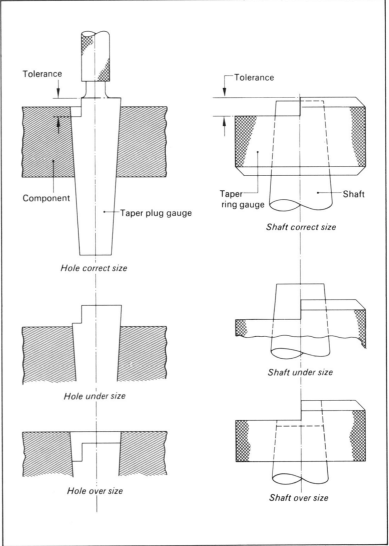

Fig. 4.44 Taper plug and ring gauges

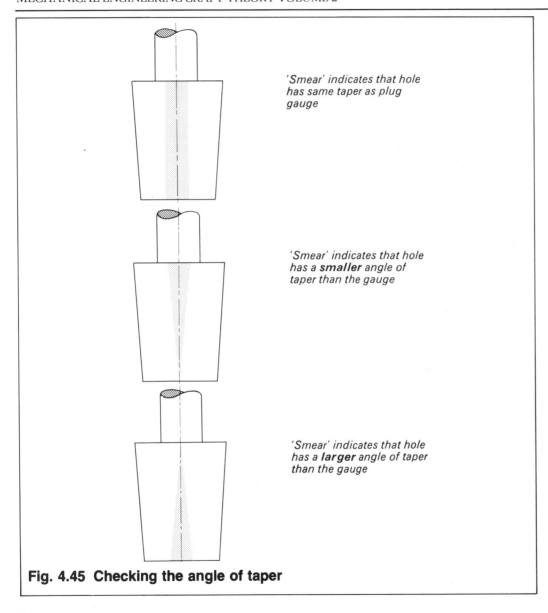

'Smear' indicates that hole has same taper as plug gauge

*'Smear' indicates that hole has a **smaller** angle of taper than the gauge*

*'Smear' indicates that hole has a **larger** angle of taper than the gauge*

Fig. 4.45 Checking the angle of taper

Exercises

1. Figure 4.46 shows the micrometer adjustment for a machine slide. Complete Table 4.7.

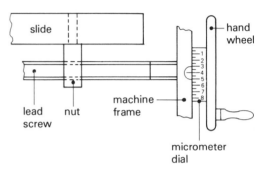

Fig. 4.46

2. Answer the following questions concerning micrometers. Illustrate your answers with clear sketches if necessary.
   (a) Explain why a micrometer cylinder gauge is superior to an inside micrometer for reading the diameter of deep holes. Sketch a typical cylinder gauge.
   (b) Explain what is meant by, and the purpose of, the fiducial indicator found on a bench micrometer.
   (c) Show why the scales of a depth micrometer are reversed to those of a micrometer caliper.

3. (a) Sketch a 50 division vernier and main scales to show a reading of 35·24 mm.

Table 4.7

Lead of screws (mm).	Number of divisions on micrometer dial	Distance moved by the slide for each dial division (mm)
5	100	
	120	0·05
8		0·02

(b) With the aid of sketches show how a vernier caliper may be used for both internal and external measurements. What allowance has to be made when the vernier caliper is used for an internal reading?

4. Tabulate the advantages and limitations of the vernier caliper compared with a micrometer caliper.

5. Show how the reading accuracy of a micrometer caliper can be improved by the addition of a vernier scale. Sketch the scales to show a reading of 22·572 mm.

6. Sketch a vernier protractor scale to show the following readings:
(a) 17° 25′, (b) 20° 35′, (c) 0° 15′.

7. Show, with the aid of sketches, the following applications of a dial test indicator (DTI).
(a) (i) Comparative measurement
(ii) Machine setting
(iii) Detecting out of roundness
(iv) Testing concentricity
(v) Use as a fiducial indicator when mounted on a vernier height gauge.

(b) Explain, with the aid of sketches what is meant by **cosine error** when using dial test indicators.

8. Sketch in good proportion a plunger type dial test indicator and a lever and scroll type dial test indicator. List the advantages and limitations of each type.

9. (a) Sketch a 200 mm sine bar set to an angle of 35° using slip gauges.
(b) From the set of slip gauges listed in Table 4.8 select a suitable stack of gauges to give the angle of 35° in part (a).

Table 4.8

Range (mm)	Steps (mm)	Pieces
1·01 to 1·49	0·01	49
0·50 to 9·50	0·50	19
10·00 to 50·00	10·00	5
75·00 and 100·00	—	2
1·0025	—	1
1·005	—	1
1·0075	—	1

(c) What precautions should be taken when:
(i) handling slip gauges,
(ii) wringing slip gauges together,
(iii) separating slip gauges.

10. With the aid of sketches explain what is meant by:
(a) maximum and minimum metal conditions for a hole,
(b) hole and shaft basis systems of limits and fits,
(c) limits of size and tolerance,
(d) interference, transition and clearance fits.

11. With reference to BS4500: pt 1, sketch and dimension a shaft and hole of nominal diameter 30 mm to give an H8/f7 fit.

12. (a) Calculate the dimensions for the GO and NOT GO elements of a plug gauge for checking a hole of nominal diameter 30 mm and tolerance grade IT6 (Refer to BS4500: pt 2 for the necessary tables).
(b) Show how a stepped taper plug gauge is used to check the size of a taper hole and how this gauge may be used to assess the accuracy of taper using prussian blue.

5. Fitting

Location

Figure 5.1 shows two pieces of metal held together by nuts and bolts. Providing they are not pulled apart with sufficient force to break the bolts, the following conditions apply.

1 The components cannot be separated in the direction YY.

2 Only friction prevents slip in the direction XX until the clearance between the shanks of the bolts and the holes is taken up as shown in Fig. 5.1(b).

3 If the two pieces of metal are separated and re-assembled it is unlikely that they will be in exactly the same position they were in before being taken apart.

For this reason it is preferable just to use the bolts, nuts, studs, etc., as *fixings* and use other devices to provide the *location*. Some typical location devices that will be discussed in this chapter include dowels, pins, studs, fitted bolts, tenons, tongue and groove, spigot and register.

Dowels

Figure 5.2(a) shows a component restrained by screwed fastenings and located by dowels. Such a component may be removed and replaced without loss of positional accuracy until the

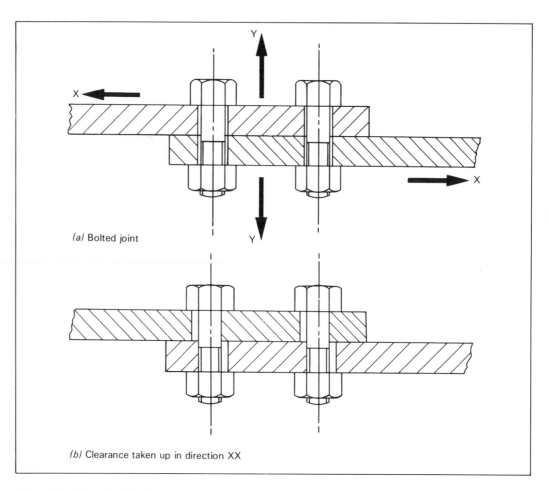

(a) Bolted joint

(b) Clearance taken up in direction XX

Fig. 5.1 A bolted joint

holes wear oversize. Figure 5.2(b) shows the steps in dowelling a component.

1 The component is lightly nipped into position using the screwed fastenings. These should be in clearance size holes to allow for slight, final adjustment, (Fig. 5.2(b)(i)).

2 The component should then be set in position. In this case it is being set parallel to a datum edge with a dial test indicator as shown in Fig. 5.2(b)(ii).

3 The screwed fastenings are tightened so that the component cannot move whilst the dowels are being fitted. After tightening the position should be re-checked and corrected if necessary.

4 The dowel holes are now drilled and reamed in situ as shown in Fig. 5.2(b)(iii).

5 The dowels are now driven home using a soft drift to avoid mushrooming or burring their heads as shown in Fig. 5.2(b)(iv). A final check is now made of the positional accuracy of the components.

For the dowel to locate a component accurately and positively it should be as large in diameter as the component will stand. Usually this is the same diameter as the fixing bolt. It must also be a precise, light drive fit in the dowel hole. The accurate machining of dowel holes will be considered on p. 98.

Taper pins

Figure 5.3(a) shows typical taper pin reamers. These are used for producing tapered holes in components required to be locked in place by a tapered pin as

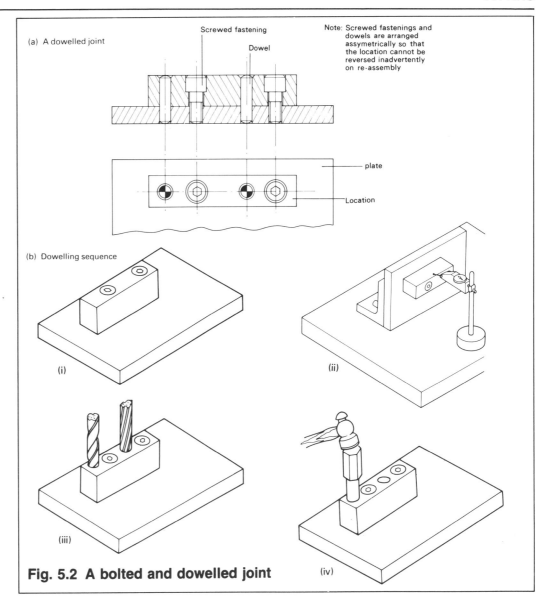

Fig. 5.2 A bolted and dowelled joint

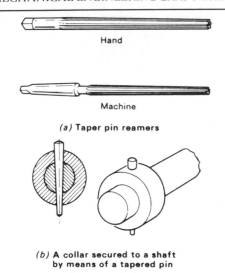

(a) **Taper pin reamers**

(b) **A collar secured to a shaft by means of a tapered pin**

Fig. 5.3 A pinned fixing

shown in Fig. 5.3(b). The tapered pin has obvious advantages over a parallel pin for such purposes. It locks up tight and is retained by a wedging action as it is driven home, but is immediately released when driven back in the reverse direction. Further, any wear in the hole is compensated for by the pin merely having to be driven a little deeper.

Studs (buttons)

Unlike the dowel that provides a positive lcoation along both the XX and YY axes in Fig. 5.1, the stud or button shown in Fig. 5.4(a) provides a location in one direction only. It will be seen that the stud is used to locate a component relative to a slot where it provides positional adjustment by allowing the

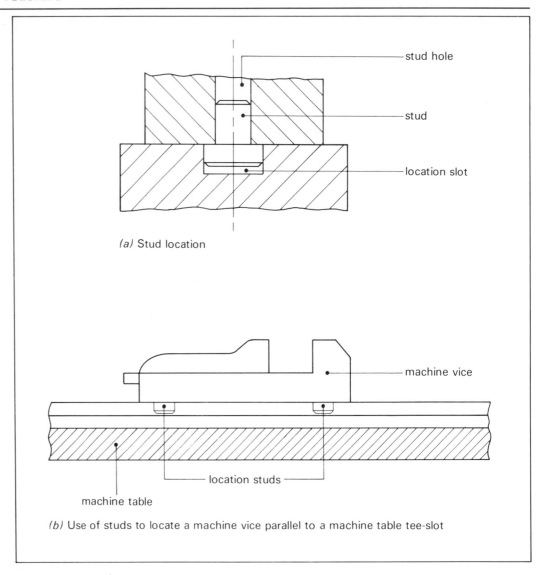

(a) Stud location

(b) Use of studs to locate a machine vice parallel to a machine table tee-slot

Fig. 5.4 Location stud

component to slide along the slot.

A typical application would be the alignment of a machine vice with the tee-slot of a machine as shown in Fig. 5.4(b). Unfortunately, the stud only makes line contact with the cheeks of the slot and wear is rapid if the vice is removed and replaced frequently. For this reason the tenon described below is often preferred. The main advantages of the stud are as follows.

1 It is located in a reamed hole that is cheap and quick to produce compared with a machined tenon slot.

2 The stud itself can be quickly and easily turned up on the lathe.

Fitted bolts

Fitted bolts have accurately ground shanks slightly larger in diameter than the diameter of the thread. Figure 5.5 shows a section through two components held together by a fitted bolt and nut. The shank is a light drive fit into a reamed hole and acts as both dowel and bolt where space is limited. To ensure that the shank alone provides the location the thread must be free to 'float'. Hence the use of a through hole and nut in the example shown.

Tenon

This is a variation on the stud described on p. 98. It will be seen from Fig. 5.6 that the fitting of a tenon is more complex and requires a location groove to be milled or shaped in the component being located. However, the tenon is more robust than the button. It can withstand a greater side thrust without

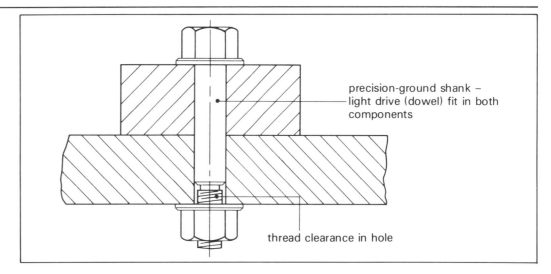

precision-ground shank – light drive (dowel) fit in both components

thread clearance in hole

Fig. 5.5 The fitted bolt

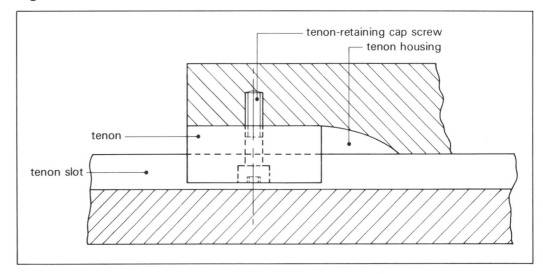

tenon-retaining cap screw

tenon housing

tenon

tenon slot

Fig. 5.6 The tenon

the likelihood of shearing off. Further, the greater contact area reduces wear and provides a more positive location.

Tongue and groove

This is a variation of the tenon block. It will be seen from Fig. 5.7 that instead of fitting a separate tenon block the tongue is machined from the solid. Although wasteful in material, it is used on small components where it saves space and the fitting time associated with a separate tenon block. Unfortunately, wear of the tongue cannot be compensated for, whereas a replacement tenon can easily be provided.

Spigot and register

This is used for fitting chucks and other turning fixtures to backplates. It will be seen from Fig. 5.8(a) that a spigot and register is a cylindrical tongue and groove. Unlike the tongue and groove which provides location in one direction only the spigot and register provides location in two directions as shown in Fig. 5.8(b).

Reamers and reaming

When producing a hole with a twist drill, that hole is most likely to be out-of-round and oversize. These faults can be overcome by drilling the hole undersize and correcting it for size, shape and finish by reaming. This can be done by hand at the bench or on the drilling machine.

  Hand reamers may have straight or

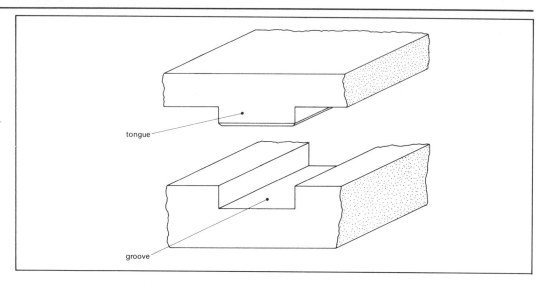

Fig. 5.7 Tongue and groove

spiral (left-hand) flutes. Unlike the machine reamer which has a morse taper shank to fit a machine spindle, the hand reamer has a square on the end of the shank so that it can be rotated by a tap wrench. It is always rotated in a clockwise direction and is not reversed when being withdrawn from the hole. A lubricant should always be used when reaming. Figure 5.9(a) shows the essential features of the hand reamer. Comparison with Fig. 5.9(b) shows that a hand reamer has a taper lead as well as a bevel lead, whereas a machine reamer only has a bevel lead. The additional taper lead is required to give guidance to the hand reamer and ensure its alignment with the original drilled hole. The parallel portion of the

reamer body has radial land and has, therefore, the characteristics of a *fluted reamer*, whilst the taper lead cuts peripherally and has, therefore, the characteristics of a *rose reamer*.

Fluted reamer   This term refers to reamers that have a cylindrical land just behind the cutting edge. Such reamers have, therefore, zero clearance and the essential metal cutting wedge is not established. Thus, little or no cutting action can take place peripherally. In fluted reamers, all the cutting action takes place at the bevel lead (or the taper lead in the case of a hand reamer) where the metal cutting wedge can be established. The terms *bevel lead* and *taper lead* are explained in Fig. 5.9 and 5.10.

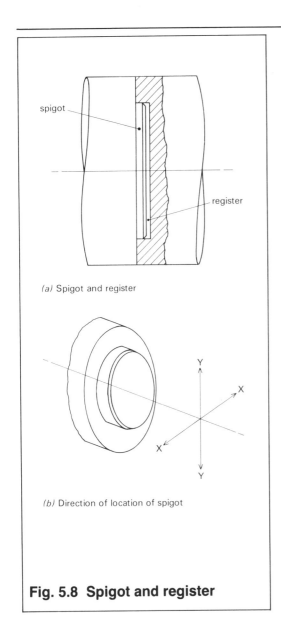

(a) Spigot and register

(b) Direction of location of spigot

Fig. 5.8 Spigot and register

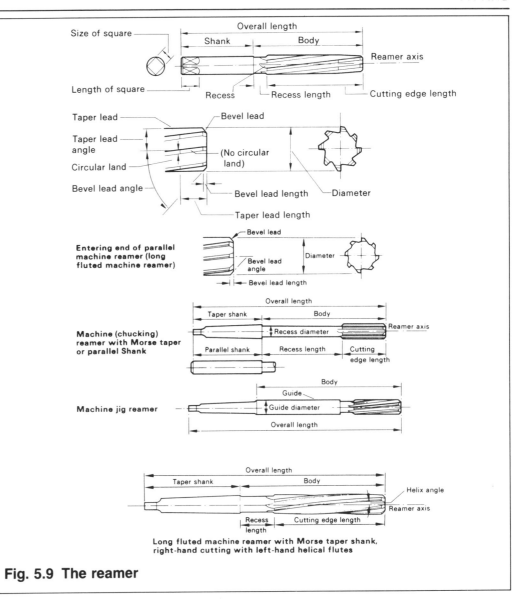

Fig. 5.9 The reamer

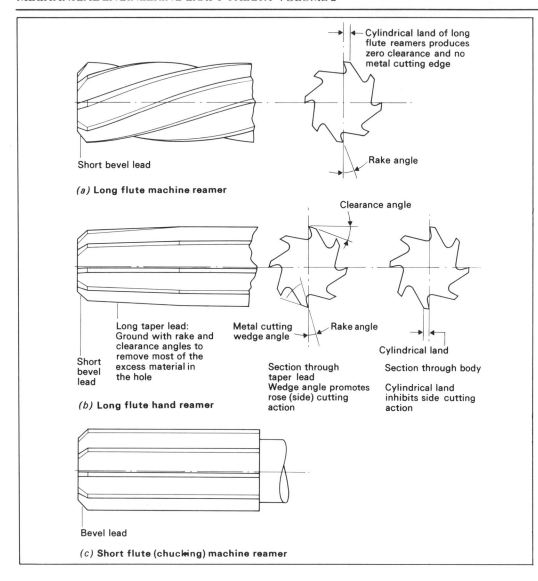

Cylindrical land of long flute reamers produces zero clearance and no metal cutting edge

Rake angle

(a) **Long flute machine reamer**

Clearance angle

Metal cutting wedge angle

Rake angle

Cylindrical land

Section through taper lead
Wedge angle promotes rose (side) cutting action

Section through body

Cylindrical land inhibits side cutting action

Long taper lead: Ground with rake and clearance angles to remove most of the excess material in the hole

Short bevel lead

(b) **Long flute hand reamer**

Bevel lead

(c) **Short flute (chucking) machine reamer**

Fig. 5.10 Reamer geometry

Rose reamer This term refers to reamers that have a definite clearance angle behind the cutting edge. Such reamers have a clearly defined metal-cutting wedge action and can cut peripherally along the full length of the flutes. Because of this, rose reamers can remove metal more rapidly but generally produce a less accurate hole than a fluted reamer where the cylindrical land gives closer control of the cutting edges. Long fluted reamers seldom have a rose cutting action, this action being found in taper pin reamers (p. 95) and machine 'chucking' reamers. The rose action is useful when cutting materials such as phosphor bronze and reinforced plastics which tend to shrink back and seize on a fluted reamer.

Hand reamers have a rose cutting action for the bevel and taper lead, but a fluted cutting action for the reamer body. This provides a satisfactory compromise between ease of metal removal and accuracy of size and finish.

A reamer can only follow the axis of a previously drilled hole. Any attempt to 'pull' the hole to correct its axial position results in ovality. Thus, to ensure a geometrically correct hole, the reamer is often mounted in a floating reamer holder as shown in Fig. 5.11.

Positioning holes

In simple applications of limited accuracy the twist drill is started in a centre punch mark at the intersection of two scribed lines. This basic method

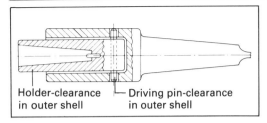

Fig. 5.11 Floating reamer holder

can be improved upon by the following techniques.
1 'Boxing' the hole.
2 Use of the optical centrescope.
3 Use of the co-ordinate table.

Boxing the hole

This technique is shown in Fig. 5.12. It will be seen that when the centre line XX is scribed on the surface of the component, two more lines parallel to XX are scribed, half the hole diameter either side of XX. These lines are AA and BB in the diagram. The component is rotated through 90° and the centre line YY is scribed together with lines CC and DD, half the hole diameter either side of YY. This forms the 'box' within which the hole should lie. Small punch marks are made at E as a witness when the hole has been drilled. A centre punch mark is made at the intersection of XX and YY and the hole is commenced. If the drill starts to run out as shown in Fig. 5.12(b), the centre must be pulled over with a chisel. Figure 5.12(c) shows the half witness marks of a correctly drilled hole.

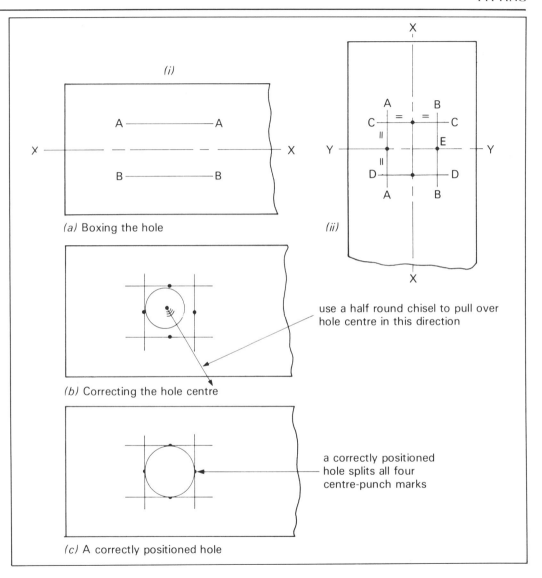

(i)

(a) Boxing the hole

(ii)

(b) Correcting the hole centre

use a half round chisel to pull over hole centre in this direction

(c) A correctly positioned hole

a correctly positioned hole splits all four centre-punch marks

Fig. 5.12 "Boxing" a hole

The optical centrescope

Although an improvement on the simple centre punch mark for starting a drilled hole, even 'boxing' the hole is inadequate for positioning the hole with any real precision.

A more accurate method of picking up the intersection of the centre lines is to use the *optical centrescope* as shown in Fig. 5.13. The centre lines are not centre-punched, the hole being started with a centre drill. Obviously, the centre lines must be very accurately scribed and a vernier height gauge is essential for this purpose. When the component has been positioned under the centrescope and clamped down so that it cannot move out of position, the centrescope is removed and a chuck holding the centre drill is placed in the machine spindle. It is essential to check that the drill chuck and arbor are clean and in good condition so that the centre drill runs true.

The co-ordinate table

The most precise method of hole location – other than using a jig-boring machine – is the use of the co-ordinate table shown in Fig. 5.14(a). The co-ordinate table shown can be set using the micrometer dials and lead screws provided to a reading accuracy of 0·01 mm, or by using slip gauges in the trays provided and the dial gauges as fiducial indicators. The table is

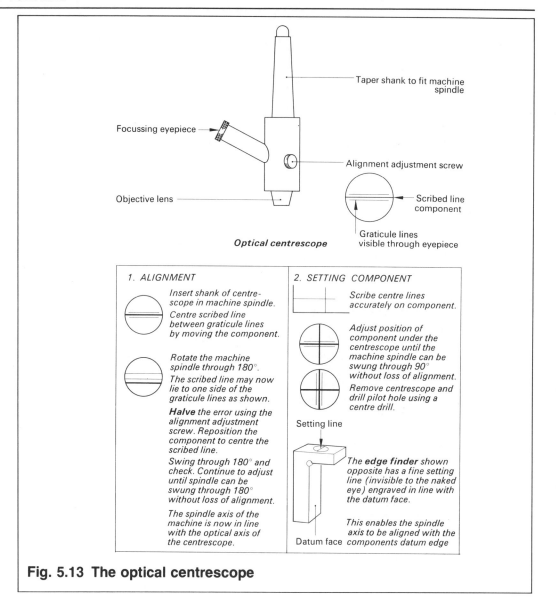

Optical centrescope

Focussing eyepiece

Taper shank to fit machine spindle

Alignment adjustment screw

Objective lens

Scribed line component

Graticule lines visible through eyepiece

1. ALIGNMENT

Insert shank of centre-scope in machine spindle. Centre scribed line between graticule lines by moving the component.

Rotate the machine spindle through 180°. The scribed line may now lie to one side of the graticule lines as shown.

Halve the error using the alignment adjustment screw. Reposition the component to centre the scribed line.

Swing through 180° and check. Continue to adjust until spindle can be swung through 180° without loss of alignment.

The spindle axis of the machine is now in line with the optical axis of the centrescope.

2. SETTING COMPONENT

Scribe centre lines accurately on component.

Adjust position of component under the centrescope until the machine spindle can be swung through 90° without loss of alignment.

Remove centrescope and drill pilot hole using a centre drill.

Setting line

The **edge finder** shown opposite has a fine setting line (invisible to the naked eye) engraved in line with the datum face.

This enables the spindle axis to be aligned with the components datum edge

Datum face

Fig. 5.13 The optical centrescope

This co-ordinate table can be set by using the micrometer dials and lead screws (reading accuracy 0·02 mm), or by using slip gauges in the trays provided and the dial gauges as fiducial indicators

(a) The co-ordinate table

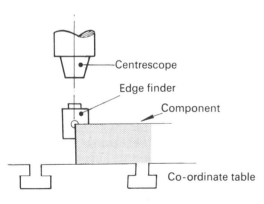

(b) Use of centrescope

1. *The edge of the component is aligned with the machine spindle axis as shown opposite. For details of the centre-scope and edge finder, see Fig. 5.13*

2. *After lining up the spindle axis with the datum edge of the component, the co-ordinate table is moved over to give the required co-ordinate dimension*

3. *The centrescope is removed and the appropriate boring equipment is mounted on the spindle*

Fig. 5.14 The co-ordinate table

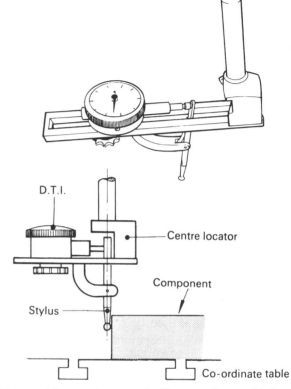

This is used for centring holes and datum edges under boring machine spindles

1. *The centre-finder is adjusted as shown so that the D.T.I. reads zero when the centre-finder is rotated through 180*

2. *The co-ordinate table is moved over the required distance **plus** the radius of the stylus*

3. *The centre-finder is removed and the hole is bored*

(c) The centre finder

clamped after positioning, but before machining commences.

This technique embodies the principles used in jig-boring machines. The spindle is centred over the datum edges of the component either by a centrescope and edge-finder (Fig. 5.14(b)) or by means of a dial gauge (Fig. 5.14(c)). The table is then moved over by means of the lead screw to the required co-ordinate setting without initially marking out the component.

No method of edge location is as accurate as positioning one hole centre to the next. Therefore, where the distance from a hole to an edge is critical, the distance is slightly increased so that a grinding allowance is left for correcting the relationship between edge and hole after machining.

No matter how accurately the component is positioned the drill may still run out. Therefore, it is preferable to single-point bore the hole between drilling out the bulk of the material and reaming it to size if it is a standard diameter hole. If non-standard the hole is left as bored.
Note: Only single-point boring can correct wander in a previously drilled hole.

Keys and keyways

Machine parts such as gears and shafts are often fastened together by keys so that a more powerful drive can be transmitted than would be possible using set screws or tapered pins. Figure 5.15 shows a selection of keys.

Saddle key   This type requires a keyway in the female component only, for example, the gear, the underside of the key is curved to suit the shaft. The key is tapered and its wedging action transmits the drive by friction alone. Therefore it is only suitable for holding parts which transmit light loads.

Flat key   This type requires a keyway in the female component and a corresponding flat on the mating shaft. The key is tapered and has greater driving power than the saddle key. Nevertheless, it is still only capable of transmitting light loads.

Sunk key   Various types of sunk key are available and will be considered in items (d) to (g). The sunk key is the strongest and most widely used type. It may be square or rectangular in section and requires a keyway to be cut both in the shaft and the mating gear or pulley.

Gib head tapered key   The gib head allows this type of sunk key to be easily removed. The taper is on the top of the key with the greatest depth at the head.

Plain tapered key   This has no head, but in all other respects it is the same as the gib head tapered key. It is used where the protruding gib head would be dangerous or where there is insufficient space for the head. Once driven home, this type of key is very difficult to remove.

Fixed or sunk feather key   This is recessed into the shaft as shown. It is retained by the tightness of its fit or by small cap screws recessed into the key. It is a parallel key and can allow axial movement of the mating parts whilst still

transmitting the rotary drive.
Sliding feather key   Several types are available but the double-headed key shown is the most popular. It is used where considerable axial movement is required as, for example, in the drive from the traverse shaft of a lathe to the saddle. Obviously, the keyway must extend to the end of the shaft so that the gear or pulley can be slid on with the key in position.

Woodruff key   This is semi-circular in shape and fits a similarly shaped keyway made with the milling cutter shown. This type of key is useful when used in conjunction with a tapered shaft and hole as it is self-aligning.

Fitting a fixed feather key

Figure 5.16 shows the keyways in the shaft and mating component ready to receive the key.
1 Clean the shaft, bore and keyway and carefully remove any sharp corners and bruises with a fine file.
2 Obtain a suitable standard key blank which will be slightly oversize to allow for fitting.
3 Check that the shaft and mating component will assemble together correctly without the key in position and that the width of the keyways are the same so that the key will not have to be stepped. Dismantle the parts and lightly oil ready for fitting the key.
4 Compare the key blank with the keyway in the shaft and file along its length until, with light tapping, it can be started into the keyway for its full length.

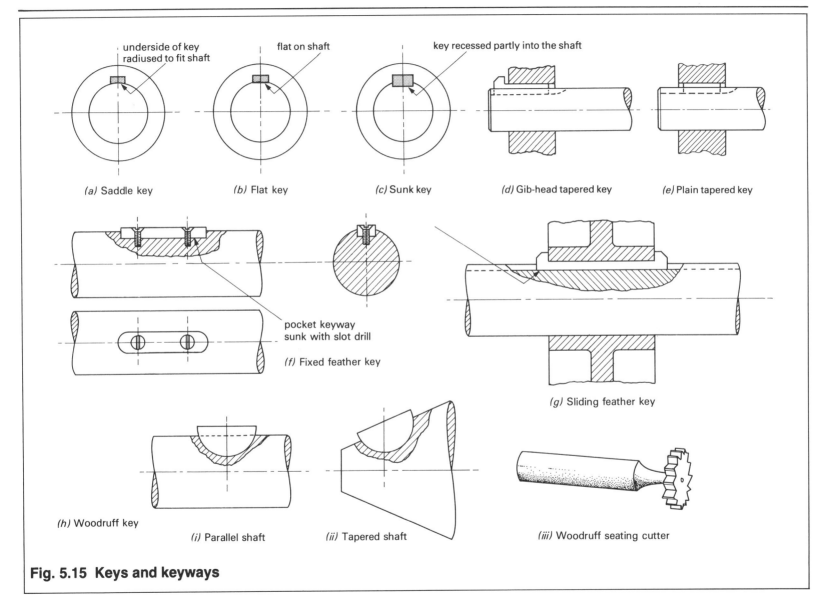

underside of key radiused to fit shaft

flat on shaft

key recessed partly into the shaft

(a) Saddle key

(b) Flat key

(c) Sunk key

(d) Gib-head tapered key

(e) Plain tapered key

pocket keyway sunk with slot drill

(f) Fixed feather key

(g) Sliding feather key

(h) Woodruff key

(i) Parallel shaft

(ii) Tapered shaft

(iii) Woodruff seating cutter

Fig. 5.15 Keys and keyways

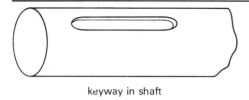

keyway in shaft

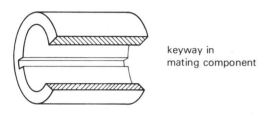

keyway in
mating component

Fig. 5.16 Fitting a fixed feather key

5 Remove the key and examine it for
high spots.
6 Carefully file or scrape away the high
spots until the key will seat on the
bottom of the keyway with a light driving
fit.
7 File the top of the key until it clears
the bottom of the keyway in the female,
mating component.
8 If necessary, the sides of the key
projecting from the shaft should be filed
until the mating parts can be
re-assembled by light tapping.

Fitting a gib head tapered key

Refer to Fig. 5.17 for details of the
technique for fitting this type of key.
Stages 1–3 on p. 104 apply here also.
1 File or scrape the sides of the key
until it is a firm push fit in the shaft

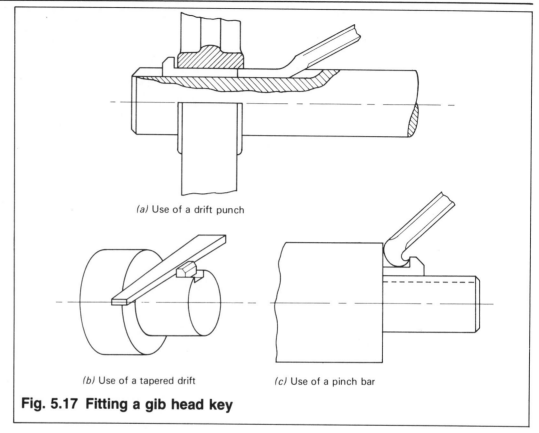

(a) Use of a drift punch

(b) Use of a tapered drift

(c) Use of a pinch bar

Fig. 5.17 Fitting a gib head key

keyway and shows a good bearing on
the sides throughout its length.
2 Check the key for bearing on the
bottom of the keyway in the shaft. Ease
any high spots until the key will bed flat.
3 Assemble the shaft and female mating
component together with the keyways in
alignment. Apply prussian blue to the
upper surface of the key and drive it
home firmly.

4 Remove the key by one of the
methods shown in Fig. 5.17, and
examine it for bearing marks. It should
show an even bearing on the bottom
and sides and high spots on the top or
tapered side.
5 File or scrape the bearing marks from
the top of the key and refit. Repeat this
procedure until an even bearing is
obtained and the head of the key is 6 to

8 mm from the face of the female component.

It is important that the key shows a good bearing on all sides before the parts are finally assembled, otherwise the key may soon become loose.

Safety   It is essential that tapered keys are accurately fitted. The fitter bears a heavy responsibility in this regard, since a key coming loose in a part such as a flywheel revolving at high speed could cause serious damage and even loss of life.

Gib-head keys should not be used in any position where they could catch on clothing, and on no account should the head of the key be permitted to project beyond the end of the shaft.

Special files

The standard files used by the fitter have already been discussed in *Part 1* of this course. However, there are many special types of file available and Fig. 5.18 shows the plan views and sections through some of these files. The files shown in Fig. 5.18 come in the normal range of sizes and have tangs to fit standard file handles.

For fine instrument and toolmaking work *Swiss files* are used. These are much smaller, with a correspondingly finer cut. They do not have a tang, the handle is integral with the file. Figure 5.19(a) shows some typical Swiss files.

For die-sinking applications where concave (hollow) surfaces have to be filed, *riffler files* are used. Again, these come in a wide range of sizes and

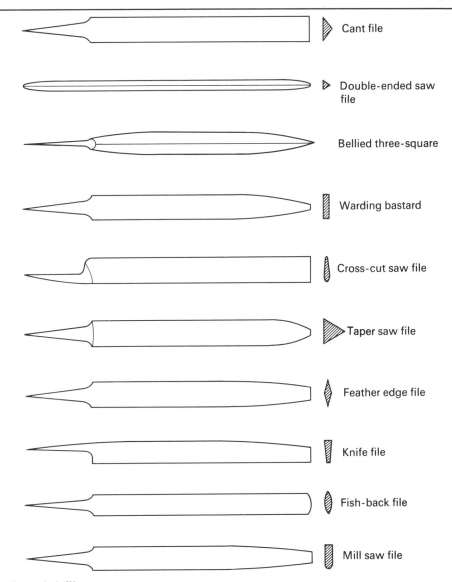

Cant file

Double-ended saw file

Bellied three-square

Warding bastard

Cross-cut saw file

Taper saw file

Feather edge file

Knife file

Fish-back file

Mill saw file

Fig. 5.18 Special files

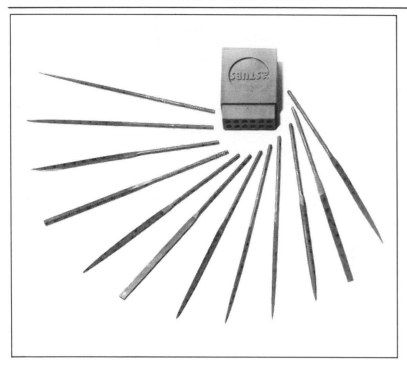

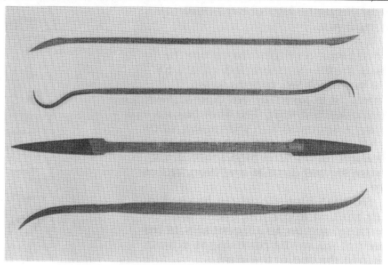

(a) Swiss files (left)
(b) Riffler files (above)

Fig. 5.19 Swiss and Riffler files

shapes but an examples of typical riffler files are shown in Fig. 5.19(b).

Scraping

Scraping is a hand-finishing operation by which very small amounts of metal can be removed locally from a surface. It is not convenient to remove metal locally from a surface with a file, only the scraper provides sufficient control to produce the accuracy and finish required. Hand scraping is a highly skilled process requiring years of practice. Figure 5.20(a) shows three basic types of scraper. Proper control of a scraper can only be maintained if the cutting edge is razor sharp. To ensure this, the cutting edge must be constantly touched up on an oilstone as shown in Fig. 5.20(b). This method of sharpening not only ensures that the scraper is kept sharp, but that the cutting edge has *negative rake*. This prevents the scraper being drawn into the work (Fig. 5.20(c)).

Before scraping can commence the high spots on the surface must be found. This is done by rubbing the component on a reference surface (surface plate or table) that has been lightly smeared with prussian blue. Figure 5.21 shows the sequence of operations to produce a flat surface.

Scraping a flat surface

1 Remove all burrs and sharp edges from the surface to be scraped by rubbing a fine, flat oilstone all over the surface as shown in Fig. 5.21(a).

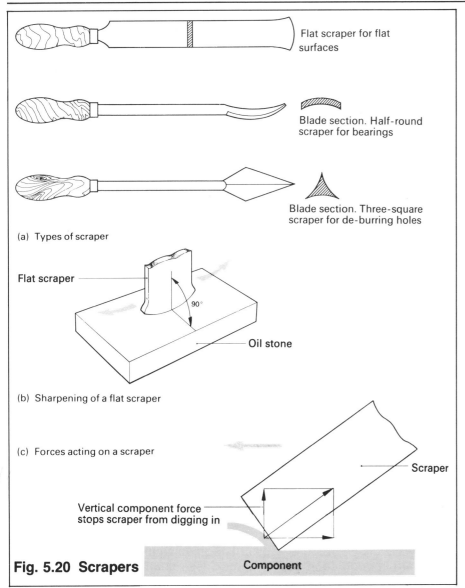

(a) Types of scraper

Flat scraper for flat surfaces

Blade section. Half-round scraper for bearings

Blade section. Three-square scraper for de-burring holes

Flat scraper

90°

Oil stone

(b) Sharpening of a flat scraper

(c) Forces acting on a scraper

Scraper

Vertical component force stops scraper from digging in

Component

Fig. 5.20 Scrapers

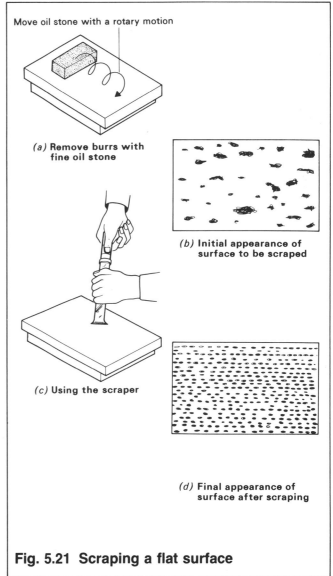

Move oil stone with a rotary motion

(a) **Remove burrs with fine oil stone**

(b) **Initial appearance of surface to be scraped**

(c) **Using the scraper**

(d) **Final appearance of surface after scraping**

Fig. 5.21 Scraping a flat surface

2 Wipe the surface clean and lightly smear prussian blue on to a surface plate.

3 Place the work upside down on the surface plate and move with a rotary motion – do not apply pressure, the weight of the component is sufficient. The appearance of the work upon separation of the surfaces will be as shown in Fig. 5.21(b). The large, dark areas (in practice smeared blue) are the high spots.

4 Holding the scraper as shown in Fig. 5.21(c), break down the high spots into a number of smaller areas.

5 De-burr with a fine oilstone and wipe clean. Check the component again on the surface plate for high spots.

6 Repeat operations 1 to 5 until the appearance of the work resembles Fig. 5.21(d). That is, there should be about 8 to 10 high spots of uniform size, uniformly distributed in each 25 mm^2 of the surface. This is an ideal bearing surface since the mating component is supported over a large area, yet there is sufficient space for an adequate reserve of lubricant between the high spots.

Common power tools

The fitter has many portable power tools at his disposal. For example: rotary drilling machines; shearing machines; nibbling machines; grinding machines; riveting machines.

These machines may be operated by compressed air (pneumatic) or by electricity. Since the single phase supply in Nigeria is 240 volts, a

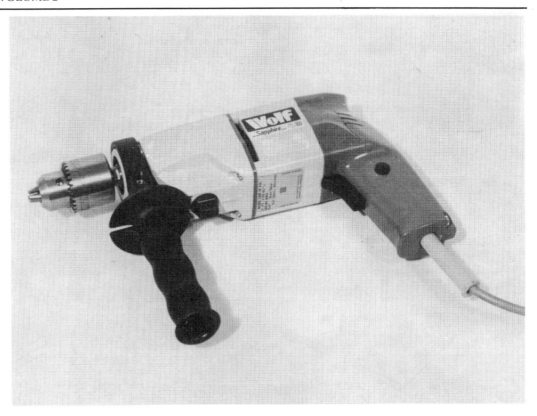

Fig. 5.22 Electric rotary drilling machine

step-down transformer between the mains and the tool should be used. Such a transformer should have an output of 110 volts centre-tapped to earth. Therefore, if the operator receives a shock to earth it will only be 55 volts which is well below the fatal voltage for human beings. Always check that the cables and plugs are in good condition and do not suspend the tool or drag it

about by its conductor. If in doubt consult a qualified electrician.

Electric rotary drilling machine

An example of one of these machines is shown in Fig. 5.22. It can be used for drilling metal with a suitable steel twist drill. Some machines have two- or three-speed gearboxes, but for industrial use it is usual to use the more robust single-speed machine and match the size and speed of the machine to the diameter drill being used.

Shearing machine

This portable power tool is used for rapid and accurate straight-line or curved cutting of material up to 4·5 mm thickness.

The machine is fitted with a pair of very narrow flat blades, one of which is usually fixed, and the other moving to and from the fixed blade at fairly high speeds. Generally these blades have a very pronounced rake to permit piercing of the material for internal cutting, and since the blades are so narrow, the sheet material can be manoeuvred easily during cutting.

The top blade is fixed to the moving member or ram, and the bottom blade on a spiral extension of the U-frame. This extension is shaped like the body of a 'throatless shear', to part the material after cutting.

There is usually provision for vertical adjustment to allow for resharpening of the blade by grinding, and an adjustment behind the bottom blade to allow for setting the cutting clearance. Figure 5.23(a) shows a typical portable, power hand-shearing machine, whilst Fig. 5.23(b) shows details of the cutting blades.

Nibbling machine

The portable nibbling machine does not operate on the same principle as the shear. A punch and die is employed instead of shearing blades, and the

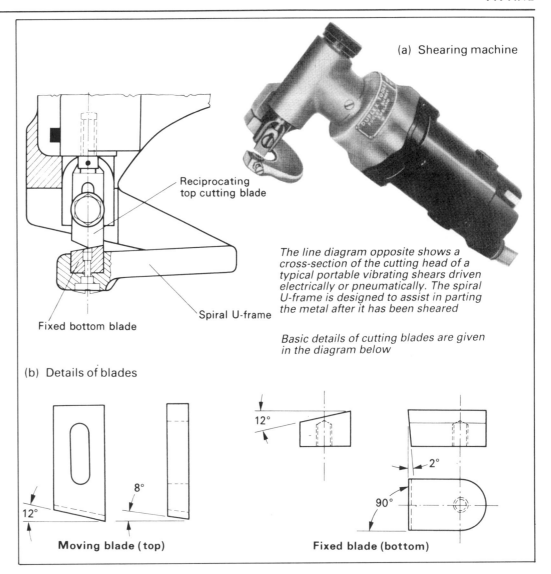

(a) Shearing machine

Reciprocating top cutting blade

Spiral U-frame

Fixed bottom blade

The line diagram opposite shows a cross-section of the cutting head of a typical portable vibrating shears driven electrically or pneumatically. The spiral U-frame is designed to assist in parting the metal after it has been sheared

Basic details of cutting blades are given in the diagram below

(b) Details of blades

12°   8°

12°

Moving blade (top)

12°

2°

90°

Fixed blade (bottom)

Fig. 5.23 Portable electric shearing machine

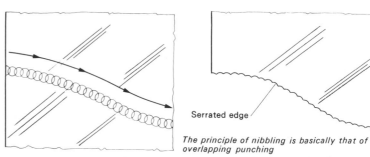

Serrated edge

The principle of nibbling is basically that of overlapping punching

The width of the cut produced by nibbling machines is determined by the diameter of the punch in relationship with the thickness of the material to be cut.   For example:

Capacity of machine −2mm **Width of cut** −8mm **Approximate cutting speed** −1·8mm/min
Capacity of machine −3·2mm **Width of cut** 9·5mm **Approximate cutting speed** −1·5mm/min

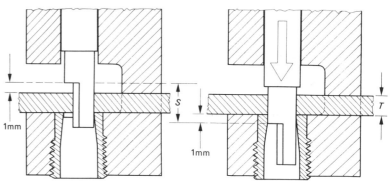

Setting of nibbling punch S = Length of stroke T = Metal thickness

The stroke is adjusted to give movement of approximately 1mm above the material and 1mm through the material, as shown in the diagram above

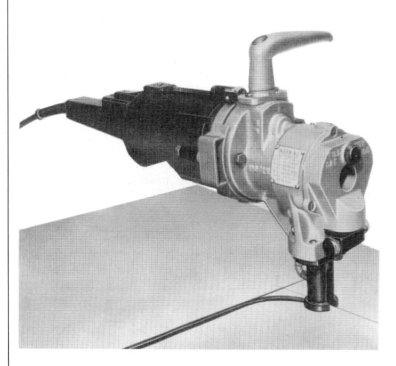

(a) Nibbling machine

(b) Principle of operation

Fig. 5.24 Portable electric nibbling machine

nibbling principle is a special application of punching.

These machines will effect certain operations that cannot be accomplished on other shearing machines. For example, they may be used to cut apertures which otherwise could be produced only by means of specially designed punches and dies set up in a powerful press.

Like the shearing machine the top cutting tool (a punch) reciprocates at fast short strokes. Punch-type nibblers are available in various sizes and the punch reciprocates at a rate of 350 to 1400 strokes per minute over a die, nibbling out the material by the simple principle of overlapping punching, and only slight finishing is necessary to produce a smooth clean edge.

One main advantage of nibbling over shearing is that there is less distortion of the work.

Figure 5.24(a) shows the punch-type nibbling machine, whilst Fig. 5.24(b) shows its principle of operation.

Portable grinding machine

Portable grinding machines are often used for smoothing down welded joints and seams and generally do many of the fabrication workshop jobs which would otherwise have to be done by laborious methods of chiselling and filing. They are also used with small mounted wheels for die finishing.

Figure 5.25 shows the two most commonly used variations of portable grinders.

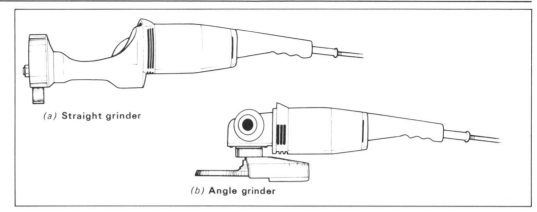

(a) Straight grinder

(b) Angle grinder

Fig. 5.25 Portable grinding machines

Riveting machines

Portable hand-riveting machines are usually compressed air (pneumatically) powered. These machines provide light, rapid blows that form the head of the rivet quickly and with less distortion to the surrounding metal than when using a manually wielded hammer. Further, a lighter hold up or 'dolly' is required to support the rivet. Different types and sizes of snap can be fitted to the hand riveter depending upon the type of head that is to be formed on the rivet. A typical hand-riveting machine is shown in Fig. 5.26.

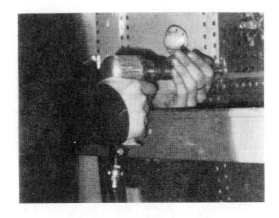

Fig. 5.26 Portable hand riveting machine

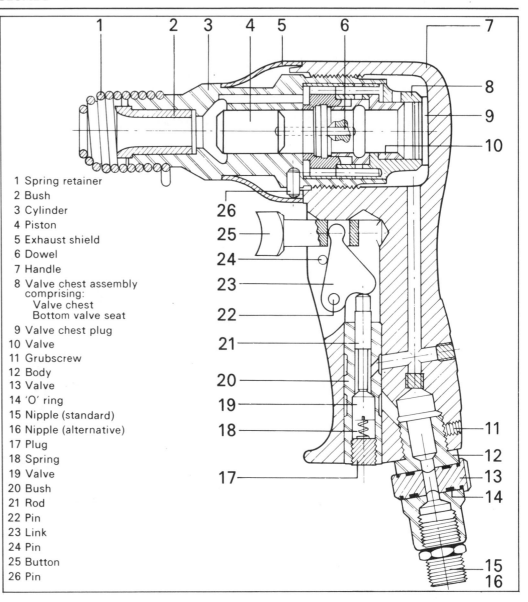

1 Spring retainer
2 Bush
3 Cylinder
4 Piston
5 Exhaust shield
6 Dowel
7 Handle
8 Valve chest assembly
  comprising:
    Valve chest
    Bottom valve seat
9 Valve chest plug
10 Valve
11 Grubscrew
12 Body
13 Valve
14 'O' ring
15 Nipple (standard)
16 Nipple (alternative)
17 Plug
18 Spring
19 Valve
20 Bush
21 Rod
22 Pin
23 Link
24 Pin
25 Button
26 Pin

Exercises

1. With the aid of sketches show how the following devices are used to locate components when they are being fitted together:
   (i) dowels,
   (ii) pins,
   (iii) studs,
   (iv) fitted bolts,
   (v) tenons.
2. Discuss the relative advantages and limitations of using studs or tenons for locating work holding devices in the tee slots of machine tables.
3. Describe with the aid of sketches the procedures for
   (a) fitting location dowels,
   (b) locating a collar on a shaft using a taper pin.
4. With the aid of sketches explain the essential differences between fluted reamers and rose reamers.
5. With the aid of sketches explain what is meant by 'boxing' a hole and show how this can be used to improve the positional accuracy of the hole.
6. With the aid of sketches show how a hole centre may be positioned under the axis of a drilling machine spindle using:
   (a) a centrescope,
   (b) a co-ordinate table.
   Having positioned the work, describe how the hole is started so that it does not wander out of position.

7. (a) Sketch in good proportion the following types of key.
      (i) Saddle key
      (ii) Flat key
      (iii) Gib head tapered key
      (iv) Sliding feather key
      (v) Woodruff key
   (b) Describe the procedure for fitting a gib head tapered key. Use sketches to illustrate your answer.
8. Describe, with the aid of sketches, the procedure for hand scraping a flat surface using a surface plate as a reference plane.
9. Show, with the aid of sketches, the principle of operation of the following portable power tools:
   (a) Shearing machine.
   (b) Nibbling machine,
10. Discuss the safety precautions that must be taken when using portable power operated machines and, in particular, portable grinding machines.

6. The centre lathe

Further work between centres

The centre lathe, as a machine for producing cylindrical surfaces was introduced in *Mechanical Engineering Craft Theory and Related Studies, Part 1*. Various methods of work-holding were considered, including turning between centres. In this section the techniques for using centres will be considered in greater depth.

If work held between centres is to be turned accurately then it is essential that the centres are in alignment and that their common axis is parallel to the slideways of the lathe bed. Also, the headstock, or live, centre must run true with the spindle. Figure 6.1 shows the live centre being checked for true running with a dial test indicator. Alternatively, a soft centre may be used and turned up to a 60° cone after it is inserted in the spindle. Since the centre and the workpiece revolve at the same speed there is no wear between them, and a soft centre will be quite satisfactory.

The tailstock centre is always hardened. This is because the tailstock centre remains stationary whilst the work rotates causing wear between them. Great care must be taken to lubricate the centre and it must be

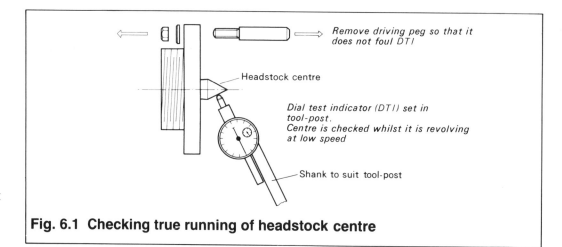

Remove driving peg so that it does not foul DTI

Headstock centre

Dial test indicator (DTI) set in tool-post.
Centre is checked whilst it is revolving at low speed

Shank to suit tool-post

Fig. 6.1 Checking true running of headstock centre

carefully adjusted so that it is neither too loose so that the job is not firmly located, nor too tight so that it overheats and burns out. Long work tends to heat up and expand whilst being machined, so the tailstock centre should be eased from time to time.

Although more bulky, a revolving centre allows the lathe to be run faster and heavier cuts to be taken without wear of the centre taking place. Figure 6.2 shows a typical revolving centre.

Use of steadies

When turning long, slender work it

tends to deflect or kick away from the cutting tool. In extreme cases it may even ride over the cutting tool and spring out from between the centres.
Travelling steady To balance the cutting forces and prevent the component deflecting a travelling steady is used. This is shown in Fig. 6.3. The steady is clamped to the saddle of the lathe and moves along with it. It is carefully adjusted to resist the cutting forces without itself deflecting the component.
Fixed steady The fixed steady, as its name implies, is fixed to the bed of the lathe and is used to support the end of

long components that cannot be held on a centre. Figure 6.4(a) shows such a component.

The component is set up as follows.

1 The 80 mm diameter end is filed flat.
2 The end is centred by marking out with a combination square centre-finder as shown in Fig. 6.4(b).
3 The centre hole is carefully drilled with a portable electric drill.
4 The flange of the component is chucked, and the opposite end held on the tailstock centre.
5 A track for the fixed steady is turned as shown in Fig. 6.4(c) (unless a suitable diameter has to be turned anyway).
6 The steady is fixed in position on the lathe bed and closed around the component. It is then adjusted to support the component and the tailstock removed.

Figure 6.4(d) shows the steady in position ready for the end of the bar to be machined.

Three-jaw chuck (soft jaws)

In *Part 1*, the three-jaw self-centring chuck and the four-jaw independent chuck were introduced. It was shown that, for second operation work on a component, the four-jaw chuck has to be used if accuracy of concentricity is required.

However, where a batch of similar components is to be produced or where a thin component has to be held, setting the four-jaw chuck is too time-consuming and costly.

Alternatively, *soft jaws* are often used

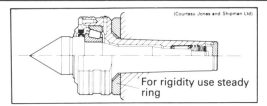

(Courtesy Jones and Shipman Ltd)

For rigidity use steady ring

Fig. 6.2 Revolving tailstock centre

in self-centring chucks and these can be turned or bored true and to suit a particular job. They are frequently used for small batch repetition work, where the time required for setting in a four-jaw chuck would be too costly. When machining the jaws it is important to remove the backlash between the scroll and the jaws. Figure 6.5 shows some applications of soft jaws and the techniques for machining them.

The parallel mandrel (snug)

The taper mandrel was introduced in *Part 1* of this course; it is used to turn the faces and outside diameter of a component true to its bore. However, some components, such as the example shown in Fig. 6.6, are too thin to be held in this manner. Such a component can best be held on a parallel mandrel as shown in Fig. 6.7(a). Such a mandrel is particularly useful if a number of similar components are to be produced.

Should the mandrel be re-used from time to time, it can be re-set in a four-jaw chuck using a dial test indicator (DTI) as shown in Fig. 6.7(b).

The parallel mandrel is also used for turning very thin components which can

(Courtesy Colchester Lathe Co.)

(a) **The travelling steady mounted on the Saddle**

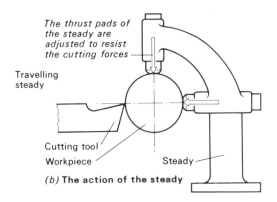

The thrust pads of the steady are adjusted to resist the cutting forces

Travelling steady

Cutting tool

Workpiece

Steady

(b) **The action of the steady**

Fig. 6.3 The travelling steady

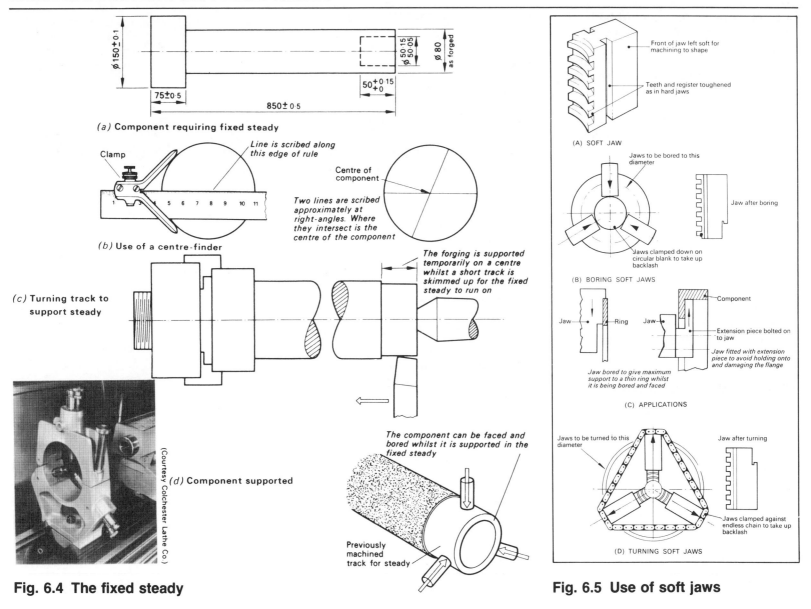

(a) Component requiring fixed steady

Clamp

Line is scribed along this edge of rule

Centre of component

Two lines are scribed approximately at right-angles. Where they intersect is the centre of the component

(b) Use of a centre-finder

(c) Turning track to support steady

The forging is supported temporarily on a centre whilst a short track is skimmed up for the fixed steady to run on

(Courtesy Colchester Lathe Co.)

(d) Component supported

The component can be faced and bored whilst it is supported in the fixed steady

Previously machined track for steady

Fig. 6.4 The fixed steady

Front of jaw left soft for machining to shape

Teeth and register toughened as in hard jaws

(A) SOFT JAW

Jaws to be bored to this diameter

Jaw after boring

Jaws clamped down on circular blank to take up backlash

(B) BORING SOFT JAWS

Jaw — Ring

Jaw — Component

Extension piece bolted on to jaw

Jaw fitted with extension piece to avoid holding onto and damaging the flange

Jaw bored to give maximum support to a thin ring whilst it is being bored and faced

(C) APPLICATIONS

Jaws to be turned to this diameter

Jaw after turning

Jaws clamped against endless chain to take up backlash

(D) TURNING SOFT JAWS

Fig. 6.5 Use of soft jaws

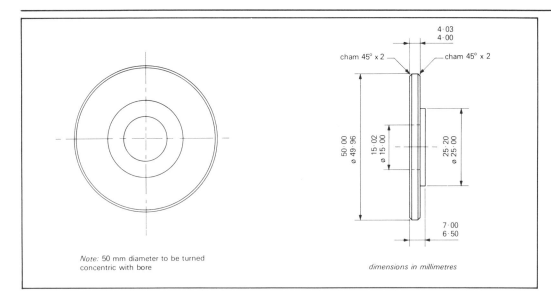

Note: 50 mm diameter to be turned concentric with bore

dimensions in millimetres

Fig. 6.6 Example of parallel mandrel work

be mounted in batches as shown in Fig. 6.7(c). Not only does this reduce production time, but the components tend to support each other against the cutting forces.

The face plate

The work-holding devices previously described are designed so that a diameter may be machined true to an existing diameter. However, the face-plate enables the component to be located so that a diameter can be turned parallel or perpendicular to a previously machined flat surface. This flat surface is the datum from which the diameter is set as shown in Fig. 6.8.

In the example shown in Fig. 6.8(a) the axis of the bore will be

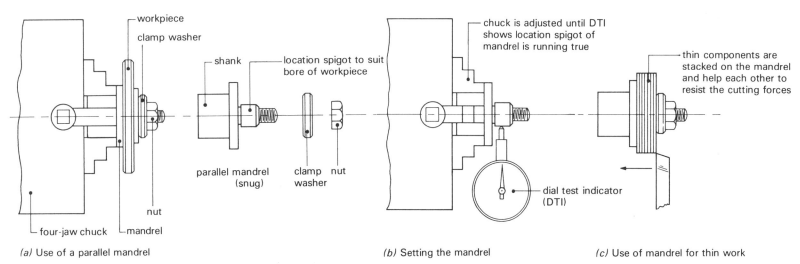

(a) Use of a parallel mandrel

(b) Setting the mandrel

(c) Use of mandrel for thin work

Fig. 6.7 Setting and use of the parallel mandrel

perpendicular to the datum surface. In the example shown in Fig. 6.8(b), the axis of the bore will be parallel to the datum which, in this case, is the base of the workpeice.

The restraints acting on a component held on a face plate are shown in Fig. 6.8(c). The advantages and limitations of this method of work-holding are considered in Table 6.1.

It will be seen that a balance weight is used to prevent out-of-balance forces damaging the spindle bearings and causing chatter when turning. It also prevents the work swinging round, after the machine has been stopped, and trapping the operator whilst he takes measurements or sets the tool.

Simple static balance can be achieved by applying the principle of moments as shown in Fig. 6.9. For purposes of calculation, the weights of the component and its counter-balance act through their respective centres of gravity.

Example 6.1 To calculate the distance L that a 15 N balance weight must be placed from the centre of the face plate to balance the component and angle plate.

Solution

$$\text{clockwise moments} = \text{anti-clockwise moments}$$

$$\text{force} \times \text{distance} = \text{force} \times \text{distance}$$

$$25 \times 100 = 15 \times L$$

$$L = \frac{25 \times 100}{15}$$

$$L = \underline{166.7 \text{ mm}}$$

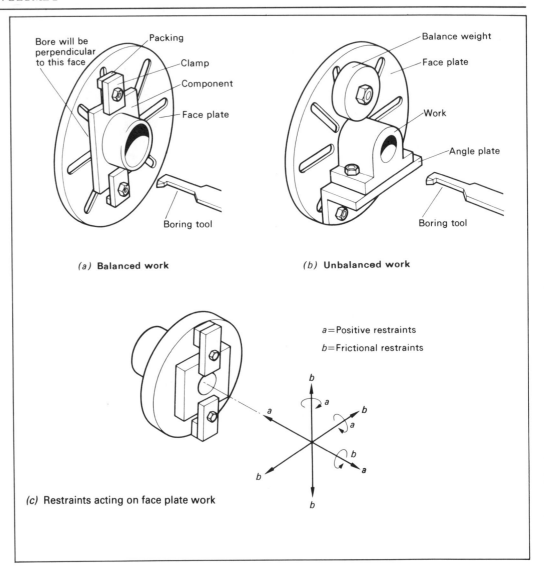

(a) **Balanced work**

(b) **Unbalanced work**

a = Positive restraints

b = Frictional restraints

(c) Restraints acting on face plate work

Fig. 6.8 The face plate

Table 6.1 The face plate

Advantages	Limitations
1. A wide range of regular and irregular components can be held.	1. The face-plate is slow and tedious to set up. Not only must the workpiece be clocked up to run true, clamps must also be set up on the face-plate to retain the component.
2. Work can be set to a datum surface. If the datum surface is parallel to the workpiece axis, it is set on an angle plate mounted on the face-plate. If the datum surface is perpendicular to the workpiece axis, the workpiece is set directly on to the face-plate.	2. Considerable skill is required to clamp the component so that it is rigid enough to resist both the cutting forces, and those forces that will try to dislodge the work as it spins rapidly round.
3. Work on the end face of the job is possible.	3. Considerable skill is required to avoid distorting the workpiece by the clamps.
4. The work can be bored.	4. Irregular jobs have to be carefully balanced to prevent vibration, and the job rolling back on the operator.
5. The work can be set to run concentrically or eccentrically at will.	5. The clamps can limit the work that can be performed on the end face.
6. There are no moving parts to lose their accuracy with wear.	
7. The work can be rigidly clamped to resist heavy cuts.	

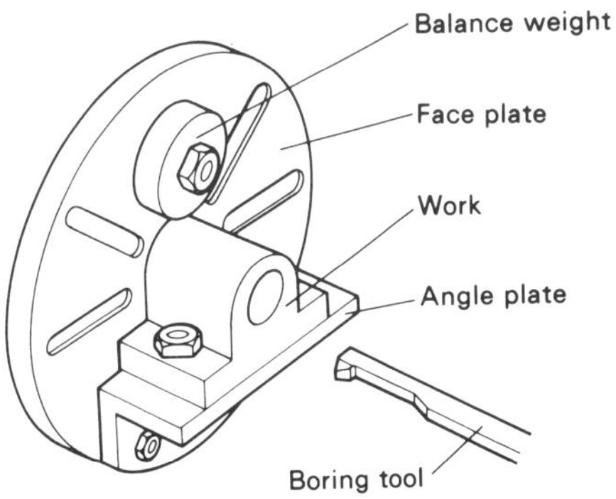

(a) **Boring an out of balance component**

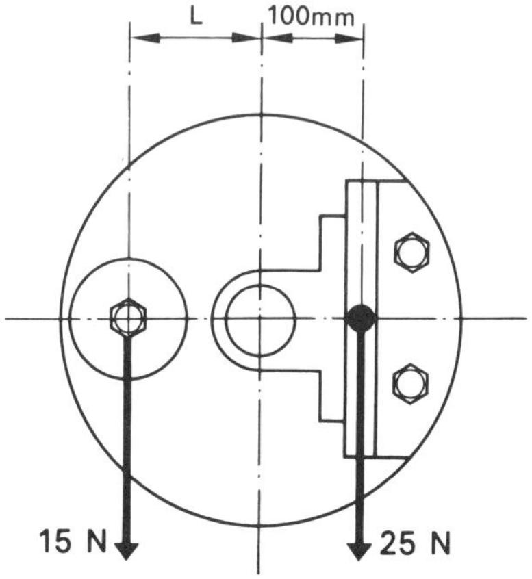

Fig. 6.9 Static balancing

(b) **Positioning the balance weight**

15 N   25 N

c.g. of casting and angle plate

Balancing is also considered in Chapter 9 in the interests of safety and surface finish. The example shown for balancing a grinding wheel uses two balance weights. This technique can also be used with advantage for balancing a face plate.

Figure 6.8(b) shows a hole being bored parallel to the datum surface of the work piece. Whilst single-point boring is the only possible means of removing wander and giving a high degree of positional accuracy, it suffers from the following limitations.

1 Chatter and poor surface finish especially on small diameter holes where only a slender tool can be used.

2 The hole tends to be oval and bell-mouthed due to deflection of the boring tool shank. These defects become less severe as the hole diameter increases, thus allowing an increasingly more rigid boring tool.

3 An alternative method of boring is shown in Fig. 6.10. This is only possible when the cross slide or saddle is fitted with a tee-slotted upper surface to act as a boring table. Since the boring bar is supported at both ends, there is less chance of chatter and geometrical errors.

Taper turning

So far, great stress has been placed on the importance of maintaining the axial alignment of the headstock and tailstock, and upon the cutting tool moving parallel, to this axis if a truly cylindrical component is to be

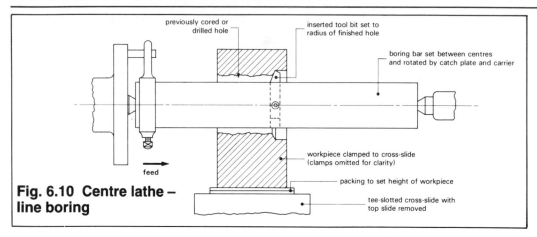

previously cored or drilled hole

inserted tool bit set to radius of finished hole

boring bar set between centres and rotated by catch plate and carrier

feed

workpiece clamped to cross-slide (clamps omitted for clarity)

packing to set height of workpiece

tee-slotted cross-slide with top slide removed

Fig. 6.10 Centre lathe – line boring

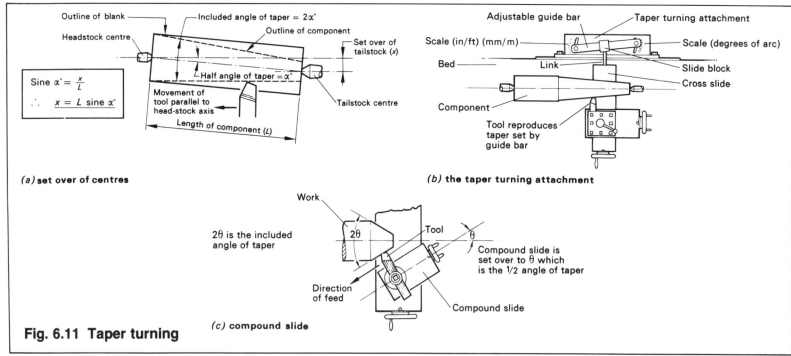

Outline of blank

Headstock centre

Included angle of taper = $2\alpha°$

Outline of component

Set over of tailstock (x)

$$Sine\ \alpha° = \frac{x}{L}$$
$$\therefore\quad x = L\ sine\ \alpha°$$

Half angle of taper = $\alpha°$

Movement of tool parallel to head-stock axis

Tailstock centre

Length of component (L)

(a) **set over of centres**

Adjustable guide bar

Taper turning attachment

Scale (in/ft) (mm/m)

Scale (degrees of arc)

Bed

Link

Slide block

Cross slide

Component

Tool reproduces taper set by guide bar

(b) **the taper turning attachment**

Work

2θ is the included angle of taper

2θ

Tool

θ

Direction of feed

Compound slide is set over to θ which is the 1/2 angle of taper

Compound slide

(c) **compound slide**

Fig. 6.11 Taper turning

produced. Similarly a conical component is produced if these basic alignments are disturbed. Taper turning involves the controlled disturbance of these alignments so that the tool moves in a path that is inclined at a given angle to the workpiece axis. This inclination is relative; it does not matter whether the workpiece axis is offset or whether the tool path is offset. Three methods of taper turning will now be described:

Off-set tailstock   Using the lateral adjusting screws, the body of the tailstock and, therefore, the tailstock centre can be offset. This inclines the axis of a workpiece held between centres relatively to the path of the cutting tool as shown in Fig. 6.11(a). The advantages and limitations of this technique are summarised in Table 6.2.

Even for a small angle the amount of set-over required is substantial. This results in excessive wear of the centres and centre holes. To avoid this, a ball centre should be used.

Taper-turning attachment   Another way in which tapers may be produced is by the use of a taper-turning attachment. These attachments are usually an optional extra and have to be purchased separately to the lathe. They vary in detail from make to make but a typical example is shown in Fig. 6.11(b)

The advantages and limitations of this technique are summarised in Table 6.2.

Compound slide   Setting over the compound slide is the simplest method of producing a taper although it has some limitations. Figure 6.11(c) shows a typical application. The advantages and

Table 6.2 Comparison of taper-turning techniques

Method	Advantages	Limitations
Set over of tailstock	1. Power traverse can be used 2. The full length of the bed used	1. Only small angles can be accommodated 2. Damage to the centre holes can occur 3. Difficulty in setting up 4. Only applies to work held between centres
Taper turning attachments	1. Power traverse can be used 2. Ease of setting 3. Can be applied to chucking and centre work	1. Only small angles can be accommodated 2. Only short lengths can be cut (304–457 mm (12–18 in) depending on make)
Compound slide	1. Very easy setting over a wide range of angles. (Usually used for short, steep tapers and chamfers) 2. Can be applied to chucking can centre work	1. Only hand traverse available 2. Only very short lengths can be cut. Varies with m/c but is usually limited to about 76–101 mm (3–4 in)

limitations of this technique of taper turning are summarised in Table 6.2.

Profile turning

As well as simple cylinders, plane surfaces and cones (tapers), shaped components also have to be turned. Figure 6.12 shows some form tools being used to produce a chamfer, a radius, and a simple form.

Although widely used on capstan and automatic lathes, form tools are not very successful on the centre lathe due to lack of rigidity which causes chatter.

Where an extensive profile has to be cut it is usual to use a single-point tool and a template as shown in Fig. 6.13. Turning by using a template requires a great deal of skill on the part of the operator. It is usual to engage the longitudinal power traverse at a fine rate of feed, while the operator controls the cross traverse. The template edge is coated with prussian blue which wipes off on any high spots. The profile is gradually turned into the component until a suitably selected control diameter becomes size.

Note: In all taper turning and form tool

123

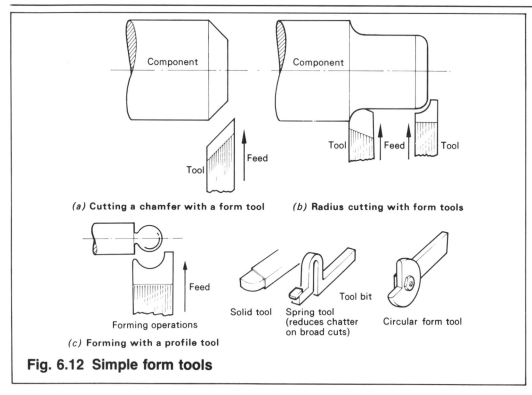

(a) Cutting a chamfer with a form tool   (b) Radius cutting with form tools

(c) Forming with a profile tool

Fig. 6.12 Simple form tools

work it is essential that the tool is exactly on centre. If it is high, or low, a true form will not be obtained.

Where many components requiring profile turning are to be manufactured and a high degree of accuracy is required, it is more usual to use a copy-turning attachment as shown in Fig. 6.14.

The attachment itself is fastened to the lathe carriage and moves with it as it traverses along the bed of the machine. The template or model is fastened to the bed of the lathe and remains stationary. As the carriage traverses along the bed of the lathe, a stylus on the copying attachment traces the profile of the template. This stylus controls the movement of the cutting tool by means of hydraulic pressure, and reproduces the shape of the template on the component.

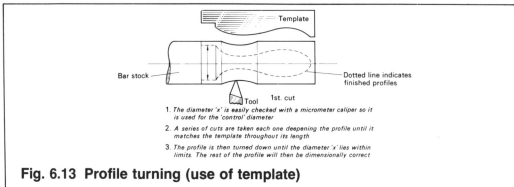

1. The diameter 'x' is easily checked with a micrometer caliper so it is used for the 'control' diameter

2. A series of cuts are taken each one deepening the profile until it matches the template throughout its length

3. The profile is then turned down until the diameter 'x' lies within limits. The rest of the profile will then be dimensionally correct

Fig. 6.13 Profile turning (use of template)

Fig. 6.14 Copy turning

Screw cutting

Figure 6.15(a) shows a helix. The **helix** is defined as: **the path of a point travelling around an imaginary cylinder so that its axial and circumferential velocities maintain a constant ratio.**

In Fig. 6.15(a) the lead and pitch of the helix appeared to be the same. This is because it is a *single-start* helix.

The helix shown in Fig. 6.15(b) is a *two-start* helix. That is, one helix is wound within the other. This enables the lead of the helix to be increased without increasing the pitch. **The screw thread is a practical example of the helix.**

Screw threads may have any number of starts, therefore the general term for all threads other than the single start is *multi-start*.

A practical example of a multi-start thread is found in the screw of a fly press used for sheet metal press work. It enables the pitch, and therefore the depth, of the thread to be kept to a reasonable size, whilst allowing a rapid axial movement of the screw.

The thread of an ordinary screw or bolt is right-handed. That is with clockwise rotation of the bolt it moves into the nut. With a left-hand bolt clockwise rotation would cause it to move out of the nut.

A practical example of left-hand and right-hand threads is found on the double-ended tool grinder. Viewed from the front, the left-hand end of the spindle has a left-hand thread and retaining nut. The right-hand end of the

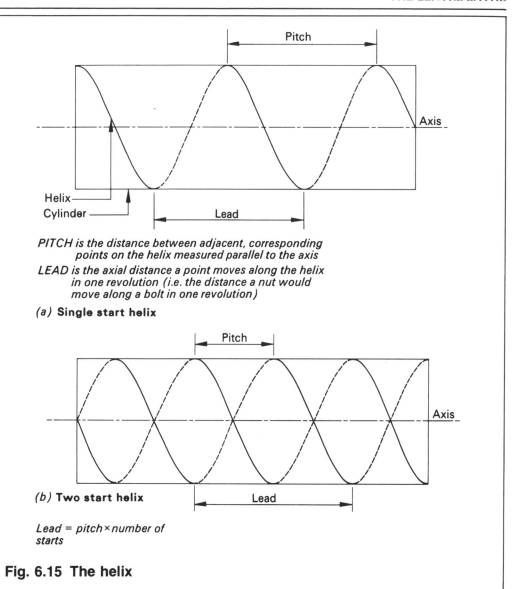

PITCH is the distance between adjacent, corresponding points on the helix measured parallel to the axis

LEAD is the axial distance a point moves along the helix in one revolution (i.e. the distance a nut would move along a bolt in one revolution)

(a) **Single start helix**

(b) **Two start helix**

Lead = pitch × number of starts

Fig. 6.15 The helix

spindle has a right-hand thread and nut. This arrangement prevents the left-hand nut spinning off when the machine is started up.

When screw-cutting, the spindle of the lathe provides the rotational movement and the lead screw provides the axial movement necessary when generating a helix. It has already been stated that the rotational and axial velocities must maintain a constant ratio, therefore, the drive between the spindle and the lead screw must be positive (without slip). Usually a gear train is used. On modern machines the ratio of velocities can be changed by means of a gear box as shown in Fig. 6.16. On older machines the end gear train is itself changed for each desired pitch being cut as shown in Fig. 6.17. (See also pp 10–16.)

There are two main considerations when screw cutting.

1 **Thread** The screw cutting tool is ground to the correct profile using a *centre gauge*. This gauge is also used to set the tool square to the workpiece (Fig. 6.18).

2 **Lead** The means by which the velocity of the lead screw may be set relative to the velocity of the spindle has already been discussed. Where change gears are used they may be calculated quite simply by the following formula, where tpi = threads per inch.

$$\frac{driver}{driven} = \frac{tpi\ lead\ screw}{tpi\ to\ be\ cut}$$
$$= \frac{lead\ to\ be\ cut}{lead\ of\ lead\ screw}$$

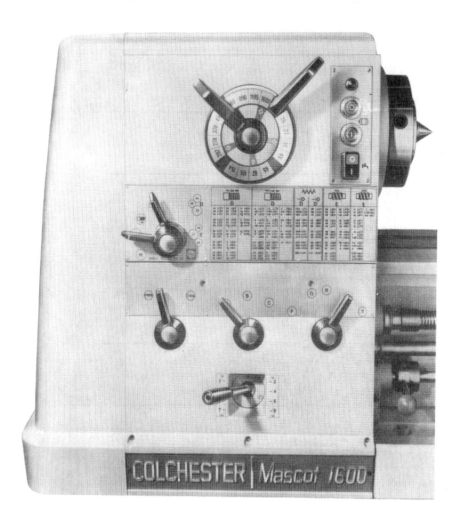

Fig. 6.16 Screw-cutting gear box

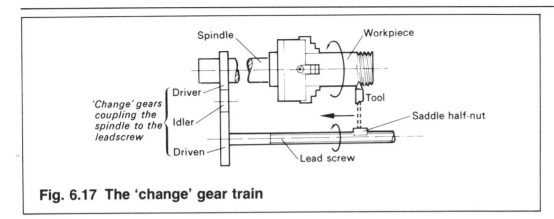

Fig. 6.17 The 'change' gear train

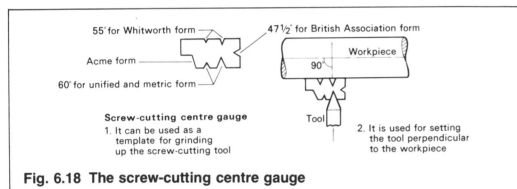

Fig. 6.18 The screw-cutting centre gauge

This formula can be used for cutting:
1 English pitches on a lathe with an English lead screw;
2 metric pitches on a lathe with a metric lead screw.

The standard gears supplied are 20-tooth (2); 25-tooth to 120-tooth, in steps of 5 teeth.

Example 6.2 Calculate the gears to cut a 12 tpi thread on a lathe with a 6 tpi lead screw.

Solution

$$\frac{\text{driver}}{\text{driven}} = \frac{\text{tpi lead screw}}{\text{tpi to be cut}}$$

$$= \frac{6}{16}$$

$$= \frac{6 \times 5}{16 \times 5} \quad \text{(multiplying top and bottom by 5 to fit standard gears)}$$

$$= \frac{30}{80}$$

i.e. a 30-tooth gear driving an 80-tooth gear.

Example 6.3 Calculate the gears to cut a 1·5 mm pitch thread on a lathe with a 6 mm pitch lead screw.

Solution

$$\frac{\text{driver}}{\text{driven}} = \frac{\text{pitch to be cut}}{\text{pitch of lead screw}}$$

$$= \frac{1·5}{6·0}$$

$$= \frac{1·5 \times 5}{6·0 \times 5} \quad \text{(multiplying top and bottom by 5 to fit standard gears)}$$

$$= \frac{7·5}{30}$$

Multiply top and bottom by a further common factor to make gear sizes more convenient if necessary:

$$\frac{\text{driver}}{\text{driven}} = \frac{7·5 \times 4}{30 \times 4} = \frac{30}{120}$$

i.e. a 30-tooth gear driving a 120-tooth gear.

Example 6.4 To cut a thread of 1·5 mm pitch on a lathe with a 6 tpi lead screw using the following formula:

$$\frac{\text{driver}}{\text{driven}} = \frac{5\,LN}{127}$$

where: L = the lead to be cut in mm,
N = tpi of the lead screw.

Solution

$$\frac{\text{driver}}{\text{driven}} = \frac{5\,PN}{127}$$

where: P = 1·5 mm, N = 6 tpi.

$$\frac{\text{driver}}{\text{driven}} = \frac{5 \times 1·5 \times 6}{127}$$

$$= \frac{45}{127}$$

127

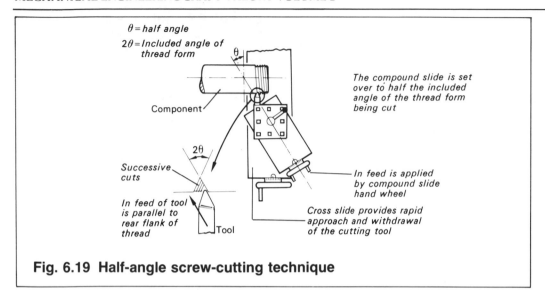

θ = half angle

2θ = Included angle of thread form

The compound slide is set over to half the included angle of the thread form being cut

Component

2θ

Successive cuts

In feed of tool is parallel to rear flank of thread

In feed is applied by compound slide hand wheel

Cross slide provides rapid approach and withdrawal of the cutting tool

Tool

Fig. 6.19 Half-angle screw-cutting technique

i.e. a 45-tooth gear driving a 127-tooth gear.

Therefore, when cutting metric threads on a lathe fitted with an English lead screw, a 127-tooth conversion gear is required in addition to the standard range of gears.

Note: In the above three examples no reference has been made to the 'hand' of the thread, since lead screws are normally right-handed.

1 To cut a right-hand thread, job and lead screw rotate in the same direction (one idler gear).

2 To cut a left-hand thread, job and lead screw rotate in opposite directions (two idler gears).

In a simple gear train the idler gears only control the direction of rotation of the first and last gear, they do not affect the speed of rotation.

There are various techniques used for cutting the thread. One of the most successful is the *half-angle technique* shown in Fig. 6.19. It gets its name from the fact that the compound slide is set over to half the included angle of the thread being cut.

The lathe is set in motion and the micrometer dial on the compound slide is set to zero. The cross-slide is fed in until the tool just touches the workpiece and then the cross-slide micrometer dial is set to zero. After this the cross-slide is only used for quick withdrawal of the tool at the end of each cut, the tool being repositioned by bringing the cross-slide back to zero again. The depth of cut is controlled by the compound slide. This method of screw

cutting enables the tool to be ground with true cutting angles since it cuts on one lip only. The advantages of this technique over the plunge cut technique are:

1 better finish (less chatter);

2 more rapid stock removal;

3 no need to remember the previous setting after each tool withdrawal – the cut is applied progressively by the compound slide.

It is not possible, except for fine instrument threads, to cut the thread to its full depth in one pass of the tool. Therefore, a number of cuts must be taken, each one being successively deeper. The tool must follow the identical path of each previous cut otherwise a series of grooves will be cut side by side. The device by which the lathe operator judges the correct moment to engage the half nut with the lead screw is called the *chasing dial*. These vary with different machines and the maker's handbook should always be consulted before using the chasing dial on a strange machine.

Thread chasing

It is not possible to cut a full thread form with a single point tool. The reason for this is shown in Fig. 6.20(a). In order to radius the crest of the thread a multi-tooth form tool has to be used. Such a tool is referred to as a *chasing* tool. Examples of internal and external form tools are shown in Fig. 6.20(b). These chasers should be fitted with a substantial wooden handle; they are used to trim the thread to size as shown

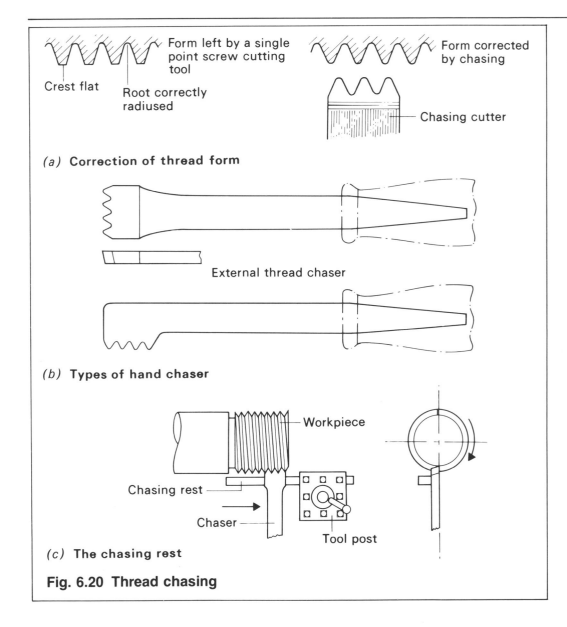

(a) **Correction of thread form**

Crest flat
Root correctly radiused
Form left by a single point screw cutting tool
Form corrected by chasing
Chasing cutter

External thread chaser

(b) **Types of hand chaser**

Workpiece
Chasing rest
Chaser
Tool post

(c) **The chasing rest**

Fig. 6.20 Thread chasing

in Fig. 6.20(c). Note that the chasing rest must be kept close up to the workpiece so that the chaser cannot be dragged down between the rest and the workpiece. (Compare this with the setting of the tool rest on a grinding machine.) When chasing, the thread is cut slightly over-size. The thread is then trimmed down to size with the chaser, constantly checking the thread with a ring gauge.

Alternatively, a full thread may be cut from the solid using a circular form tool as shown in Fig. 6.21(a). The form on the tool is slightly modified, to allow for the distortion caused by the rake angle, so that a true form is cut. Such form tools are very expensive compared with a single-point tool and care must be taken not to chip them by incorrect usage. A button die in a tailstock die-holder may also be used to finish threads to size, and even cut them from the solid when machining low-strength materials, see Fig. 6.21(b).

Square thread

Figure 6.22 shows a square thread. It also shows how the helix angle affects the setting of the cutting tool. It will be seen from Fig. 6.22(a) that the heel of the cutting tool will interfere with the flank of the thread if the tool is set in the normal manner. Increasing the side clearance or reducing the depth of the tool will weaken it considerably. This is not desirable, as cutting a square thread puts a considerable strain on the tool due to the width of the cut. It is preferable to incline the tool as shown

129

in Fig. 6.22(b) so that the tool is tangential to the helix of the thread and the side clearance can be kept to a minimum.

Multi-start screw threads

The lathe is set up in the usual way for a single-start thread but the lead and pitch will differ.

lead = pitch × number of starts

The gears are set so that the *lead* of the thread will be cut as shown in Fig. 6.23(a). When the thread has been cut to depth, the compound slide, and therefore the tool, is advanced by a distance equal to the pitch of the thread as shown in Fig. 6.23(b). With the same settings as previously the thread is again cut to depth. This procedure is repeated until the required number of starts has been obtained. The thread can be finished with a chaser of the correct pitch.

Cutting tools

The more common cutting-tool materials can be listed as shown in Table 6.3.

A cutting-tool material must have the following properties.
1 Sufficient strength to resist the cutting forces.
2 Sufficient hardness to resist wear and give an adequate life between re-grinds.
3 It must retain its hardness at the high temperatures generated at the tool point when cutting.

(a) **Circular form tool (screw cutting)**

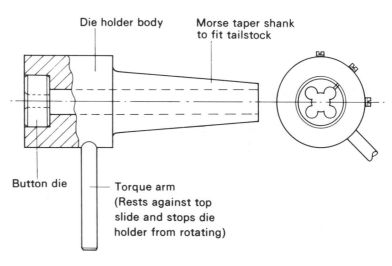

(b) **Button die and holder**

Fig. 6.21 Form tool and die

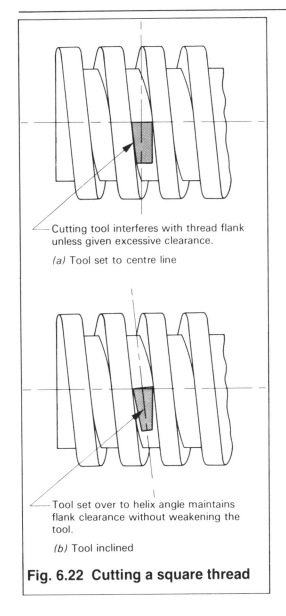

Cutting tool interferes with thread flank unless given excessive clearance.

(a) Tool set to centre line

Tool set over to helix angle maintains flank clearance without weakening the tool.

(b) Tool inclined

Fig. 6.22 Cutting a square thread

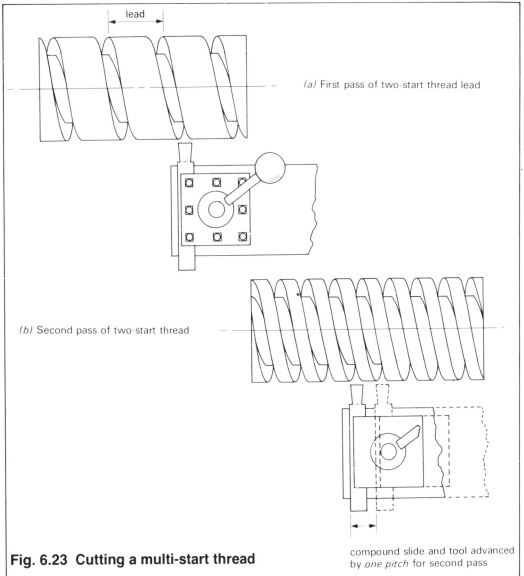

lead

(a) First pass of two-start thread lead

(b) Second pass of two-start thread

Fig. 6.23 Cutting a multi-start thread

compound slide and tool advanced by *one pitch* for second pass

Table 6.3 Cutting-tool materials

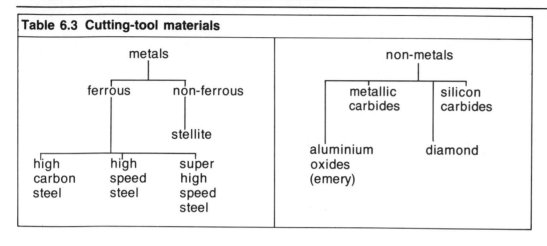

Figure 6.24 shows the relationship between hardness and temperature for ceramic, tungsten carbide, high-speed steel, stellite and plain carbon steel, but it excludes diamond for which comparative figures are not available. The hardness of diamond and the temperatures at which it remains hard are greater than any other material. Unfortunately, its high cost and low mechanical strength (brittleness) make it unsuitable except for very specialised applications.

High-carbon steels

These were introduced in *Part 1* of this course and are plain carbon steels in the hyper-eutectoid range; that is, their carbon content exceeds 0·87 per cent carbon. Steels containing from 1·0 to 1·2 per cent carbon are widely used for hand tools and for wood-machining tools running at low speeds where the heat generation is relatively low. However, even for wood machining, they are now largely supplanted by high-speed steel and stellite. It will be see from Fig. 6.24 that, at room temperature, high carbon steels are harder than high-speed steels and for this reason they are preferred for knives and hand 'edge' tools where their keen cutting properties are an advantage. High-carbon steels are rarely used for machining metals under present-day production conditions as their hardness falls off rapidly at relatively low tempering temperatures, as can be seen from Fig. 6.24.

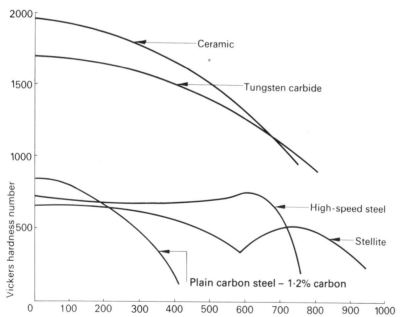

Fig. 6.24 Hardness/temperature curves for cutting-tool materials

High-speed steel

High-speed steels are the most widely used cutting-tool materials in engineering today. In the annealed condition they can be forged and machined with relative ease into single-point tools, twist drills, milling cutters and the most complex form cutters. Yet, when hardened, they combine the strength to work unsupported with high positive rake angles, with a reasonable hardness that is retained almost to red heat, as can be seen from Fig. 6.24. Table 6.4 lists some typical high-speed steels.

Super high-speed steel

A typical super high-speed steel consists of:

carbon	0·8%
chromium	5·0%
tungsten	21·0%
vanadium	1·5%
molybdenum	0·5%
cobalt	11·5%
iron	remainder

This alloy has much more cobalt than the ordinary high-speed steels listed in Table 6.4. This has the following effects.
1 Increases the temperature at which steel will still remain sufficiently hard to cut efficiently.
2 Increases the strength and toughness of the steel so that it can resist the cutting forces met with when machining modern high-strength alloys.
3 Increases the cost of the alloy so that it is only economical to use it when high rates of production are required or when difficult materials are being cut.

Stellite

This is a cobalt-based alloy containing little or no iron. It can only be cast to shape and requires no heat treatment to make it hard. It cannot be softened to make it machinable so it must be ground. Although slightly softer than high-speed steel, it retains its hardness even when it glows red-hot due to the heat being generated by the cutting process. Because of the large amount of tungsten and cobalt present in the alloy it is considerably more expensive than high-speed and super high-speed steels. It can be deposited by welding on to plain carbon and alloy steels to provide built-up hard facings. It is also available in the form of tool 'bits' to fit standard tool holders. A typical composition is:

cobalt	50%	carbon	3%
tungsten	33%	various	14%

High-speed steel, super high-speed steel and stellite are available in standard size tool bits and, since they have a relatively high transverse strength, they may be used in standard tool holders of the pattern shown in Fig. 6.25(a). Alternatively, high-speed steel and super high-speed steel are available butt-welded to medium-carbon steel shanks as shown in Fig. 6.25(b). These types of tool are very robust and are suitable for the heaviest cuts.

Cemented carbides

Pre-formed tool tips made from metallic

Table 6.4 Typical high speed steels

Type of steel		Composition (%)						Hardness (NVP)	Uses
		C	Cr	W	V	Mo	Co		
18% tungsten	Remainder iron	0·68	4·0	19·0	1·5			800–850	Low quality alloy, not much used.
30% tungsten		0·75	4·7	22·0	1·4			850–950	General-purpose cutting tools for jobbing work shops.
6% cobalt		0·8	5·0	19·0	1·5	0·5	6·0	800–900	Heavy-duty cutting tools.
Super HSS 12% cobalt		0·8	5·0	21·0	1·5	0·5	11·5	850–950	Heavy-duty cutting tools for maching high-tensile materials.

The chemical symbols used are: C = carbon, Cr = chromium, W = tungsten, V = vanadium, Mo = molybdenum, Co = cobalt.

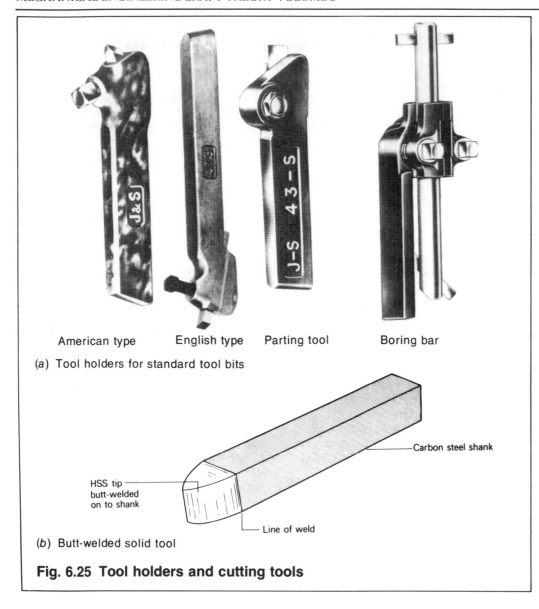

American type   English type   Parting tool   Boring bar

(a) Tool holders for standard tool bits

Carbon steel shank

HSS tip
butt-welded
on to shank

Line of weld

(b) Butt-welded solid tool

Fig. 6.25 Tool holders and cutting tools

carbides are produced by a technique known as *sintering*. They are much harder than stellite, can operate at the same temperatures, and are slightly cheaper than stellite but more difficult to shape. Carbide cutting tools fall into two categories:

1 tungsten carbide;
2 mixed carbides (tungsten and titanium carbides).

Tungsten carbide This is very hard and brittle and is used for cutting cast irons and cast bronzes which have the following properties.

1 A relatively low tensile strength.
2 Form a discontinuous chip.
3 Have a highly abrasive skin.

Owing to its low strength and brittleness tungsten carbide is not suitable for cutting ductile, high-strength materials which form a continuous chip. In addition, tungsten carbide is porous and particles of the metal being cut can become embedded in the matrix of carbide. Although the metal being cut will not chip weld direct to the tungsten carbide, it will chip weld to the embedded particles of metal and this leads to the formation of a built-up edge on the tool.

Mixed carbides These are mixtures of titanium carbide and tungsten carbide. They are less hard than tungsten carbide alone but they are very much stronger. They are used for cutting high-tensile materials. They are less porous than tungsten carbide with the result that there is less tendency for particles of metal to become embedded in the carbide matrix and, therefore,

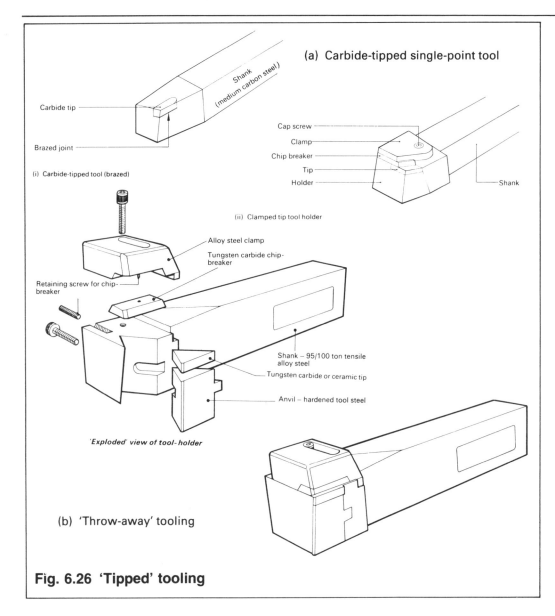

(a) Carbide-tipped single-point tool

Carbide tip

Shank (medium carbon steel)

Brazed joint

(i) Carbide-tipped tool (brazed)

Cap screw

Clamp

Chip breaker

Tip

Holder

Shank

(ii) Clamped tip tool holder

Alloy steel clamp

Tungsten carbide chip-breaker

Retaining screw for chip-breaker

Shank – 95/100 ton tensile alloy steel

Tungsten carbide or ceramic tip

Anvil – hardened tool steel

'Exploded' view of tool-holder

(b) 'Throw-away' tooling

Fig. 6.26 'Tipped' tooling

there is less tendency for a built-up edge to form.

Carbides are very brittle and must be securely supported by the tool shank to which they may be brazed or clamped (see Fig. 6.26(a)). Modern practice favours clamping because the brazing may soften at the high temperatures at which the tip operates under modern cutting conditions. This would allow the tip to come loose.

Ceramics

Ceramic tips are even harder than those made from metallic carbides and also more brittle. The ceramic material most commonly used is sintered aluminium oxide (Al_2O_3), either commercially pure or mixed with other metallic oxides such as chromic oxide. The oxides are prepared by ball-milling alumina powder, together with any suitable additives, to the appropriate grain size. After adding water to form a stiff clay, the tool tips are pressed to shape in moulds and dried. Considerable shrinkage takes place and the moulds must be oversize to allow for this. The tips are then fired at 1600 °C and slowly cooled to avoid shrinkage-cracking. The hardness of the ceramic tips is about 2000 VPN, which is about three times the hardness of high-speed steel and is substantially harder than tungsten carbide. Unlike carbide tips, ceramic tips cannot be brazed to steel shanks and they have to be clamped in place (see Fig. 6.26(b)).

Ceramic tips are weak in tension and susceptible to edge chipping. Therefore, they are only used for finishing cuts at high speeds and fine feeds. Because they are so hard, ceramic tips can only be ground with diamond-impregnated wheels with some difficulty. Therefore, since they are relatively cheap to manufacture, they are used on a 'throw-away' basis.

Machines used with ceramic tooling must be very powerful and rigid to exploit this tool material's special properties. Cutting speeds of 150 to 300 m/min are common when using ceramic tooling, but any vibration or chatter will cause immediate failure of the cutting edge. Because of its low transverse strength, ceramic tooling is normally used with a negative rake angle of 5° to 7° and the chips are frequently seen to be red-hot as they leave the tool. (Another proof of the high power necessary to exploit ceramic tooling.)

Diamond

Diamond – a crystalline allotrope of carbon – is the hardest substance known. Because of its hardness the industrial applications of diamonds are constantly being widened. Usually, cutting tools are made from chips of black or brown diamonds which are unacceptable as gemstones. Although very hard, diamonds are also extremely brittle and great care must be taken to preserve the cutting edge. When turning with diamond-tipped tools the depth of cut should not exceed 0·1 mm and the feed rate should not exceed 0·05 mm/rev. Machine tools for use with

diamond tools should be free from vibration and should be fitted with fine feed and traverse controls. The diamonds are set in holders, either by brazing or by mechanical means such as peening over the edge of the seating, and are cut to a wedge shape to help key them into their seatings. The most common use of diamond tools is for finish machining components made from non-ferrous alloys that cannot be ground satisfactorily, e.g. the aluminium alloy pistons of motor-car engines.

Negative rake

High-speed steel cutting tools have a fairly high transverse strength as well as the hardness necessary in a cutting tool. This enables them to be ground with a positive rake angle and enables them to be used with little support. For example, a tool bit in a standard lathe tool holder is stressed as a self-supporting cantilever.

Unfortunately, the more brittle cutting-tool materials such as the metallic carbides and the metallic oxides (ceramics) cannot be treated in this manner as their transverse strengths are very low. Furthermore, they are invariably used to cut high-strength materials. In order to provide adequate support for the cutting-tool material a different tool geometry is often used, as shown in Fig. 6.27. By employing a negative rake angle the major cutting force is resisted by the full cross-section of the tool shank.

Previously, it has been stated that a

positive rake angle is necessary to promote efficient cutting, to reduce chip thickness and to ease the path of the chip over the tool. It may appear strange, therefore, that a tool with a negative rake angle can cut effectively. However, the increased cutting speeds possible with carbide- and ceramic-tipped tools, coupled with the negative rake geometry, have the effect of transferring the greater part of the work done to the chip. This results in reduced abrasive wear of the tool, less tendency for chip welding and reduced chip force on the rake face of the tool. Furthermore, the work and tool tend to remain cool whilst the chips may become red-hot. This renders the chip more ductile and is the main reason for the reduced force on the tool.

Cutting fluids

Engineers are continually striving to maintain maximum production at minimum cost in the face of increasingly closer design tolerances, tougher materials and the demand for closer control of surface finish. Cutting-tool wear has a significant influence on these goals, since excessive wear results in frequent shutdowns for tool replacement. Downtime results in lost production and increased costs. Extensive tool wear also means excessive tool regrinding and replacement costs. To obtain maximum uninterrupted rates of metal removal and, at the same time, maintain maximum tool service life it is usually

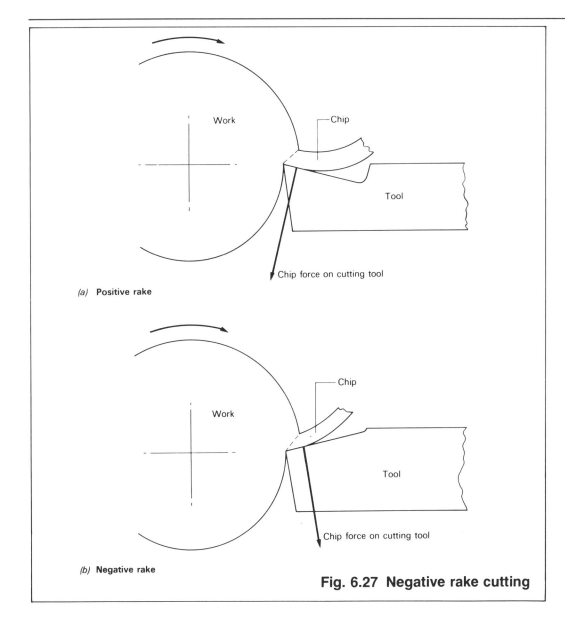

(a) **Positive rake**

(b) **Negative rake**

Fig. 6.27 Negative rake cutting

necessary both to lubricate and to cool the cutting zone. The topic of cutting fluids was introduced in *Part 1* of this course and will now be considered in greater detail.

Cutting fluids are designed to fulfil one or more of the following functions.
1 To cool the tool and workpiece.
2 To lubricate the chip/tool interface and reduce tool wear due to friction and abrasion.
3 To prevent chip welding (formation of a built-up edge).
4 To improve the surface finish of the workpiece.
5 To flush away the chips.
6 To prevent corrosion of the work and machine.

Experiments have shown that for the majority of machining processes the cooling and flushing action of the cutting fluid is the most important. It has also been shown that the tool wear rate is extremely sensitive to small changes in temperature in the region of the wearing surfaces. For these reasons, emulsified cutting fluids are used in the majority of workshop applications because the high water content improves the cooling action.

However, the lubricating action of the cutting fluid becomes of prime importance in reducing the wear rate of the tool in such operations as tapping, broaching, gear cutting, etc., where expensive form tools are used. In these types of operation the cutting speeds are relatively low and the chip force on the rake face of the tool is very high. Therefore, straight or neat (no water added) cutting lubricants are used. Often an extreme pressure additive is present in the lubricant.

Except for very light machining operations, normal mineral lubricating oils are not successful as cutting fluids. They are too viscous and have too low a specific heat capacity to be effective coolants, and they have too low a lubricity to withstand the forces encountered in metal-cutting processes. The shaft in a bearing is supported on a film of oil drawn between itself and the bearing shell. However, in metal-cutting the sliding velocity of the chip over the rake face of the tool is too low to form the essential hydrodynamic wedge of oil found under normal bearing conditions. Also, the chip force is concentrated on a very small area of lubricant and pressures are built up that are in excess of those normally found in a plain bearing. Under these conditions a mineral lubricant would not only break down but, because of the high temperatures encountered in the cutting zone, would give off large volumes of noxious fumes. Such fumes are not only unpleasant but are a health hazard to the operator. Where a neat cutting oil has to be used to provide lubrication, it is essential to use one of the special oils that have been developed.

Cutting fluids in general use can be categorised as follows: soluble oils; synthetic fluids; chemical solutions; straight cutting oils.

Soluble oils

High temperatures adversely affect cutting tools by causing tool softening and reducing their resistance to wear. High temperatures also promote chip welding and accelerate corrosive chemical reactions between the material being cut and the tool. In some instances, a decrease in temperature of only 14 °C can increase tool life by 150 per cent. Because of thermal expansion, control of temperature can also have an effect on maintaining cutting accuracy and preventing distortion of the workpiece. Therefore, cooling the cutting zone is an important function of cutting fluids and this can be accomplished in two ways.

1 Direct removal of heat energy.
2 Indirect cooling by reducing the heat generated through friction at the chip/tool interface.

The effectiveness of direct cooling is influenced by a number of factors, especially the temperature of the fluid and its thermal and physical properties. It is immediately apparent that the cooler the cutting fluid the greater will be the temperature difference between the fluid and the tool, and the greater will be the amount of heat energy absorbed from the cutting zone. Water, because of the low resistance it offers to the transfer of heat, its high latent heat of vaporisation (boiling) and its high specific heat capacity, is about twice as effective a coolant as a light machine oil. However, water is a poor cutting fluid used neat since it causes rusting and has negligible lubricating properties. However, when it is mixed with soluble oils or synthetic and chemical additives, cutting fluids are produced which have the benefits of water cooling without the disadvantages.

Indirect cooling results from any reduction in friction brought about by introducing a lubricant between the chip and the rake face of the tool. It also improves the surface finish of the cut material. However, as already discussed above, lubrication of the chip/tool interface is very difficult except for the lightest cuts and, therefore, indirect cooling is far less important than the direct cooling effect in the majority of workshop applications.

When water and oil are mixed together they remain separate. Addition of an emulsifier, in the form of a detergent, breaks up the oil into droplets and spreads it through the water as shown in Fig. 6.28. This is what happens when the 'soluble' oils are added to water. The milky appearance of these emulsions is due to the light being refracted by the oil droplets. Since the oil is highly diluted with water, these emulsions are very cheap to use and form the most widely used group of cutting fluids to be found in the machine shop.

Obviously, the dilution with water must reduce the lubricating properties. As a result soluble oils are not suitable for the very severe conditions found on many automatic machines or on machines using form cutters such as broaching and gear-cutting machines. However, the high water content makes them excellent coolants and for the

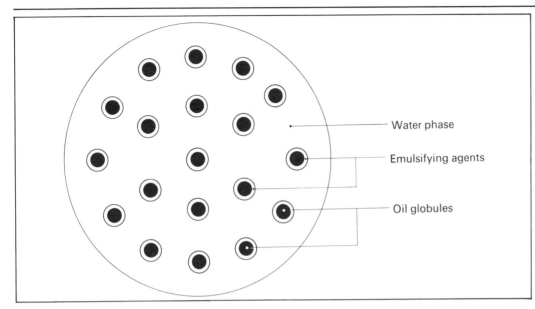

Water phase

Emulsifying agents

Oil globules

Fig. 6.28 Emulsified oil

general machine shop they are ideal. They are especially useful for manually operated machines taking fast but light cuts, and where the operator would be affected by the fumes given off by neat oils. The dilution also helps to reduce the tendency for mineral oils to produce skin diseases. The addition of a disinfectant helps to reduce the transmission of disease from one operative to another, and also helps to prevent the emulsion breaking down under bacteriological attack when it is standing.

Emulsified oils must be properly mixed. Generally modern oils are very stable, but incorrect mixing and storing can cause the oil to separate out.

1 Mixing must be carried out in clean containers, using carefully measured quantities of oil and of fresh, clean water.
2 The oil must be added to the water (never the reverse) whilst the mixture is vigorously and continuously stirred with a paddle.
3 If the emulsion is for stock, then dirt must not be allowed to drop into it. The emulsion must, however, be open to fresh air and periodically stirred. This oxygenation of the emulsion prevents it becoming stagnant and subject to bacteriological attack.

Milky-white opaque emulsions (suds) are used for most machining operations where a reasonable degree of tool life

and performance is required under jobbing and batch-production conditions. Rust inhibitors can be incorporated in this type of soluble oil to prevent corrosion of the work and the machine when high dilution ratios are used.

Translucent or semi-opaque emulsions are formed when very small globules of mineral oil are suspended in the water. Although more expensive, translucent emulsions are generally more stable than the conventional opaque types when mixed at high dilutions. Furthermore, they generally have better anti-corrosive, wetting out and swarf-settling properties than opaque types.

For a given water/oil ratio, oil globules in translucent emulsion are smaller and more finely dispersed in the water and consequently the lubricating action (indirect cooling) is improved. Translucent emulsions are less greasy than conventional opaque types and are favoured for light-duty, high-speed machining operations, including grinding. A further advantage of translucent emulsions is that the cutting tools, fixtures and components can all be seen during the machining operation. This is a considerable asset for craftsmen engaged on intricate work of high precision.

Rust inhibitors can also be added to translucent emulsified cutting oils in order to enhance their anti-corrosion properties and enable high dilution ratios to be achieved.

Synthetic fluids

In this group of cutting fluids the mineral-oil base of conventional cutting oils – both emulsified and neat – are replaced by aqueous solutions of inorganic chemicals, together with corrosion inhibitors and extreme pressure lubricating additives. These solutions are transparent, but colouring agents are added to differentiate them from water and soda solutions. Having a high water content, chemical cutting fluids possess excellent cooling properties.

Other benefits include a high level of cleanliness in the cooling system and of the machine tool slideways. They have long-term stability, easily removable residual films and no tendency to foaming. Being transparent, they give improved visual control of intricate machining operations. Some of the advantages claimed for synthetic fluids are:
1 Absence of fire risk. Some oil-based cutting fluids are highly flammable.
2 Greater stability of water emulsions, especially in hard-water areas.
3 Reduced health hazards for operators.
4 Spent fluid may be disposed of as a normal trade effluent without first having to be rendered environmentally safe by complex and expensive chemical treatment.

Chemical solutions

These consist of carefully chosen chemicals in dilute solution with water. They possess a good flushing action, a good cooling action and are non-corrosive and non-clogging. Since they are non-clogging they are widely used for grinding and sawing. One of the earliest chemical solutions was of sodium carbonate (soda-ash) in water. This was purely a corrosion-inhibited coolant widely used for sawing and grinding. However, it attacked painted surfaces of the machines on which it was used and also caused minor skin irritations amongst the machine operators. Modern chemical solutions do not affect the machines on which they are used and present no health hazard. Unlike oil-based lubricants, chemical solutions are non-flammable and safer to store and use.

Lubricants

Where greater lubrication of the chip/tool interface is required, this can be obtained at the expense of some of the cooling properties of the cutting fluid by using one of the following lubricants: straight mineral oils; straight fatty oils; compounded oils; extreme pressure lubricants.

Straight mineral oils The term 'straight' when applied to lubricants and coolants, means undiluted. Anyone who has tried using an ordinary lubricating oil as a cutting fluid will have discovered that:
1 it gives off a cloud of unpleasant smoke and fumes;
2 it has little effect as a cutting fluid.

The chip and tool have a small area of contact, therefore the load per unit area on the lubricant is much higher than in a bearing. The film strength of the oil is not sufficient to withstand this load and it ceases to act as a lubricant, that is, the chip punctures the oil film and comes into contact with the tool face. Furthermore, mineral oils are relatively poor coolants.

The only widely used application is that of kerosene (crude paraffin) for machining aluminium and its alloys. However, this is being replaced now by specially designed emulsified oils which are more effective, do not produce noxious fumes, and present a lesser fire hazard.

Straight fatty oils Lard oils and vegetable oils have the advantage of much higher film strength (oiliness) than mineral oils. Unfortunately, they are not stable and rapidly lose their lubricating properties when contaminated with impurities. Neither are they satisfactory coolants as they have a high viscosity. They are much more expensive and less plentiful than mineral oils. Nevertheless, they were used for heavy-duty machining and pressing operations for a long time. Today, lard oil is mainly used on the bench for thread cutting with taps and dies.

Compounded or blended oils These are mixtures of mineral and fatty oils. The film strength of fatty oils is retained, even when diluted with 75 per cent mineral oil. As a result they are much cheaper and more fluid than the neat fatty oils. They are very versatile and can be used on most machining operations, especially on light- and medium-duty automatic machines.

Extreme pressure lubricants It has already been stated that the high pressures existing at the chip/tool interface during machining do not allow conventional fluid film and boundary layer lubrication to be achieved, to any significant extent, under severe cutting conditions. In fact, experimentation has proved that the lubricating action of cutting fluids, operating under severe conditions, is mainly of a chemical nature.

For example, the lubricating effect of tetrachloromethane under normal bearing conditions is negligible. Tetrachloromethane (CCl_4) is the thin, spirit-like solvent used for dry-cleaning clothing. However, it proves to be a most effective lubricant when machining copper. Because of its small molecular size the fluid is able to diffuse into the strained crystal lattice of the copper where it is deformed at the point of cutting. A layer of copper chloride is produced by chemical action and this acts as a boundary layer lubricant that can withstand higher temperatures and pressures than conventional lubricants. Tetrachloromethane must not be used as a lubricant outside the laboratory because of its toxic properties. When heated it gives off the very dangerous and poisonous gas called phosgene.

In practice, extreme pressure cutting fluids are bought ready compounded. They consist of safe chlorine and sulphur compounds added to compounded oils or to soluble oils.

Sulphurised oils are probably the most useful single group of extreme pressure cutting fluids available either as straight oils or as soluble oils. They should be compounded so that there is no free sulphur present which would attack and stain copper and high-nickel alloys. Sulphurised oils are used mainly for their lubrication factor in heavy lathe work, gear cutting, thread grinding, screwing and automatic lathe work.

Sulphured oils contain free or elemental sulphur which is completely dissolved in a mineral or compounded oil. The sulphur is in a very active state, and although exhibiting extreme pressure characteristics, they will attack and stain copper and high-nickel-based alloys.

Table 6.5 Recommended cutting lubricants for use with high-speed steel tools

Material	Cutting lubricants
Aluminium and aluminium alloys	Soluble oil, paraffin (do not use alkali solutions).
Magnesium and magnesium alloys	Dry. If possible, keep the drill cooled with a jet of compressed air.
Copper	Soluble oil, lard oil.
Brass	Dry, soluble oil.
Phosphor-bronze	Soluble oil, lard oil.
Slate	Dry. If possible, keep the drill cooled with a jet of compressed air.
Monel metal	Soluble oil, sulphurised oil.
Bakelite	Dry. If possible, keep the drill cooled with a jet of compressed air.
Cast iron	Dry. If possible, keep the drill cooled with a jet of compressed air.
Chilled cast iron	Soluble oil.
Malleable iron	Soluble oil.
Nimonic	Neat oil, lard oil.
Wrought iron	Soluble oil, sulphurised oil.
Zinc	Soluble oil.
Mild steel	Soluble oil, sulphurised oil.
Alloy steel – all tensile strengths	Soluble oil, sulphurised oil.
High manganese steel	Sulphurised oil.
Steel forgings	Soluble oil, sulphurised oil.
Stainless steels (austenitic, martensitic and ferritic – standard grades)	Small diameters: tallow or turpentine. Large diameters: soluble oil.
Stainless steels (free-cutting grades)	Small diameters: sulphurised oil. Large diameters: soluble oil.

Application of cutting fluids

Having selected the correct cutting fluid, it is equally essential to apply it effectively to the cutting zone. All too often the chip or the tool masks the chip/tool interface and prevents the cutting fluid from doing its job properly.

Normally, coolant should be applied in a generous flow at low pressure, but occasionally a more restricted high-pressure jet is required as in deep-hole drilling and boring. As machining proceeds there is a continual loss in volume of the coolant circulating. This arises from splashing, misting and carryover in machined parts, and swarf. Therefore, regular topping up of the coolant tank is necessary.

If the coolant volume falls low, the cutting fluid becomes overheated, leading to fuming and lack of effective cooling and lubrication. If the flow becomes intermittent, thermal cracking of the cutting tools can occur.

Some typical applications It has only been possible to deal with the complex problems of cutting fluids in a general way. The major oil companies publish many helpful booklets on this subject and it is recommended that these are consulted. Table 6.5 gives a guide as to the selection of cutting fluids for the general machining of various materials using high-speed steel cutting tools.

Exercises

1. Describe, with the aid of sketches, typical applications of (a) a fixed steady, (b) a travelling steady.
2. (a) Explain how 'soft jaws' may be used in a three-jaw self-centring chuck to improve the concentricity for second-operation work.
   (b) With the aid of sketches show the precautions that must be taken when machining soft jaws to ensure concentricity.
3. Why is it often necessary to use balance weights when turning components fastened to the face plate? What problems and hazards arise from not fitting balance weights?
4. With the aid of sketches show a typical application of the parallel mandrel (snug).
5. With the aid of sketches show **three** methods of generating tapers in the centre lathe.
6. Describe the techniques of screw-cutting on the centre lathe (a) by the 'plunge-cut' method, (b) by the 'half-angle' method. Discuss the advantages and limitations of each method.
7. To cut an M20 × 2·5 vee form screw thread on a centre lathe fitted with a 6 mm lead, lead screw,
   (i) calculate the change gears necessary;
   (ii) describe the process of cutting the thread using the half-angle technique using sketches to illustrate your answer;
   (iii) describe a method of 'picking-up' the thread on successive cuts;
   (iv) explain with the aid of sketches why the thread has to be finished with a chaser.
8. Explain with the aid of sketches how to cut a two start square thread in a centre lathe and show how the tool has to be set to compensate for the helix angle.
9. (a) Compare the advantages and limitations of the following cutting tool materials:
      (i) high speed steel,
      (ii) cemented carbides,
      (iii) ceramics.
   (b) With the aid of sketches show what is meant by negative rake cutting and explain the advantages of this technique.
10. (a) List the six main functions of a cutting fluid.
    (b) Discuss the advantages and limitations of soluble oil (suds) as a cutting fluid, and describe the precautions that must be taken in mixing and storing soluble oil so that it does not deteriorate.

7. Shaping, planing and slotting

The ram-head sub-assembly

The ram-head sub-assembly is shown in Fig. 7.1(a). It consists of three basic elements: the *tool slide*, the *clapper box* and the *tool post*. The clapper box was introduced in *Mechanical Engineering Craft Theory and Related Studies: Part 1*.

The tool slide controls the in-feed of the cutting tool into the workpiece; that is, it controls the depth of cut and is adjusted by a lead screw and nut fitted with a micrometer dial. Since the vibration of cutting tends to move the screw, a slide clamp is often provided so that the setting can be locked. It also removes the cutting forces from the screw and nut and helps to preserve their accuracy. Many larger, modern machines are provided with a power feed to the tool slide for use when machining surfaces which are perpendicular or inclined to the machine table. It will be seen from Fig. 7.1(a) that the ram head sub-assembly is fitted with a protractor scale. This is used when the tool slide has to be inclined at an angle to the vertical as shown in Fig. 7.1(b).

Setting the clapper box

The clapper box allows the cutting tool

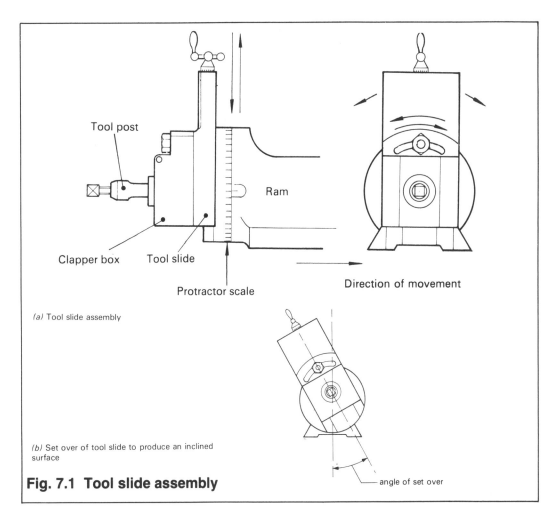

(a) Tool slide assembly

(b) Set over of tool slide to produce an inclined surface

Fig. 7.1 Tool slide assembly

to lift on the return stroke, as shown in Fig. 7.2(a). If the tool were rigidly fixed to the tool slide it would be dragged back through the uncut workpiece as the latter traverses across for the next cut. This would result in damage to the workpiece and damage to the cutting edge of the tool. In order to provide clearance for the tool on the return stroke when cutting surfaces that are perpendicular to, or inclined to, the work table the clapper box is set over as shown in Fig. 7.2(b). The clapper box is always adjusted so that the tool is swung towards the work as shown. When cutting a surface parallel to the worktable the clapper box is centralised.

The *tool post* carries the cutting tool in the same way as it does on the lathe.

Setting the tool-slide

The ram head sub-assembly, and therefore the tool slide, can be inclined for machining angular surfaces. For this reason it is important to check the tool slide for perpendicularity before machining horizontal and perpendicular surfaces, in case it has been disturbed. Figure 7.3(a) shows how a large try-square is clamped to the machine table so that a dial test indicator (DTI) can be used to check the tool slide. The DTI is either secured to the tool slide by a magnetic scribing block or by an adaptor clamped in the tool post. The tool slide is wound up or down so that the stylus of the DTI follows the edge of the try-square blade. If the tool slide is perpendicular the reading of the DTI should remain constant.

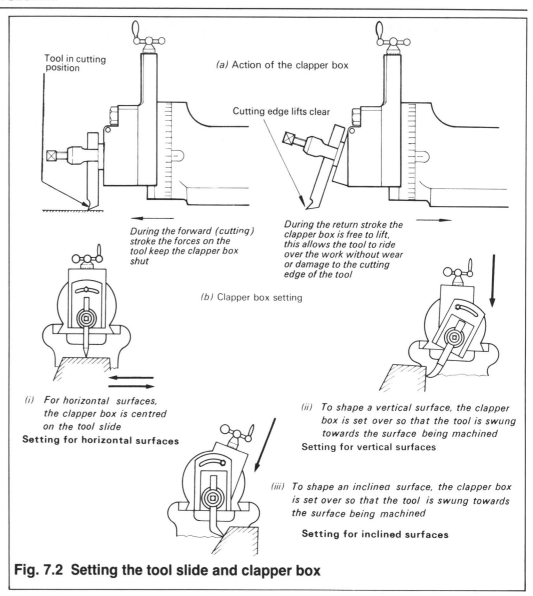

(a) Action of the clapper box

Tool in cutting position

Cutting edge lifts clear

During the forward (cutting) stroke the forces on the tool keep the clapper box shut

During the return stroke the clapper box is free to lift, this allows the tool to ride over the work without wear or damage to the cutting edge of the tool

(b) Clapper box setting

(i) For horizontal surfaces, the clapper box is centred on the tool slide

Setting for horizontal surfaces

(ii) To shape a vertical surface, the clapper box is set over so that the tool is swung towards the surface being machined

Setting for vertical surfaces

(iii) To shape an inclined surface, the clapper box is set over so that the tool is swung towards the surface being machined

Setting for inclined surfaces

Fig. 7.2 Setting the tool slide and clapper box

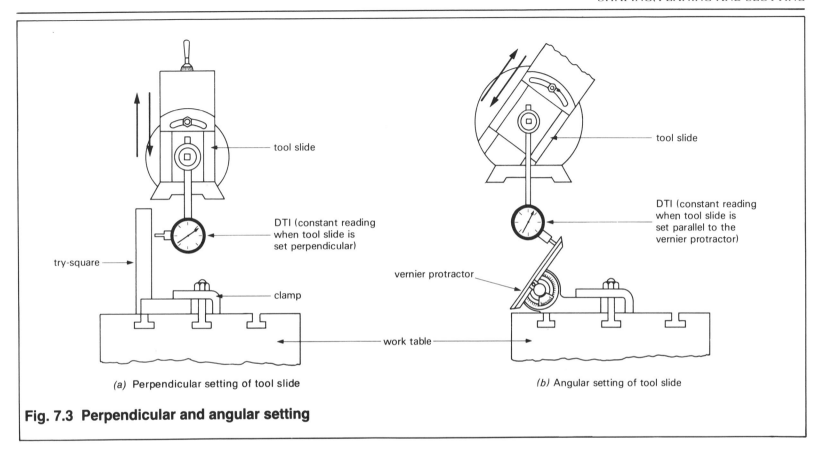

(a) Perpendicular setting of tool slide

(b) Angular setting of tool slide

tool slide

DTI (constant reading when tool slide is set perpendicular)

try-square

clamp

work table

tool slide

DTI (constant reading when tool slide is set parallel to the vernier protractor)

vernier protractor

work table

Fig. 7.3 Perpendicular and angular setting

Figure 7.3(b) shows how a vernier protractor can be used for off-setting the tool slide when an angular surface is to be machined. The procedure is the same as that previously described, except that the vernier protractor is substituted for the try-square.

Setting the tilting table

Some shaping machines are fitted with a tilting table so that tapered work can be machined. Figure 7.4 shows a typical tilting table. One method of setting a tilting table is to use a device called a *clinometer*.

The clinometer is an instrument

which uses a precision level to measure or set angles. A typical instrument is shown in Fig. 7.5 and Fig. 7.6 shows how the instrument is used to adjust the tilting table of a shaping machine.
1 A dial test indicator is used to set the table parallel to the cross rail slide.
2 The clinometer is placed on the machine table and the bubble is

145

centralised in the vial. Note this initial clinometer reading.

3 Set the clinometer to the required reading ± the initial reading obtained in 2. Set the table over until the bubble is again central in the vial.

Note: Whether the reading obtained in 2 is added to or subtracted from the required angle will depend upon its direction relative to the desired angle of tilt:

same direction *add*
opposite direction *subtract*

After the tilting table has been inclined, it must always be reset to the horizontal position using a parallel and dial test indicator as shown in 1 above.

Fig. 7.4 Tilting table

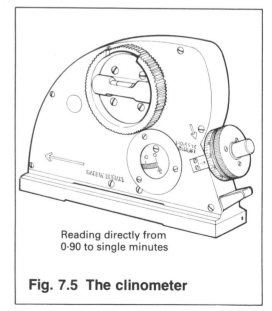

Reading directly from
0·90 to single minutes

Fig. 7.5 The clinometer

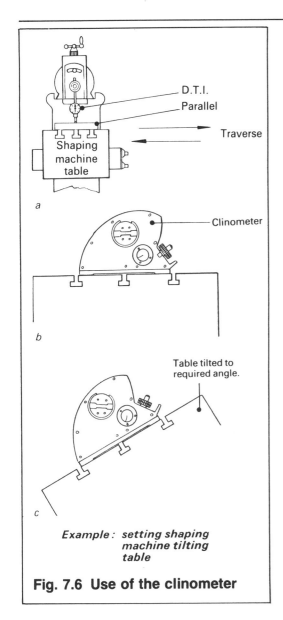

a

b

c

Example: setting shaping machine tilting table

Fig. 7.6 Use of the clinometer

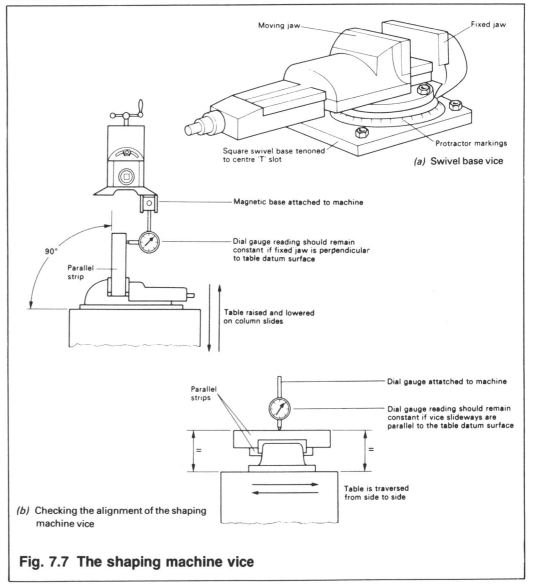

(a) Swivel base vice

(b) Checking the alignment of the shaping machine vice

Fig. 7.7 The shaping machine vice

Setting the machine vice

There are several ways of holding the workpiece on a shaping machine. The most usual is to use a swivel base vice as shown in Fig. 7.7(a). In order to produce accurate work, it is essential that the fixed jaw and upper surfaces of the slides of the vice are accurately aligned with the machine work table. After the vice has been positioned for a particular job, it should be checked for alignment as shown in Fig. 7.7(b).

Like all machine vices, the moving jaw slideways are subject to wear. The *couple* formed by the clamping force and the workpiece reaction force tends to tilt the moving jaw as it is tightened as shown in Fig. 7.8(a). This tends to lift the work off the parallels and causes lack of parallelism and perpendicularity between the machined surfaces as shown in Fig. 7.8(b). There are various ways by which this effect can be overcome providing the wear is not excessive. A badly worn vice is dangerous since the work will not be securely held. Figure 7.9 shows how the workpiece may be set in the shaping machine vice.

The method shown in Fig. 7.9(a) is only suitable for bright drawn mild steel or previously machined blanks and the vice must be in good condition so that the lift of the moving jaw is negligible. Even then, it will be necessary to tap the work down on to the parallels after the vice is finally tightened.

In Fig. 7.9(b) a piece of rod has been inserted between the work and the

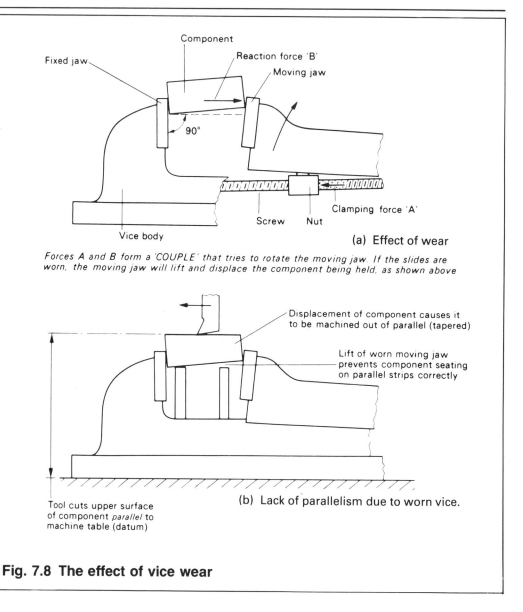

(a) Effect of wear

Forces A and B form a 'COUPLE' that tries to rotate the moving jaw. If the slides are worn, the moving jaw will lift and displace the component being held, as shown above

(b) Lack of parallelism due to worn vice.

Fig. 7.8 The effect of vice wear

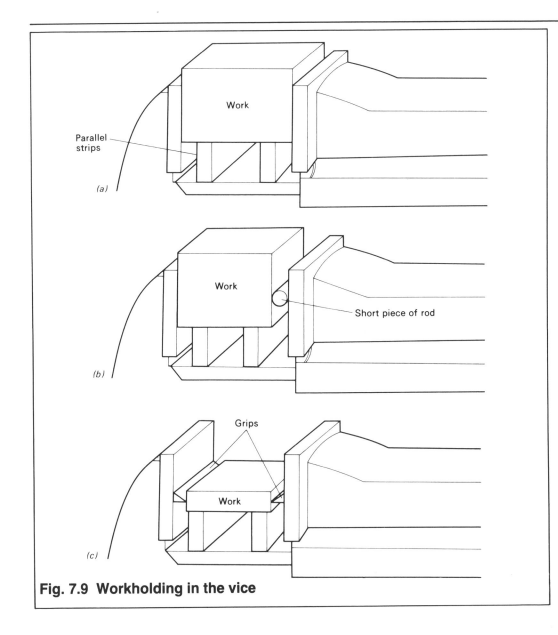

Parallel
strips

Work

(a)

Work

Short piece of rod

(b)

Grips

Work

(c)

Fig. 7.9 Workholding in the vice

moving jaw. Any lift in the moving jaw merely causes the rod to roll up the side of the component which remains securely clamped against the fixed jaw.

In Fig. 7.9(c) triangular grips have been used. These ensure that the work is pulled securely down on to the parallels. They tend to mark the work and are usually used for hot-rolled (black) bar and rough castings. They are also useful when machining plate as shown in the diagram. It is possible for the tool to clear both sides of the job when cutting right across the upper surface, yet mount the job well down in the vice. If held directly in the jaws, the work would have to be packed up until it was only being held on the tips of the jaws which is bad practice. Figure 7.10 shows an enlarged view of one of the grips. It will be seen that the angle at B is slightly greater than 90°. (It has been exaggerated in the diagram.) As the vice is tightened the face AB of the grip tries to close against the vice jaw, depressing the point of the grip C. This drags the work down hard on to the parallel strips. Any attempt by the work to lift, causes C to lift and forces the corner A against the vice jaw. Since the grip and the jaw are solid, no movement can take place. Thus the gripping action is very powerful indeed, and the work is securely held.

Usually it is good practice to cut against the fixed jaw of a vice so that the cutting forces are resisted by a solid abutment. Figure 7.11(a) shows the restraints that apply when work is set in this manner. However, this is not

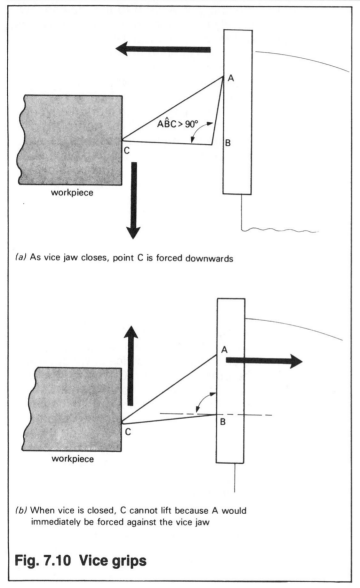

(a) As vice jaw closes, point C is forced downwards

(b) When vice is closed, C cannot lift because A would immediately be forced against the vice jaw

Fig. 7.10 Vice grips

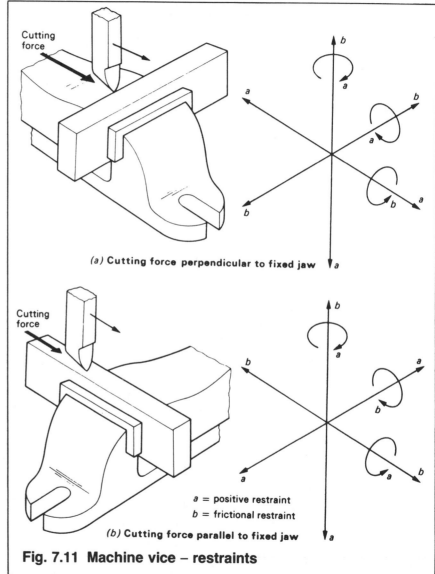

(a) Cutting force perpendicular to fixed jaw

a = positive restraint

b = frictional restraint

(b) Cutting force parallel to fixed jaw

Fig. 7.11 Machine vice – restraints

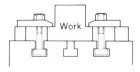

Work clamped to machine table

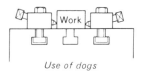

Use of dogs

(a) *Large work can be fastened directly to the shaping machine table*

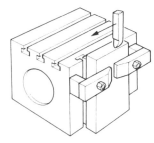

(b) *Large work can be fastened directly to the side of the shaping machine table for squaring up the ends*

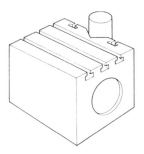

(c) *Large cylindrical work can also be fastened into the vee slot on the side of the shaping machine table*

Fig. 7.12 Alternative methods of work-holding

possible on a shaping machine when long components are being machined, as the shaping machine works more efficiently when set to a long stroke, so that the arrangement shown in Fig. 7.11(b) is often used on this machine. It will be seen that the main cutting force is only restrained by friction, and care must be taken in setting the work to prevent it being dislodged.

Large jobs may be mounted directly on to the machine table using clamps or dogs as shown in Fig. 7.12(a). Surfaces may be machined perpendicular to each other using the side of the table as shown in Fig. 7.12(b). The side of the table is often provided with a vee slot for holding cylindrical work as shown in Fig. 7.12(c).

Work holding will be referred to again in Chapter 10 when the shaping of some typical components is considered.

Shaping machine tools and tool-holding

One of the great advantages of the shaping machine for jobbing-shop work is the fact that it uses cheap, single point tools similar to lathe tools. Further, these tools can be ground off-hand when it is necessary to change their shape to suit a particular job or to re-sharpen them. Some typical shaping machine tools are shown in Fig. 7.13(a) when their similarity to lathe tools will be evident. Figure 7.13(b) shows the basic tool angles.

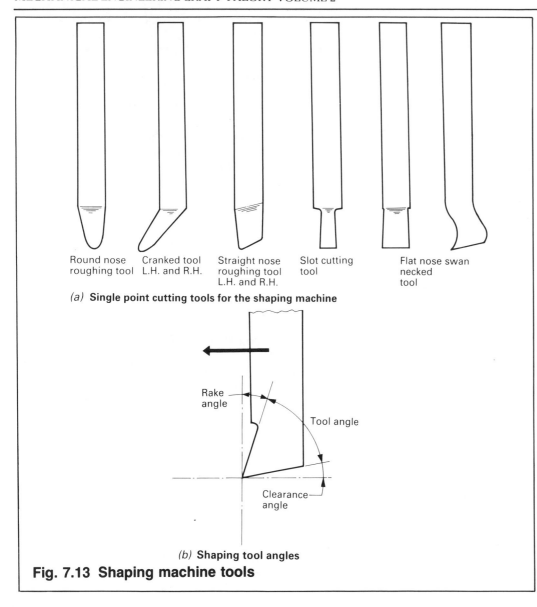

Round nose roughing tool

Cranked tool L.H. and R.H.

Straight nose roughing tool L.H. and R.H.

Slot cutting tool

Flat nose swan necked tool

(a) **Single point cutting tools for the shaping machine**

Rake angle

Tool angle

Clearance angle

(b) **Shaping tool angles**

Fig. 7.13 Shaping machine tools

The shaping machine tool is held in a tool post similar to that used on the lathe. Figure 7.14(a) shows the forces acting on the tool and the tool holder, whilst Fig. 7.14(b) shows the restraints acting on a shaping tool held in a simple, single tool post.

The shaping machine tool often has to operate with greater overhang from the tool post than is customary on the lathe. This leads to springing of the tool shank and chatter, especially when using a broad nose finishing tool. The swan-necked tool shank shown in Fig. 7.15(a) is sometimes used to prevent chatter and digging in. If the cutting load becomes sufficient to deflect the tool it bends about the point P, and it will be seen that this causes the cutting edge to lift away from the work reducing the depth of cut and therefore the load on the tool. This continues until equilibrium is established with the cutting force and the spring back of the shank in balance.

However, any deflection will cause an ordinary straight shank tool, as shown in Fig. 7.15(b), to dig deeper into the cut. Since this increases the load on the tool the shank deflects further, again increasing the load. This will continue progressively until the machine stalls or the cutting edge fractures.

The planing machine

Figure 7.16 shows a typical modern planing machine. Like the shaping machine, it generates plane surfaces by ruling with a single-point cutting tool.

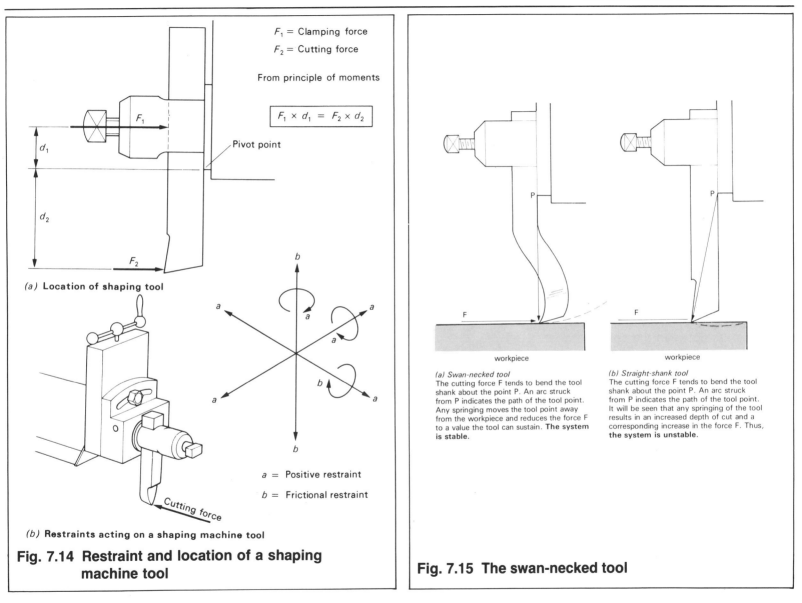

F_1 = Clamping force

F_2 = Cutting force

From principle of moments

$$F_1 \times d_1 = F_2 \times d_2$$

Pivot point

(a) **Location of shaping tool**

a = Positive restraint

b = Frictional restraint

Cutting force

(b) **Restraints acting on a shaping machine tool**

Fig. 7.14 Restraint and location of a shaping machine tool

(a) Swan-necked tool
The cutting force F tends to bend the tool shank about the point P. An arc struck from P indicates the path of the tool point. Any springing moves the tool point away from the workpiece and reduces the force F to a value the tool can sustain. **The system is stable.**

(b) Straight-shank tool
The cutting force F tends to bend the tool shank about the point P. An arc struck from P indicates the path of the tool point. It will be seen that any springing of the tool results in an increased depth of cut and a corresponding increase in the force F. Thus, **the system is unstable.**

workpiece

workpiece

Fig. 7.15 The swan-necked tool

153

However, the planing machine can deal with very much bigger components than the shaping machine because it is more rigid and more powerful. It is used to machine the beds of machine tools as well as other large and heavy components. Unlike the shaping machine, it is the table of the planing machine that moves backwards and forwards, and the tool head that traverses from side to side. For this reason the bed of a planing machine is twice as long as the table to give it support throughout its stroke. The slides of the planing machine have to support the heavy table as well as the large and heavy workpiece; they must be adequately lubricated and kept free from dust and dirt. The table slideways are protected by telescopic covers. The size of a planing machine is specified by the length of its stroke and the width that will pass between the column supporting the cross rail. There are four tool heads on this machine so that the component can be cut on three sides at one setting.

Table drive

Planing machine tables may be driven mechanically or by hydraulic means. Figure 7.17 shows the layout for a typical skew gear and rack drive to the table. The main drive motor is permanently coupled to the drive and is a direct current variable speed and reversing motor. It is provided with variable voltage from a special motor generator set. Reversal of the polarity is provided through switches actuated by

Fig. 7.16 A planing machine

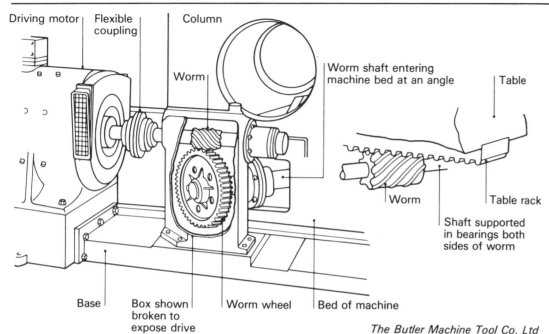

Fig. 7.17 (a) **Planing machine drive**

Driving motor | Flexible coupling | Column | Worm | Worm shaft entering machine bed at an angle | Table | Worm | Table rack | Shaft supported in bearings both sides of worm

Base | Box shown broken to expose drive | Worm wheel | Bed of machine

The Butler Machine Tool Co. Ltd

Fig. 7.17(b) **Planing machine drive**

adjustable trip dogs attached to the table. The constant reversal of the motor and drive sets up considerable mechanical and electrical stresses. This is so particularly when a heavy component has to be accelerated at the start of the stroke and brought to rest again before it is reversed at the end of the stroke. Although the electro-mechanical planing machine has been brought to a high degree of reliability, the hydraulic drive is far simpler and places less stress on the drive mechanism.

Fig. 7.18 **Planing machine movements**

Above Power lift to tool holders
Left General arrangement of cutting tool slides

155

Fig. 7.19 Planing a large casting

Cutting tools and tool-holding

The cutting tools for planing machines are similar to those used on the lathe and on the shaping machine except that they are very much more robust to support the greater cutting forces associated with the heavier work of the planing machine. The tool slides are provided with vertical and horizontal feeds both manual and automatic. Provision is also made for inclining the tool heads. Tool boxes are also provided on vertical slides on the side columns for machining perpendicular surfaces. Figure 7.18(a) shows the arrangement of the cutting tool slides of a planing machine.

Unlike the shaping machine, planing machine tool boxes are fitted with power lift to the tool for the return stroke. The tools and their mounting are too heavy for the conventional clapper box, see Fig. 7.18(b).

Work-holding and setting

The table of the planing machine rests on the bed and the load of the workpiece is transmitted directly through the bed to the foundations supporting the machine. This results in rigidity and freedom from deflection and vibration.

Generally, the work machined on the planer is bolted directly to the table by a combination of clamps, dogs and packing or jacks. Great skill is required on the part of the operator to ensure that the work is adequately supported

Fig. 7.20 Planing a 'string' of smaller castings

so that it does not deflect under its own weight or under the force of the clamps. Because of the power of the machine, the operator must also ensure that the clamping is adequate to resist the cutting forces. Some typical examples of planing machine work are shown in Figs 7.19 and 7.20.

The slotting machine

Figure 7.21(a) shows a typical slotting machine and names its more important features. Like the planing and the shaping machines the slotting machine also produces plane surfaces by a reciprocating tool. The slotting machine has the added advantage that the work table can rotate and this feature is used to generate radiused components as shown in Fig. 7.21(b).

The drive mechanism to the ram of the slotting machine can be a variation of the slotted link mechanism used on shaping machines, or it can be the Whitworth quick return mechanism shown in Fig. 7.21(c). Figure 7.21(d) shows a typical slotting machine set up.

Slotting machine tools

At first sight the tools for slotting machines appear to have their cutting angles upside down. However, this is due to the fact that the tool moves in the vertical plane and not in the horizontal plane. Figure 7.22 shows some typical slotting machine tools and their cutting angles.

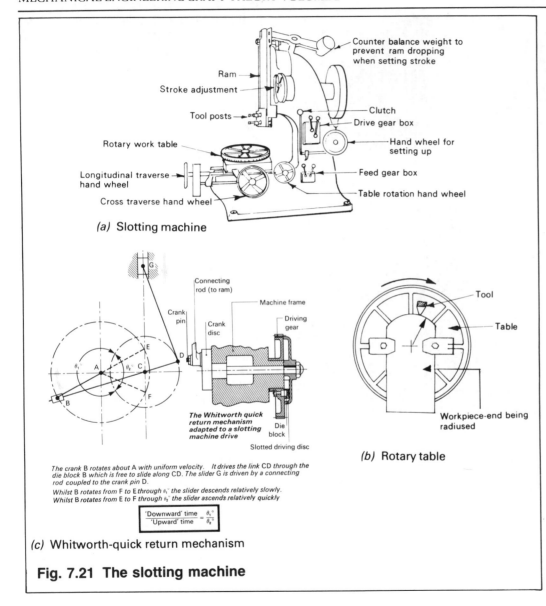

(a) Slotting machine

(c) Whitworth-quick return mechanism

The Whitworth quick return mechanism adapted to a slotting machine drive

Slotted driving disc

The crank B rotates about A with uniform velocity. It drives the link CD through the die block B which is free to slide along CD. The slider G is driven by a connecting rod coupled to the crank pin D.
Whilst B rotates from F to E through θ_1 the slider descends relatively slowly.
Whilst B rotates from E to F through θ_2 the slider ascends relatively quickly

$$\frac{\text{'Downward' time}}{\text{'Upward' time}} = \frac{\theta_1{}^\circ}{\theta_2{}^\circ}$$

(b) Rotary table

Workpiece-end being radiused

Fig. 7.21 The slotting machine

Slotting a keyway

The slotting machine is useful for such operations as cutting keyways in single components where the cost of a broach is not warranted. Figure 7.23(a) shows a typical component whilst Fig. 7.23(b) shows a typical set up. The operation sequence would be as follows:

1 Set component on the slotting machine table as shown in Fig. 7.23(b). Support the component on parallels so that the tool may clear the bottom of the component without marking the work table, and tighten the clamps.

2 Rotate the work table until the marked-out centre line is parallel with the cross-slide of the machine. A sticky pin can be used to check the setting.

3 Use a keyway tool slightly narrower than the keyway being cut. Set stroke so that the tool just clears the top and bottom of the component.

4 Start cutting in the centre of the marked-out keyway, and feed the tool slowly by hand into the component.

Fig. 7.21(d)

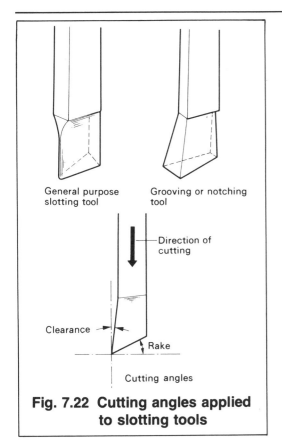

General purpose slotting tool

Grooving or notching tool

Direction of cutting

Clearance

Rake

Cutting angles

Fig. 7.22 Cutting angles applied to slotting tools

Check the depth of cut using inside calipers or a telescopic gauge and a micrometer. An inside micrometer may also be used if the slot is wide enough.
5 Before bottoming out, withdraw the tool and clean out the keyway on one side only.
6 Using slip gauges, check the width of the slot and open out the keyway to size. Finally bottom out and check for correct depth as in 4.

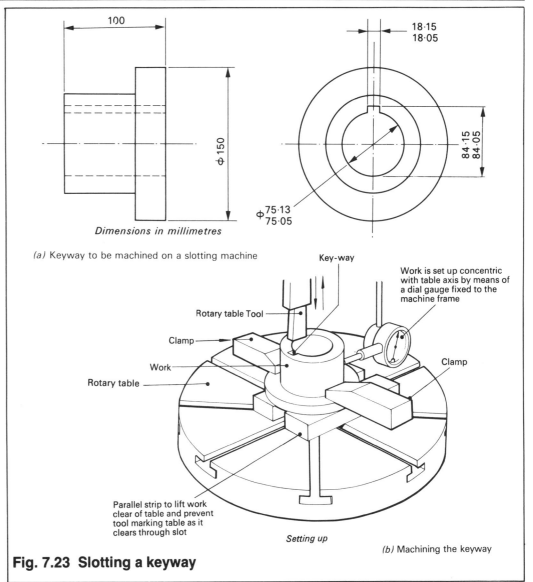

100

18·15
18·05

ϕ 150

84·15
84·05

ϕ 75·13
75·05

Dimensions in millimetres

(a) Keyway to be machined on a slotting machine

Key-way

Work is set up concentric with table axis by means of a dial gauge fixed to the machine frame

Rotary table Tool

Clamp

Work

Clamp

Rotary table

Parallel strip to lift work clear of table and prevent tool marking table as it clears through slot

Setting up

(b) Machining the keyway

Fig. 7.23 Slotting a keyway

159

Exercises

1. With the aid of diagrams describe the essential difference between shaping and slotting machines.

2. With the aid of diagrams, show how the tool slide and clapper box should be set when machining vertical and inclined surfaces on a shaping machine.

3. Describe with the aid of sketches, the settings of the tool slide and clapper box of a shaping machine to make the component shown in Fig. 7.24. List the operations.

4. Explain, with the aid of sketches, how the tilting table of a shaping machine can be set to produce a wedge shaped component. Angle of taper of wedge $5° \pm 15'$. A clinometer may be used as a setting aid.

5. Explain, with the aid of diagrams, how the use of cutting tools with 'swan-neck' shanks reduces chatter when taking broad finishing cuts on planing and shaping machines.

6. (a) With the aid of sketches show the position and movement of the tool slides of a large planing machine, and thus show how perpendicular and inclined surfaces can be planed as well as horizontal surfaces.

   (b) Explain briefly the essential difference between a shaping machine clapper box and a planing machine clapper box.

7. By means of a sketch show how the cutting angles of a slotting machine tool differ from those of a shaping machine tool.

8. Describe with the aid of diagrams how the keyway in the bush shown in Fig. 7.25 can be machined on a slotting machine. Pay particular attention to the method of setting and clamping the component on the machine.

9. Explain, with the aid of sketches, how the tool slide can be set: (a) at 90° and (b) at 65° to the machine table surface.

10. (a) With the aid of diagrams, show how:
    (i) a thin plate may be held in the vice using grips,
    (ii) a plate may be held directly on to the machine table using clogs,
    (iii) a 'lift' in the moving jaw of a worm machine vice may be overcome.

    (b) From the following data calculate the number of cycles/min (double strokes) and the feed per double stroke for a shaping machine.
    Stroke length = 200 mm
    Cutting speed = 45 m/min
    Table traverse screw lead = 6 mm
    Ratchet wheel = 30 teeth
    Increment = 3 teeth/double stroke

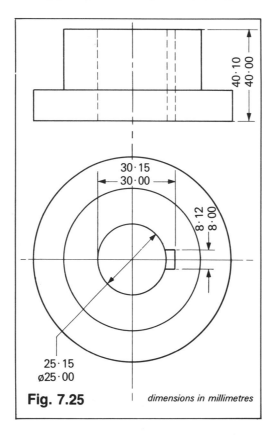

25·15
ø25·00

Fig. 7.25   *dimensions in millimetres*

Material: mild steel

dimensions in millimetres

▽ Machine
◊ Do not machine

Fig. 7.24

8. Milling

Milling stepped components

The milling machine has already been introduced in *Part 1* of this course for machining plain surfaces, where its multi-tooth cutter removed metal more rapidly than the single-point tool of the shaping machine.

Figure 8.1(a) shows a stepped component that is to be machined from a blank that has already been squared up. In this example only the step is to be milled. For this operation a *side and face* milling cutter is used and an example is shown in Fig. 8.1(b). This type of cutter has the added advantage that it can machine the side and bottom of the step at the same time. The procedure for milling the slot using a side and face milling cutter on a horizontal milling machine will now be described.

To ensure that the slot is parallel with the sides of the blank, the vice must be set square as shown in Fig. 8.2(a).
1 The dial gauge is clamped to the arbor as shown and the plunger is brought into contact with the fixed jaw.
2 The table is traversed to and from the column of the machine. If the vice is correctly set the dial gauge should show a constant reading as it moves along the jaw.

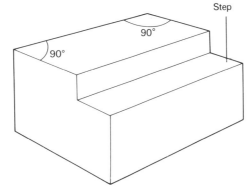

(a) Stepped component

(b) Side and face milling cutter

Fig. 8.1 Milling a stepped component

3 The machine vice fixing bolts are now tightened up and the jaw is re-checked to ensure it has not moved. If the ends of the blank have been machined square to the sides the step will be parallel to the sides of the blank.

The component is now secured in the vice as shown in Fig. 8.2(b) and it is set as follows:
1 The table is raised so that the gap between the cutter and the component can be checked with feeler gauges as shown in Fig. 8.2(b).
2 The table is lowered until the cutter clears the component. The table is then moved over, using the cross-traverse micrometer dial to measure the movement, an amount which is equal to the width of the step plus the thickness of the feeler gauge.
3 A series of cuts are taken until the step is the required depth. The depth of the step is controlled by the micrometer dial coupled to the table-elevating screw. The step is checked using a depth micrometer (Chapter 4).

Straddle and gang milling

Single cutters are only used for jobbing and small batch production. Where large quantities of components with complex surfaces are to be milled it is

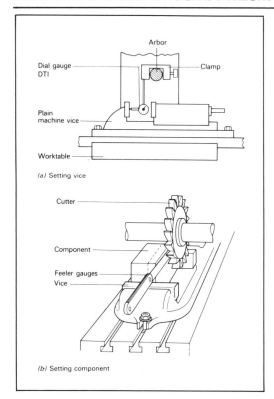

(a) Setting vice

(b) Setting component

Fig. 8.2 Setting a stepped component

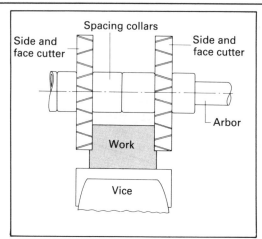

Fig. 8.3 Straddle milling

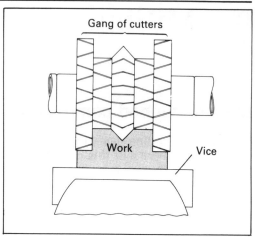

Fig. 8.4 Gang milling

often an advantage to combine several cutters together on a single arbor, as shown in Figs 8.3 and 8.4.

Straddle milling

This is the name given to the operation shown in Fig. 8.3. It will be seen that two side and face milling cutters are used and that they are cutting mainly on the sides. Therefore, *straddle milling* is only a sizing operation used to control the width of the component. The diameters of the cutters do not have to be exactly matched, but the space between them is critical and is adjusted by shim steel washers or an adjustable spacing collar.

Gang milling

This is a much more complex operation in which the faces as well as the sides of the component are machined. This is shown, in Fig. 8.4. The spacing between the cutters and their relative diameters are both important. It is normal to keep the whole gang of cutters together permanently on a spare mandrel. When re-grinding the cutters, they have to be reground as a set to maintain their relative diameters.

If helical tooth cutters are used in straddle milling and gang milling

set-ups, it is usual to use cutters that are a combination of left-hand and right-hand helices in order to balance out the end thrust on the arbor as much as possible.

Slot milling

Slots can be milled on both horizontal and vertical milling machines using such cutters as side and face milling cutters, slot milling cutters, slitting saws, end-milling cutters and slot drills. Examples of these types of milling cutter are shown in Fig. 8.5, together with a tee-slot cutter.

Side and face milling cutters can remove metal faster than the plain-sided slot mill, but tend to wander and to cut over size. Figure 8.6 shows key slots milled in a shaft using a slot milling cutter on a horizontal milling machine, and an end mill or slot drill on a vertical milling machine. It will be seen that unless the cutter can be arranged so as to clear the workpiece, provision must be made for the radius of the cutter.

End-milling cutters cannot be sunk into a solid blank because of their tooth form. Where a slot or a recess is 'blind' a slot drill must be used. Figure 8.7 shows a typical slot drill and the situations where it can be used. Since the slot drill has only two teeth, it cannot cut as quickly or leave as good a finish as an end mill.

A tee-slot cutter is shown in Fig. 8.5. It is used to undercut the tee-slots in machine tables. The slot is first of all gashed out using one of the above cutters, and then finished off by under-cutting with the tee-slot cutter. The shank of the tee-slot cutter is just clearance in the initial slot if a standard tee-slot is being machined and this helps to support and guide the shank of the tee-slot cutter.

Angle milling cutters

Figure 8.8 shows a range of angle milling cutters. These are *not* form-relieved cutters since the tooth form is made up from straight lines and they can be reground on the 'land' or primary clearance face.

Single angle cutters Figure 8.8(a) shows how these cutters may be used to produce chamfers and serrations.

Double angle cutters Figure 8.8(b) shows how these cutters may be used to produce a vee-groove. Usually they are

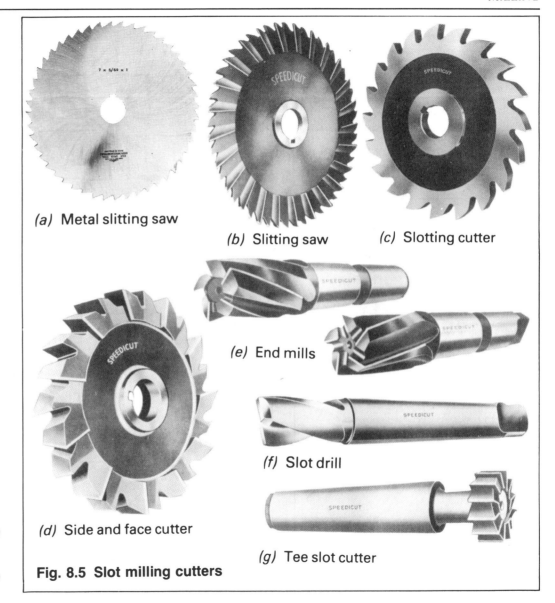

(a) Metal slitting saw

(b) Slitting saw

(c) Slotting cutter

(d) Side and face cutter

(e) End mills

(f) Slot drill

(g) Tee slot cutter

Fig. 8.5 Slot milling cutters

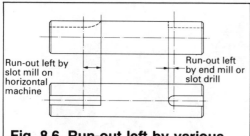

Run-out left by slot mill on horizontal machine

Run-out left by end mill or slot drill

Fig. 8.6 Run-out left by various slot milling cutters

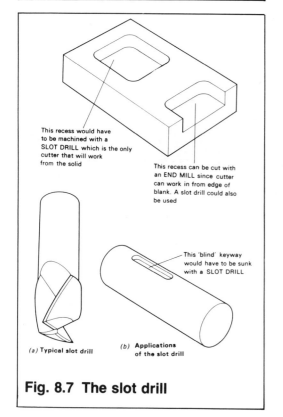

This recess would have to be machined with a SLOT DRILL which is the only cutter that will work from the solid

This recess can be cut with an END MILL since cutter can work in from edge of blank. A slot drill could also be used

This 'blind' keyway would have to be sunk with a SLOT DRILL

(a) Typical slot drill

(b) Applications of the slot drill

Fig. 8.7 The slot drill

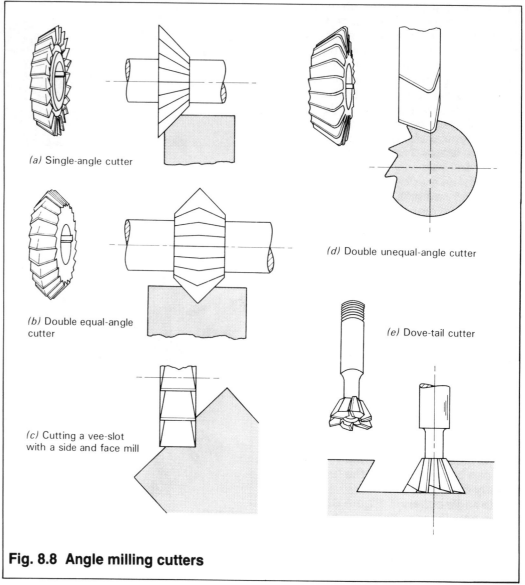

(a) Single-angle cutter

(b) Double equal-angle cutter

(c) Cutting a vee-slot with a side and face mill

(d) Double unequal-angle cutter

(e) Dove-tail cutter

Fig. 8.8 Angle milling cutters

used in gang milling set-ups, since it is often cheaper and more convenient to use a side and face milling cutter or a shell-end mill and incline the workpiece for a one-off or small batch of components (Fig. 8.8(c)).

Double unequal-angle cutters These are used in the production of other milling cutters and reamers. Figure 8.8(d) shows how a double unequal-angle cutter can be used to produce the tooth form of a reamer.

Dove-tail cutter These cutters are used to undercut dove-tail slides as shown in Fig. 8.8(e). Like tee-slot cutters, their slender shank renders them rather fragile and great care must be taken when using these cutters.

Form-relieved milling cutters

Figure 8.9 shows a range of typical concave and convex cutters together with an involute cutter for producing gear teeth. These cutters differ from those previously described in that the form of the tooth is relieved and they are reground only on the rake-face in order to retain the form of the tooth. They are used to radius corners and to produce concave slots such as the flute of a twist drill. It will be seen that the profile of the involute gear cutter is that of the space between the teeth of the gear and not that of the tooth itself.

Inserted tooth cutters

The cost of super-high-speed and

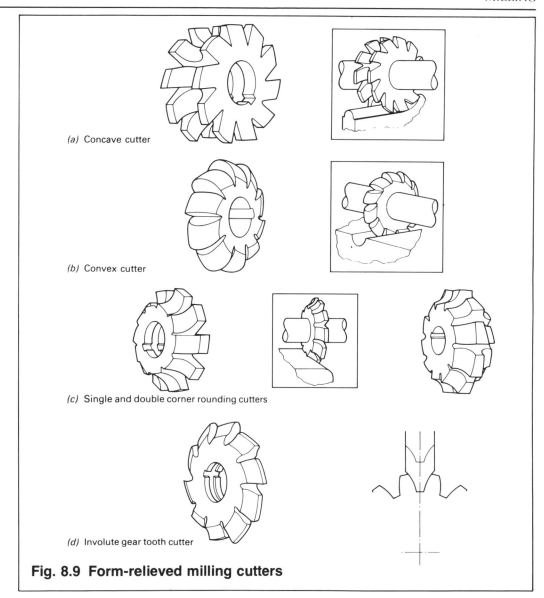

(a) Concave cutter

(b) Convex cutter

(c) Single and double corner rounding cutters

(d) Involute gear tooth cutter

Fig. 8.9 Form-relieved milling cutters

high-speed steel is constantly rising as the cost of energy and the alloying elements in the steel keeps rising. It is, therefore, no longer economical to make cutters from solid blanks of high-speed steel except in the smaller sizes.

Face mills and staggered tooth side and face mills in the larger sizes are usually built up from carbon steel bodies with inserted teeth of high-speed steel. This not only reduces the initial cost but allows individual teeth to be replaced if accidentally damaged. Figure 8.10(a) shows a typical example of these cutter types.

Tungsten carbide and ceramic cutting tool materials are too fragile to be used by themselves and have to be supported by a stronger steel body. The teeth may be brazed into place as shown in Fig. 8.10(b) or clamped into place as shown in Fig. 8.10(c). These inserted teeth can be rotated to present fresh cutting edges and then discarded when all the cutting edges have been used. This is often more economical than attempting to regrind the carbide inserts which require special skills and equipment.

Figure 8.11 shows a fly-milling cutter as used on a vertical milling machine. These are frequently used when machining aluminium and the weaker aluminium alloys. The large cutting diameter allows the full surface to be covered in one pass. The large cutting diameter also increases the cutting speed to a suitable magnitude for light alloys whilst keeping the spindle speed

(a) Inserted tooth cutter

(b) Brazed tip cutter

(c) Clamped tip cutter

Fig. 8.10 Cutter construction

Table 8.1 Cutting speeds and feeds for H.S.S. milling cutters

Material being milled	Cutting speed m/min	Feed per tooth (chip thickness) (Millimetres)					
		Face mill	Slab mill	Side & face	Slotting cutter	Slitting saw	End mill
Aluminium	70–100	0·2–0·8	0·2–0·6	0·15–0·4	0·1–0·2	0·05–0·1	0·1–0·4
Brass (alpha) (ductile)	35–50	0·15–0·6	0·15–0·5	0·1–0·3	0·07–0·15	0·035–0·075	0·07–0·3
Brass (free-cutting)	50–70	0·2–0·8	0·2–0·6	0·15–0·4	0·1–0·2	0·05–0·1	0·1–0·4
Bronze (phosphor)	20–35	0·07–0·3	0·07–0·25	0·05–0·15	0·04–0·07	0·02–0·04	0·04–0·15
Cast Iron (grey)	25–40	0·1–0·4	0·1–0·3	0·07–0·2	0·05–0·1	0·025–0·05	0·05–0·2
Copper	35–45	0·1–0·4	0·1–0·3	0·07–0·2	0·05–0·1	0·025–0·05	0·05–0·2
Steel (mild)	30–40	0·1–0·4	0·1–0·3	0·07–0·2	0·05–0·1	0·025–0·05	0·05–0·2
Steel (medium carbon)	20–30	0·07–0·3	0·07–0·25	0·05–0·15	0·04–0·07	0·02–0·04	0·04–0·15
Steel (alloy-high tensile)	5–8	0·05–0·2	0·05–0·15	0·035–0·1	0·025–0·05	0·015–0·025	0·025–0·1
Thermosetting plastic (low speed due to abrasive properties)	20–30	0·15–0·6	0·15–0·5	0·1–0·3	0·07–0·15	0·035–0·075	0·07–0·3

Notes:
1. The above feeds and speeds are for ordinary H.S.S. cutters. For *super* H.S.S. cutters the feeds would remain the same, but the cutting speeds could be increased by 10% to 15%.
2. The *lower* speed range is suitable for heavy, roughing cuts.
The *higher* speed range is suitable for light, finishing cuts.
3. The feed is selected to give the required surface finish and rate of metal removal.

down to a reasonable value. Such cutters are usually 'homemade' for a specific job and the tool inserts are standard lathe tool bits. Such cutters must be carefully guarded because at high speeds the cutter-bar becomes almost invisible and the chips fly off with a very high velocity.

Speeds and feeds for milling

Calculations involving milling cutters are treated rather differently from those considered for lathes and drilling machines because the milling cutter is a

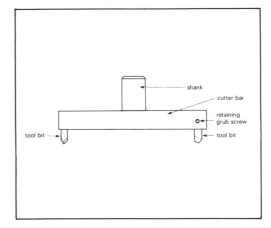

Fig. 8.11 Fly cutter

multi-tooth cutter. When milling, the feed is given as a rate per tooth not as a rate per revolution as on a centre lathe. Milling cutters are more difficult to re-grind than single-point tools and greater care must be taken to avoid overloading and overheating the teeth.

The speed and feed values given by cutter manufacturers are only an approximate guide. As in all machining operations the actual rates chosen will depend upon such factors as: surface finish, material strength, rigidity of work and cutter, breadth of cut, depth of cut, cutter tooth form, type of cutter, coolant.

Some typical feeds and speeds for milling a range of materials with high speed steel cutters are given in Table 8.1.

Example 8.1 Calculate the spindle speed in rev/min for a milling cutter 125 mm diameter, operating at a cutting speed of 30 m/min.

Solution

$$N = \frac{1000S}{\pi D}$$

where: N = spindle speed, S = 30 m/min, π = 3, D = 125 mm.

$$N = \frac{1000 \times 30}{3 \times 125}$$
$$= \underline{80 \text{ rev/min}}$$

Example 8.2 Calculate the table feed in mm/min for a 12 tooth cutter revolving at 80 rev/min when the feed per tooth is 0·1 mm.

Solution

Feed/rev = feed/tooth × number of teeth.
$$= 0·1 \times 12$$
$$= 1·2 \text{ mm/rev}$$
Table feed = feed/rev × rev/min.
$$1·2 \times 80$$
$$\underline{96 \text{ mm/min}}$$

Example 8.3 Using the following data calculate the time taken to complete a 270 mm long cut using a slab mill. Diameter of cutter = 125 mm, number of teeth = 6, feed/tooth = 0·05 mm, cutting speed = 45 m/min.

Solution

$$N = \frac{1000S}{\pi D}$$

where: N = spindle speed,
S = 45 m/min,
π = 3,
D = 125 mm.
$$N = \frac{1000 \times 45}{3 \times 125}$$
$$= 120 \text{ rev/min} ....(1)$$
Feed/rev = feed/tooth × number of teeth
$$= 0·05 \times 6$$
$$= 0·3 \text{ mm/rev.}$$
Table feed/min = feed/rev × rev/min (from 1)
$$= 0·3 \times 120$$
$$= 36 \text{ mm/min} .... (2)$$
Time to complete 270 mm cut
$$= \frac{\text{length of cut}}{\text{table feed/min}}$$
$$= \frac{270}{36} \quad \text{(from 2)}$$
$$= \underline{7·5 \text{ min}}$$

Work-holding on the milling machine

When a workpiece is being cut, both the tool and the workpiece are subject to forces which tend to distort and displace them. Thus, it is necessary to support and clamp both the tool and the workpiece in such a manner that distortion and displacement cannot occur. In order to locate and restrain the tool and the workpiece effectively it is necessary to understand certain basic principles.

A body in space, free of all restraints, is able to:
1 move back and forth along the Z axis;
2 move from side to side along the X axis;
3 move up and down along the Y axis;
4 rotate in either direction about the Z axis;
5 rotate in either direction about the X axis;
6 rotate in either direction about the Y axis.

That is, the metal block shown in Fig. 8.12(a) has six degrees of freedom.

In order that a body may be worked upon by hand or by machine it must be located in a given position by restraining its freedom of movement.

Figure 8.12(b) shows how a block of metal can be located in a given position by the application of suitable restraints. The baseplate supports the block and locates it in the vertical plane by restraining its downward movement. At the same time it restrains rotation about the X and Z axes of the block.

The addition of three location pegs adds restraint along the X and Z axes and positions the block on the plate.

Finally screw clamps are provided to complete the restraint of the block by ensuring its contact with the plate and the location pegs at all times. Since the block is restrained by contact with solid metal abutments in every direction it is said to be subjected to positive restraint.

Restraint may be positive or frictional and the difference is explained in

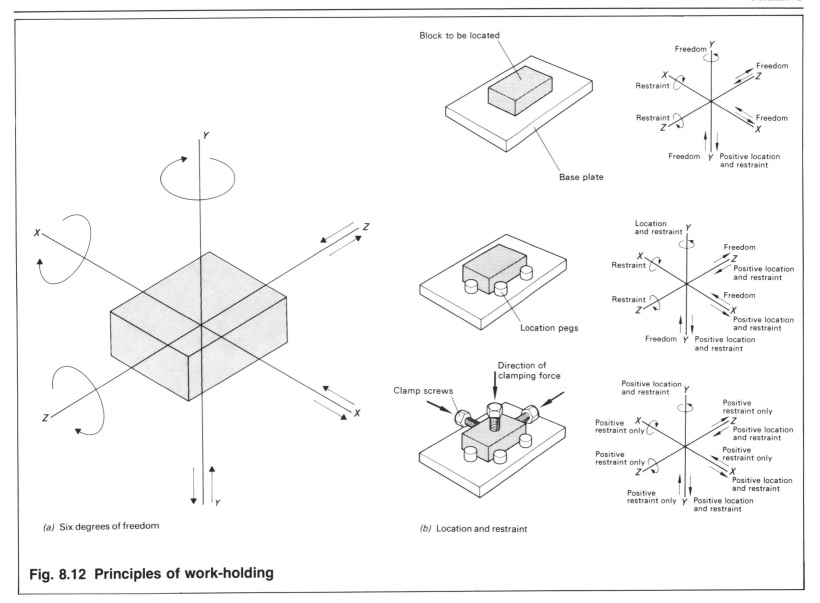

(a) Six degrees of freedom

(b) Location and restraint

Fig. 8.12 Principles of work-holding

Fig. 8.13. Wherever possible cutting forces should be resisted by positive restraints (solid abutments) and not by frictional restraint alone. For example, a component should be positioned in a vice so that the main cutting force is resisted by the fixed jaw, that is, the cutting force should be perpendicular to the fixed jaw and not parallel to it.

Various methods of work-holding are available on the milling machine. Small components are usually held in a machine vice which is itself bolted to the milling machine table. To avoid having to set the vice with a dial test indicator every time it is moved, the vice is often provided with tenon blocks to locate in the milling machine table tee-slots. An example of work-holding in a milling machine vice, together with the locations and restraints acting on the workpiece, is shown in Fig. 8.14(a).

Large components such as castings are supported directly on the machine table as shown in Fig. 8.14(b). Care must be taken when tightening the clamps to avoid distorting the workpiece. Jacks and wedges should be used to ensure adequate support unless a previously machined datum surface is available. The restraints and locations for the example shown are also given.

Figure 8.14(c) shows work-holding using the dividing head. This device is used when it is necessary to mill slots round the periphery of a circular blank. For example: keyways, splines, gear teeth, etc. In the set-up shown, the dividing head is connected to the table

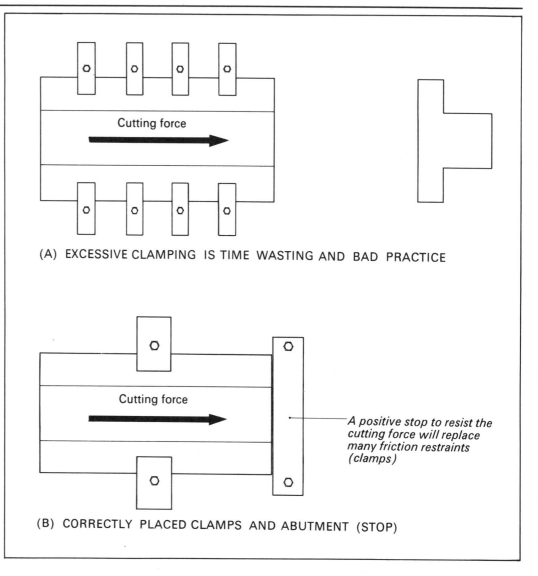

(A) EXCESSIVE CLAMPING IS TIME WASTING AND BAD PRACTICE

Cutting force

Cutting force

A positive stop to resist the cutting force will replace many friction restraints (clamps)

(B) CORRECTLY PLACED CLAMPS AND ABUTMENT (STOP)

Fig. 8.13 Positive and frictional restraints

lead screw by a gear train. This would be used to mill a spiral flute when making a twist drill. The work may be held between centres as shown or in a chuck mounted on the spindle nose of the dividing head. The restraints and locations shown in Fig. 8.14(c) are for work located between centres. The dividing head will be considered in greater detail on pp. 172–82.

The forces acting on the workpiece when using a vertical milling machine are very different from those acting on the workpieces in a horizontal milling machine. As well as tending to push the component along the table, the cutter of the vertical milling machine also tends to spin the job round. Figure 8.15(a) shows a component held in a fixture on a vertical milling machine, whilst Fig. 8.15(b) shows how the side abutments should be positioned to prevent the component spinning. The dog point screws are used to clamp the work-piece and prevent it lifting. For this reason the screws should be given a downward inclination (Fig. 8.15(c)).

Cylindrical components that do not have to be indexed can be held on the milling machine, using vee-blocks either in the vice or between the work and the machine table. Figure 8.16(a) shows the use of a vee-block to give three-point support when mounting cylindrical work vertically in the milling machine vice. The vee-block should be inserted between the work and the fixed jaw. Figure 8.16(b) shows cylindrical work mounted on the milling machine table. The vee-blocks must be a matched pair

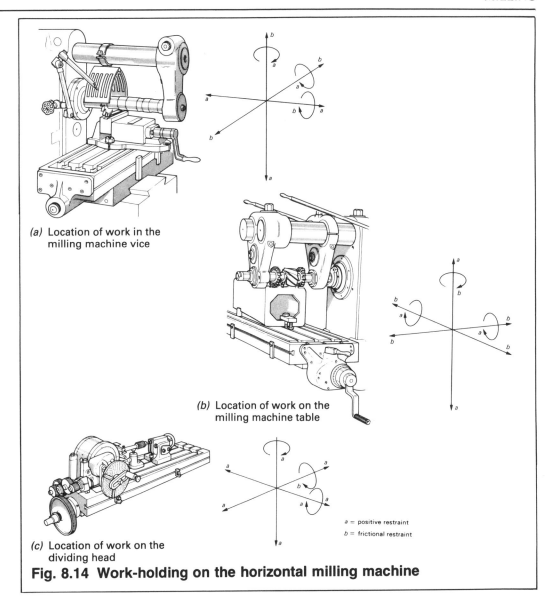

(a) Location of work in the milling machine vice

(b) Location of work on the milling machine table

(c) Location of work on the dividing head

a = positive restraint
b = frictional restraint

Fig. 8.14 Work-holding on the horizontal milling machine

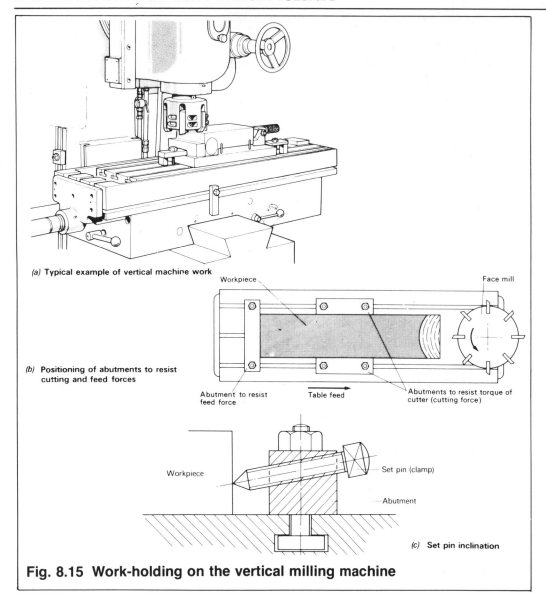

(a) Typical example of vertical machine work

(b) Positioning of abutments to resist cutting and feed forces

Workpiece

Face mill

Abutment to resist feed force

Table feed

Abutments to resist torque of cutter (cutting force)

Workpiece

Set pin (clamp)

Abutment

(c) Set pin inclination

Fig. 8.15 Work-holding on the vertical milling machine

so that the workpiece axis is parallel to the machine table.

Simple indexing

Sometimes it is necessary to make a series of cuts around the periphery of a component; for example when cutting splines on a shaft. Such an operation is called indexing, and Fig. 8.17 shows a simple dividing head suitable for such work. The index plate in this machine locates the spindle directly, whereas the more sophisticated universal dividing head, shown in Fig. 8.21, incorporates a worm and worm wheel between the indexing arm and the spindle (see p. 176). In Fig. 8.17 the index plate has only two rows of holes. In practice it has many more rows of holes and this provides a wide range of circular division. For example, to index through three equal divisions, the plunger is rotated through four holes in the 12-hole circle between each division. Figure 8.18(a) shows a typical component where this would be necessary, and Fig. 8.18(b) shows the general arrangement for work-holding between centres. If the work cannot be held in this manner, then a chuck can be mounted on the dividing head spindle in place of the catch plate.

The universal dividing head

A typical universal dividing head and its construction is shown in Fig. 8.19. This type of dividing head is capable of a wide range of work. Angular division to

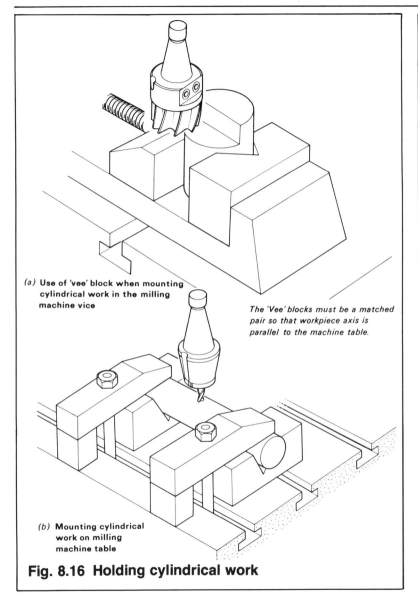

(a) **Use of 'vee' block when mounting cylindrical work in the milling machine vice**

The 'Vee' blocks must be a matched pair so that workpiece axis is parallel to the machine table.

(b) **Mounting cylindrical work on milling machine table**

Fig. 8.16 Holding cylindrical work

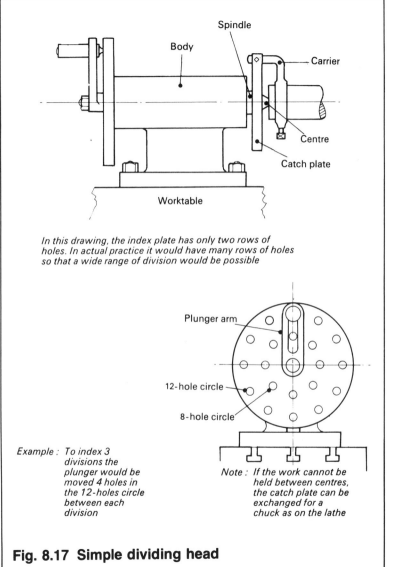

In this drawing, the index plate has only two rows of holes. In actual practice it would have many rows of holes so that a wide range of division would be possible

Example : To index 3 divisions the plunger would be moved 4 holes in the 12-holes circle between each division

Note : If the work cannot be held between centres, the catch plate can be exchanged for a chuck as on the lathe

Fig. 8.17 Simple dividing head

fine limits is possible, and it is possible to link the dividing head to the table lead screw for helical milling and cam milling operations (see pp. 177–81)

Unlike the simple dividing head shown in Fig. 8.17, the spindle of the universal dividing head is driven by a worm and worm-wheel having a standard ratio of 40:1. Simple indexing is possible on the universal dividing head by disengaging the worm and worm wheel and using the *direct dividing* plate which is attached to the spindle immediately behind the catch plate (see Fig. 8.19). However, for most applications the worm and worm wheel are kept in engagement and the indexing plate on the side of the dividing head is used. Since the ratio between the worm and worm wheel is 40:1, the spindle only rotates through $\frac{1}{40}$ of a turn for each complete revolution of the plunger arm. Details of this drive mechanism are shown in Fig. 8.20.

The total movement of the plunger arm for any given number of divisions is given by the expression:

$$\text{index arm setting} = \frac{40}{N}$$

where: N = the number of divisions required.

Angular division is possible using the expression:

$$\text{index arm setting} = \frac{\text{angle required}}{9}$$

since $\frac{1}{40}$ of a revolution = $\frac{360°}{40}$ = 9°.

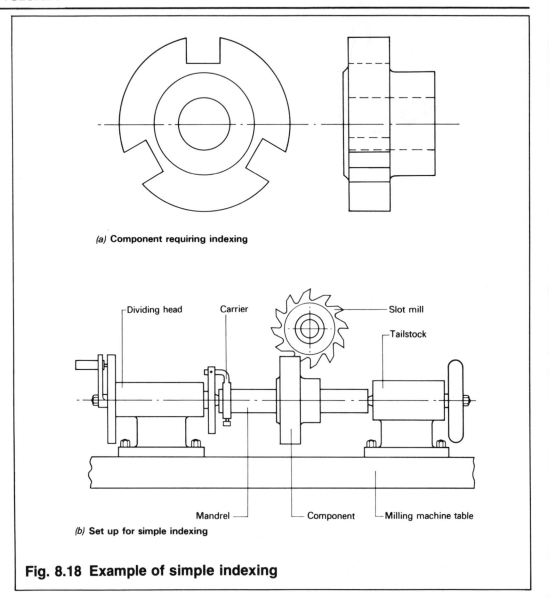

(a) **Component requiring indexing**

(b) **Set up for simple indexing**

Fig. 8.18 Example of simple indexing

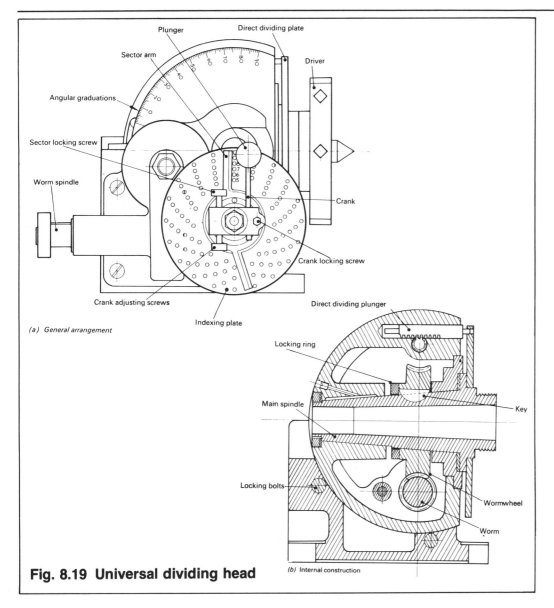

(a) General arrangement

(b) Internal construction

Fig. 8.19 Universal dividing head

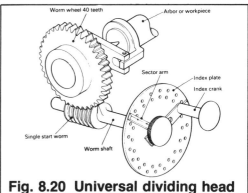

Fig. 8.20 Universal dividing head drive mechanism

Example 8.4 Calculate the index arm setting required to give 13 equally spaced divisions. The index plate has the following number of holes: 24, 25, 28, 30, 34, 37, 38, 39, 41, 42, 43.
Solution

$$\text{Index arm setting} = \frac{40}{N}$$

where: N = required number of divisions.

$$\text{index arm setting} = \frac{40}{13}$$
$$= 3\tfrac{1}{13}$$

From inspection of the index plate the actual indexing will be 3 whole turns and 3 holes in the 39-hole circle.

Example 8.5 Using the same index plate as in the previous example, calculate the index arm setting to give an angular division of the work piece of 15° 18′.

Solution

$$\text{Index arm setting} = \frac{\text{required angle}}{9}$$

$$= \frac{15°\ 18'}{9}$$

$$= \frac{918}{9 \times 60}$$

(calculation in minutes of arc)

$$= \frac{102}{60}$$

$$= 1\frac{21}{30}$$

From inspection of the index plate it will be seen that the actual indexing will be 1 whole turn and 21 holes in the 30-hole circle.

Differential indexing

Divisions outside the range of a standard index plate can be obtained by differential indexing.

Instead of the index plate being clamped to the body of the dividing head, it is coupled to the work spindle by a gear train as shown in Fig. 8.21. Thus, as the index arm is rotated through the required number of turns, the index plate is advanced or retarded through a small amount automatically.

The following expression is used to obtain the gear ratio of the drive coupling the work spindle to the index plate:

$$\frac{\text{driver}}{\text{driven}} = \frac{N_1 - N_2}{N_2} \times 40$$

where: N_1 = required divisions, N_2 = actual divisions available on the index plate.

Example 8.6   Calculate the gear train to give an indexing of 113 divisions. The index plate available has: 24, 25, 28, 30, 34, 37, 38, 39, 41, 42, 43 holes. The gears available are: 24(2), 28, 32, 40, 48, 56, 64, 72, 86, 100 teeth.

Solution   From Example 8.4 it will be seen that the required indexing is $\frac{40}{113}$ but this is not available with the index plate supplied, therefore, a near approximation is selected as a basis for calculation. For example $\frac{40}{120}$ which can be indexed as $\frac{14}{42}$. That is, 14 holes in a 42-hole circle.

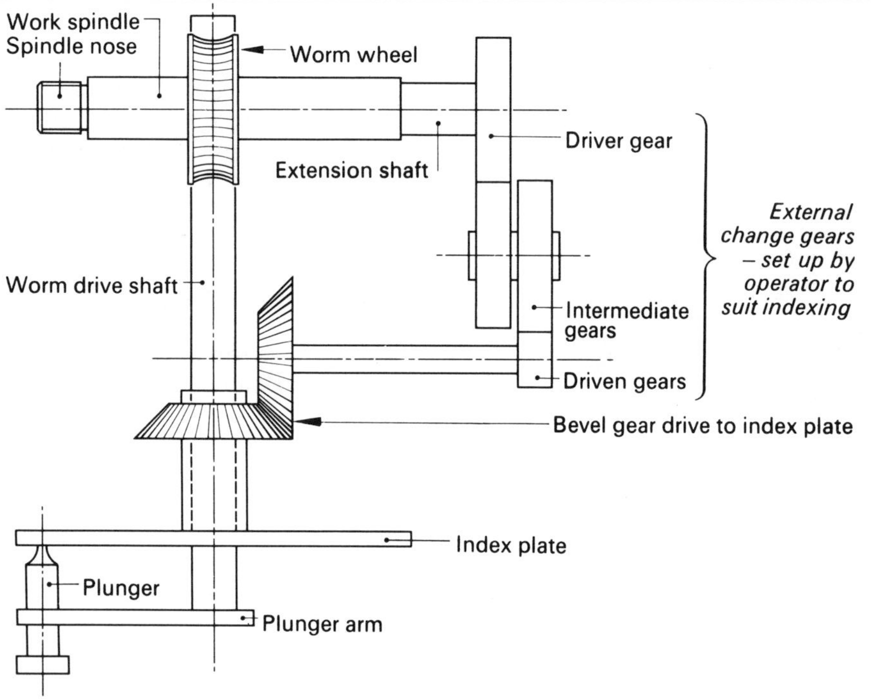

Fig. 8.21 **Differential indexing**

$$\frac{\text{driver}}{\text{driven}} = \frac{N_1 - N_2}{N_2} \times 40$$

where: N_1 = 113, N_2 = 120.

$$\frac{\text{driver}}{\text{driven}} = \frac{113 - 120}{120} \times 40$$

$$= -\frac{7}{120} \times 40$$

(the minus sign can be disregarded as it only indicates the direction of rotation)

$$= \frac{7}{3}$$

$$= \frac{56}{24} \quad \text{from the gears available.}$$

Therefore, when indexing 14 holes in a 42-hole circle with a 56-tooth gear driving a 24-tooth gear, the actual number of divisions on the specimen will be 113, and not 120 as it would be if the index plate were fixed.

The negative sign in the calculation indicates that the plate rotates with the index arm. A positive sign indicates that the plate rotates against the index arm.

Sector arms

To save having to count the holes in the index plate every time the dividing head is operated, sector arms are provided, as shown in Fig. 8.22(a). The method of using the sector arm is as follows.
1 The sector arms are set so that between arm A and arm B there is the required number of holes plus the starting hole a.
2 The plunger and index arm is moved from hole a to hole b against sector arm B.
3 The sector arms are rotated so that arm A is now against the plunger in hole b.
4 For the next indexing the plunger is moved to hole c against the newly positioned arm B.

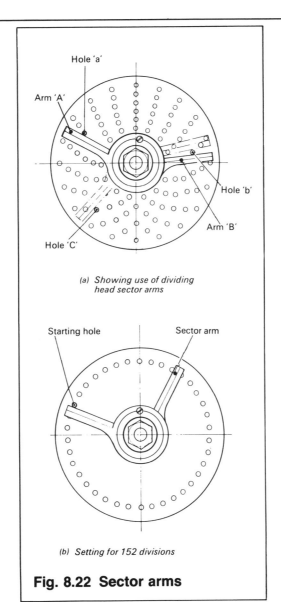

Hole 'a'

Arm 'A'

Hole 'b'

Arm 'B'

Hole 'C'

(a) Showing use of dividing head sector arms

Starting hole   Sector arm

(b) Setting for 152 divisions

Fig. 8.22 Sector arms

5 The process is repeated for each indexing.

Figure 8.22(b) shows the setting of the sector arms for indexing 10 holes in a 38-hole circle, that is, 152 divisions round the workpiece.

Helical milling

The operation of milling a helical groove along a cylindrical component, for example, when cutting the flutes in a large twist drill, has become known, quite incorrectly, as spiral milling. A spiral is, in fact, the shape of the groove in the scroll of a self-centring lathe chuck.

In helical milling, the table lead provides the axial movement and the dividing head provides the circumferential movement. The method of coupling the table lead screw to the dividing head by a gear train is shown in Fig. 8.23(a).

If the dividing head was coupled to the milling machine table by gears having a ratio of 1:1 then, because of the worm and worm-wheel in the dividing head, the table lead screw would have to rotate 40 times for the workpiece to rotate once. During those 40 revolutions the table and the work would traverse 40P millimetres, where P would be the pitch of the table lead screw. Since a single-start lead screw is invariably used, pitch is equal to lead in this instance. This distance of 40P millimetres is referred to as the lead of the machine. For any given helix the ratio of the gears is:

$$\frac{driver}{driven} = \frac{lead\ of\ machine}{lead\ of\ helix\ to\ be\ cut}$$

Example 8.7 Calculate the gear train to cut a helix of 480 mm on a milling machine fitted with a table lead screw having a lead of 6 mm.

Solution

Lead of machine = 40P = 40 × 6
            = 240 mm

$$\frac{driver}{driven} = \frac{lead\ of\ machine}{lead\ of\ helix\ to\ be\ cut}$$
$$= \frac{240}{480}$$
$$= \frac{1}{2}$$

From the gears normally available a 32-tooth gear would be used to drive a 64-tooth gear. Whether or not one or two idler gears would be introduced between the driver and the driven gears would depend upon the 'hand' of the helix being cut.

To prevent the cutter from interfering with the sides of the groove being cut it is necessary to swing the table of the milling machine round until the cutter is lying in the path of the helix as shown in Fig. 8.23(b). It is not possible to set over the table of a plain horizontal milling machine, so that helical milling is only possible on universal horizontal milling machines which are provided with the requisite table movements.

Even when the table is swung round to the helix angle of the groove it is not possible to mill a groove with straight sides. The only way that straight-sided grooves may be produced is on a

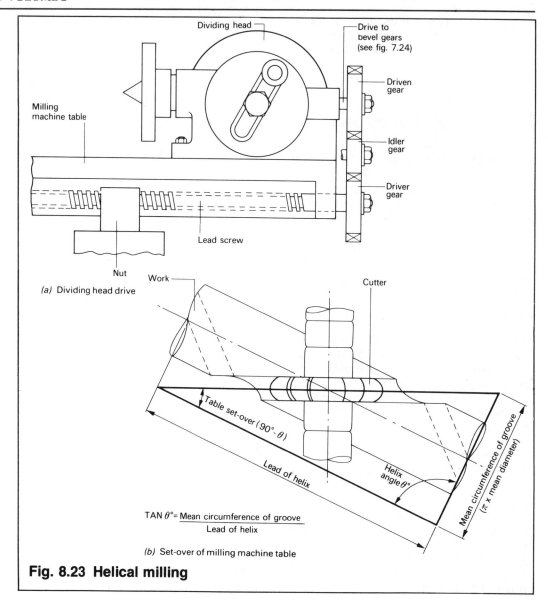

(a) Dividing head drive

$$TAN\ \theta° = \frac{Mean\ circumference\ of\ groove}{Lead\ of\ helix}$$

(b) Set-over of milling machine table

Fig. 8.23 Helical milling

vertical milling machine using an end mill or a slot drill. Under these conditions the table does not need to be set over. Unfortunately, the metal removal rate for an end mill is low compared with a side and face milling cutter. For this reason the groove should not be designed with straight sides if quantity production is envisaged.

Example 8.8 With reference to Fig. 8.23(b) calculate the angle of set-over when milling a groove with a lead of 480 mm. The mean diameter of the groove is 50 mm.

Solution

$$\text{Tan } \theta° = \frac{\text{lead of work}}{\text{mean circumference}}$$
$$= \frac{480}{50 \times \pi}$$
$$= 3.06$$
$$\therefore \theta° = 71° \, 54'$$

Set-over angle of table
$$= 90° - \theta°$$
$$= 90° - 71° \, 54'$$
$$= \underline{18° \, 06'}$$

Note: For practical purposes the table would be set over by 18°.

Cam milling

Snail cams of the type shown in Fig. 8.24(a) can be milled using a universal dividing head geared to the table lead screw of a vertical milling machine as shown in Fig. 8.24(b). As the table feeds the cam blank into the cutter the dividing head rotates the blank. The

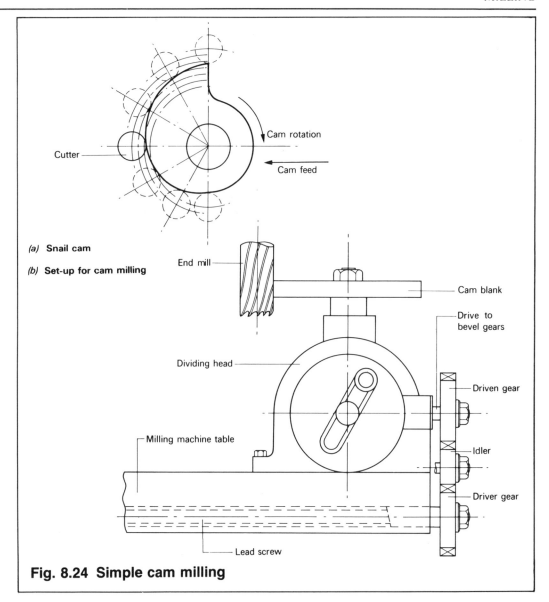

(a) **Snail cam**

(b) **Set-up for cam milling**

Fig. 8.24 Simple cam milling

dividing head has been set with its spindle vertical in Fig. 8.24(b). The gear ratio to provide a given cam lift can be calculated from the expression:

$$\frac{\text{driver}}{\text{driven}} = \frac{\text{lead of machine}}{\text{lift per revolution of cam}}$$

Example 8.9 Calculate the gear ratio to cut a cam that has a lift of 15 mm in 90° rotation if the table lead screw has a pitch of 6 mm.

Solution

Lead of machine = 40P = 40 × 6
= 240 mm

Lift of cam per revolution
= 15 mm $\times^{360°}/_{90°}$ = 60 mm

$$\frac{\text{driver}}{\text{driven}} = \frac{\text{lead of machine}}{\text{lift per revolution}}$$
$$= \frac{240}{60} = \frac{4}{1}$$

Unfortunately, the ratio of lift to lead rarely works out so conveniently in practice and some means has to be used to obtain intermediate values from the standard gears supplied. With the dividing head spindle set vertically the lift generated on the cam is a maximum for any given gear ratio. However, with the dividing head and the milling machine spindle set horizontally, as shown in Fig. 8.25(a), only a cylindrical surface will be generated and the lift will be zero. Thus, some setting intermediate between these extremes will give the required lift.

To cam mill, an inclinable-head vertical milling machine is required. A gear ratio is then selected that gives a lift larger than that required, and the machine head and the dividing head are

inclined to give the actual lift required, as shown in Fig. 8.25(b).

$$\text{Sin }\theta = \frac{\text{Lift per revolution of cam produced (x)}}{\text{table movement per revolution of cam (L)}}$$

and $L = \dfrac{x}{\sin \theta}$

But *L* is the maximum lift per revolution for any given gear train, and:

$$\frac{\text{driver}}{\text{driven}} = \frac{\text{lead of machine}}{L}$$

$$= \frac{\text{lead of machine}}{x/\sin\theta} \text{ when inclined at } \theta°$$

$$= \frac{\text{lead of machine} \times \sin\theta}{x}$$

Thus: $\sin\theta = \dfrac{x}{\text{lead of machine}} \times \dfrac{\text{driver}}{\text{driven}}$

where *x* = the required lift per revolution of the cam.

where *x* = the required lift per revolution of the cam.

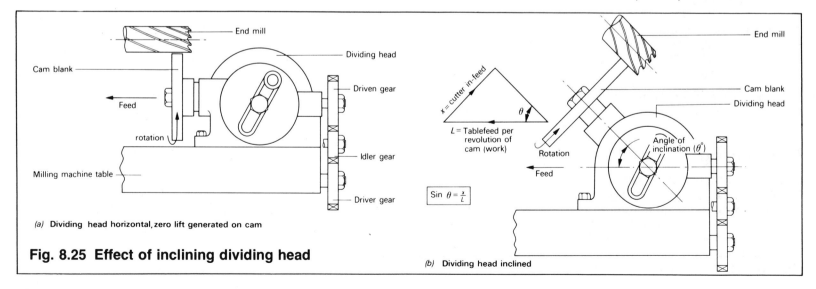

(a) **Dividing head horizontal, zero lift generated on cam**

$\text{Sin }\theta = \frac{x}{L}$

x = cutter in-feed

L = Tablefeed per revolution of cam (work)

θ

End mill

Cam blank

Dividing head

Angle of inclination ($\theta°$)

Rotation

Feed

(b) **Dividing head inclined**

End mill

Cam blank

Driven gear

Idler gear

Driver gear

Feed

rotation

Milling machine table

Fig. 8.25 Effect of inclining dividing head

Example 8.10 Calculate the gears and spindle inclination to cut a cam whose lift is 23·5 mm in 83° on a vertical milling machine whose lead is 240 mm.

Solution

Lift per revolution of cam

$$= \frac{23{\cdot}5 \times 360}{830} = 101{\cdot}9 \text{ mm/rev}$$

The nearest convenient gear ratio greater than this lift would be:

$$\frac{\text{driver}}{\text{driven}} = \frac{\text{lead of machine}}{\text{maximum lift per revolution}}$$

$$= \frac{240}{105}$$

$$= \frac{48}{21}$$

To find the angle of inclination (θ):

$$\text{Sin } \theta = \frac{x}{\text{lead of machine}} \times \frac{\text{driver}}{\text{driven}}$$

$$= \frac{101{\cdot}9}{240} \times \frac{48}{21}$$

$$= 0{\cdot}9705$$

$$\therefore \theta = 76° \ 3'$$

Miscellaneous indexing devices

The rotary table

Figure 8.26(a) shows a typical rotary table that is used for indexing flat plates that cannot be conveniently held on the dividing head. The main scale surrounding the working surface is calibrated in degrees of arc (360°). The working surface is driven by a worm and worm wheel as in the dividing head.

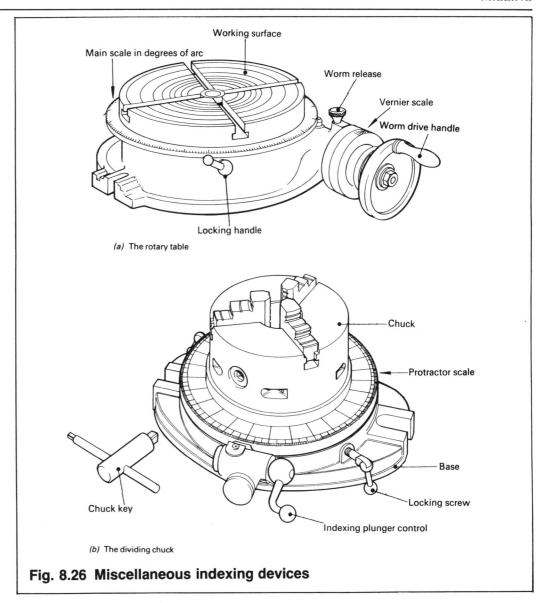

(a) The rotary table

(b) The dividing chuck

Fig. 8.26 Miscellaneous indexing devices

However, the ratio is not standardised and will depend on whether smaller increments than 1° of arc are obtained by an index plate or a vernier scale. The example shown in Fig. 8.26(a) is equipped with a vernier scale. The worm and worm wheel can be disengaged for setting purposes.

The dividing chuck

For cylindrical work which is not convenient to hold on the rotary table, the dividing chuck shown in Fig. 8.26(b) can be used. Although the universal dividing head can be inclined through 90°, the dividing chuck is less bulky and is more convenient to use when only simple indexing is required.

Gear cutting

Usually, only gears required for maintenance or experimental purposes are cut on a milling machine. The process is too slow and uneconomical for quantity production purposes. Also, the tooth form is only an approximate involute and such gears are only suitable for light and medium duties.

Ideally each size of gear would require a special cutter to give a true tooth form. However, this is not practical and a system of eight involute cutters has been devised which are a compromise. These cutters are listed in Table 8.2. One of these cutters is shown in Fig. 8.10.

Generally involute gears have module (m) pitches ranging from about 1 mm (m) to 16 mm (m). Since the height of

Table 8.2 Involute Gear Cutters
In accordance with Rotary Gear Cutter practice the standard group for any given pitch shall consist of eight cutters, numbered 1 to 8 inclusive, for milling gears having the numbers of teeth specified in the following table:
No. 1 will cut wheels from 135 teeth to a rack.
No. 2 will cut wheels from 55 to 134 teeth.
No. 3 will cut wheels from 35 to 54 teeth.
No. 4 will cut wheels from 26 to 34 teeth.
No. 5 will cut wheels from 21 to 25 teeth.
No. 6 will cut wheels from 17 to 20 teeth.
No. 7 will cut wheels from 14 to 16 teeth.
No. 8 will cut wheels from 12 to 13 teeth.

the tooth is *twice the module pitch*, the corresponding tooth height ranges from 2 mm to 32 mm. For teeth larger than 12 mm (m) the tooth dimensions are more often given in terms of their circular pitch, P, where: $P = \pi(m)$ millimetres.

The following precautions should be taken when cutting a gear.
1 Check that the gear blank and its mandrel run true so that the teeth are concentric with the axis of the gear.
2 Make sure that the cutter is sunk into the blank to the correct depth. This is usually marked on the side of the cutter, but it can be calculated by multiplying the module pitch by 2·25. For example the depth of cut for an 8 (m) cutter is $8 \times 2\cdot25 = 18$ mm.
3 To avoid overloading a fragile and expensive cutter it is advisable not to cut to the full depth in one pass, but to go round the gear at least twice leaving a small amount of metal to be removed

with a finishing out.
4 The cutter must be accurately centred over the gear blank as shown in Fig. 8.27(a). One method of centring the cutter is shown in Fig. 8.27(b). The knee

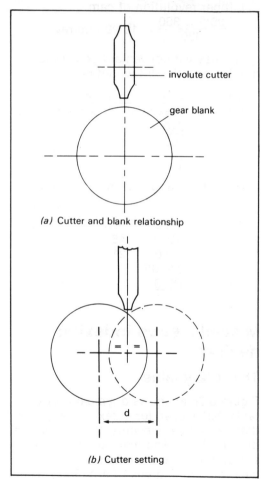

(a) Cutter and blank relationship

(b) Cutter setting

Fig. 8.27 Gear cutting

is raised so that the cutter can be brought into contact with the side of the wheel blank as shown by the full circle, and actual contact is obtained by feeding the saddle across until the rotating cutter just touches the blank. The readings of the cross traverse and knee-elevating dials are noted. The knee is lowered and the table is traversed across for a distance slightly greater than d in the figure. The knee is raised to its original height and the table is traversed across until contact is again made with the blank. The difference between the first and second readings of the cross traverse dial is the distance d. The table is then moved over by a distance d/2 and the cutter is centred over the blank.

Unfortunately any backlash in the cross traverse screw and nut leads to inaccuracy and allowance must be made for this.

Exercises

1. Compare the advantages and limitations of side and face milling cutters with end milling cutters for machinery slots and steps in components.
2. With the aid of sketches show the difference between straddle milling and gang milling.
3. Explain with the aid of sketches the difference in construction and use of slot drills and end mills.
4. With the aid of sketches show typical applications of the following milling cutters.
   (i) Single angle
   (ii) Double angle
   (iii) Double unequal angle
   (iv) Concave cutter
   (v) Convex cutter
5. (a) Compare the advantages and limitations of inserted tooth cutters with solid milling cutters.
   (b) With the aid of sketches show a typical fly-milling cutter for machining light alloys.
6. (a) List **eight** factors upon which the feed and speed rates for a milling cutter depend.
   (b) Calculate the spindle speed in rev/min for a milling cutter 200 mm diameter, operating at a cutting speed of 30 m/min (take π as 3).
7. Using the following data, calculate the time taken to complete a 300 mm long cut using a slab mill. (Take π as 3).

Diameter of cutter	100 mm
Number of teeth	6
Feed/tooth	0·025
Cutting speed	33 m/min.

8. (a) Calculate the index arm setting and gear train for milling 59 divisions around a component. The index plate has: 24, 25, 28, 30, 34, 37, 38, 39, 41, 42, 43 holes.
   The gears available are: 24 (2), 28, 32, 40, 48, 56, 64, 72, 86, 100 teeth.
   A universal dividing head with an internal drive ratio of 40:1 is to be used.
   (b) Describe the advantages of using sector arms and how they would be set in this example.
9. (a) Calculate the gear train to cut a helix of 500 mm lead on a machine fitted with a table lead screw having a lead of 6 mm, and using a universal dividing head with an internal gear drive of 40:1.
   The gears available are 24 (2), 28, 32, 40, 48, 56, 64, 72, 86, 100 teeth.
   (b) Calculate the angle of set-over of the machine table if the mean diameter of the helical groove in (a) is 50 mm.
10. (a) Calculate the gear ratio and spindle inclination to cut a cam whose lift is 24·5 mm in 87° on a vertical milling machine. Dividing head internal gear drive is 40:1. Table lead screw has a lead of 6 mm. Use the gears listed in question 9 (a).
    (b) Sketch the set-up to cut this cam.

9. Precision grinding

Fundamental principles

Grinding is the name given to those processes which use abrasive particles for material removal. The abrasive particles are made by crushing hard, crystalline solids such as aluminium oxide (emery) and silicon carbide.

Grinding wheels consist of large numbers of abrasive particles, called *grains*, held together by a *bond* to form a multi-tooth cutter similar in its action to a milling cutter. Since the grinding wheel has many more 'teeth' than a milling cutter, and because this reduces the 'chip clearance' between the teeth, it produces a good surface finish but a low rate of material removal. The fact that the cutting points are irregularly shaped and randomly distributed over the active face of the tool enhances the surface finish produced by a grinding process. Figure 9.1 shows the dross from a grinding wheel highly magnified. The dross consists of particles of abrasive material stripped from the grinding wheel together with metallic chips which are remarkably similar to the chips produced by the milling process.

The grains at the surface of the wheel are called *active grains* because they actually perform the cutting operation.

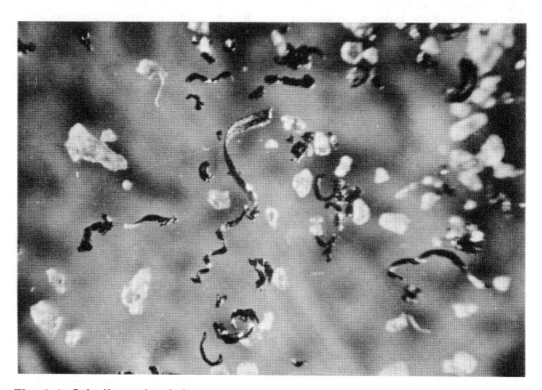

Fig. 9.1 Grinding wheel dross

In peripheral grinding, each active grain removes a short chip of gradually increasing thickness in a similar way to the tooth of a milling cutter as shown in Fig. 9.2. As grinding proceeds, the cutting edges of the grains become dulled and the forces acting on the grains increase until either the dulled grains fracture and expose new cutting surfaces, or the whole of the dulled grains are ripped from the wheel exposing new active grains. In this way, grinding wheels are self-sharpening.

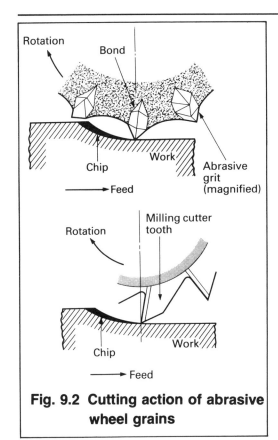

Fig. 9.2 Cutting action of abrasive wheel grains

Grinding wheel specification

A grinding wheel consists of two constituents.
1 The *abrasive* grains that do the cutting.
2 The *bond* that holds the grains together.

The specification of a grinding wheel gives a clue to its construction and to its suitability for a particular operation. For

Table 9.1 Abrasive types

Manufacturer's Type code	BS code	Abrasive	Application
–	A	Aluminium oxide	A high strength abrasive for hard, tough materials
32	A	Aluminium oxide	Cool; fast cutting, for rapid stock removal
38	A	Aluminium oxide	Light grinding of very hard steels
19	A	Aluminium oxide	A milder abrasive than 38A used for cylindrical grinding
37	C	Silicon carbide	For hard, brittle materials of high density such as cast iron
39	C (green)	Silicon carbide	For very hard, brittle materials such as tungsten carbide

Note: In the above examples, the manufacturer's type code is based upon Norton abrasives.

example, a wheel carrying the marking:

$$38A60 - J5V$$

would indicate that the wheel has an aluminium oxide abrasive; that the abrasive grit is medium to fine in grain size; that the grade of the wheel is soft; that the structure has a medium spacing, and that a vitrified bond has been used.

Abrasive This must be chosen to suit the material being cut. The following general classification can be used.
1 Brown aluminium oxide is used for grinding tough materials.
2 White aluminium oxide is used for grinding hard die steels.
3 Green silicon carbide is used for grinding very hard materials

with low tensile strengths such as cemented carbides.

Table 9.1 indicates how the abrasive type may be coded and is based upon *Norton* abrasives. The British Standard marking system only calls for A for aluminium oxide abrasives or C for silicon carbide abrasives. However, it does permit the use of a prefix to the A or the C so that specific abrasives can be identified within each broad classification.

Grain size The number indicating the grain size represents the number of openings per linear 25 mm in the sieve used to size the grains. The larger the grain size number, the finer the grain. Table 9.2 gives a general classification. The sizes listed as *very fine* are referred

Table 9.2 Grit size

Coarse	Medium	Fine	Very fine
10	30	70	220
12	36	80	240
14	40	90	280
16	46	100	320
20	54	120	400
24	60	150	500
		180	600

to as 'flours' and are used for polishing and super-finishing processes.

Grade This indicates the strength of the bond and therefore the hardness of the wheel. In a *hard* wheel the bond is strong and securely anchors the grit in place, thus reducing the rate of wear. In a *soft* wheel the bond is weak and the grit is easily detached resulting in a high rate of wear.

The bond must be carefully related to the use for which the wheel is intended. Too hard a wheel will result in dull, blunt grains being retained in the periphery of the wheel causing the generation of excessive heat at the tool/wheel interface with the resultant softening (blueing) of the tool being ground. Too soft a wheel would be uneconomical due to rapid wear and would also result in lack of control of dimensional accuracy in the workpiece when precision grinding. Table 9.3 gives a general classification of hardness using a literal code.

Structure This indicates the amount of bond between the grains and the closeness of adjacent grains. In milling

Table 9.3 Grade

Very soft	Soft	Medium	Hard	Very hard
EFG	HIJK	LMNO	PQRS	TUWZ

cutter parlance it indicates the *chip clearance*. An open-structured wheel cuts freely tends to generate less heat in the cutting zone, and removes material rapidly. However, it will not produce such a good finish as a closer structured wheel. Table 9.4 gives a general classification of structure.

Table 9.4 Structure

Close spacing	Medium spacing	Wide spacing
0 1 2 3	4 5 6	7 8 9 10 11 12

Bond There is a wide range of bonds available and care must be taken to ensure that the bond is suitable for a given application because the safe use of the wheel is very largely dependent upon this selection.

1 **The vitrified bond** is the most widely used bond and is similar to glass in composition. It has a high porosity and strength which give a wheel suitable for high rates of material removal. It is not adversely affected by water, acid, oils or ordinary temperature conditions.
2 **The rubber bond** is used where a small amount of flexibility is required in the wheel, such as in thin cutting-off wheels and centreless grinding control wheels.
3 **The resinoid (bakelite) bond** is used for high-speed wheels where the bursting forces are great. Such wheels are used in foundries for dressing castings. Resinoid bond wheels are also used for the larger sizes of cutting-off wheels. They are strong enough to withstand considerable abuse.
4 **The shellac bond** is used for heavy-duty, large-diameter wheels, where a fine finish and cool cutting are required. Such wheels are used for grinding mill rolls.

Table 9.5 lists the literal code used to specify the bonding materials discussed above.

Table 9.5 Bond

Type of bond	BS code
Vitrified bond	V
Resinoid bond	B
Rubber bond	R
Shellac bond	E

Wheel selection

The correct selection of a grinding wheel depends upon many factors, only general guide lines are given here and manufacturers literature should be consulted for more precise information.

Material to be ground

1 Aluminium oxide abrasives should be used on materials with relatively high tensile strengths.

2 Silicon carbide abrasives should be used on materials with relatively low tensile strengths.

3 A fine grain wheel can be used on hard, brittle materials.

4 A coarser grain wheel should be used on soft, ductile materials.

5 When considering the *grade*, a general guide is to use a soft grade of wheel for a hard workpiece, and a hard grade of wheel for a soft workpiece.

6 When considering the *structure*, it is permissible to use a close structured wheel on hard, brittle materials, but a more open-structured wheel should be used for soft, ductile materials.

7 The *bond* is seldom influenced by the material being ground.

Rate of stock removal

1 A coarse-grain wheel should be used for rapid stock removal, but it will give a comparatively rough finish. A fine-grain wheel should be used for finishing operations requiring low rates of stock removal.

2 The structure of the wheel has a major effect on the rate of stock removal. An open-structured wheel with a wide grain spacing is used for maximum stock removal and cool cutting conditions.

3 It should be noted that the performance of a grinding wheel can be

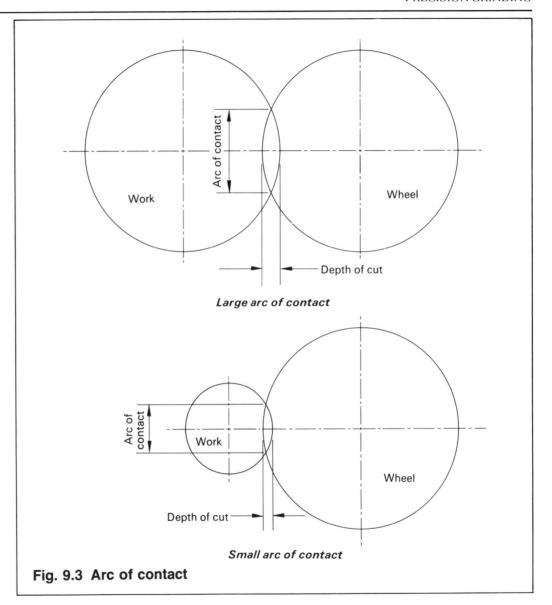

Large arc of contact

Small arc of contact

Fig. 9.3 Arc of contact

appreciably modified by the method of dressing (see below) and the operating speed.

Arc of contact   Figure 9.3 explains the meaning of *arc of contact*. It may be large or small depending on the relative sizes of the wheel and the work.

1 For a small arc of contact a fine-grained wheel may be used, whereas for a large arc of contact a coarser grained wheel should be used to prevent overheating.

2 For a small arc of contact a 'hard' wheel may be used, whereas for a large arc of contact a 'soft' wheel should be used as the cutting edges will become dulled more quickly.

3 For a small arc of contact a close-structure wheel may be used, with the advantage of improved surface finish and closer dimensional control. For a large arc of contact an open-structured wheel should be used to maintain free-cutting conditions.

Bond   The bond is selected for its mechanical properties (p. 186). It must achieve a balance between strength to resist the rotational, bursting forces and the applied cutting forces, and the requirements of cool cutting together with the controlled release of dulled grains and the exposure of fresh cutting edges.

Type of grinding machine   A heavy, rigidly constructed machine can produce accurate work using softer grade wheels. This reduces the possibility of overheating the workpiece and *drawing* its temper (i.e. reducing its hardness) or, in extreme cases, causing surface cracking of the workpiece. Furthermore, broader wheels can be used and this increases the rate of metal removal without loss of accuracy.

Wheel speed   Variation in the surface speed of a grinding wheel has a profound effect upon its performance. Increasing the speed of the wheel causes it to behave as though it were of a harder grade than that marked upon it. Conversely, reducing the surface speed of a grinding wheel causes it to behave as though it were of a softer grade than that marked upon it.

Care must be taken when selecting a wheel to ensure that the bond has sufficient strength to resist the bursting effect of the rotational forces. **Never exceed the safe working speed marked on the wheel.**

Grinding defects

Loading   When a soft material, such as a non-ferrous metal, is ground with an unsuitable wheel, the spaces between the grains become clogged with metal particles. Under such circumstances the particles of metal can often be seen embedded in the wheel. This condition is referred to as *loading* and it is detrimental to the cutting action of the grinding wheel. Loading destroys the clearance between the grains, causing them to rub rather than to cut. This results in excessive force being used to press the work against the wheel in an attempt to make the wheel cut. This in itself may be sufficient to fracture the wheel. In addition, considerable heat is generated by the wheel rubbing instead of cutting and this may not only adversely affect the hardness of the component, but it may cause the wheel to overheat, the bond to weaken, and the wheel to burst.

Glazing   A wheel consisting of relatively tough grains, strongly bonded together, will only exhibit the self-sharpening action discussed on p. 184 to a small degree and will quickly develop a shiny, or *glazed*, appearance. This is due to large worn areas on the active crystals which cause excessive friction resulting in overheating of the workpiece. Grinding under these conditions is inefficient and the force required to make the wheel cut may be sufficiently excessive to cause the wheel to burst. The only permanent remedy for glazing is the use of a softer grade of wheel.

Wheel dressing and truing

To correct either loading or glazing or to 'true' the wheel so that its circumference is concentric with the spindle axis, the wheel must be dressed. There are various devices used to dress grinding wheels but they all have similar aims.

1 To remove blunt grains from the matrix of the bond.

2 To fracture the blunt grains so that they exhibit fresh, sharp cutting edges.

3 To remove any foreign matter that may be embedded in the wheel.

Huntington-type wheel dresser   This is shown in Fig. 9.4(a). The star wheels dig into the wheel and break out the blunt grains and any foreign matter that may be clogging it. Since the star wheels rotate with the grinding wheel little abrasive action takes place and wear of the star wheels is minimal. This type of wheel dressing device is widely used for pedestal type, off-hand grinding machines, but it is not suitable for dressing and truing the wheels of precision grinding machines.

The diamond wheel dresser Generally, Brown Burt stones from Africa are used since these are useless as gem stones, and are therefore relatively cheap. The diamond cuts the wheel to shape and is used for dressing and truing the wheels on precision grinding machines, such as surface and cylindrical grinding machines. The diamond holder should be rotated from time to time to maintain the shape of the stone and prevent it from becoming blunt.

Figure 9.4(b(i)) shows the diamond being used incorrectly. Used in this way, the diamond will develop a 'flat', and this will blunt the new grains as they are exposed.

Figure 9.4(b(ii)) shows the correct way to use the diamond. It should trail the direction of rotation of the wheel, but lead the centre of rotation slightly. This will maintain the shape of the diamond so that it will keep sharp and dress cleanly.

The effective structure of the wheel can also be controlled to some extent by the way in which the wheel is dressed. Traversing the diamond rapidly across the face of the wheel has the effect of

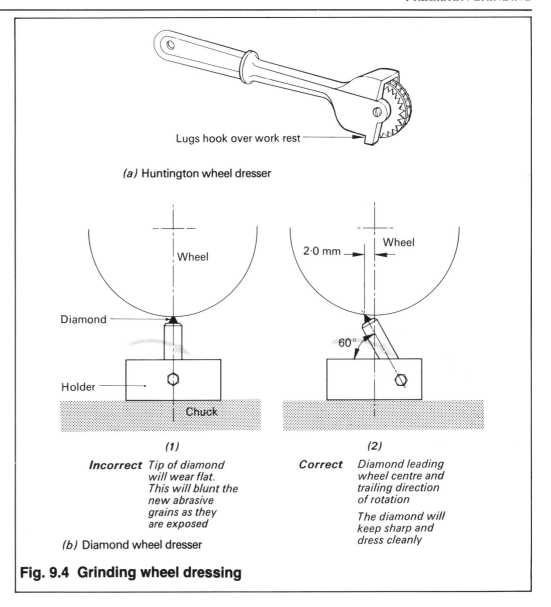

(a) Huntington wheel dresser

Lugs hook over work rest

Wheel

Diamond

Holder

Chuck

2·0 mm

Wheel

60°

(1)

Incorrect *Tip of diamond will wear flat. This will blunt the new abrasive grains as they are exposed*

(2)

Correct *Diamond leading wheel centre and trailing direction of rotation*

The diamond will keep sharp and dress cleanly

(b) Diamond wheel dresser

Fig. 9.4 Grinding wheel dressing

opening the structure, whilst a slow traverse has the effect of making the wheel cut as though it had a close structure.

The dressing stick This consists of a stick of coarse abrasive crystals. It is used for removing the sharp corners from grinding wheels and for dressing small, mounted wheels.

Balancing the grinding wheel

Precision grinding machines make provision for balancing the grinding wheel and its hub. An out-of-balance wheel produces vibration causing a 'chess board' pattern on the finished surface. If allowed to continue, this causes wear and damage to the spindle bearings.

Large and heavy grinding wheels also need to be balanced, since the out-of-balance forces can be great and may cause the wheel to burst.

The grinding wheel should be trued before balancing and it may require re-balancing from time to time as it wears (down in size).

Figure 9.5(a) shows how crescent balancing weights are fitted to the grinding wheel hub. Grub screws are provided for clamping the balance weight in position when the balance point is reached.

To balance the wheel and hub they are first mounted on a mandrel which, in turn, is supported on the knife edges of the balancing stand as shown in

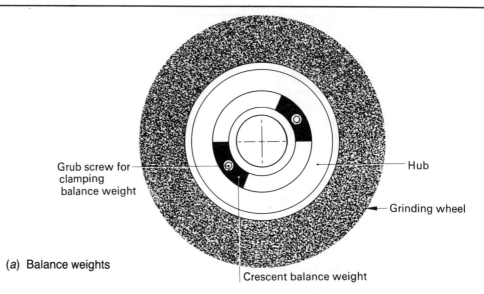

Grub screw for clamping balance weight

Hub

Grinding wheel

Crescent balance weight

(a) Balance weights

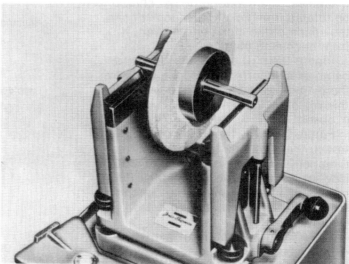

(b) Balancing stand

Fig. 9.5 Grinding wheel balancing

Fig. 9.5(b). The balance procedure is as follows.

1 Supported on the knife edges and free to rotate, the wheel will roll back and forth until it stops with the heaviest part of the assembly at the bottom.

2 Without disturbing the wheel, the top of the wheel is marked (X) with a pencil or chalk as shown in Fig. 9.6(a).

3 Move the balance weights to the position shown in Fig. 9.6(b), that is, they are moved until A and B are at 90° to the original chalk mark (XO) and the wheel is again allowed to rotate until it comes to rest. The top point is again carefully marked.

4 The balance weights are moved to a symmetrical position relative to the new balance point such that the wheel will balance in any position without rolling (see Fig. 9.6(c)).

The grinding wheel and hub are removed from the mandrel and are carefully mounted on the grinding machine spindle, where the wheel is re-trued ready for use.

Grinding wheel applications

Off-hand grinding machine

Figure 9.7(a) shows a typical off-hand grinding machine widely used in workshops for sharpening cutting tools.

Because of its apparent simplicity the double ended off-hand grinding machine comes in for more than its fair share of abuse. For *safe* and *efficient* cutting the grinding wheel must be mounted and used correctly. Only

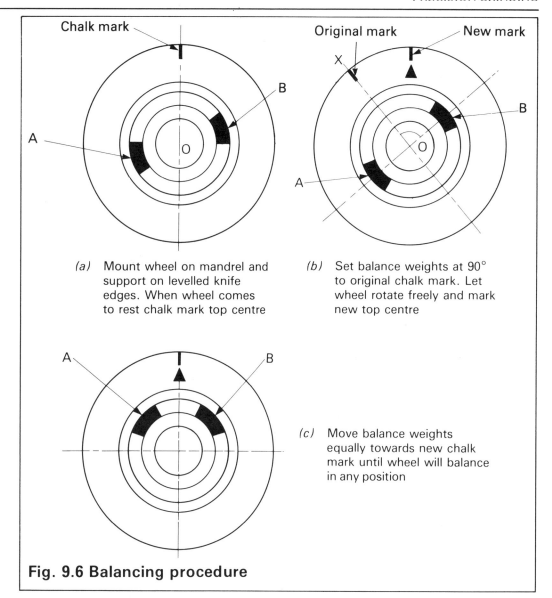

(a) Mount wheel on mandrel and support on levelled knife edges. When wheel comes to rest chalk mark top centre

(b) Set balance weights at 90° to original chalk mark. Let wheel rotate freely and mark new top centre

(c) Move balance weights equally towards new chalk mark until wheel will balance in any position

Fig. 9.6 Balancing procedure

certificated persons should change and mount a grinding wheel. To mount a new wheel see Fig. 9.7(b) and the procedure described below.

1 Clean the spindle and wheel flange to remove traces of the old wheel and any burrs that may be present.

2 Check that the new wheel is suitable as shown in Fig. 9.8(a) and, in particular, check that the operating speed is suitable. Nowadays the spindle speed must be marked on all grinding machines.

3 Check that the wheel is not cracked or faulty by 'ringing' it as shown in Fig. 9.8(b). To do this the wheel to be tested is freely suspended on stout twine and *lightly* tapped with a wooden rod. If the wheel is free from cracks or manufacturing faults such as voids, it will 'ring' with a clear note.

4 Slip the wheel on to the spindle. The lead bush in the centre of the wheel should be an easy fit. If it is tight, the wheel may twist and crack as the flanges are tightened up. Tight bushes should be opened up with a three-square scraper so that the wheel may float into position as shown in Fig. 9.8(c).

5 Check that the 'blotters' on the side of the wheel are slightly larger than the flanges and that the diameter of the flanges is at leat half the diameter of the wheel. The 'blotters' prevent the sharp edges of the flanges from biting into the wheel and starting a crack.

6 Tighten the flange retaining nut sufficiently to grip the wheel securely. Overtightening may crack the wheel.

(a) Typical machine

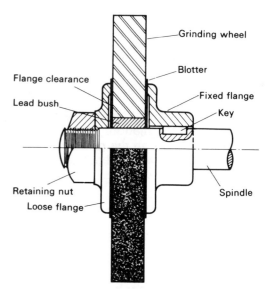

Grinding wheel

Blotter

Flange clearance

Fixed flange

Lead bush

Key

Retaining nut

Spindle

Loose flange

(b) The wheel mounting

Fig. 9.7 The double ended off-hand grinding machine

7 Replace the wheel guard and adjust the work rest as shown in Fig. 9.9. Grinding wheel guards and burst containment will be considered in greater detail on pp. 199–200.

8 Test the wheel by running it up to speed. **Do not stand in front of the wheel in case it shatters.**

9 Finally, the wheel is trued up ready for use.

Because of their relatively flimsy construction and high rotational speeds the grinding wheel is potentially dangerous. A large wheel stores very high kinetic energy which can be released with disastrous results if it is burst by incorrect mounting or misuse. Hence the emphasis that has been placed on the correct mounting procedure in this section and the additional notes on the safe handling and use of grinding wheels to be found on pp. 199–200.

Surface grinding machines

Surface grinding machines can be divided into four categories.

1 Horizontal spindle – reciprocating table.
2 Horizontal spindle – rotary table.
3 Vertical spindle – reciprocating table.
4 Vertical spindle – rotary table.

Figure 9.10(a) shows a typical horizontal spindle surface grinding machine of the type used in tool rooms for precision grinding. It has a table traverse that is infinitely variable from zero to 25 m/minute and a cross feed that is variable from about 0·2 mm to about 5 mm per pass of the wheel. The

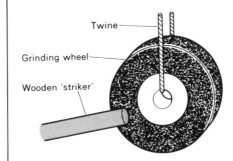

Courtesy of Norton Grinding Wheel Co.

(a) **Checking the new wheel**

Grinding wheel marking

38A 46-K5VBE

'38' Alundum brand of abrasive

Grain size

Grade (hardness) or bond strength)

Type of vitrified bond

Vitrified bond

Structure (grain spacing)

1. Check that wheel is correct grade
2. Check that wheel is correct size
3. Check that operating speed is correct
4. Visually inspect wheel for damage :- chips :- cracks :- etc.

(b) **'Ringing' a grinding wheel**

'Ringing' the wheel

1. *The wheel to be tested is freely suspended on stout twine.*
2. *It is **lightly** struck with a wooden rod.*
3. *If the wheel is free from cracks or manufacturing faults such as voids, it will 'ring' with a clear note.*

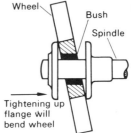

1. *Incorrect – if the lead bush in the centre of the wheel is too tight a fit on the spindle, there is a danger that the wheel will crack as the flanges are tightened up.*

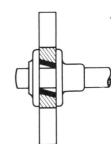

2. *Correct – the bush is eased out with a 3 square scraper until the wheel can float on the spindle it will then pull up square to the fixed flange without cracking*

Note : in the above examples the out of alignment of the bush has been exaggerated for clarity.

(c) **Fitting the bush**

Fig. 9.8 Mounting a grinding wheel

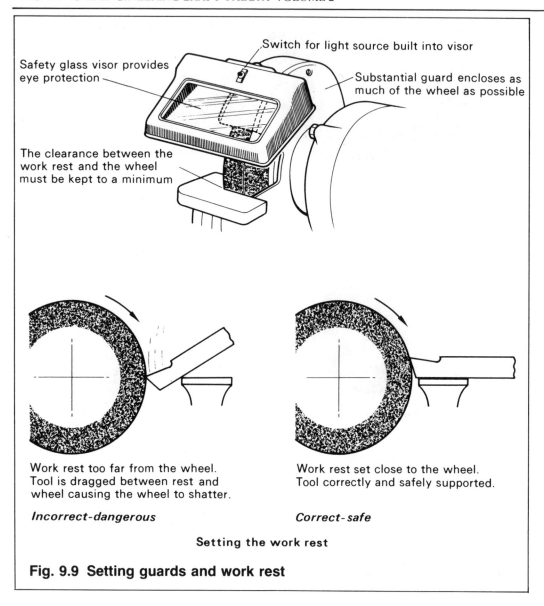

Switch for light source built into visor

Safety glass visor provides eye protection

Substantial guard encloses as much of the wheel as possible

The clearance between the work rest and the wheel must be kept to a minimum

Work rest too far from the wheel. Tool is dragged between rest and wheel causing the wheel to shatter.

Incorrect-dangerous

Work rest set close to the wheel. Tool correctly and safely supported.

Correct-safe

Setting the work rest

Fig. 9.9 Setting guards and work rest

vertical infeed of the wheel is very precisely controlled in increments of 0·005 mm. This type of machine uses grinding wheels that cut mainly on the periphery and, if wheel wear is to be kept to a minimum in the interest of dimensional accuracy, stock removal is rather limited. Precision surface grinding wheels are normally mounted on hubs containing balance weights as described on p. 190, and for this reason do not have the lead bush of the wheels illustrated on p. 193. Usually, the surface grinder operator keeps a number of wheels of different specifications ready mounted on spare hubs so that they can be interchanged quickly as required.

Figure 9.10(b) shows a horizontal surface grinding machine with a rotary table suitable for production grinding small components. The wheels used are similar to those shown in Fig. 9.13.

Figure 9.10(c) shows a vertical spindle machine with a reciprocating table whilst Fig. 9.10(d) shows a vertical spindle machine with a rotary table. Both these machines are used for production grinding and are suitable for much larger components than those previously described. The smaller machines use cup- and ring-shaped grinding wheels as shown in Fig. 9.11(a), whilst the largest machines use segmental wheels built up in a chuck as shown in Fig. 9.11(b).

Work-holding on surface grinding machines is usually effected by means of a magnetic chuck of circular or rectangular form. Fig 9.12(a) shows a section through such a chuck in the *on*

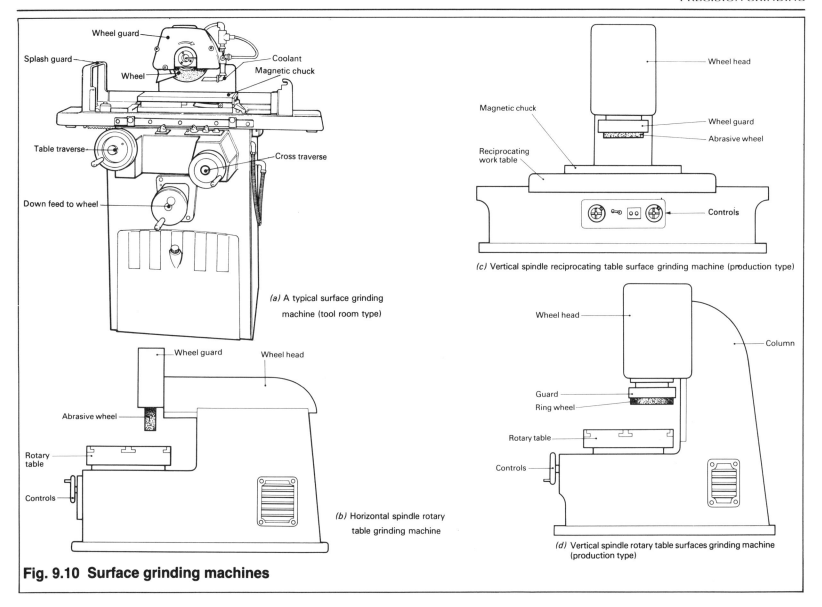

Fig. 9.10 Surface grinding machines

(a) A typical surface grinding machine (tool room type)

(b) Horizontal spindle rotary table grinding machine

(c) Vertical spindle reciprocating table surface grinding machine (production type)

(d) Vertical spindle rotary table surfaces grinding machine (production type)

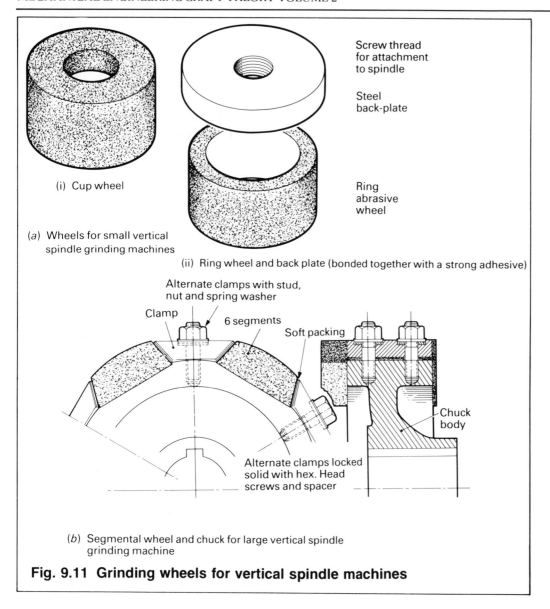

(i) Cup wheel

Screw thread
for attachment
to spindle

Steel
back-plate

Ring
abrasive
wheel

(a) Wheels for small vertical
spindle grinding machines

(ii) Ring wheel and back plate (bonded together with a strong adhesive)

Alternate clamps with stud,
nut and spring washer

Clamp

6 segments

Soft packing

Chuck
body

Alternate clamps locked
solid with hex. Head
screws and spacer

(b) Segmental wheel and chuck for large vertical spindle
grinding machine

Fig. 9.11 Grinding wheels for vertical spindle machines

position. It will be seen that the lines of flux pass through the workpiece which must be made of a magnetic material. The magnets are mounted in a grid which can be off-set by the operating handle. When this is moved to the *off* position as shown in Fig. 9.12(b), the magnetic circuit field no longer passes through the component. The flux field does not hold the component against the cutting forces directly, but provides a friction force between the component and the chuck. It is the friction that prevents the component from moving. Mechanical clamping has to be used for non-magnetic materials.

Cylindrical grinding

Figure 9.13(a) shows a typical cylindrical grinding machine. As in the case of the horizontal spindle surface grinding machine, the wheels are mounted on hubs fitted with crescent balance weights.

Invariably the wheel and workpiece rotate in opposite directions when cylindrically grinding so that the grit will enter the work gradually and produce a wedge-shaped chip such as that produced when milling conventionally.

If the work and wheel rotated in the same direction the grit would contact the work at the maximum depth of cut as in climb milling. This shock load would break the grains from the wheel before they had finished cutting resulting in excessive wheel wear and loss of accuracy.

Since the surface speed of the wheel is 10 to 20 times greater than the

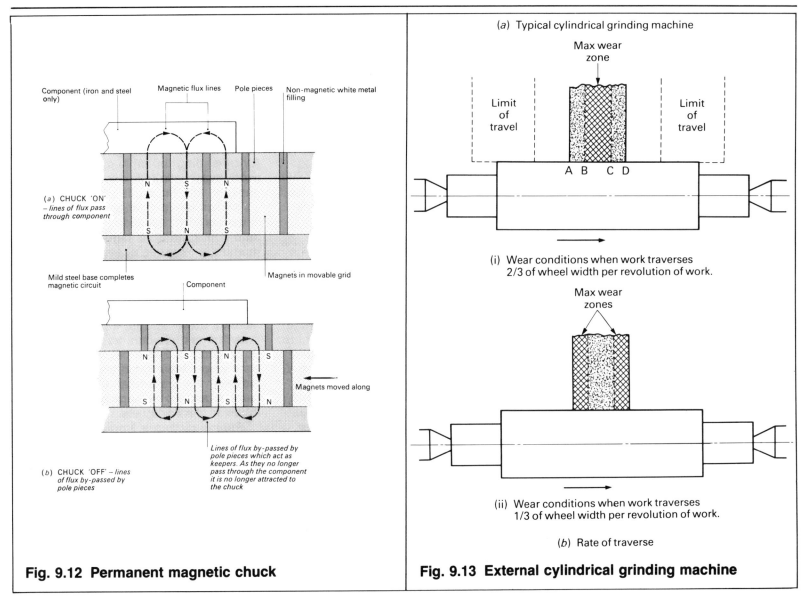

Component (iron and steel only)

Magnetic flux lines

Pole pieces

Non-magnetic white metal filling

(a) CHUCK 'ON' – lines of flux pass through component

Mild steel base completes magnetic circuit

Magnets in movable grid

Component

Magnets moved along

Lines of flux by-passed by pole pieces which act as keepers. As they no longer pass through the component it is no longer attracted to the chuck

(b) CHUCK 'OFF' – lines of flux by-passed by pole pieces

Fig. 9.12 Permanent magnetic chuck

(a) Typical cylindrical grinding machine

Max wear zone

Limit of travel

Limit of travel

A B   C D

(i) Wear conditions when work traverses 2/3 of wheel width per revolution of work.

Max wear zones

(ii) Wear conditions when work traverses 1/3 of wheel width per revolution of work.

(b) Rate of traverse

Fig. 9.13 External cylindrical grinding machine

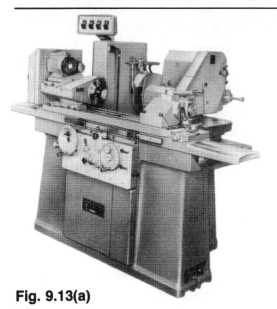

Fig. 9.13(a)

surface speed of the work, it is usual to quote the *actual* surface speed of the workpiece rather than the relative surface speed between the workpiece and wheel.

The surface speed of the workpiece depends upon a number of factors of which the following are most important.
1 Rigidity of work and machine.
2 Proportions of the workpiece.
3 Arc of contact between wheel and work (see Fig. 9.3).
4 Hardness of the workpiece.
5 Rate of feed and finish required.

In general the *work-speed* should be two-thirds the surface speed normally used for finish-turning workpieces made from the same material.

If the grinding wheel exhibits 'hard' characteristics, or if the workpiece is soft, then the work-head spindle speed should be increased. Conversely, if the wheel is exhibiting 'soft' characteristics and rapid wear with corresponding loss of dimensional accuracy, the work-head spindle speeds should be reduced. Furthermore, slender or hollow work should rotate faster than the norm to prevent local overheating.

Longitudinal feed of the grinding wheel is much more rapid than the feed associated with turning and is usually equal to two-thirds the width of the wheel for each revolution of the workpiece as this gives the most economical rate of wheel wear. Reference to Fig. 9.13(b) shows that when the work movement is from left to right the portion AC of the wheel is cutting, whilst the portion BD is cutting when movement of work is from right to left. Thus the centre third of the wheel BC wears most rapidly and produces a wheel that has a slightly concave working face. If the feed is reduced to one-third of the width of the wheel per revolution of the workpiece, then the outer two-thirds of the wheel does most of the work and the wheel wears convex and loses its shape twice as quickly. The wheel should not be allowed to run off the end of the work and there should always be two-thirds of the wheel in contact with the work.

Radial feed or *infeed* will vary between 0·005 mm and 0·05 mm per pass of the workpiece depending upon the size of the machine and the rigidity

of the workpiece. This is the amount the wheel is fed into the workpiece at the start of each cut. The diameter of the work will be reduced by twice this amount. On the last cut the wheel is allowed to 'spark out' with no extra feed to allow for spring in the work and machine.

Tapered work is ground on a 'universal' cylindrical grinding machine by off-setting the table complete with work-head, tailstock, and workpiece, through half the angle of taper required as shown in Fig. 9.14(a). The table is separate from the slide that carries it and is pivoted at its centre. A scale marked in degrees of arc or taper per unit length is fitted to the end of the table for approximate setting. A fine-adjustment screw is provided, and the table is usually fitted with a knurled headed dowel so that it can be quickly reset on-centre when parallel work has to be ground. Since the table sets over as a whole there is no loss of alignment between the work-head and tailstock centres and no damage to the centre holes in the workpiece.

Plunge cutting is employed when the workpiece is shorter than the grinding wheel width as shown in Fig. 9.14(b). The wheel is dressed parallel with the workpiece axis and then gently wound in until the correct diameter is reached. To even up the wear on the wheel, a slight rocking action of ± 3 mm is an advantage.

Internal grinding is also performed on the cylindrical grinding machine using a high speed *quill* fitted with small

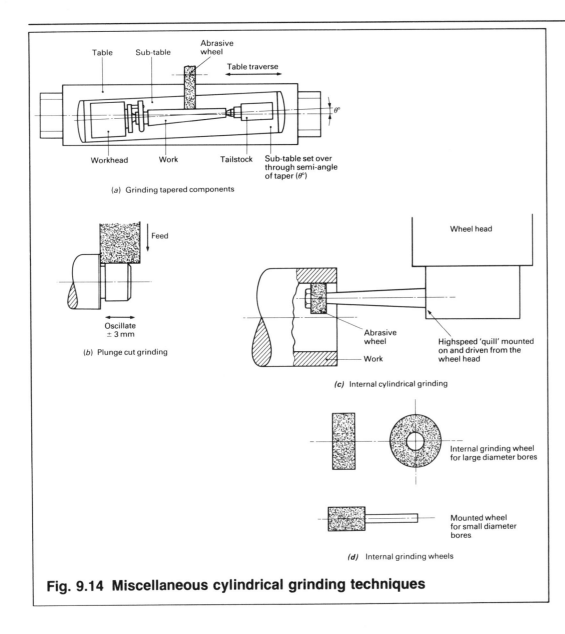

(a) Grinding tapered components

Table · Sub-table · Abrasive wheel · Table traverse · Workhead · Work · Tailstock · Sub-table set over through semi-angle of taper ($\theta°$) · $\theta°$

(b) Plunge cut grinding

Feed · Oscillate ± 3 mm

(c) Internal cylindrical grinding

Wheel head · Abrasive wheel · Work · Highspeed 'quill' mounted on and driven from the wheel head

(d) Internal grinding wheels

Internal grinding wheel for large diameter bores · Mounted wheel for small diameter bores

Fig. 9.14 Miscellaneous cylindrical grinding techniques

diameter wheels. To prevent glazing and chatter the wheels have to be relatively soft and free cutting. Figure 9.14(c) shows a typical internal grinding attachment, whilst Fig. 9.14(d) shows some typical wheels and methods of mounting them.

Safety in the use of grinding wheels

Most of the accidents involving grinding machines fall into two categories.
1 Contact with the revolving wheel.
2 Inadequately guarded wheels bursting whilst revolving a high speed. The kinetic energy stored in a rapidly revolving grinding wheel is very high, and serious or even fatal accidents can occur if the fragments of bursting wheel are not adequately contained.

An abrasive wheel means not only a wheel consisting of bonded abrasive particles with which there is a recognised risk of bursting. The definition also includes, for example, coated abrasive discs, wheels made from wood and metal with a surface of abrasive material. With abrasive wheels of these latter kinds there is no risk of bursting, but guarding is required to protect the operator against the risk of contact or entanglement.

Some of the more important factors governing the safe use of grinding wheels may be summarised as follows.
1 At all times grinding wheels must only be handled by suitably trained and certificated personnel.

2 Wheels should be handled and stored carefully as they are relatively fragile. They should not be dropped, bumped or rolled on hard surfaces. Suitable racks, bins, or drawers should be provided to accommodate the various types of wheels in use. Most plain or tapered wheels are best supported on edge on a shelf formed to cradle the wheel or on a rod through the centre bush of the wheel where such a bush is provided. Thin wheels should be placed on their sides and corrugated paper or other cushioning material should be placed between adjacent wheels.

3 The grinding wheel must be carefully selected for the work it has to do and care must be taken to ensure that the safe working speed declared on the wheel is not exceeded.

4 Grinding wheels must only be fitted by trained and certificated personnel who must also ensure that the wheel is regularly dressed to avoid loading or glazing (see p. 188) and to keep the wheel true and balanced to avoid vibration. The guard and the work-rest must also be regularly adjusted to compensate for the reduction in diameter that occurs as the wheel wears down.

5 A guard of suitable strength and design must be in place all the time the wheel is in use. It must not only prevent accidental contact with the wheel, but it must be of sufficient strength and suitably designed to contain the fragments of wheel in the event of the wheel breaking (adequate burst containment).

Exercises

1. (a) With the aid of a sketch show how a grinding wheel cuts metal.
   (b) What is meant by the marking 38A80 – k5V on a grinding wheel.

2. Explain what is meant by the following terms used in grinding wheel selection.
   (i) Grain size
   (ii) Grade
   (iii) Structure
   (iv) Bond

3. Explain how the following factors influence grinding wheel selection.
   (i) Material to be ground
   (ii) Rate of stock removal
   (iii) Arc of contact
   (iv) Type of machine
   (v) Wheel speed

4. (a) Describe what is meant by the terms 'loading' and 'glazing' with respect to grinding wheels.
   (b) Describe two methods of turning and dressing grinding wheels.

5. With the aid of sketches, describe how a grinding wheel mounted on a hub fitted with crescent balance weights can be balanced. Why is balancing essential?

6. Describe in detail the correct and safe procedure for changing the abrasive wheel on an 'off-hand' grinding machine. Pay particular attention to the re-fitting of the guard and the adjustment of the work rest.

7. Use sketches to show how the magnetic chuck used on a surface grinding machine works.

8. (a) Describe with the aid of sketches the effect of longitudinal feed rate on grinding wheel wear when cylindrically grinding. How does this affect accuracy?
   (b) Show by means of a sketch how the cylindrical grinding machine is set to grind a tapered work piece.

9. State **five** important safety factors that must be observed when using grinding wheels and grinding machines.

10. (a) When cylindrically grinding, why is it preferable for the wheel and workpiece to rotate in opposite directions?
    (b) List **five** factors that influence the choice of surface speed for a given workpiece.
    (c) Explain, with a sketch, what is meant by plunge cut grinding.

10. Operation planning and general machining

Introduction to planning

Figure 10.1 shows a simple component that is to be produced from a mild steel blank that has been machined to size. The skilled craftsman would quickly review the four alternative methods:
1 drill and tap hole; machine slot; machine angle
2 machine angle; machine slot; drill and tap hole
3 machine slot; machine angle; drill and tap hole
4 machine slot; drill and tap hole; machine angle

The craftsman would, from experience, reject 1 since it is easier to tap a 'through' hole than a blind hole; and 2 and 3 since in both cases the drill and the tap would have to start at an angle to the component surface. He would accept 4 because it presents the fewest difficulties.

Without realising it, the craftsman has *planned* the sequence of operations.

For a more complicated component a written plan is advisable. Then if the job is interrupted or handed over to someone else, as is often the case with the specialisation of modern industry, the original plan can be completed.

A plan, informal or formal, must ensure the following.

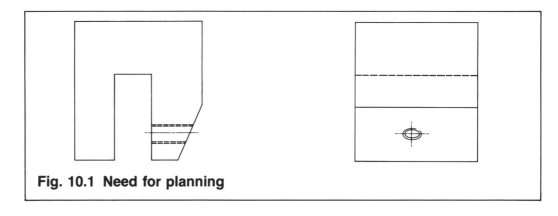

Fig. 10.1 Need for planning

1 Correct choice of datums.
2 Correct process for each operation.
3 Adequate provision is made for work-holding.
4 Adequate quality and dimensional checks are made.
5 The equipment required is available.

Figure 10.2(a) shows a more complicated component and Fig. 10.2(b) shows a suitable *operation schedule*.

Turning operations

Centres

It is a golden rule of lathe work that where two or more diameters are to be strictly concentric they must be turned at the same setting.

Figure 10.3(a) shows a component with a number of concentric diameters. No matter what method of work-holding is employed, it is impossible to turn all the diameters at the same setting. At some stage in its manufacture the component must be turned end for end. Since the component is not hollow, it can be held readily between centres and this will ensure the best chance of the diameters turned at the two settings being concentric. The operation sequence is shown in Fig. 10.3(b) and some precautions to be taken when centring the blank are shown in Fig. 10.4. The importance of aligning the centres was considered in Chapter 6.

Op. No.	Description	Equipment
1.	Chuck bar, in centre lathe.	3 Jaw chuck.
2.	Rough turn all diameters and face end.	Turning Tools 0-25, 25-50 micrometers rule, odd-leg calipers.
3.	Drill & Ream ⌀12·0 Hole.	Centre drill, drills. ⌀12·0 Reamer.
4.	Part off.	Parting Tool.
5.	Face to length.	Vernier caliper.
6.	Mount on Mandrel	⌀12·0 Mandrel Mandrel Press.
7.	Set between centres in centres lathe.	Catchplate, carrier
8.	Finish turn all diameters, chamfer and undercut.	Turning tools, depths micrometer.
9.	Set in milling machine using Vee block against Vice Jaw (horizontal or vertical)	Vee block, machine vice ⌀8·0 cutter.
10.	Centre cutter - Take Trial Cut.	
11.	Mill to depth & open up slot to size.	Slip gauges.
12.	Set in Vee block & mark out position of tapped hole.	Vernier height gauge, Surface plate, centre punch.
13.	Drill and tap 2.B.A. Hole.	Tapping size drill set 2.B.A. taps Tap wrench.
14.	De-burr, check all dimensions.	File.

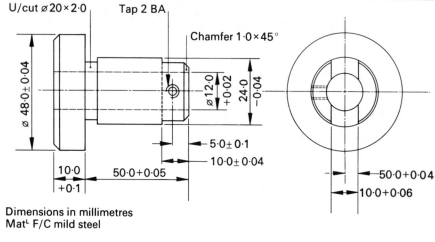

Dimensions in millimetres
Mat\ F/C mild steel

(a) The planning sheet   (b) Component to be planned

Fig. 10.2 A simple planning sheet

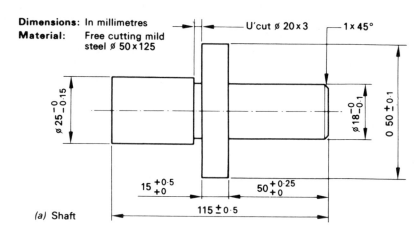

(a) Shaft

Fig. 10.3 Turning between centres

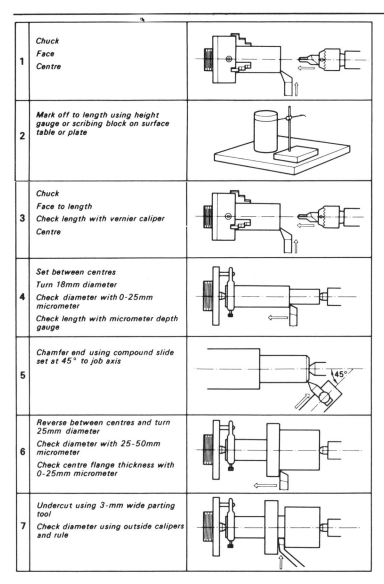

1	*Chuck* *Face* *Centre*	
2	*Mark off to length using height gauge or scribing block on surface table or plate*	
3	*Chuck* *Face to length* *Check length with vernier caliper* *Centre*	
4	*Set between centres* *Turn 18mm diameter* *Check diameter with 0-25mm micrometer* *Check length with micrometer depth gauge*	
5	*Chamfer end using compound slide set at 45° to job axis*	45°
6	*Reverse between centres and turn 25mm diameter* *Check diameter with 25-50mm micrometer* *Check centre flange thickness with 0-25mm micrometer*	
7	*Undercut using 3-mm wide parting tool* *Check diameter using outside calipers and rule*	

Fig. 10.3 Turning between centres

(b) Planning sheet

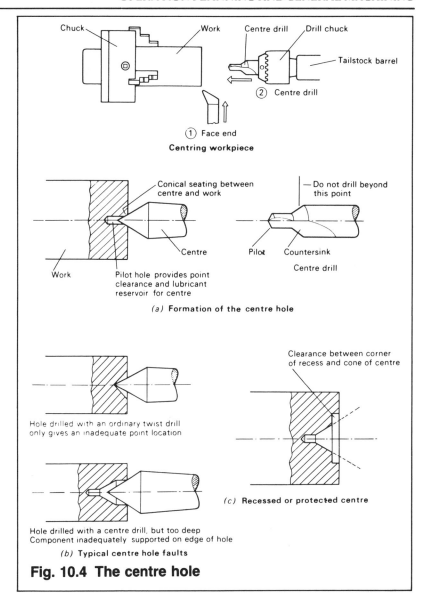

(1) Face end

Centring workpiece

(a) Formation of the centre hole

Conical seating between centre and work

Do not drill beyond this point

Centre

Pilot   Countersink

Centre drill

Work

Pilot hole provides point clearance and lubricant reservoir for centre

Hole drilled with an ordinary twist drill only gives an inadequate point location

Hole drilled with a centre drill, but too deep Component inadequately supported on edge of hole

Clearance between corner of recess and cone of centre

(c) Recessed or protected centre

(b) Typical centre hole faults

Fig. 10.4 The centre hole

Chuck   Work   Centre drill   Drill chuck

Tailstock barrel

(2) Centre drill

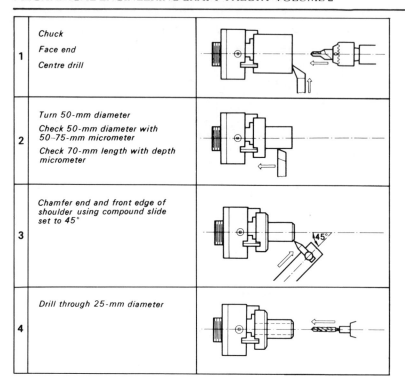

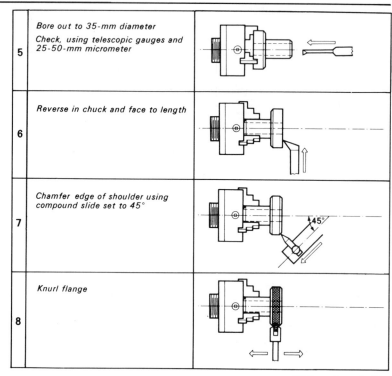

(b) Operation schedule

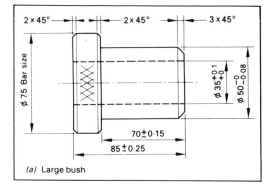

(a) Large bush

Fig. 10.5 Turning in three-jaw chuck

Three-jaw chuck

Because of its ease and quickness when setting up, the three-jaw, self-centring chuck is the most popular work-holding device on the lathe. However, unless it is used with care it also gives the *least accurate results*. Figure 10.5(a) shows a typical short, stumpy component that is ideal for holding in the three-jaw chuck.

In planning the operations for this component it should be noted that only the 35 mm diameter and the 50 mm diameter have to be concentric. The knurled collar does not have to have a greater accuracy of concentricity than the three-jaw chuck can provide. Second, it should be remembered that any drilled hole will be out-of-round, oversize and its axis will most likely have wandered. The bore must be finished with a single-point boring tool at the same setting as the 5 mm external diameter. A bored hole is sometimes oval, in which case the bore could be finished with a reaming operation between operations 5 and 6.

Figure 10.5(b) shows a suitable operation sequence and Fig. 10.6 shows a knurling tool for finishing the collar.

Tapered mandrel

If the component in Fig. 10.5 had the proportions shown in Fig. 10.7(a) it would have had to be turned on a

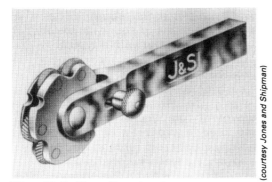

Fig. 10.6 Knurling tool

(courtesy Jones and Shipman)

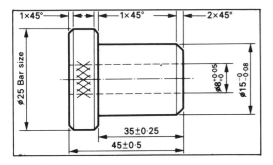

(a) Small bush

Fig. 10.7 The tapered mandrel

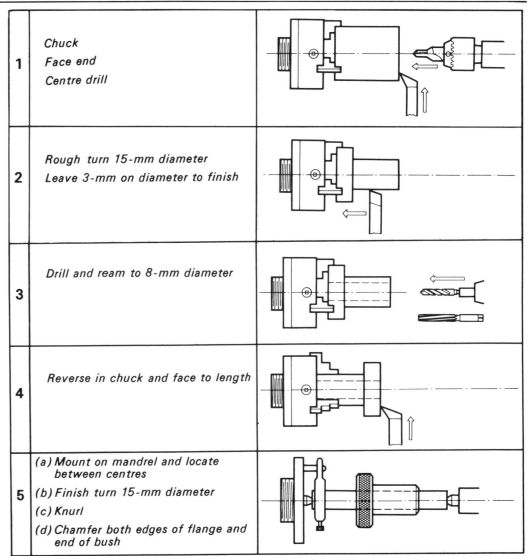

1	*Chuck* *Face end* *Centre drill*	
2	*Rough turn 15-mm diameter* *Leave 3-mm on diameter to finish*	
3	*Drill and ream to 8-mm diameter*	
4	*Reverse in chuck and face to length*	
5	*(a) Mount on mandrel and locate between centres* *(b) Finish turn 15-mm diameter* *(c) Knurl* *(d) Chamfer both edges of flange and end of bush*	

(b) Operation sequence

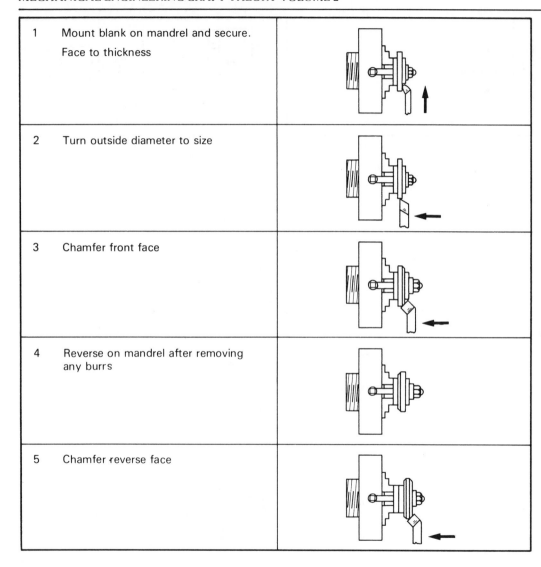

1 Mount blank on mandrel and secure. Face to thickness	
2 Turn outside diameter to size	
3 Chamfer front face	
4 Reverse on mandrel after removing any burrs	
5 Chamfer reverse face	

Fig. 10.8 Parallel mandrel work

mandrel. A boring bar for this component would have to be excessively slender for its length. This would cause it to deflect causing chatter, ovality, and bell-mouthing.

Since the tolerance on the hole permits the use of a standard reamer, it is preferable to drill and ream the bore. The bore then becomes the datum for turning the external diameters whilst the bush is mounted on a mandrel. The operation sequence is shown in Fig. 10.7(b).

The parallel mandrel (snug) The parallel mandrel or snug was introduced on p. 117 together with a typical component in Fig. 6.6. Unlike the tapered mandrel which is used for a variety of components, snugs are usually specially made just for one design of component. The snug is mounted in a four-jaw chuck and adjusted until it is running true as shown by a DTI. The operation sequence for making the component in Fig. 6.6, is shown in Fig. 10.8.

Four-jaw chuck

The four-jaw chuck has already been introduced as a means of holding round, regular and irregularly shaped components. It is used where components must be set up to a high accuracy of concentricity with an existing diameter. Alternatively, it is used where a specific degree of eccentricity is required. Figure 10.9(a) and (b) show two methods of setting work in the four-jaw chuck, whilst Fig. 10.9(c) shows how work can be re-set.

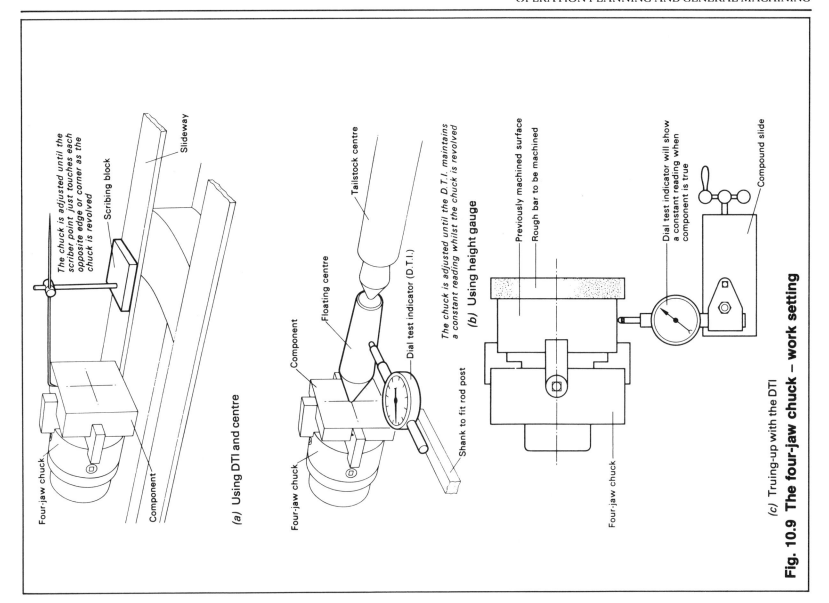

The chuck is adjusted until the scriber point just touches each opposite edge or corner as the chuck is revolved

Slideway

Scribing block

Four-jaw chuck

Component

(a) Using DTI and centre

Tailstock centre

Floating centre

Dial test indicator (D.T.I.)

Component

Four-jaw chuck

Shank to fit rod post

The chuck is adjusted until the D.T.I. maintains a constant reading whilst the chuck is revolved

(b) Using height gauge

Previously machined surface

Rough bar to be machined

Dial test indicator will show a constant reading when component is true

Compound slide

Four-jaw chuck

(c) Truing-up with the DTI

Fig. 10.9 The four-jaw chuck – work setting

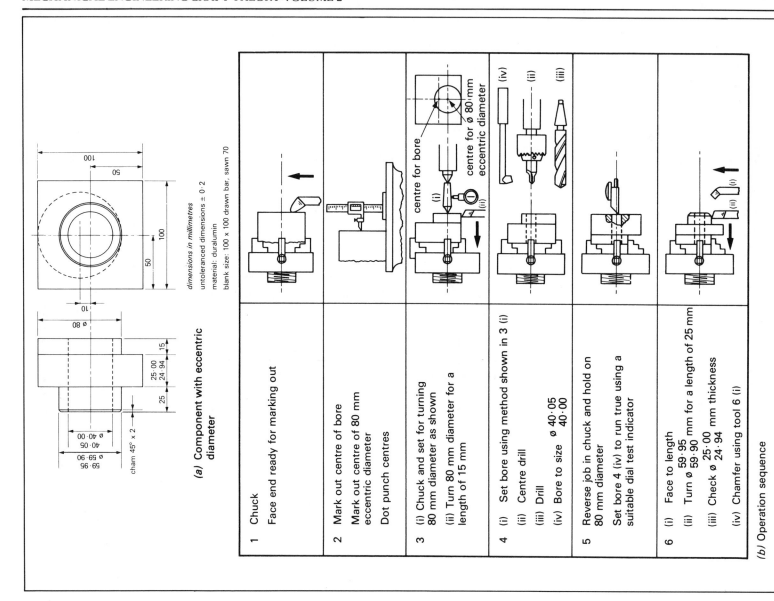

dimensions in millimetres
untoleranced dimensions ± 0.2
material: duralumin
blank size: 100 x 100 drawn bar, sawn 70

(a) Component with eccentric diameter

1   Chuck
    Face end ready for marking out

2   Mark out centre of bore
    Mark out centre of 80 mm eccentric diameter
    Dot punch centres

3   (i) Chuck and set for turning 80 mm diameter as shown
    (ii) Turn 80 mm diameter for a length of 15 mm

4   (i)   Set bore using method shown in 3 (i)
    (ii) Centre drill
    (iii) Drill
    (iv) Bore to size ∅ 40·05 40·00

5   Reverse job in chuck and hold on 80 mm diameter
    Set bore 4 (iv) to run true using a suitable dial test indicator

6   (i)   Face to length
    (ii) Turn ∅ 59·95 59·90 mm for a length of 25 mm
    (iii) Check ∅ 25·00 24·94 mm thickness
    (iv) Chamfer using tool 6 (i)

(b) Operation sequence

Fig. 10.10 Eccentric turning

Figure 10.10(a) shows a typical example of a component with an eccentric diameter, whilst Fig. 10.10(b) shows the operation schedule for this component. The combination of eccentricity and the square section blank make it an ideal four-jaw chuck exercise.

The face-plate

In the examples considered so far, the prime consideration has centred around maintaining concentricity of the turned diameters. The face-plate is used where the axis of a turned diameter has to be perpendicular (at right angles) or parallel to a datum surface. In the bearing housing shown in Fig. 10.11(a) the datum surface (AA) is perpendicular to the axis of the bore. In this example the 50 mm diameter bore has to be enlarged to take a replacement bearing. The component is mounted on a face-plate as shown in Fig. 10.11(b), and the original bore is trued up with the aid of a dial test indicator (DTI). After this the housing is bored to size.

Typical shaping operations

Small components

As well as squaring up blanks, the shaping machine can be used to machine slots, steps and chamfers. The relative settings of the tool slide and clapper box when machining such surfaces have already been discussed in Chapter 7.

A component exploiting these movements is shown in Fig. 10.12(a),

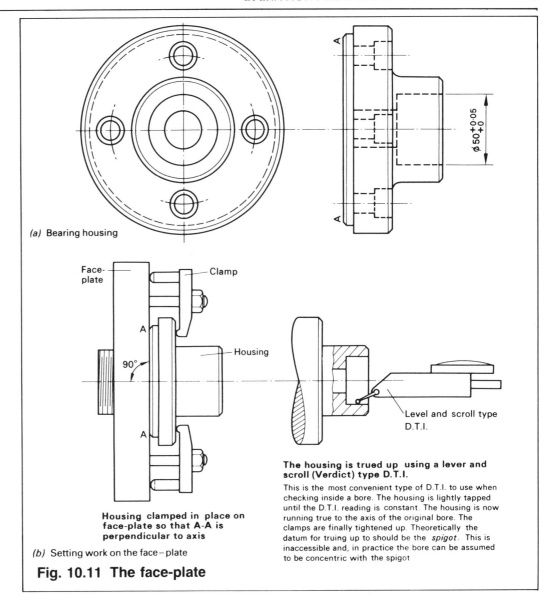

(a) Bearing housing

(b) Setting work on the face-plate

Housing clamped in place on face-plate so that A-A is perpendicular to axis

The housing is trued up using a lever and scroll (Verdict) type D.T.I.

This is the most convenient type of D.T.I. to use when checking inside a bore. The housing is lightly tapped until the D.T.I. reading is constant. The housing is now running true to the axis of the original bore. The clamps are finally tightened up. Theoretically the datum for truing up to should be the *spigot*. This is inaccessible and, in practice the bore can be assumed to be concentric with the spigot

Fig. 10.11 The face-plate

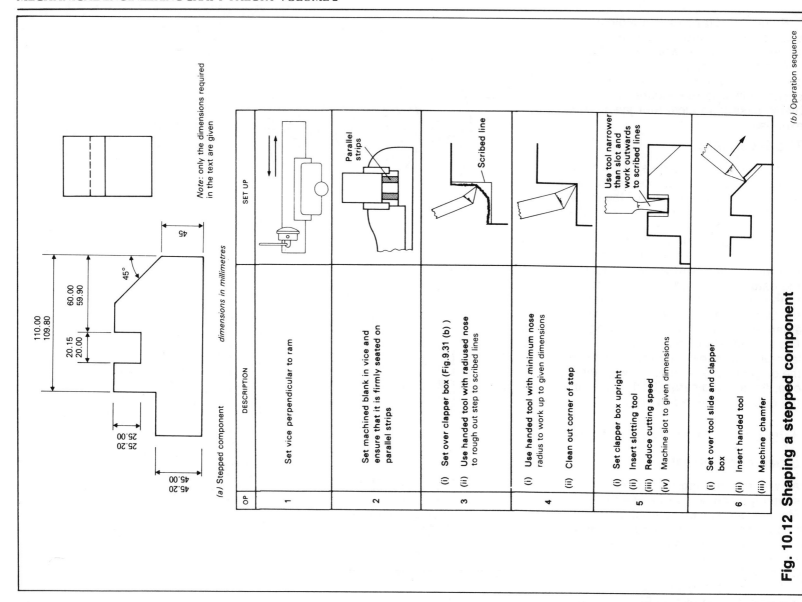

Note: only the dimensions required in the text are given

(a) Stepped component   *dimensions in millimetres*

OP	DESCRIPTION	SET UP
1	Set vice perpendicular to ram	
2	Set machined blank in vice and ensure that it is firmly seated on parallel strips	**Parallel strips**
3	(i) Set over clapper box (Fig. 9.31 (b)) (ii) Use handed tool with radiused nose to rough out step to scribed lines	Scribed line
4	(i) Use handed tool with minimum nose radius to work up to given dimensions (ii) Clean out corner of step	
5	(i) Set clapper box upright (ii) Insert slotting tool (iii) Reduce cutting speed (iv) Machine slot to given dimensions	Use tool narrower than slot and work outwards to scribed lines
6	(i) Set over tool slide and clapper box (ii) Insert handed tool (iii) Machine chamfer	

(b) Operation sequence

Fig. 10.12 Shaping a stepped component

whilst the operations to produce this more complex component are outlined in Fig. 10.12(b).

It is assumed that the blank has already been squared up previously. To machine the step, slot and chamfer this component would be held in the machine vice so that it is perpendicular to the movement of the ram. Thus the first operation would be to place a ground parallel strip in the vice and check that the vice is correctly set using a DTI as shown in Fig. 10.12(b), operation 1. Next, the tool slide would need to be set perpendicular using a DTI and try-square. Normally the slide would be set to the machine table, but since the component is being held in the machine vice, the moving jaw slideways are being used as the horizontal datum in this instance. The table rise and fall cannot be used for machining the step and the slot as the vertical feed mechanism is not sufficiently sensitive or accurate.

Once the vice and tool slide are correctly set, the blank would be clamped firmly in the vice on two parallel strips as shown. Care must be taken to ensure that an adequate gap is left so that a micrometer can be used to measure the 45·20/45·00 mm dimension without disturbing the setting of the component in the vice.

The step and slot would be machined before the chamfer in order to leave a datum edge to measure from. Commencing with the step, this would be roughed out to within 1 mm of the scribed line using a round-nosed,

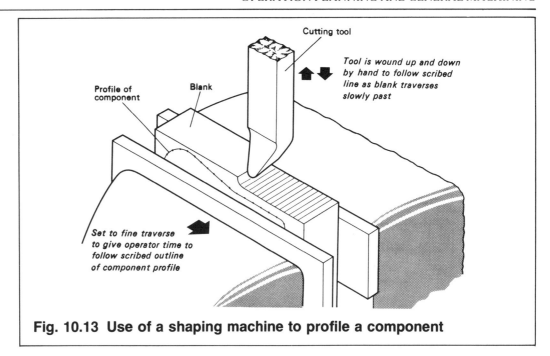

Fig. 10.13 Use of a shaping machine to profile a component

handed tool. The round nose would give strength to the tool and enable the surplus material to be removed rapidly. A series of horizontal and vertical cuts would be taken leaving the corner as sharp as the nose radius would allow. A finishing tool with minimum nose radius would then be used to complete the operation. The corner radius would be cleaned out and horizontal cuts would be taken until the 45·20/45·00 mm dimension is achieved. This dimension would be checked using a 25–50 mm micrometer without removing the component from the vice. Vertical cuts would then be taken using the tool slide

on the ram. The 110·00/109·80 mm would be checked using a vernier caliper, and when this dimension has been achieved, the corner would be finally squared out.

Next the slot would be machined. A parting or slotting tool would be used as shown. The initial slot would be cut in the middle of the scribed lines and then the slot would be gradually opened up to the right until the 60·00/59·90 mm dimension has been achieved. This dimension would be checked using a vernier caliper.

The slot width would then be opened up to the left until the slot is

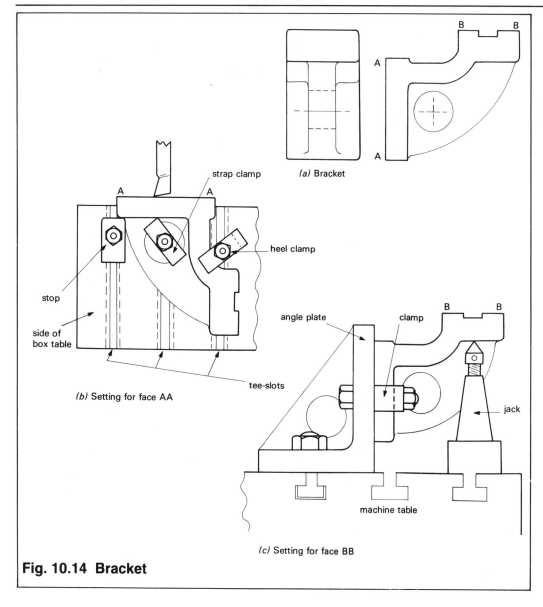

(a) Bracket

(b) Setting for face AA

strap clamp

heel clamp

stop

side of
box table

tee-slots

angle plate

clamp

jack

machine table

(c) Setting for face BB

Fig. 10.14 Bracket

20·15/20·00 mm wide as checked using telescopic gauges and a micrometer caliper. When the correct width has been achieved the slot would be taken down to the correct depth as indicated by a depth micrometer. Once the 25·20/25·00 mm depth has been achieved, the slot would be correct in size and position.

Finally the chamfer would be machined. Neither the angle nor the position of the chamfer is toleranced, so the tool slide can be set over using the protractor scale on the ram head. The chamfer can then be machined down to the scribed line. The component would then be removed from the vice and any burrs would be removed with a file.

Profiles for such components as press tool punches can easily be cut out on the shaping machine as shown in Fig. 10.13. A very fine cross traverse is set and the machine is run more slowly than usual. As the job traverses under the tool, the operator winds the tool slide up and down to follow the scribed line. This requires very considerable skill and, since the operator is facing the cut, goggles *must* be worn.

Large components

It has already been shown (Chapter 7) that large components can be mounted directly on to the shaping machine table. Two typical examples will now be considered:

The faces AA and BB of the bracket shown in Fig. 10.14(a) are to be machined at right angles to each other.

The operation sequence could be as follows.

1 Clamp the bracket to the side of the shaping machine table so that the base AA is uppermost as shown in Fig. 10.14(b). Use feeler gauges between the tool point and the casting to get the surface being machined as nearly horizontal as possible.

Some difficulty may be experienced in getting a rough, and possibly distorted, casting to lie flat against the machine table. A wad of paper between the casting and the table will help to prevent damage to the machined surface of the table and also help the casting to bed down. However, if it is too irregular or distorted, shims should be arranged so that the clamps do not spring the casting as they are tightened.

2 After the base has been machined the bracket is removed from the side of the table and secured to an angle plate. The angle plate is, itself, then secured to the machine table as shown in Fig. 10.14(c). Note the use of screw jacks to support the casting immediately under the point of cutting.

Figure 10.15(a) shows a machine slide with re-entrant surfaces. That is, the tee-slots and the dove-tail slideways. The following operation sequence assumes that the cast iron blank has been machined on all faces ready for finishing.

1 Clamp the blank to the machine table with the edge parallel to the movement of the ram. Using a parting tool, machine the slots down to depth and, using the same tool, open up the width

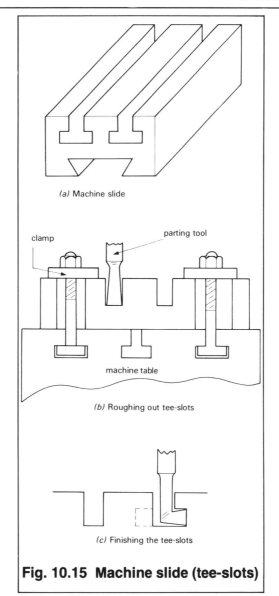

(a) Machine slide

clamp   parting tool

machine table

(b) Roughing out tee-slots

(c) Finishing the tee-slots

Fig. 10.15 Machine slide (tee-slots)

of the slots and correct their centre distance. The width of the slots can be checked with slip gauges and the depth can be checked with a depth micrometer (see Fig. 10.15(b)).

2 The undercut of the tee-slot is then machined by a tool specially ground for the purpose. For operations 1 and 2 the tool slide and clapper box are set central. Figure 10.15(c) shows the set up at this stage. Cutting the tee-slot requires considerable skill and concentration as the tool has to be lifted clear by hand at the end of each stroke. For this reason the machine should be set to the slowest speed and to a longer stroke than usual.

3 After completing the tee-slots, the casting is turned over and clamped down to the machine table. The vee-slide is roughed out as shown in Fig. 10.16(a).

4 The tool slide is inclined at 60° and a suitable handed tool is put into the tool holder. Remember that this is an *inside*, or *re-entrant* vee. Therefore the clapper box is swung away from the vee and *not* towards it as described on p. 144 where an *outside* vee was being machined. Machine one side to size using the tool slide and cross traverse (see Fig. 10.16(b)).

5 Reverse the tool head and clapper box and use a cutting tool of opposite hand to machine the second vee. The size of the vee and the gap between them is checked with rollers and slip gauges from a calculated dimension, as shown in Fig. 10.16(c).

6 Remove all sharp corners with a file.

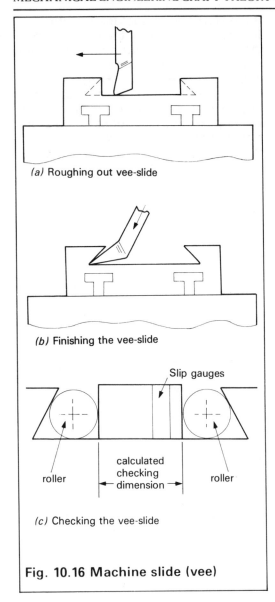

(a) Roughing out vee-slide

(b) Finishing the vee-slide

Slip gauges

roller

calculated
checking
dimension

roller

(c) Checking the vee-slide

Fig. 10.16 Machine slide (vee)

Milling

Vice work

Figure 10.17(a) shows a small vee-jaw from some work-holding device. The component is to be machined from a case-hardening quality mild steel and the dimensions given allow for grinding after case-hardening. Therefore, the tolerances are quite generous as the grinding operation will impart the final accuracy.

It is often difficult to determine when a vee is the correct size. In this example, the draughtsman has given a dimension over a standard roller. Having centred his double equal-angle milling cutter, the craftsman has merely to increase the depth of cut until the checking dimension is reached. The vee will then be the required size. The draughtsman is not always so obliging and the craftsman may often have to make the calculation himself using trigonometry. Basic trigonometry was introduced in Chapter 1 of this book.

One area of discussion is the slot at the bottom of the vee which provides corner clearance for the component being clamped. The alternative procedures are as follows.
1 Mill the slot first and then the vee.
2 Mill the vee first and then the slot.

Method 1 has the advantage of removing the cutting load from the corner of the angle-cutter teeth. This is good practice as the corners of the teeth are liable to chip under these

conditions. However, it is difficult to cut a deep, narrow slot with a slitting saw and great care has to be taken to prevent the saw from jamming in the slot and breaking. It may also wander in a deep slot.

Method 2 puts more strain on the angle cutter and a number of shallow cuts have to be taken. On the other hand, there is less chance of breaking the saw.

In the operation schedule, Fig. 10.17(b), a double-angle cutter is used to cut the vee. A good craftsman will have little trouble with a 6 mm thick slitting saw in a vee this size and, in any case, a broken slitting saw is cheaper than a damaged angle cutter.

Method 2 is satisfactory where the vee is produced using a more robust cutter, such as a shell end mill, as shown in Fig. 10.17(c). In this alternative set up, a vertical spindle milling machine is used with the head inclined at 45°.

Table mounted work

Figure 10.18(a) shows a cast iron angle plate which is to be machined on the two faces as indicated. This example exploits the ability of a horizontal milling machine to generate a surface at right angles to the machine table when using a face mill on a stub arbor as shown in Fig. 10.18(b).

When setting a rough casting on a machine table the following points must be noted.
1 The rough casting must not damage the ground reference surface of the

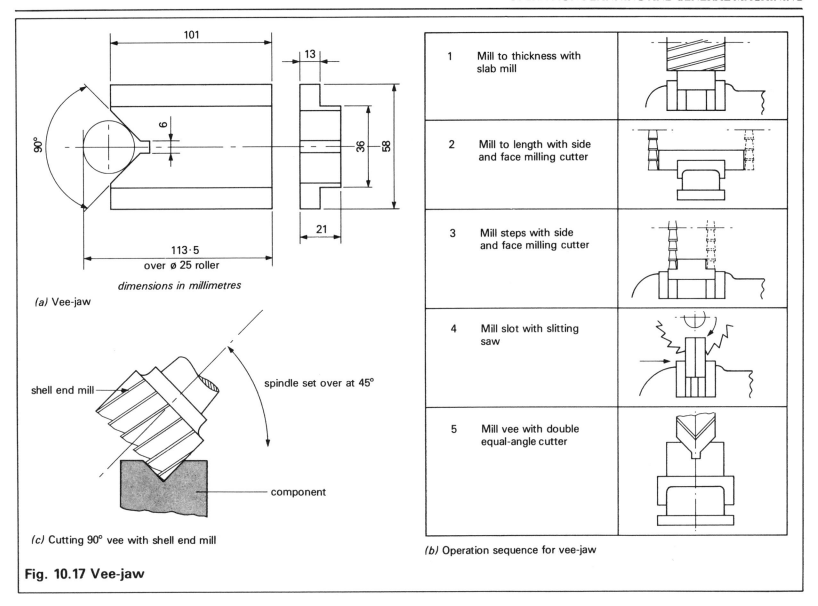

1	Mill to thickness with slab mill	
2	Mill to length with side and face milling cutter	
3	Mill steps with side and face milling cutter	
4	Mill slot with slitting saw	
5	Mill vee with double equal-angle cutter	

101

13

6

90°

36

58

21

113·5
over ø 25 roller

dimensions in millimetres

(a) Vee-jaw

shell end mill

spindle set over at 45°

component

(c) Cutting 90° vee with shell end mill

Fig. 10.17 Vee-jaw

(b) Operation sequence for vee-jaw

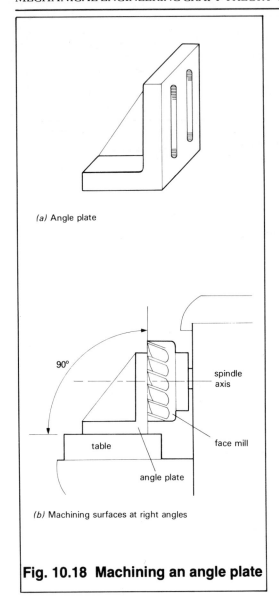

(a) Angle plate

90°

spindle axis

table

face mill

angle plate

(b) Machining surfaces at right angles

Fig. 10.18 Machining an angle plate

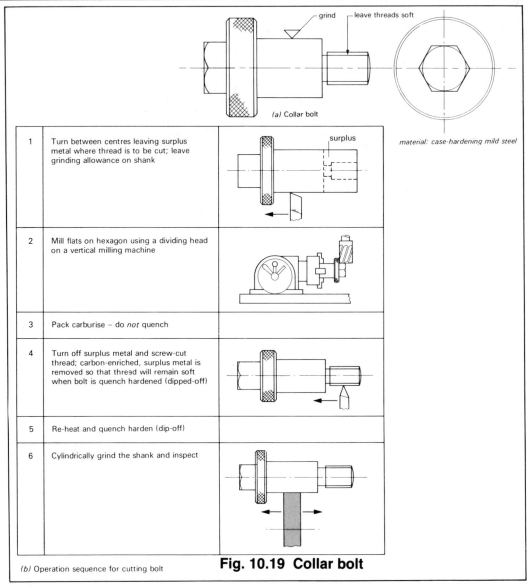

grind   leave threads soft

(a) Collar bolt

material: case-hardening mild steel

1	Turn between centres leaving surplus metal where thread is to be cut; leave grinding allowance on shank	surplus
2	Mill flats on hexagon using a dividing head on a vertical milling machine	
3	Pack carburise – do *not* quench	
4	Turn off surplus metal and screw-cut thread; carbon-enriched, surplus metal is removed so that thread will remain soft when bolt is quench hardened (dipped-off)	
5	Re-heat and quench harden (dip-off)	
6	Cylindrically grind the shank and inspect	

(b) Operation sequence for cutting bolt

Fig. 10.19 Collar bolt

machine table.

2 The clamping should be arranged so that the casting is not distorted.

Providing that one surface of the casting is reasonably flat the casting can often be bedded down on several thicknesses of newspaper. This keeps the rough casting off the ground surfaces and provides a reasonable bed for the casting. However, if the casting is severely distorted, packing may be necessary.

Care must be taken to ensure that on the first cut, the tips of the cutter teeth are operating below the hard and abrasive skin of the casting. Preferably an inserted, carbide-tipped face mill should be used with cast iron.

Combined operations

So far the components discussed in this chapter have been made entirely on one type of machine. In practice, most components have a large number of operations performed upon them requiring a range of machines and bench-fitting operations.

Figures 10.19 and 10.20 show two components that require a range of operations to complete them together with outline operation sequences. Detailed discussion of the operations would be too lengthy here, but attention is drawn to the more important operations. Figure 10.21 gives details of the technique of button-boring which is required for the component shown in Fig. 10.20(a).

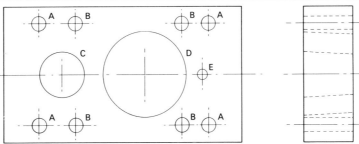

(a) Press tool die-pierce and blank progression tool

Holes
A – clearance M8 x 1 cap screw
B – ream to fit ø dowel
C – cutton bore ø30·50/30·00 back off at 3° inclusive
D – button bore ø 50·05/50·00 back off at 3° inclusive
E – ream ø 7 for stop shank

dimensions in millimetres
material: K9 die steel

1	Machine die blank all over to remove scale and at least 3 mm decarburised metal underscale Square up ready for working out.	Shaping machine with carbide-tipped tool
2	Mark out all hole centres accurately.	Surface plate Vernier height gauge.
3	Drill all A holes ø 8·5 mm Drill and ream all B holes ø 8·00 mm Drill tapping size 2BA centre of C and D holes for button-retaining screw. Drill and ream E hole ø 7 for peg stop shank	Pillar drilling machine
4	Tap 2BA holes at centre of C and D for button-retaining screws.	Bench vice, taps and tap wrench
5	Set up buttons for boring C and D. See Fig. 10.21	Surface plate, slip gauges, depth micrometer
6	Bore holes C and D to size; relieve back of bores at 3° inclusive taper to allow easy drop for blanks and piercing slugs	Centre lathe with face plate and single-point turning tool
7	Remove all sharp edges and corners.	Bench, file
8	Harden and temper	Salt-bath furnaces, quenching bath
9	Surface grind both faces	Surface grinding machine

(b) Operation sequence for press tool die

Fig. 10.20 Press tool die

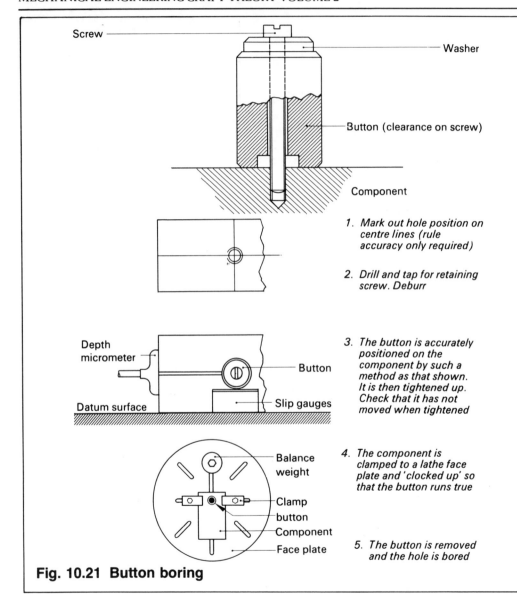

1. Mark out hole position on centre lines (rule accuracy only required)

2. Drill and tap for retaining screw. Deburr

3. The button is accurately positioned on the component by such a method as that shown. It is then tightened up. Check that it has not moved when tightened

4. The component is clamped to a lathe face plate and 'clocked up' so that the button runs true

5. The button is removed and the hole is bored

Fig. 10.21 Button boring

Exercises

1. Explain why operation planning is essential before commencing manufacture of a component.
2. Draw up an operation schedule for turning the component shown in Fig. 10.22 on a centre lathe.

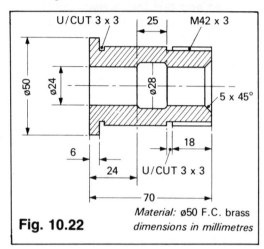

Material: ø50 F.C. brass
Fig. 10.22 *dimensions in millimetres*

3. Draw up an operation schedule for turning the component shown in Fig. 10.23 between centres on a lathe.

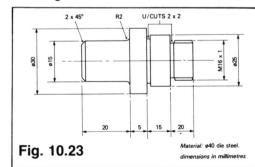

Fig. 10.23 *Material: ø40 die steel. dimensions in millimetres*

4. Draw up an operation schedule for boring and facing a cast iron bracket on a centre lathe as shown in Fig. 10.24. The base AA is already machined and should be used as a datum. Pay particular attention to setting up on a centre lathe face plate to ensure the bore is the correct distance from, and parallel to the datum AA, and that the set up is balanced.

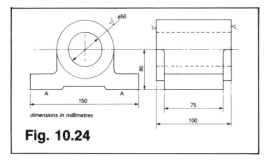

dimensions in millimetres

Fig. 10.24

5. Draw up an operation schedule for producing the component shown in Fig. 10.25 on a shaping machine from a sawn mild steel blank. Machine all over.

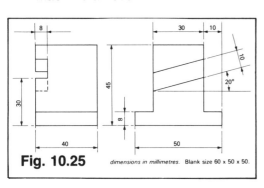

Fig. 10.25 dimensions in millimetres. Blank size 60 x 50 x 50.

6. Draw up an operation schedule for producing the component shown in question 5 on a horizontal milling machine.

7. Draw up an operation for producing the component shown in question 5 on a vertical milling machine.

8. Draw up an operation schedule for machining the slots in the component shown in Fig. 10.26 on a slotting machine.

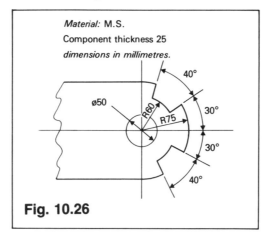

Material: M.S.

Component thickness 25

dimensions in millimetres.

Fig. 10.26

9. Draw up an operation schedule for machining the slots in the 12 mm thick by 150 mm diameter duralumin plate shown in Fig. 10.27. The plate is supplied ready faced and bored. The slots penetrate through the plate.

10. The plate shown in question 9 is to be modified by reducing its O/D to 140 mm.
    (i) Sketch a design for a 'snug' to

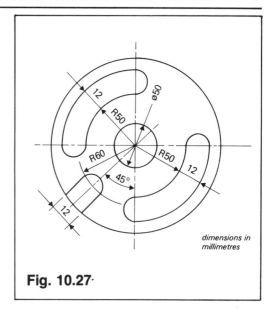

dimensions in millimetres

Fig. 10.27·

fit the 50 mm bore to locate the plate true whilst it is clamped through the slots to a face plate.
(ii) Draw up an operation schedule for making the snug.

11. Maintenance

The need for maintenance

Nigerian companies invest huge amounts of money to acquire the machines, equipment and tools needed in order to be able to manufacture their products. The money spent on these items is part of a company's capital and the equipment represents that company's assets. A company is wise to protect its assets by an efficient maintenance programme so that its machines and equipment will yield the anticipated profit. Unfortunately the climate in West Africa causes rapid deterioration in all metal objects and machines and tools are no exception.

The maintenance department of any company and the craftsmen in that department are responsible for the following work:

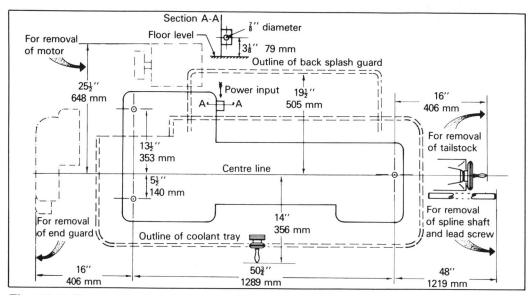

Fig. 11.1 Typical foundation plan for centre lathe

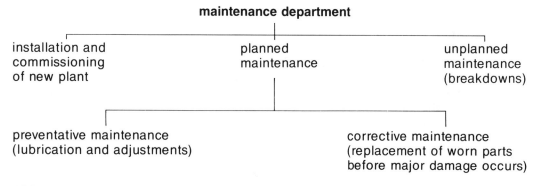

Installation

Before new machines are installed it is necessary to make adequate preparations.
1 The foundation must be prepared. Small machines can often stand upon the existing workshop floor but larger machines have to have strong concrete foundations specially prepared for them. Figure 11.1 shows a typical foundation plan for a centre lathe.

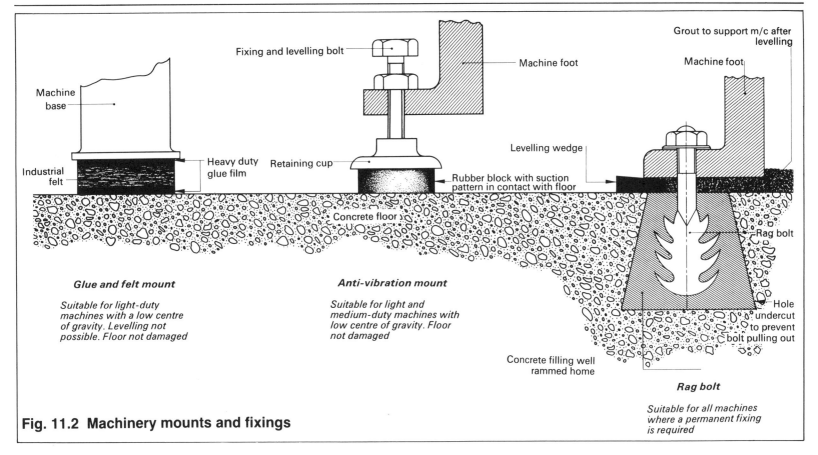

Fig. 11.2 Machinery mounts and fixings

Glue and felt mount

Suitable for light-duty machines with a low centre of gravity. Levelling not possible. Floor not damaged

Anti-vibration mount

Suitable for light and medium-duty machines with low centre of gravity. Floor not damaged

Rag bolt

Suitable for all machines where a permanent fixing is required

2 The method of fixing the machine to the foundation or floor has to be chosen. Figure 11.2 shows three methods of mounting machines. The choice of which method is used will depend upon such factors as:
 a) the material from which the foundation is made,
 b) the degree of vibration produced by the machine,
 c) the sensitivity of the machine to outside vibration,
 d) whether the machine tends to 'walk',
 e) whether the machine is to be temporarily or permanently fixed,
 f) where the centre of gravity of the machine lies.

3 Services such as an electrical supply and often a compressed air supply must be planned and brought up to the site ready for coupling to the machine. It may also be necessary to provide for fume extraction and suitable ducting and extractor fans must be prepared.

Once the site has been prepared for the machine its movement into position must be considered. Large works are usually fortunate in having overhead cranes and other mechanical handling devices. However in most medium and small firms the machine is delivered to the workshop doors on a lorry and then manhandled into position. Great care has to be taken to avoid strains and injury. To remove a machine from a lorry a temporary tripod and hoist can be erected as shown in Fig. 11.3, or the machine can be slid down a ramp of strong planks supported at various points as shown in Fig. 11.4(a). To avoid the machine running away down the ramp a drag rope should be used as shown in Fig. 11.4(b).

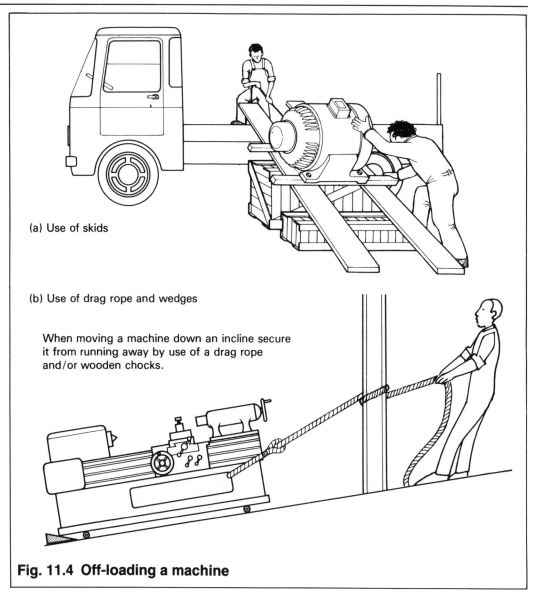

(a) Use of skids

(b) Use of drag rope and wedges

When moving a machine down an incline secure it from running away by use of a drag rope and/or wooden chocks.

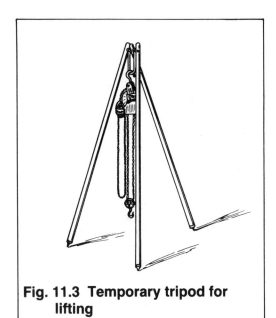

Fig. 11.3 Temporary tripod for lifting

Fig. 11.4 Off-loading a machine

Once the machine is on level ground it is normal to move it on rollers using a crow bar as shown in Fig. 11.5. Three rollers are normally used so that as the machine is moved off the rear roller, that roller can be carried round to the front so that the machine is never supported on less than two rollers.

When the machine is on its foundation it has to be levelled to ensure it is not twisted in any way as this would throw it out of alignment. Usually spirit levels are used to check that the machine is properly positioned and free from twist. Some machines are fitted with levelling bolts, but others have to be levelled by adjusting steel wedges between the bed of the machine and the foundation as shown in Fig. 11.6.

Once the machine has been levelled and the services connected it is ready for a test run. First ensure that it has been prepared in accordance with the maker's instructions. For example, that any temporary locking devices have been released, that any rust preventative plastic films or varnishes have been washed from the slides with paraffin and that the machine has been correctly and thoroughly lubricated. It is usual to test the machine's performance before finally accepting it and it should run smoothly and quietly throughout its entire range of speeds and feeds. If there is any vibration or unusual noise it should be stopped immediately and the maker's service engineer sent for. However, if all is well, alignment tests should next be carried out. Figure 11.7

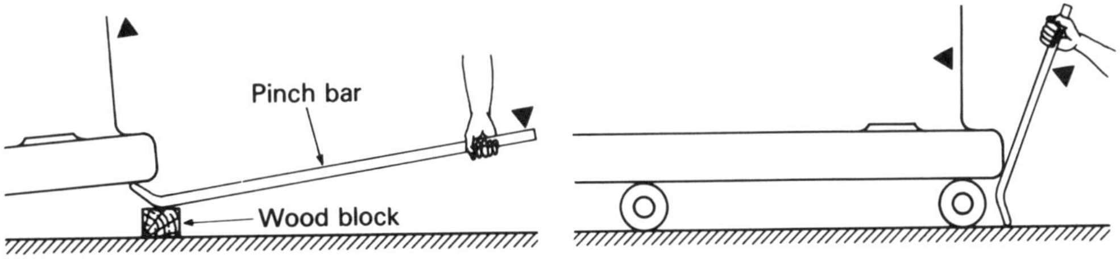

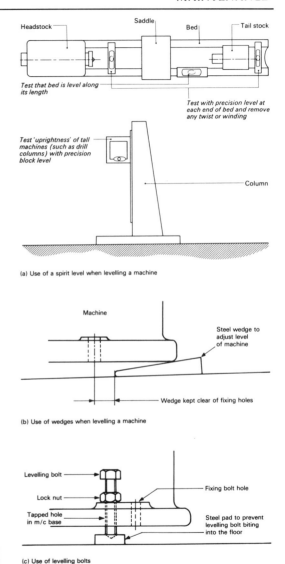

Test that bed is level along its length

Test with precision level at each end of bed and remove any twist or winding

Test 'uprightness' of tall machines (such as drill columns) with precision block level

Column

(a) Use of a spirit level when levelling a machine

Machine

Steel wedge to adjust level of machine

Wedge kept clear of fixing holes

(b) Use of wedges when levelling a machine

Levelling bolt

Lock nut

Fixing bolt hole

Tapped hole in m/c base

Steel pad to prevent levelling bolt biting into the floor

(c) Use of levelling bolts

Fig. 11.6 Levelling a machine

Pinch bar

Wood block

(a) Using a pinch (crow) bar to raise a machine so that rollers can be placed under it

(b) Using a pinch (crow) bar to propel a machine mounted on rollers

Fig. 11.5 Use of a pinch (crow) bar

Test to be applied	Test diagram	Gauge and methods	Tolerances
Spindle Bore true and size to gauge (internal taper)	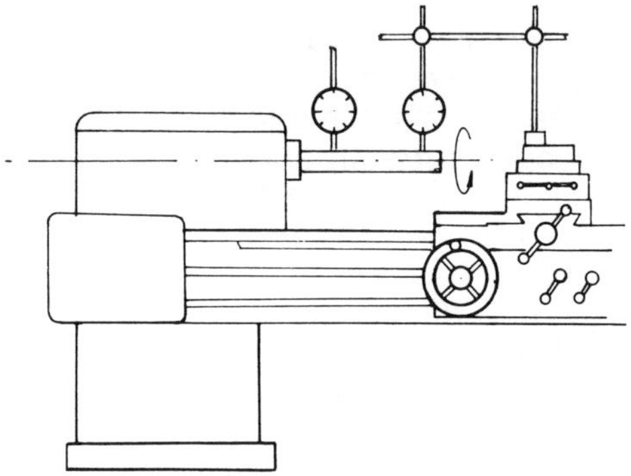	Mandrel 250 mm long, one end a gauge for spindle. Dial test indicator (D.T.I.) and stand	0·02 mm maximum eccentric error
Axis parallel with bed in a vertical plane		Stationary mandrel (as above). Dial test indicator and stand	0 to +0·02 mm per 250 mm from end of mandrel
Axis parallel with bed in a horizontal plane		Free end of mandrel inclined towards tool pressure	0 to 0·02 mm per 250 mm from end of mandrel

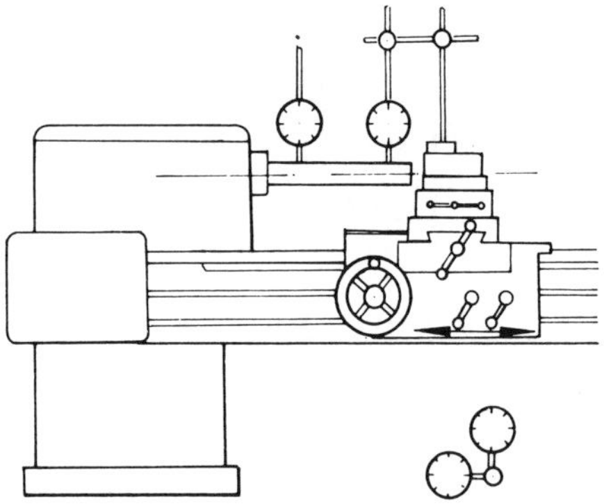

Fig. 11.7 Alignment tests for a centre lathe

Test to be applied	Test diagram	Gauge and methods	Tolerances
Saddle Movement of upper slide parallel with spindle. Vertical plane		Stationary mandrel. D.T.I. in tool post. Test over mandrel. Set at zero and traverse top slide by hand	0·02 mm in its movement
Movement of lower slide at 90°		D.T.I. in tool post. Test across straight edge on face plate	0 to 0·02 mm per ⌀ 250 mm concave only. D.T.I. reading to be minus at centre
Quill movement parallel with bed. Vertical plane		D.T.I. and stand. Test over quill which is clamped. Centre must rise	0 to 0·02 mm in its movement
Quill movement parallel with bed. Horizontal plane		As above. Test side of quill. Inclination towards tool pressure	0 to 0·01 mm in its movement

225

shows tests that are suitable for a centre lathe.

Preventative maintenance

As its name implies, preventative maintenance is the planned and regular servicing of a machine in accordance with the procedures laid down in the operator's manual in order to prevent expensive breakdowns. This servicing includes such items as:

1 lubrication,
2 adjustment of slideways,
3 adjustment of belts,
4 adjustment of brakes, clutches and safety devices.

Lubrication

The principles of lubrication have already been discussed in Chapter 2. The maintenance engineer is interested in the application of these principles to machines. For example, Fig. 11.8 shows a typical machine tool lubrication chart. This gives information on the points which need daily, weekly or monthly attention. This is essential to ensure the safe and efficient running of the machine. Only the lubricants recommended by the manufacturer should be used, as the use of inferior or incorrect lubricants can lead to rapid wear and even failure of the machine. In addition, the incorrect lubrication of the machine can invalidate the maker's guarantee.

The gear boxes are fitted with sight glasses and should be filled to the

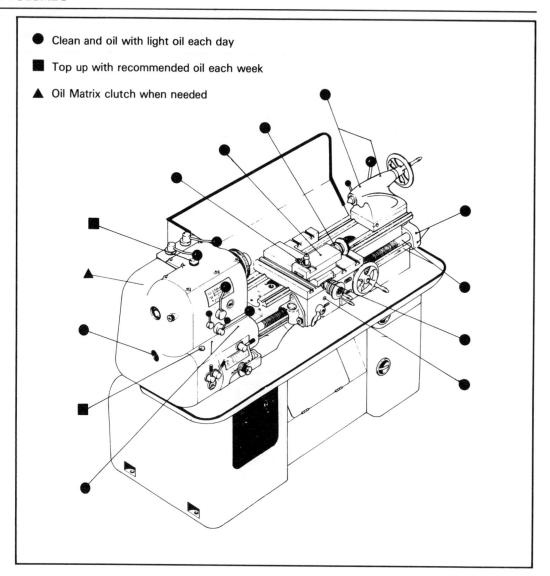

● Clean and oil with light oil each day

■ Top up with recommended oil each week

▲ Oil Matrix clutch when needed

Fig. 11.8 Lubrication chart

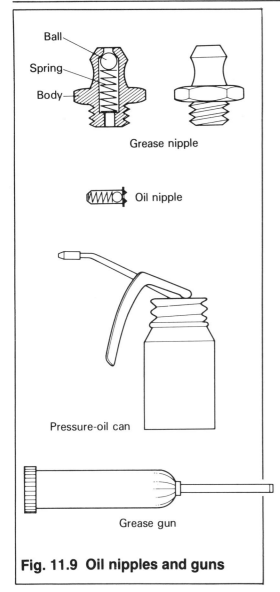

Fig. 11.9 Oil nipples and guns

correct level. It is bad practice to overfill a gear box, just as it is bad practice to let it run with insufficient oil. After the first 150 to 200 hours the gear boxes should be drained, flushed out with a suitable flushing oil and refilled with the correct grade of lubricating oil. This should be repeated half-yearly thereafter as oil not only deteriorates in use, but it can become contaminated with abrasive dust and moisture from the atmosphere.

The motor bearings should be checked periodically to ensure that they have an adequate supply of grease as recommended by the manufacturer. The bearings of the coolant pump and motor should also be checked at the same time. In this latter case a water-repellent grease should be used.

Some examples will now be given of the more common methods of lubrication found in the engineering workshop. Oil holes are rarely provided nowadays as they tend to clog up with dirt. Generally, some form of nipple is provided that only allows the oil and grease to be injected under pressure, a spring-loaded ball valve keeping out any dirt. They are generally charged by grease-guns, oil-guns and pressure oil-cans. This equipment is shown in Fig. 11.9.

In some cases the oil needs to be fed to the bearings in small quantities at regular intervals. Two ways of doing this are shown in Fig. 11.10. The wick feed oiler in Fig. 11.10(a) uses an absorbent wick – similar to a lamp-wick – to syphon the oil from the oil cup to the bearing. It also acts as a filter and stops

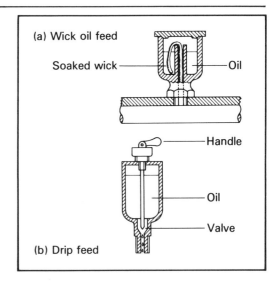

Fig. 11.10 Oilers

dirt getting into the bearing and damaging it. The drip feed oiler shown in Fig. 11.10(b) uses an adjustable needle valve to regulate the supply of oil to the bearing. A sight glass is usually provided so that the number of 'drips per minute' can be counted to check if the needle valve is correctly adjusted.

Another method of lubricating a slow running shaft and bearing is the 'chain' or 'ring' oiling system as shown in Fig. 11.11. The chain or ring rests loosely on the shaft and rotates with it, transferring oil from the oil well.

Where a large number of lubrication points have to be fed, it is not only time-wasting to feed them individually, there is always the chance that a vital nipple may be missed. Wherever

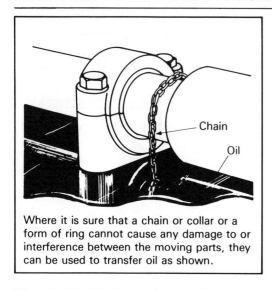

Where it is sure that a chain or collar or a form of ring cannot cause any damage to or interference between the moving parts, they can be used to transfer oil as shown.

Fig. 11.11 Chain or ring oil feed

possible, all the lubrication points should be piped to a single panel fed by a pump. This is known as 'one-shot' lubrication and an example of such a system is shown in Fig. 11.12(a).

Gearboxes are usually lubricated by a 'splash' system as shown in Fig. 11.12(b) or by an 'oil-gallery' as shown in Fig. 11.12(c). The gearboxes are generally filled by pouring direct from measuring cans. Sight glasses are provided in the wall of the gearbox to indicate the correct level.

The use of grease on machine tools is gradually diminishing as speeds increase. It is most commonly used on electric motor bearings. Its advantage is that only occasional application is required, e.g. only once a year. It is

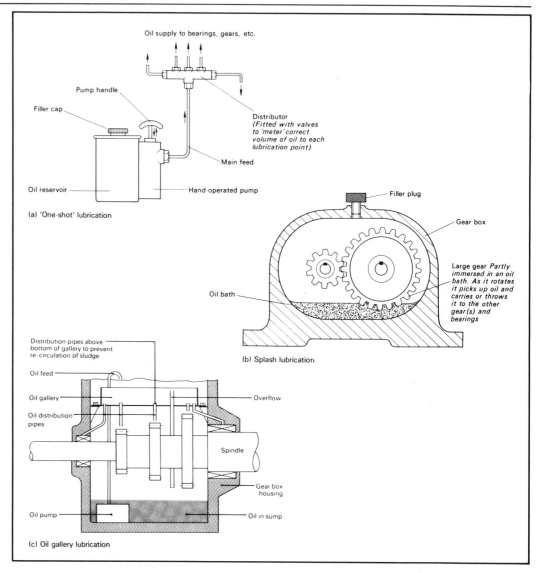

Fig. 11.12 Methods of lubrication

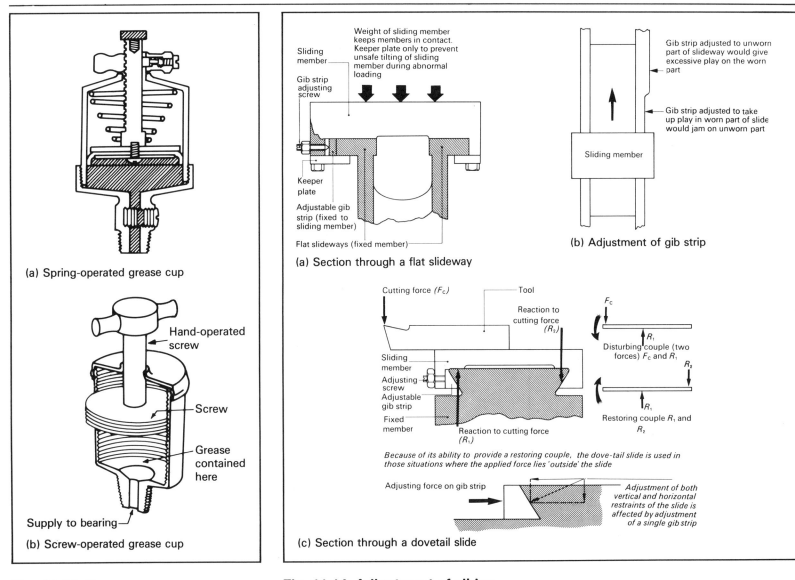

(a) Spring-operated grease cup

Weight of sliding member keeps members in contact. Keeper plate only to prevent unsafe tilting of sliding member during abnormal loading

Sliding member

Gib strip adjusting screw

Keeper plate

Adjustable gib strip (fixed to sliding member)

Flat slideways (fixed member)

(a) Section through a flat slideway

Gib strip adjusted to unworn part of slideway would give excessive play on the worn part

Gib strip adjusted to take up play in worn part of slide would jam on unworn part

Sliding member

(b) Adjustment of gib strip

Cutting force (F_c)

Tool

Reaction to cutting force (R_2)

Sliding member

Adjusting screw

Adjustable gib strip

Fixed member

Reaction to cutting force (R_1)

F_c

R_1

Disturbing couple (two forces) F_c and R_1

R_2

R_1

Restoring couple R_1 and R_2

Because of its ability to provide a restoring couple, the dove-tail slide is used in those situations where the applied force lies 'outside' the slide

Adjusting force on gib strip

Adjustment of both vertical and horizontal restraints of the slide is affected by adjustment of a single gib strip

(c) Section through a dovetail slide

Hand-operated screw

Screw

Grease contained here

Supply to bearing

(b) Screw-operated grease cup

Fig. 11.13 Grease cups

Fig. 11.14 Adjustment of slides

disastrous to use grease in the wrong bearing; if in doubt use oil.

As well as using grease-guns to charge grease nipples with lubricant, grease cups, shown in Fig. 11.13, can also be used. Two types of grease cup are shown. That in Fig. 11.13(a) relies upon spring pressure to feed the grease into the bearing, whilst Fig. 11.13(b) shows a screw feed system. This is more positive but relies upon the operator remembering to screw it down periodically.

Adjustment of slideways

Slideways are linear bearings. As well as being lubricated so that they slide easily, they must be adjusted so that they prevent movement in certain directions whilst offering the greatest possible ease of movement in other directions.

The flat slide.   This is shown in Fig. 11.14(a). Wear is taken up by adjusting the *gib strip*. Unfortunately most machine slides receive uneven wear and care has to be taken in adjusting the gib strip so that it does not jam on the unworn areas of the slide. If wear becomes too uneven the slideway has to be reground or scraped flat again (Fig. 11.14(b)).

The dovetail slide.   This is shown in Fig. 11.14(c). Adjustment of the gib strip simultaneously takes up horizontal and vertical components of wear. This type of slide is widely used on machine tools.

The vee slide.   This type of slide is self-adjusting for wear and is found on most modern lathe beds. Figure 11.15

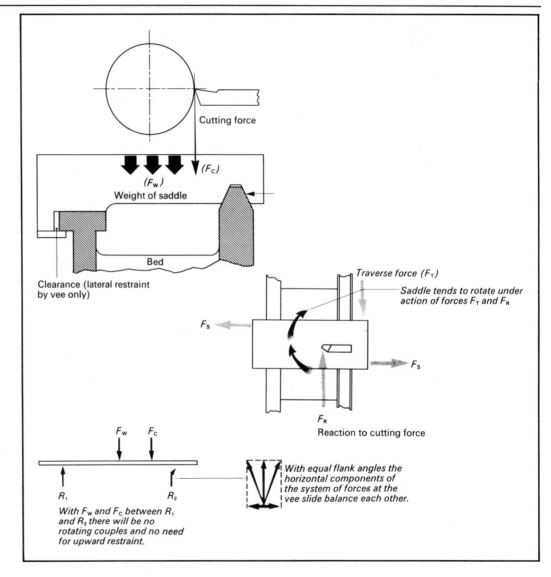

Fig. 11.15 The vee slide

shows a typical vee slide and flat slide combination. Two vee slides should never be used as it is not possible to make them perfectly parallel and so the slides would fight against each other in guiding the sliding carriage.

Adjustment of belt and chain drives

Belt drives are widely used to couple driving motors to machine tools. The principles of belt drives and some typical applications were considered in Chapter 2, together with some examples of tensioning devices. Figure 11.16(a) shows a further method of belt tensioning. Great care is essential when tensioning driving belts. Insufficient tension causes slip, overheating of the belt, and rapid wear or even failure; whilst excessive tension causes premature stretching of the belt and excessive wear on the bearings carrying the belt pulley. Figure 11.16(b) shows a flat belt drive. Flat belts are usually made of leather and are joined by 'lacing' the ends together. One such method of wire lacing is shown in Fig. 11.16(c). Flat belts require very careful setting up or they will continually run off the belt pulleys, which do not have flanges to keep the belt on, but are slightly domed in the middle. Such pulleys are often said to be 'crowned'. Leather belts should be regularly treated with a proprietory dressing to keep them supple and to prevent slip.

Chain drives are tensioned in the same way as belts. Since they do not

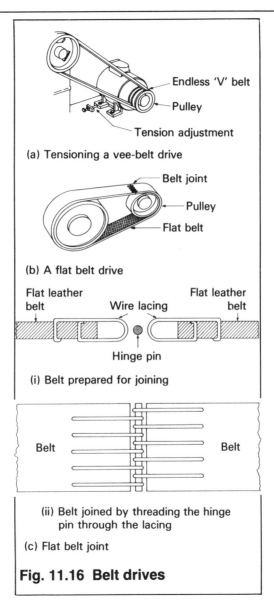

(a) Tensioning a vee-belt drive

Endless 'V' belt
Pulley
Tension adjustment

Belt joint
Pulley
Flat belt

(b) A flat belt drive

Flat leather belt — Wire lacing — Flat leather belt
Hinge pin

(i) Belt prepared for joining

Belt — Belt

(ii) Belt joined by threading the hinge pin through the lacing

(c) Flat belt joint

Fig. 11.16 Belt drives

slip, some slack can be left to prevent premature stretching and wear. However, excessive slackness results in the chain being thrown from its sprockets. Figure 11.17 shows a typical chain drive. Unlike belts, which are made from non-corrosive materials and can operate in hostile environments for long periods without attention, chains require regular lubrication and cleaning if exposed. If possible they should run in a chain case, not only for safety but to protect them from dust and dirt. The chain case should also contain an oil bath for the chain to pass through to keep it constantly lubricated.

Adjustment of brakes and clutches

Brakes are fitted to many machine tools so that they can be stopped quickly when the clutch is disengaged. Brakes are also fitted to prevent machine spindles turning whilst the work or cutters are mounted.

Clutches are used to engage and to disengage the driving motor and so control the starting and stopping of the machine. They are often interlinked with the brake mechanism. There are many types of clutch and brake mechanism and they must always be regularly checked for proper adjustment. A slipping clutch prevents the machine from operating properly and reduces its output and profitability. It also causes premature wear of the clutch plates. However a clutch that has been overtightened will 'nibble' and keep moving the machine slowly even when in the disengaged position. This is very dangerous as the operator may become trapped whilst setting work or taking measurements.

Since the operator's safety depends upon the correct operation of the brake and clutch of his machine, they should only be adjusted by a skilled and experienced maintenance engineer or under his supervision.

Corrective maintenance

In addition to the planned maintenance already discussed, machines should be periodically taken out of service for more extensive maintenance. Figure 11.18 shows a hydraulic pump which has been removed for servicing. Such maintenance includes:
1 the replacement of worn belts,
2 the replacement of worn brake linings and clutch plates,
3 the replacement of worn lead screws and nuts. (Figure 11.19).

The maintenance engineer should also listen for unusual noises coming from the machine so that faults can be corrected by replacing worn components before a major breakdown occurs. For instance a worn gear may shed a tooth which can fall between other gears in a gear box. These in turn have their teeth stripped off and there is a major failure resulting in damaged gears, bearings and bent shafts having to be replaced at very high cost not only in labour and parts but also in lost production. Therefore worn parts

should be replaced before they become liable to fail. Where people's live are at stake, as in road vehicles and aircraft, corrective maintenance is mandatory and key components have, by law, to be replaced before they reach such a dangerous condition that they are liable to failure. Maintenance engineers looking after such equipment and the more dangerous machines used in industry are responsible for the lives of their workmates and should take their duties very seriously.

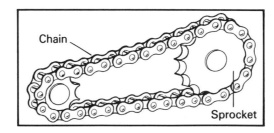

Fig. 11.17 A chain drive

Unplanned maintenance (breakdown)

No matter how well a machine is maintained it will, from time to time, break down. Some of the causes of breakdown are given below.

Metal fatigue. Although metals seem strong, solid and indestructible, they can get 'tired' and fail by fatigue – usually at a sharp corner. This is one reason why engineering designers usually ask for corners to be radiused. Vibration and stress reversals can cause

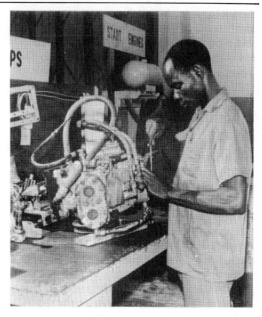

Fig. 11.18 A fitter servicing a hydraulic pump

metals to become fatigued more quickly. This is why it is important that moving parts should be balanced and run smoothly.

Operator error. Another cause of breakdown is rough and careless use by the operator. A sudden application of the brake or sudden engagement of the clutch can cause undue wear. Overloading the machine or careless setting causing the cutter or work to jam is another cause of breakdown. Overtightening the work holding devices by using a hammer or lengthening any handle or levers with

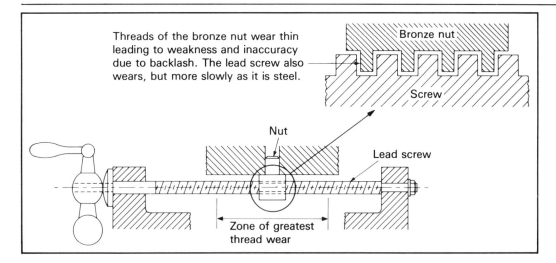

Threads of the bronze nut wear thin leading to weakness and inaccuracy due to backlash. The lead screw also wears, but more slowly as it is steel.

Bronze nut

Screw

Nut

Lead screw

Zone of greatest thread wear

Fig. 11.19 Worn lead screw and nut

tubing can also overstress the components concerned and cause breakage.

Seized bearings. These occur when the lubrication system fails either by lack of attention or by blockage of an oilway due to dirt getting into the system.

Whatever the cause of a breakdown it invariably involves the partial dismantling of the machine and this, in turn, can mean the removal of heavy components and sub-assemblies.

Dismantling a machine

Before commencing work on a machine make sure that it is electrically isolated so that it cannot be accidentally started. If the isolating switch cannot be locked in the off position, the fitter should

remove the fuses and keep them in his pocket or lock them away where only he has access to them. In the case of prime-movers, the ignition system and/or fuel system should be disconnected before commencing work.

Except for small components and sub-assemblies, mechanical lifting aids should be used when dismantling a machine. Apart from preventing personal strain and injury, there is less likelihood of damage to the machine when a lifting aid is used. A number of such aids are shown in Fig. 11.20.

1 The ratchet jack shown in Fig. 11.20(a) can be used for lifting machines. The 'toe' of the jack which can be inserted into a barring hole in the base of the machine is also useful.

2 In many workshops small mobile

hoists are available and one is shown in Fig. 11.20(b).

3 The 'pul-lift' shown in Fig. 11.20(c) is useful both for moving heavy components as well as lifting them.

When using lifting tackle care must be taken to ensure that it is not overloaded. The safe working load (SWL) must be clearly marked on each piece of equipment and care must be taken not to exceed the stated value. When using slings and chains to attach the load to the hoist, the precautions shown in Fig. 11.21 must be observed.

During the lifting of large pieces of machinery using a crane, the maintenance engineer must give clear signals to the crane driver. The international signals recommended for slingers are shown in Fig. 11.22. The precautions that must be taken when using a crane to lift and move heavy objects are summarised in Table 11.1.

When repairing large pieces of equipment, it is often necessary to work underneath it. It is highly dangerous to work under equipment that is suspended from a hoist, and the assembly should be supported at a convenient height on trestles as shown in Fig. 11.23(a). With the increasing use of motorised transport in and around factories, many types of motor vehicle have to be regularly serviced and repaired. It is very dangerous to work under any vehicle when it is only supported on jacks. The vehicle should be supported on axle stands, as shown in Fig. 11.23(b), before the maintenance engineer gets under it.

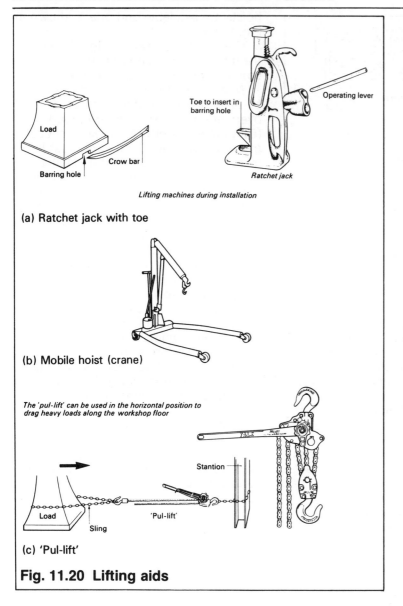

(a) Ratchet jack with toe

(b) Mobile hoist (crane)

The 'pul-lift' can be used in the horizontal position to drag heavy loads along the workshop floor

(c) 'Pul-lift'

Fig. 11.20 Lifting aids

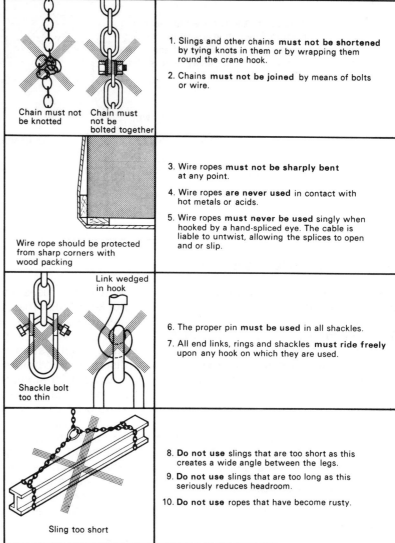

1. Slings and other chains **must not be shortened** by tying knots in them or by wrapping them round the crane hook.

2. Chains **must not be joined** by means of bolts or wire.

3. Wire ropes **must not be sharply bent** at any point.

4. Wire ropes **are never used** in contact with hot metals or acids.

5. Wire ropes **must never be used** singly when hooked by a hand-spliced eye. The cable is liable to untwist, allowing the splices to open and or slip.

6. The proper pin **must be used** in all shackles.

7. All end links, rings and shackles **must ride freely** upon any hook on which they are used.

8. **Do not use** slings that are too short as this creates a wide angle between the legs.

9. **Do not use** slings that are too long as this seriously reduces headroom.

10. **Do not use** ropes that have become rusty.

Fig. 11.21 Care and use of slings

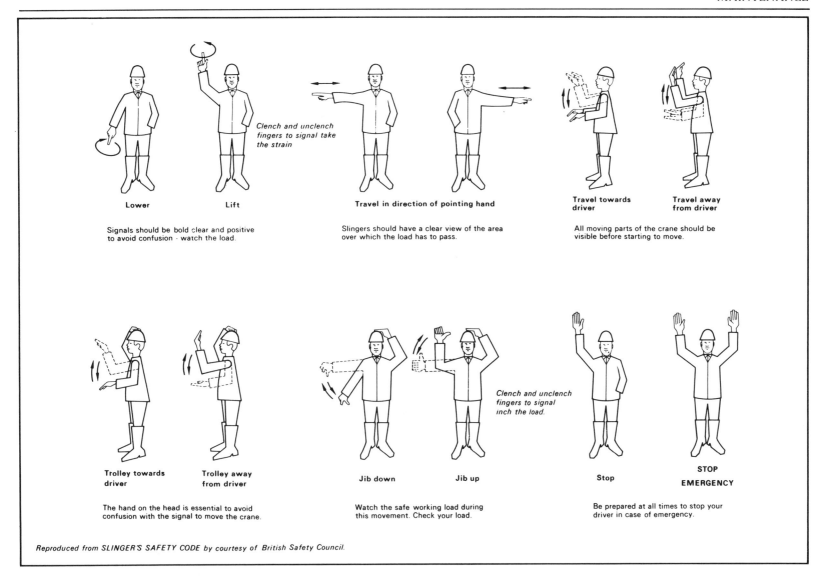

Reproduced from SLINGER'S SAFETY CODE by courtesy of British Safety Council.

Fig. 11.22 Slingers' signals

Table 11.1 Precautions when using hoists and cranes

When loading...

Slings should be protected from sharp edged loads by packing soft wood or other suitable material between the load and the sling – bricks are not a suitable packing.

Ensure that the load is evenly distributed to avoid excessive stresses on one side of a sling.

Avoid letting the load rest on a wire rope as it may crush strands and render the rope unsafe.

Reduce the possibility of a bogie tipping up by placing the load in the centre.

Before lifting...

Ensure that the load is securely slung before taking the lift.

Always see that the crane hook is centrally placed over the load to prevent swinging when the load is being raised.

Take your hands away from chains and ropes before the crane takes the load.

See that the load is free from lifting.

Give warning to persons to keep clear of the load.

During lifting...

Signals shown in Fig. 11.22 must be given by the one person responsible for the lift, and nobody else.

Hooks slings not in use should not be carried on the carrying hook, as these may cause the sling carrying the load to ride on the nose of the hook.

Never ride on a crane load, nor allow any other person to do so.

Never allow the load to be carried over the heads of other persons.

Chains, slings, hooks or loads should never be dragged along the floor.

When unloading...

Make sure that you have a firm foundation for your stack, and make provision for the removal of slings without disturbing the stack.

Stack material securely and make provision for safe access for its subsequent removal.

Vehicles should be loaded in such a manner that there are no dangerous projections, and the load is safe for transport.

Vehicles should not be overloaded.

Material should not be stacked within three feet of any moving object or crane track.

When dismantling a machine the parts should be placed in clean trays on the bench. The parts should be laid out systematically and each part should be carefully examined for wear and damage. Exposed parts should be washed off in paraffin to remove congealed dirt, grease and oil so that any cracks or other defects can be easily seen.

Pulleys and wheels are removed from shafts using an extractor of the type shown in Fig. 11.24(a). Bushes can be driven out using a drift (Fig. 11.24(b)) or an extractor as shown in Fig. 11.24(c).

Machine repairs

Wherever possible, machines should be repaired using replacement components supplied by the original manufacturer. This ensures that the repaired machine is restored to a satisfactory level of operating efficiency. Sometimes it is not possible to obtain replacement parts and new parts have to be made locally or the old parts refurbished so that they can be re-used. The fitting of keys and keyways has already been dealt with in Chapter 5.

Treatment of worn shafts. There are various ways of reclaiming a worn shaft without manufacturing a new one.

1 Regrind the bearing journals to remove scoring and ovality. This obviously reduces the diameter of the shaft, but this can be compensated for by making new bushes, bored to fit the reground shaft.

2 Build up the shaft by depositing weld

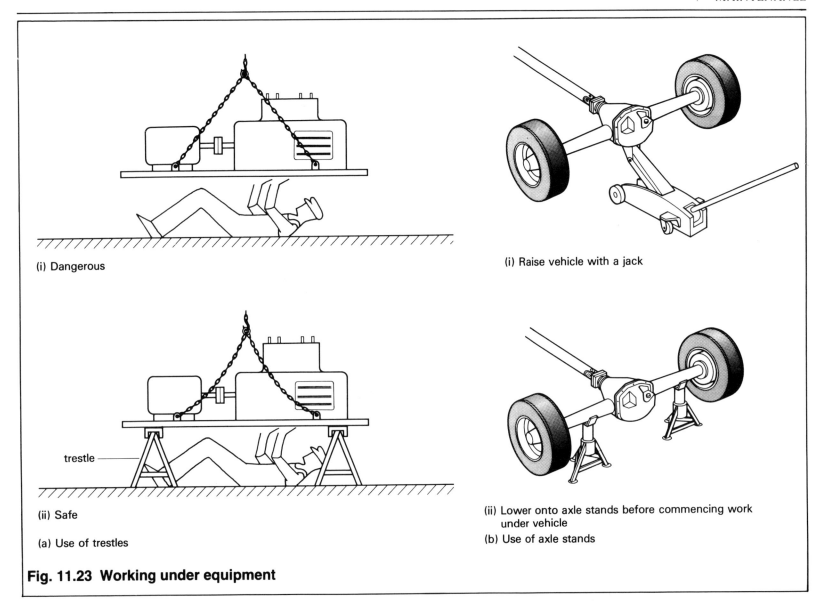

(i) Dangerous

(i) Raise vehicle with a jack

trestle

(ii) Safe

(a) Use of trestles

(ii) Lower onto axle stands before commencing work under vehicle

(b) Use of axle stands

Fig. 11.23 Working under equipment

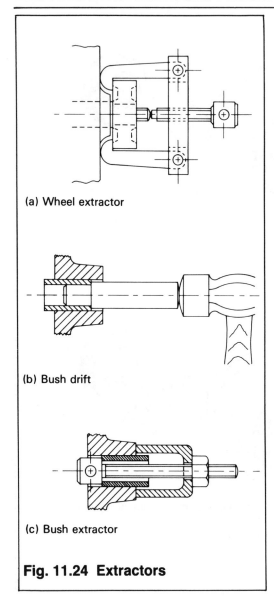

(a) Wheel extractor

(b) Bush drift

(c) Bush extractor

Fig. 11.24 Extractors

metal at the worn surfaces as shown in Fig. 11.25. After welding, the shaft is remachined to size. This is used where the shaft runs in ball or roller bearings and must be built up to fit a standard size bearing.

3 Metalising, in which molten metal is sprayed onto the worn surface, is an alternative to welding. This gives better control and less machining is required than for welding. Unfortunately special spraying equipment is required.

4 Electro-plating is also used. Hard nickel and hard chromium deposits can be very effective on surfaces subject to heavy wear. The deposit is not even and subsequent grinding is required.

Treatment of worn bearings.   There is not so much latitude in repairing bearings. Ball and roller bearings cannot be repaired, but must be replaced by new ones. Plain bearings can be reclaimed to a limited extent.

1 Split bearings can take up a certain amount of wear by removing metal from the joint faces of the bearing cap so as to close the bearing down on the shaft. The bearing is then scraped into the shaft using prussian blue to indicate the high (tight) spots.

2 White metal bearings may be relined as shown in Fig. 11.26. After melting out the old metal, the shell is scraped clean and slightly roughened to act as a key. The shell is mounted in a fixture as shown in Fig. 11.26. Its inner surface is fluxed and the shell is warmed to avoid chilling the cast metal and preventing proper adhesion. The molten

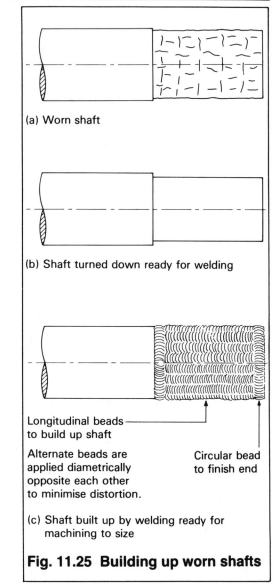

(a) Worn shaft

(b) Shaft turned down ready for welding

Longitudinal beads to build up shaft

Alternate beads are applied diametrically opposite each other to minimise distortion.

Circular bead to finish end

(c) Shaft built up by welding ready for machining to size

Fig. 11.25 Building up worn shafts

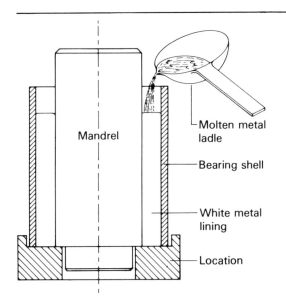

Fig. 11.26 Relining a white metal bearing

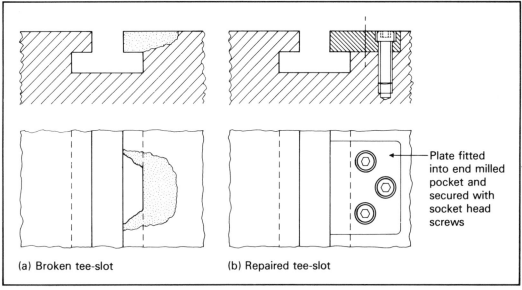

(a) Broken tee-slot   (b) Repaired tee-slot

Fig. 11.27 Repairing a casting

white metal is poured into the gap between the bearing shell and the mandrel.

Patching damage. Figure 11.27 shows a broken tee slot in a machine table. It may be rebuilt with weld metal and remachined or, as shown in Fig. 11.27(b), a patch may be inserted and screwed into position after previously milling a pocket to receive it.

The above examples of machine repairs are in no way exhaustive but are just a few indications as to how the imaginative maintenance engineer can use his skill and ingenuity to keep the machines in his care operational.

The re-assembly of machines

When re-assembling machines every care must be taken to avoid damage to the machined surfaces.

1 Only soft faced mallets must be used, or soft metal drifts between the component and the hammer.

2 Bearings and bushes must be started square with the hole into which they are to be inserted.

3 Fitted surfaces must be wiped perfectly clean and checked for burrs.

4 Undue force must be avoided and a suitable lubricant should be used.

5 The free-running and correct alignment between components should be checked at every stage.

6 The lubrication system should be checked before the machine is restarted.

7 Finally the supply to the machine is reconnected and it is given a trial run.

Sometimes it is necessary to fit a direct coupled motor to a pump or compressor using flanged couplings as shown in Fig. 11.28(a). It is essential that the motor shaft and the shaft of the machine it is driving are in exact alignment. The height of the shafts can be adjusted by placing shims (thin pieces of steel fail) under the motor or the driven unit. It is also important to check that the flange faces are parallel using feeler gauges as shown in Fig. 11.28(b). Alternatively flexible couplings may be used as shown in Fig. 11.28(c) and although these are less critical than solid couplings any major error of alignment causes vibration and rapid wear of the coupling.

Many modern machines have hydraulic and pneumatic systems as well as low pressure coolant systems. Therefore the maintenance engineer must be familiar with some basic techniques of pipe-filling. Figure 11.29 shows some typical screwed fittings and a screwed joint. The thread on the pipe is tapered (1 in 16) so that it will lock into the parallel thread of the fitting. A jointing compound is used to seal the joint. Although this type of joint is easy to make, it has the disadvantage that valves and other fittings cannot be readily removed from the pipe run for maintenance or replacement. Further, if the pipe is cranked a large amount of room is required to swing it round as it is screwed home.

To overcome these limitations a number of 'unions' have to be left in the pipework as shown in Fig. 11.30(a). These allow the joints to be made without rotating the pipes. However, the pipes have to be sprung by the length of the cones to separate the pipes and, for large and rigid pipes, flanged joints are used. Figure 11.30(b) shows a high pressure flanged joint, whilst Fig. 11.30(c) shows a simpler, low pressure flanged joint.

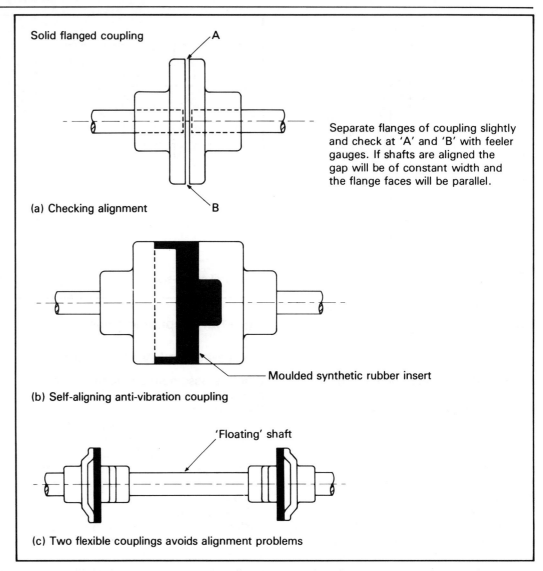

Solid flanged coupling

Separate flanges of coupling slightly and check at 'A' and 'B' with feeler gauges. If shafts are aligned the gap will be of constant width and the flange faces will be parallel.

(a) Checking alignment

Moulded synthetic rubber insert

(b) Self-aligning anti-vibration coupling

'Floating' shaft

(c) Two flexible couplings avoids alignment problems

Fig. 11.28 Couplings

Compression joints are becoming increasingly used in place of screwed joints for smaller pipe sizes. Not only do they save time in installation, as the pipe does not have to be threaded, but lighter gauge pipe can be used since it is not weakened by the screw thread. (See Fig. 11.31(a).) Originally compression joints were made from brass and limited to copper pipework and pressures of 1 MN/m² (10 bar). More recently, compression joints have become available in steel for pressures up to 40 MN/m² (400 bar). Figure 11.31(b) shows two typical compression joints.

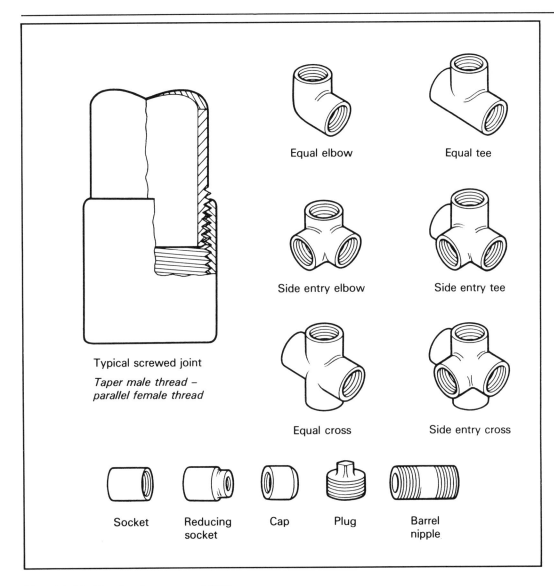

Equal elbow

Equal tee

Side entry elbow

Side entry tee

Equal cross

Side entry cross

Typical screwed joint

Taper male thread – parallel female thread

Socket

Reducing socket

Cap

Plug

Barrel nipple

Fig. 11.29 Typical screwed fittings

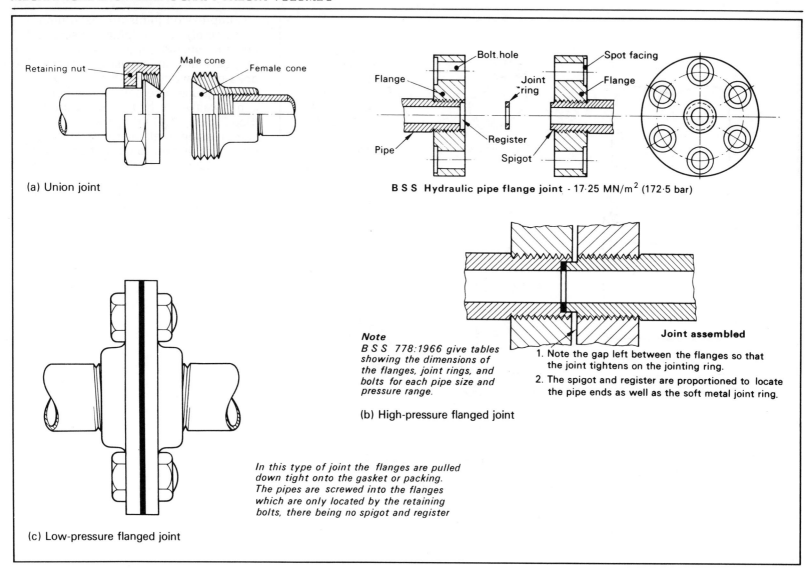

(a) Union joint

B S S Hydraulic pipe flange joint - 17·25 MN/m^2 (172·5 bar)

Note

B S S 778:1966 give tables showing the dimensions of the flanges, joint rings, and bolts for each pipe size and pressure range.

(b) High-pressure flanged joint

Joint assembled

1. Note the gap left between the flanges so that the joint tightens on the jointing ring.
2. The spigot and register are proportioned to locate the pipe ends as well as the soft metal joint ring.

In this type of joint the flanges are pulled down tight onto the gasket or packing. The pipes are screwed into the flanges which are only located by the retaining bolts, there being no spigot and register

(c) Low-pressure flanged joint

Fig. 11.30 Pipe couplings

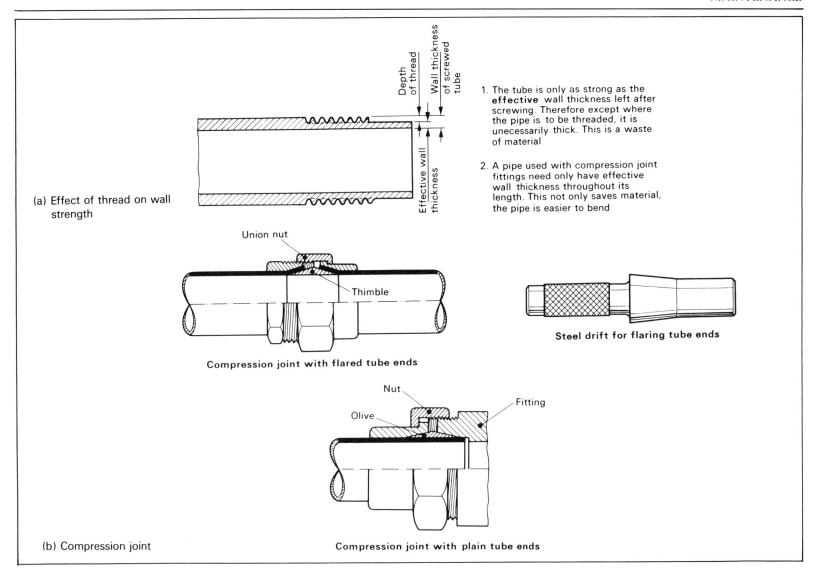

Depth of thread

Wall thickness of screwed tube

Effective wall thickness

(a) Effect of thread on wall strength

1. The tube is only as strong as the **effective** wall thickness left after screwing. Therefore except where the pipe is to be threaded, it is unecessarily thick. This is a waste of material

2. A pipe used with compression joint fittings need only have effective wall thickness throughout its length. This not only saves material, the pipe is easier to bend

Union nut

Thimble

Compression joint with flared tube ends

Steel drift for flaring tube ends

Nut

Olive

Fitting

Compression joint with plain tube ends

(b) Compression joint

Fig. 11.31 Compression joints

12.   Forging and heat treatment

The forging process

Second to casting, forging is the oldest process used to form metal components. It may be described briefly as the manipulation of metals by hammering, squeezing and bending after they have been rendered more plastic by heating them above their temperature of re-crystallisation (see *Mechanical Engineering Craft Theory and Related Studies: Part 1*).

Some metals that may be forged to shape are listed in Fig. 12.1 together with the range of temperatures within which forging may take place. Overheating may cause weakness due to grain growth and oxidation of the crystal boundaries (burning). Forging below the minimum temperature may cause work-hardening and cracking. Only materials that are *malleable* may be forged.

Generally, the properties of a material are improved with forging and show a notable increase in toughness. The improvement in toughness is dependent upon two factors:
1 grain refinement (reduction in crystal size);
2 grain orientation.

If a forging is cut in half and etched so that its grain structure becomes visible, then it will be seen that after forging the grain flow follows the profile of the component. This orientation of the grain of a forging to its profile is shown in Fig. 12.2 which compares a gear blank machined from the bar with a forging. Metal – like wood – breaks more easily along the grain than across it, so that teeth cut in the forged gear blank will be stronger than those cut in the blank machined from a bar.

The raw material for forging is either bar stock or billets cut from bar stock. This is obviously more expensive than

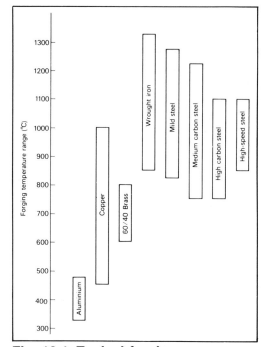

Fig. 12.1 Typical forging temperatures

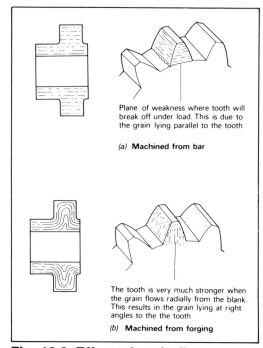

Plane of weakness where tooth will break off under load. This is due to the grain lying parallel to the tooth

(a) **Machined from bar**

The tooth is very much stronger when the grain flows radially from the blank. This results in the grain lying at right angles to the the tooth

(b) **Machined from forging**

Fig. 12.2 Effect of grain flow on component strength

the raw material for casting, and forging is usually only resorted to where the special strength characteristics of a forging are required or where the forging is simple in shape and can be made from standard tooling. The special tooling required for the drop-forging process (see p. 247) only becomes economical for the quantity production of such components as motor-car connecting-rods, crankshafts, etc. Large components, such as the steam drums for power station boilers, are forged from cast ingots.

Small components may be forged by hand or with the aid of small power hammers. This is known as blacksmithing. Large components are formed by the same basic processes, but the force to make the metal flow is provided by a hydraulic press or a steam hammer. Where repetitive forging is required, as in the manufacture of motor-car components, pre-formed dies are used in drop-stamping and upset forging machines.

The basic forging operations are: drawing down; upsetting or jumping up; punching or piercing; cutting with hot or cold chisels; swaging; bending and twisting; forge welding. These operations were described in detail in *Mechanical Engineering Craft Theory and Related Studies: Part 1*.

Forging large components

The pneumatic hammer shown in Fig. 12.3 is used to extend the work of blacksmithing to larger work beyond the

Fig. 12.3 Pneumatic hammer

scope of the hand hammer. The aircompressor is built into the machine body and the ram is capable of giving single or repeated blows.

For even larger work the steam hammer shown in Fig. 12.4 is used. In older hammers the steam was only used to raise the *tup* and the forging blow was delivered by the tup dropping under the action of gravity. However, modern hammers are *double-acting*, that is, steam is used not only to raise the tup but also to drive it down again and deliver a greater blow. Standard forging tools such as swages and fullers may be fitted to the tup and the anvil of the hammer, as well as simple closed dies (p. 247).

The sharp blow of any type of hammer tends to modify the grain structure of the forging more at its surface than at its centre. Thus, hammers are unsuitable for forgings of considerable cross-sectional thickness. For the largest forgings, which may have a mass of 200 tonnes, the hydraulic forging press is used, as shown in Fig. 12.5(a). The ponderous strength of these huge machines is an awe-inspiring sight as they slowly squeeze the white-hot steel to size under a closing force of many meganewtons. (Equivalent to crushing the metal under the combined weight of several thousand medium-sized motor cars.) The slow squeeze of the hydraulic press allows time for the metal to flow internally throughout the mass of the forging.

Very heavy work is carried on a porter

Fig. 12.4 Steam hammer

(a) Hydraulic press

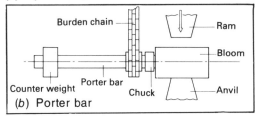

(b) Porter bar

Fig. 12.5 Hydraulic forging press
(This particular example is an 8 000 tonne
multi-stage free-forging press, designed by
Davy-Loewy Ltd, Sheffield, and manufactured
by Kobe Steel Ltd, Japan, for their own forge).

Fig. 12.6 Drop-stamp

bar as shown in Fig. 12.5(b). The porter
bar and counterweight, balance the
work under the ram of the press. In turn,
the porter bar is supported by the
burden chain. This not only supports the
combined mass of counterweight,
porter bar and work, but rotates them as
well so that all sides of the metal may be
forged.

Closed die forging

Where the quantity production of
components is required, as in the
motor-car industry, closed-die forging is
used. In place of the general smithying
tools described earlier in this chapter,
formed dies are used to produce the
finished component. The dies may be
closed by a hydraulic or mechanical
press, but usually a *drop-stamp* or
drop-hammer may be used. Figure 12.6
shows a typical drop-stamp used for
closed-die forging.

Figure 12.7 shows a section through a
pair of drop-forging dies. To ensure
complete filling of the die cavity the hot
blank is slightly larger in volume than
the finished forging. As the dies close,
the surplus metal is forced out into the
flash gutter through the flash land. The
flash land offers a constriction to the
flow of the surplus metal and holds it
back in the die cavity to ensure
complete filling. It also ensures that the
flash is thinnest adjacent to the
component being forged. This results in
a neat, thin flash line being left after the
flash has been trimmed off. The flash
land should be kept as short as possible
otherwise the dies may fail to close. The
rapping faces ensure that the
component being forged is the correct
thickness when the dies are completely
closed. The sharp 'rap' of the hardened
surfaces coming into contact tells the
hammer driver that the operation is
complete. The dies are given a 7° taper,
or draught, so that the forging can be
easily removed. An example of forging

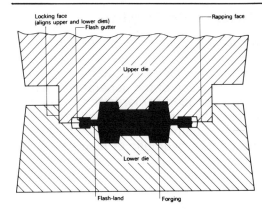

Fig. 12.7 Closed-forging die

dies and the component they produce is shown in Fig. 12.8.

Upset forging

Figure 12.9 shows an upset forging machine. Unlike the processes described so far, the header moves horizontally and strikes the stock bar end on, to force it into a pair of split dies. Figure 12.10 shows the principle of an upset forging operation. It will be seen that the bar stock is fed into the machine after being heated to the correct temperature. It is then gripped between split dies which prevent it from moving. These dies are closed by means of a crank or cam-operated toggle mechanism. A crank-operated header then moves the punch forward against the heated end of the bar stock and forces it into the cavity formed either in the gripping dies or partly in the dies and partly in the heading punch. This

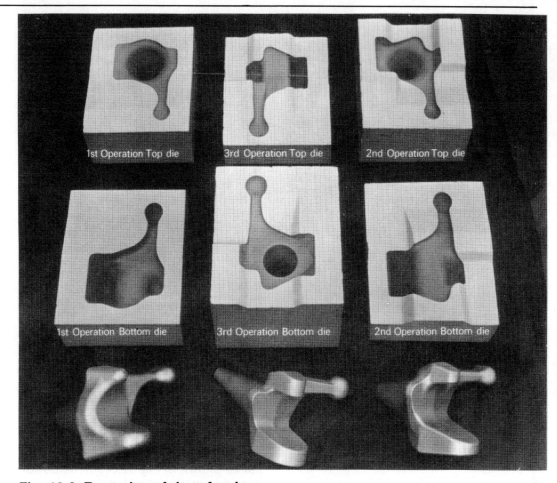

Fig. 12.8 Examples of drop forging

process is used to produce high-tensile bolt blanks, motor-car engine valve blanks, small cluster gear blanks and similar components.

Cooling curves

The heat treatment of carbon steels was introduced in *Mechanical Engineering Craft Theory and Related Studies: Part 1*, where it was stated that the metal had

Fig. 12.9 Upset forging machine

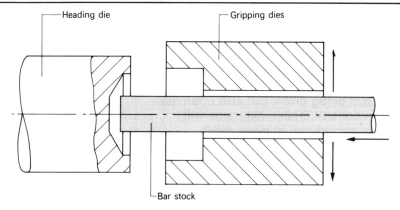

(a) **Gripping dies open whilst stock is fed in**

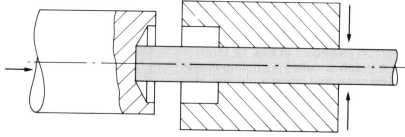

(b) **Gripping die close and heading die moves against stock**

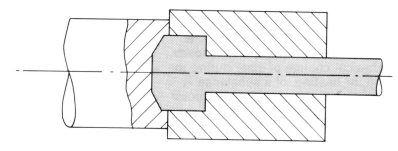

(c) **Heading dies upsets stock to fill die cavity**

Fig. 12.10 Heading dies

249

to be heated to various critical temperatures before cooling quickly or slowly depending upon the properties required. Diagrams were also introduced which showed that the temperature depended not only on the treatment being given, but also upon the carbon content. These diagrams will now be considered in more depth.

Most substances can exist in the gaseous, liquid or solid phase, depending upon their temperature. Water can exist as a gas or vapour (steam) if it is sufficiently hot; as a liquid; and as a solid (ice) if it is sufficiently cold.

If water is raised to its boiling point and allowed to cool slowly, the change in temperature with time can be plotted as a graph as shown in Fig. 12.11(a). Such a graph is called a cooling curve. It will be seen that when a change of state occurs (such as liquid water to solid ice) there is a short pause or *arrest point* in the cooling process. An arrest point occurs because the substance absorbs or gives out latent heat. Latent heat is the heat energy required to produce a change of state in a substance at a constant temperature. Phase changes can also occur in solids.

A physical change of state during the cooling, or heating, of a substance is always accompanied by an arrest point in the cooling or heating curve.

The cooling curve shown in Fig. 12.11(a) is typical of a pure substance. Plain carbon steels consist of compounds and solutions of iron and carbon as well as pure iron, and to

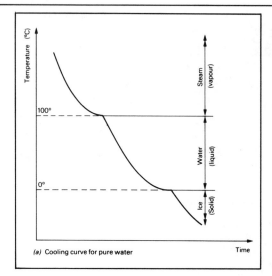

(a) Cooling curve for pure water

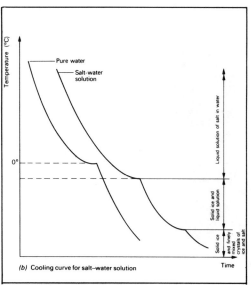

(b) Cooling curve for salt–water solution

Fig. 12.11 Cooling curves

understand the iron-carbon equilibrium diagram the arguments presented for the cooling curve of water must now be applied to a solution.

A suitable solution is that of domestic table salt (sodium chloride) in water. Figure 12.11(b) shows the cooling curve for pure water compared with the cooling curve for a salt–water solution for the temperature range covering the liquid and solid phases. It will be seen that the salt–water solution has two arrest points and that both these are below the freezing point of water.

A salt–water solution has a lower freezing point than pure water and at 0 °C no change of state occurs. However, as cooling continues, droplets of pure water separate out from the solution and immediately change into ice particles. This occurs at the upper arrest point, which is not usually too well defined, and the process of separation continues as the temperature of the remaining solution is further reduced. Thus, as the temperature continues to fall, more and more water separates out and freezes causing the concentration of the remaining salt–water to increase. When the lower arrest point is reached, even the concentrated salt–water solution freezes and no liquid phase is left. The solid so formed consists of a mixture of fine crystals of pure water (ice) and fine crystals of salt.

If the experiment is repeated several times using stronger and weaker salt–water solutions the family of cooling curves shown in Fig. 12.12

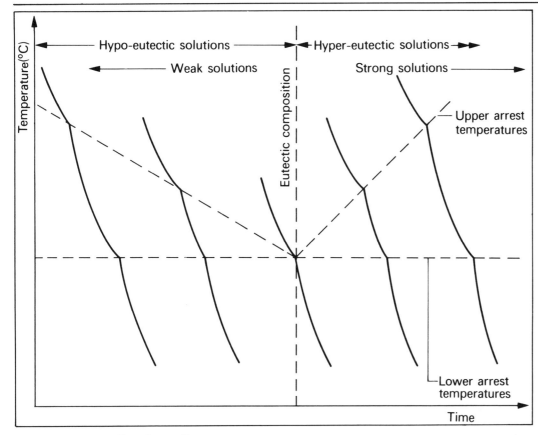

Fig. 12.12 Family of cooling curves

shows some interesting trends.
1 The temperature of the lower arrest point remains constant.
2 The temperature of the upper arrest point falls as the concentration of the solution increases until a point is reached where the temperatures of the upper and lower arrest points coincide.
3 The ratio of solid to liquid at the point

where the temperatures coincide is referred to as a *eutectic*. Solutions with a lower concentration of solid to liquid are referred to as *hypo-eutectic* solutions. Solutions with a higher concentration of solid to liquid are referred to as *hyper-eutectic* solutions.
4 When the concentration of the solution increases beyond that of the

eutectic composition the temperature of the upper arrest point rises once more.

Since water separates out as ice crystals between the arrest points of hypo-eutectic solutions, and since salt separates out between the arrest points of hyper-eutectic solutions, the remaining solution is always of a constant concentration; this concentration is the same as for the eutectic solution. Figure 12.12 is called a thermal equilibrium diagram since excess water or salt is rejected from the solution to maintain a eutectic balance. The dotted lines in Fig. 12.12 resemble the outline of the diagrams used for the heat treatment of plain carbon steels.

The iron−carbon equilibrium diagram (steel section)

In the equilibrium diagram for a common salt solution (Fig. 12.12), the arrest points were associated with changes from liquid to solid. However, such a diagram can also apply to changes in the crystal structure of an already solid material such as steel. Figure 12.13 shows the *steel section* of the iron-carbon equilibrium diagram below about 1200 °C.

The equivalent of the eutectic solution for salt and water is represented, in Fig. 12.13, as an alloy of 0·83 per cent carbon in iron. Since this is not a true eutectic it is referred to as the *eutectoid* composition for plain carbon steels. As previously discussed, plain carbon steels with a carbon

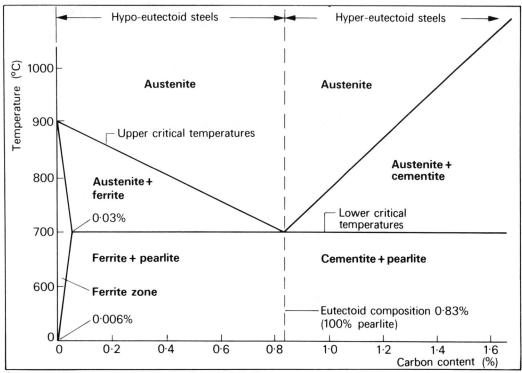

Fig. 12.13 Iron–carbon equilibrium diagram (steel section)

content lower than 0·83 per cent are referred to as hypo-eutectoid steels. Similarly, plain carbon steels with a carbon content greater than 0·83 per cent are referred to as hyper-eutectoid steels.

It will be seen that Fig. 12.13 is built up of two substances: iron and iron carbide which, in turn, form three structures. Iron and iron carbide can form many different structures. Figure 12.13 is built up from the following alloys.

Ferrite This is commercially pure iron and is, in practice, a very weak solid solution of carbon (0·006 per cent at room temperature) in iron. Ferrite is soft, ductile and relatively weak.

Cementite This is the name that engineers and metallurgists give to iron carbide. It is very hard and brittle. All the carbon present in steel is combined with iron to form iron carbide.

Pearlite This is a eutectoid alloy of ferrite and cementite. The two constituents form a structure that is

laminated like plywood. Under the microscope these crystals have a pearly sheen from which they get their name. Pearlite crystals always contain 0·83 per cent carbon and form the toughest structure present in a plain carbon steel.

Austenite This is a strong solution of carbon in iron. Usually it exists only above the upper critical temperatures for plain carbon steels. The three previous constituents and structures all change to austenite by the time the upper critical temperatures are reached. Similarly, on cooling, the austenite always changes back to ferrite, cementite and pearlite by the time the lower critical temperature is reached.

The effects of cooling the solid solution of austenite to below the upper critical temperatures will now be considered . It will be seen from Fig. 12.13 that below the upper critical temperatures the austenite commences to change back into ferrite, pearlite and cementite. The similarity with the effects described on p. 250, when the salt–water solution was cooled, will immediately become apparent.

Eutectoid steels (0·83 per cent carbon) Just as a eutectic solution changes from liquid to solid without an intermediate (semi-liquid) phase, so austenite changes directly into pearlite at the eutectoid composition of 0·83 per cent carbon. The excess carbon always forms iron carbide upon precipitation, leaving the rest of the iron present as ferrite. Thus, there is the simultaneous formation of ferrite and cementite (iron carbide), giving the fine-grained distribution which is pearlite.

Hypo-eutectoid steels   Below the upper critical temperature ferrite always separates out first in hypo-eutectoid steels, leaving the austenite at the 0·83 per cent (eutectoid) concentration. At the lower critical temperature the remaining austenite changes into pearlite, so that the final solid is ferrite and pearlite. This is similar to the process of cooling the weak solution of salt–water described on p. 251.

Hyper-eutectoid steels   Similarly for hyper-eutectoid steels, the excess carbon separates out first, as the temperature drops below the upper critical temperature, and immediately forms cementite (iron carbide). This leaves the austenite at the 0·83 per cent (eutectoid) concentration and, as it cools to the lower critical temperature, it changes into pearlite. The final solid is pearlite and cementite. This is similar to the process of cooling the strong solution of salt–water.

Figure 12.14(a) shows the appearance of typical plain carbon steels under the microscope after specimens of these steels have been polished and etched. The steel is etched by dipping it into acid so that the crystal boundaries are eaten away to make the crystals show up.

The relationship between the carbon content and the properties and structure of plain carbon steels are shown in Fig. 12.14(b). This diagram assumes that the cooling rate has been slow enough for equilibrium to have been achieved in the structures of the steels being

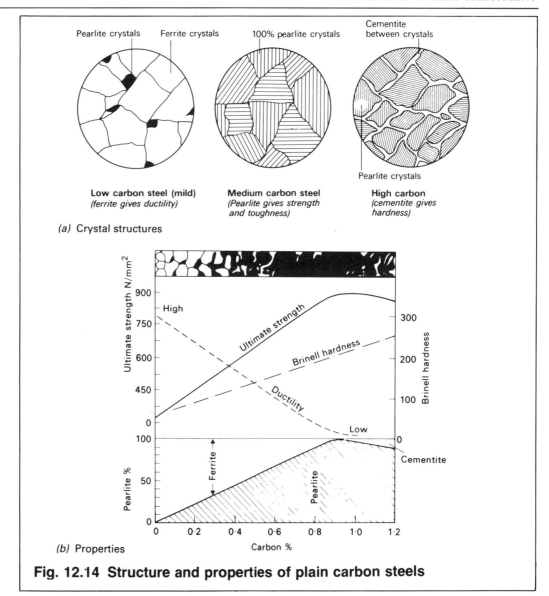

(a) Crystal structures

(b) Properties

Fig. 12.14 Structure and properties of plain carbon steels

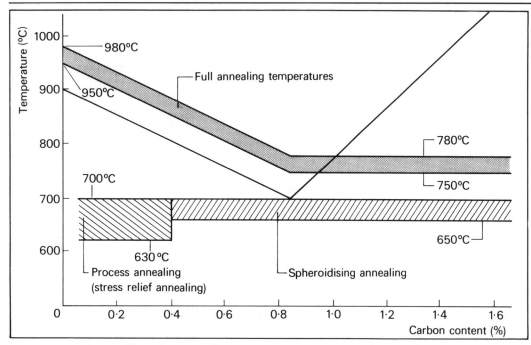

Fig. 12.15 Annealing temperatures

considered. The heat-treatment processes associated with plain carbon steels will now be considered in detail.

Annealing processes

All annealing processes are concerned with rendering the steel soft and ductile so that it can be cold-worked or machined. There are three basic annealing processes.

1 Stress-relief annealing at sub-critical temperatures (also known as process annealing and inter-stage annealing).

2 Spheroidised annealing at sub-critical temperatures.

3 Full annealing for forgings and castings.

The process chosen depends upon the carbon content of the steel, its pre-treatment processing, and its subsequent use. Figure 12.15 shows the temperature ranges for the annealing processes superimposed upon the iron–carbon equilibrium diagram. In all annealing process the cooling rate is as slow as possible and often takes place in the furnace.

Stress-relief annealing

This process is reserved for steels below

0.4 per cent carbon content. Such steels will not satisfactorily quench-harden (p. 257) but, since they are relatively ductile, they are frequently cold-worked and become *work-hardened*, that is, the crystal structure is severely deformed from its normal equilibrium condition. Re-crystallisation commences at 500 °C but, in practice, annealing is usually carried out at 630 °C to speed up the process and limit grain growth. The principles of hot- and cold-working and re-crystallisation were discussed in detail in *Part 1* of this course. To recapitulate briefly, hot-working processes are those – such as hot rolling – that are carried out above the temperature of re-crystallisation (the temperature at which crystals reform after being distorted) and crystal distortion is relieved as fast as it occurs. Cold-working processes – such as wire drawing – are carried out below the temperature of re-crystallisation, and this results in the structure of the steel becoming severely distorted. Steel in this condition is highly stressed, hard and brittle. The success of stress-relief annealing depends upon the stresses locked up in the crystals triggering off the process of nucleation at sub-critical temperatures. A seed crystal will form at each stress concentration point in the deformed crystal. These seed crystals or nuclei will continue to grow, if the temperature is maintained, until a normal equilibrium grain structure is restored. Continued heating will result in grain growth in the steel and impaired properties.

Spheroidising annealing

It has already been stated that crystals of pearlite have a laminated structure consisting of alternate layers of cementite and ferrite. When steels containing more than 0·5 per cent carbon are heated to just below the lower critical temperature (650 ° to 700 °C) the cementite in the crystals tends to 'ball up'. This is referred to as the aspheroidisation of pearlitic cementite and the process is shown diagrammatically in Fig. 12.16. Since the temperatures involved are sub-critical, no phase changes take place and the aspheroidisation of the cementite is purely a surface tension effect.

If the layers of cementite in the crystal are relatively coarse prior to annealing, they take too long to break down and tend to form coarse globules of cementite. This, in turn, leads to impaired physical properties and poor machined surfaces. Thus, grain refinement by a quench treatment prior to aspherioidisation is recommended to produce fine globules of cementite. The process is most effective when it is used to soften plain carbon tool steels that have been either work- or quench-hardened. After treatment the steel can be drawn and it will also machine freely. Furthermore, steel that has been subjected to spheroidising annealing will harden more uniformly and with less chance of cracking. As with any other annealing process, slow cooling is required after the heating cycle. It is usual to turn off the furnace

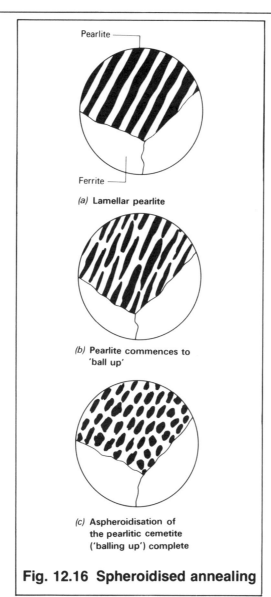

(a) Lamellar pearlite

(b) Pearlite commences to 'ball up'

(c) Aspheroidisation of the pearlitic cemetite ('balling up') complete

Fig. 12.16 Spheroidised annealing

and allow furnace and charge to cool down together.

Full annealing

Plain carbon steels solidify at temperatures well in excess of the upper critical temperatures with which the heat-treatment processes are concerned, and as a result large castings, well lagged by the sand mould, take a very long time to cool. Similarly, large forgings, although hot-worked below their melting point are, nevertheless, processed at temperatures substantially above their upper critical temperatures for relatively long periods of time. In both cases grain growth is excessive and the physical properties of the metal are impaired.

To render the steel usable it has to be re-heated to approximately 50 °C above the upper critical point for hypo-eutectoid steels and to 50 °C above the lower critical point for hyper-eutectoid steels, as shown in Fig. 12.15. This results in the formation of fine grains of austenite, which transform into finer crystals of ferrite and pearlite as the steel is slowly cooled back to room temperature, usually in the furnace.

Normalising

The normalising temperatures for plain carbon steels are shown in Fig. 12.17. The process resembles full annealing except that whilst in annealing the cooling rate is deliberately retarded, in normalising the cooling rate is

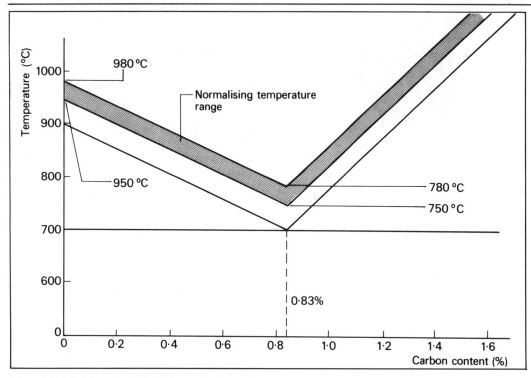

Fig. 12.17 Normalising temperatures

accelerated by taking the work from the furnace and allowing it to cool in free air. Provision must be made for the free circulation of cool air, but draughts must be avoided. This more rapid cooling results in a finer grain structure which, in turn, leads to improved physical properties and improved finishes when machining. However, the ductility is not sufficient for severe cold-working processes. Normalising is frequently used for stress-relieving between the rough machining and the

finish machining of large components to avoid subsequent 'movement' and loss of accuracy.

Hardening

If plain carbon steels are quenched (cooled rapidly) from above their upper critical temperatures there is insufficient time for the equilibrium transformations previously described to take place and the steel becomes appreciably harder. The final hardness will depend solely

upon the carbon content and the rate of cooling. Generally, steels containing less than 0·5 per cent carbon do not harden sufficiently to warrant being considered for cutting tools. Large components do not cool as rapidly as small components and may not achieve the critical cooling rate necessary for maximum hardness. Under equilibrium conditions the ferrite and cementite form a laminated structure called pearlite. In fact, pearlite can exist in several different forms and the coarsely laminated structure considered so far is called *lamellar pearlite*. Increasing the cooling rate results in the formation of finer and harder forms of pearlite. If the critical cooling rate for a given steel is exceeded, the austenite changes directly into *martensite* which is the hardest structure that can exist in plain carbon steels. The hardening temperatures for plain carbon steels are the same as for full annealing, but the hot steel is cooled very quickly (quenched) in oil or water. Figure 12.18 shows the needle-like structure of martensite.

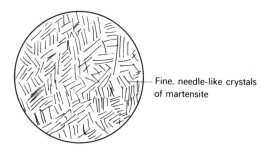

Fine, needle-like crystals of martensite

Fig. 12.18 Martensite

Quenching

Water is used for medium- and high-carbon steels where maximum hardness is required. Unfortunately, the sudden shock of being plunged into cold water can cause the hot steel to crack and distort.

Oil is less severe than water and is less likely to cause cracking and distortion. Unfortunately, it will cool the hot steel down at below the critical cooling rate for medium-carbon steels. Such steels quenched in oil tend to be toughened rather than hardened.

Tempering

A fully hardened plain carbon steel is brittle and hardening stresses are present. In such a condition it is of little practical use and it is re-heated, or tempered, to relieve the stresses and reduce the brittleness. Tempering causes the transformation of the martensite into less brittle structures. Unfortunately, any increase in toughness is accompanied by some decrease in hardness. Tempering always tends to transform unstable martensite back to the stable pearlite of the equilibrium transformations.

Tempering temperatures below 200 °C only relieve the hardening stresses, but above 220 °C the martensite starts to change into a fine pearlitic structure. This is much tougher, although somewhat softer than martensite and is the structure to be found in most carbon-steel cutting tools.

Table 12.1 Tempering temperatures

Colour*	Equivalent Temperature(°C)	Application
Very light straw	220	Scrapers; lathe tools for brass.
Light straw	225	Turning tools; steel-engraving tools.
Pale straw	230	Hammer faces; light lathe tools.
Straw	235	Razors; paper cutters; steel plane blades.
Dark straw	240	Milling cutters; drills; wood-engraving tools.
Dark yellow	245	Boring cutters; reamers; steel-cutting chisels.
Very dark yellow	250	Taps; screw-cutting dies; rock drills.
Yellow–brown	255	Chasers; penknives; hardwood-cutting tools.
Yellowish brown	260	Punches and dies; shear blades; snaps.
Reddish brown	265	Wood-boring tools; stone-cutting tools.
Brown–purple	270	Twist drills.
Light purple	275	Axes; hot setts; surgical instruments.
Full purple	280	Cold chisels and setts.
Dark purple	285	Cold chisels for cast iron.
Very dark purple	290	Cold chisels for iron; needles.
Full blue	295	Circular and band saws for metals; screwdrivers.
Dark blue	300	Helical springs; wood saws.

* Appearance of the oxide film that forms on a polished surface of the material as it is heated.

Tempering above 400 °C causes the cementite particles to 'ball up', giving a coarser structure called *sorbite*. This is tougher and more ductile than the finer pearlitic structure previously described, and is the structure used for components subjected to shock loads such as crankshafts and connecting-rods in motor-car and motor-cycle engines. It is normal to quench the steel once the tempering temperature has been reached. Table 12.1 gives the tempering temperatures for various applications of hardened plain carbon steels.

Case-hardening

Often components require a hard case to resist wear and a tough core to resist shock loads. These two properties do not exist in one steel. For toughness, the core should not exceed 0·3 per cent carbon content, whilst to give adequate hardness, the surface of the component should have a carbon content of approximately 1·0 per cent. The usual solution to this problem is *case-hardening*. This is a process by which carbon is added to the surface layers of a low-carbon steel component to a carefully regulated depth, after which the component goes through successive heat-treatment processes to harden the case and refine the core.

Thus the process has two distinct steps:
1 *carburising* (the addition of carbon)
2 *heat-treatment* (hardening and grain refinement)
   Carburising makes use of the fact that low-carbon steels (approximately 0·1 per cent carbon) absorb carbon when heated to the austenitic condition. Various carbonaceous materials are used in the carburising process.
1 *Solid media* such as bone charcoal or charred leather, together with an energiser such as sodium and barium carbonates. The energiser makes up to 40 per cent of the total composition.
2 *Fused salts* such as sodium cyanide, together with sodium carbonate and varying amounts of sodium or barium chloride. Since cyanide is a deadly poison and represents from 20–50 per cent of the total furnace content, stringent safety precautions must be taken in its use.
3 *Gases* are increasingly used now that natural gas (methane) is available. Methane is a hydrocarbon gas containing organic compounds of carbon that are readily absorbed into the steel. It is often enriched by the vapours given off by heated oils.

Pack-carburising

This involves packing the components to be carburised into heavy cast-iron or fabricated steel boxes along with the carburising media described above. The lid of the box is 'luted' into place with fire-clay to ensure a gas-tight seal. The boxes are then heated to between 900 °C and 950 °C for up to five hours, depending upon the depth of case required. The case depth should not exceed 2 mm, as thick cases tend to flake off due to cracking and brittleness.
   When carburising is complete the boxes are allowed to cool down so that they can be opened and unpacked. The components are then cleaned ready for subsequent heat treatment.

Salt-bath carburising

This involves suspending components in a mixture of molten sodium cyanide and energising salts. The composition of the mixture was given above. Large components are suspended individually from a bar lying across the top of the pot or crucible. On no account should copper wire be used as this dissolves in cyanide and the component would drop to the bottom of the pot. Small components are suspended in baskets made from a non-reactive material such as a inconel.
   Great care must be taken when using salt-bath furnaces since cold and moist components can cause an explosion when immersed in the hot, molten salts. In addition cyanide salts have the added

hazard of being extremely poisonous. When working with cyanide salts scrupulous personal cleanliness is absolutely essential. Only a few grains of cyanide under the fingernail can prove fatal if transferred to the mouth via food or a cigarette. The process has the following advantages over pack carburising for small components and where shallower cases are required, despite its inherent dangers.
1 Loading is quicker and, therefore, cheaper.
2 Heating and carburisation is more uniform with less chance of distortion.
3 The components can be hardened by quenching straight out of the cyanide without the need for further heat treatment.

Gas carburising

This is carried out in both batch-type and continuous furnaces. The components are heated at 900–950 °C in an atmosphere of methane (natural gas) which is a hydrocarbon gas. The gas is often enriched by adding hot mineral oil vapours. Oil is dripped on to a heated platinum electrode. The heat vaporises the oil and the platinum acts as a catalyst, 'cracking' the oil into its constituent elements. The gases are cleaned of moisture and carbon dioxide before being passed into the furnace. Since such gases are highly flammable, great care must be taken to prevent leakages causing the build-up of explosive mixtures of gas and air.
   Gas carburising is used for the mass production of cases up to 1 mm deep.

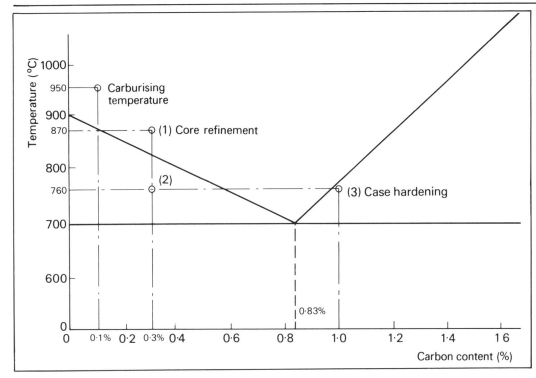

Fig. 12.19 Case hardening temperatures

Heat treatment after carburising

It is a fallacy to suppose that carburising hardens the steel. It merely adds carbon to the outer layers and leaves the steel in a fully annealed condition with a coarse grain structure. Therefore, additional heat-treatment processes are required to harden the case and refine the grain of both the case and the core in order to give adequate strength and toughness (see Fig. 12.19).

Refining the core Since the core has a carbon content of less than 0·3 per cent carbon, the correct annealing temperature is approximately 870 °C. After raising the component to this temperature it is water quenched to ensure a fine grain. The fine grain is required to ensure toughness. Although the temperature of 870 °C is correct for the core (temperature (1) in Fig. 12.19), it is excessively high for the case (temperature (2) in Fig. 12.19).

Refining and hardening the case Since the case has a carbon content of

approximately 1:0 per cent carbon its correct hardening temperature is 760 °C. Therefore, the component is reheated to this temperature (temperature (3) in Fig. 12.19), and again quenched. This hardens the case and ensures a fine grain. The temperature of 760 °C is too low to cause grain growth in the core, providing the component is heated rapidly through the range 650–750 °C during reheating and quenched without soaking at the hardening temperature.

Tempering At about 200 °C it is advisable to relieve any quenching stresses present in the case.

The above procedure is used to give ideal results. However, in the interests of speed and economy, the process is often simplified where components are lightly stressed or where alloy steels are used having less critical grain growth and quenching characteristics.

Localised case hardening

It is often not desirable to harden a component all over. For example it is undesirable to case harden screw threads. Not only would they be extremely brittle, but any distortion occurring during carburising and hardening could only be corrected by expensive thread-grinding operations.

Various means are available for avoiding the local infusion of carbon during the carburising process. Some examples follow.
1 The areas to be left soft can be heavily copper plated (this cannot be used for salt-bath treatment as copper dissolves in cyanide).

2 The areas to be left soft can be encased in fire cay.

3 The surplus metal can be left on. This is machined off, together with the infused carbon, between carburising and hardening. Although expensive this is the surest way of leaving local soft areas (see Chapter 10).

Exercises

1. Show, with the aid of sketches, the following forging processes.
   (i) Drawing down
   (ii) Upsetting (jumping up)
   (iii) Punching or piercing a hole
   (iv) Swaging

2. (a) Name **three** types of machine that are used for producing large forgings.
   (b) Draw a section through a typical drop forging die showing what is meant by the terms.
       (i) Impression
       (ii) Flash land
       (iii) Flash gutter
       (iv) Rapping faces
       (v) Locking faces

3. With the aid of sketches show the stages in upset forging a bolt head on a horizontal forging machine.

4. Sketch the steel section of the iron-carbon equilibrium diagram and use the diagram to select suitable temperatures for:
   (i) Annealing a 0·6% carbon steel,
   (ii) Quench hardening a 1·2% carbon steel tool,
   (iii) Normalising a 1·2% carbon steel forging.

5. With reference to plain carbon steels explain what is meant by.
   (i) Ferrite
   (ii) Cementite
   (iii) Pearlite
   (iv) Austenite

6. Describe the difference between:
   (i) stress-relief annealing for steels below 0·4% carbon,
   (ii) spheroidising annealing for steels above 0·5% carbon,
   (iii) full annealing.

7. Describe the following processes.
   (i) Quench hardening
   (ii) Normalising
   (iii) Full annealing

8. State the factors upon which the hardness of a quench hardened steel depend.
   What is *tempering* and why is it required after hardening?
   List the advantages and limitations of oil as a quenching bath compared with water.

9. Describe in detail the process of pack carburising mild steel components and the subsequent heat treatment to have a hard case and a tough, fine grained core.

10. Explain **three** ways in which selected features (e.g. screw threads) can be left soft when the rest of the component is case hardened.

13. Brazing and welding

Thermal joining processes

Joining metals by soft-soldering was introduced in *Mechanical Engineering Craft Theory and Related Studies: Part 1.* Low melting point tin-lead solders are used for soft-soldering and the joints produced are relatively weak.

Where a stronger joint is required *hard-soldering* or *brazing* is used. Brazing processes use silver alloy solders and brass spelters (solders) with a very much higher melting point than the soft solders considered previously.

Even stronger are joints produced by *bronze welding*. The melting point of the bronze filler rods is so high that an oxy-acetylene flame has to be used to melt them.

The strongest joints of all are produced by fusion welding. The edges of the metals being joined are melted and run together to produce a single piece of material of almost uniform strength. Additional material of similar composition to those being joined is added in the form of a filler rod. Very high temperatures are required for fusion welding.

Hard-soldering or brazing

Hard-soldering is a general term used to cover brazing and silver soldering which are very similar thermal-joining processes.

In this process, as in soft-soldering, melting or fusion of the parent metals to be joined does not take place, which means that a suitable filler material which has a lower melting point than that of the parent metal is employed.

There are a number of alloys other than the familiar *tin/lead* alloys which can be used as *solder*. They do not possess the low melting point of the soft solders, but they have other properties such as *higher strength*, which makes them preferable for certain jobs.

For many years bicycle frames have been made by joining alloy steel tubes to the brackets by a brazing operation using a grade of *brass* as the solder. The brass usually consists of 60 per cent zinc and 40 per cent copper and melts at about 850 °C, which is much higher than the soft-soldering temperatures. Such high melting point solders are called hard solders, and hard soldered or brazed joints are much stronger than ordinary soft-soldered ones.

Brazing is defined as a process of joining metals in which molten filler metal is drawn by capillary attraction into the space between closely adjacent surfaces of the parts to be joined. In general, the melting point of the filler metal is above 500 °C. In this respect, and broadly in its application, brazing lies between soft soldering and fusion welding.

Basic principles of brazing

The success of all brazing operations depends on the following conditions.
1 Selection of a suitable brazing alloy which has a melting range appreciably lower than that of the parent metals to be joined.
2 Thorough cleanliness of the surfaces to be brazed.
3 Complete removal of the oxide film from the surfaces of the parent metals and the brazing alloy by a suitable flux.
4 Complete 'wetting' of the mating surfaces by the molten brazing alloy.

The above requirements also apply to the process of silver soldering.

When a surface is wetted by a liquid, a continuous film of the liquid remains on the surface after draining. This condition is essential for brazing and silver soldering, where the flux removes the oxide film and completely covers the surfaces of the joint faces. This wetting action by the flux assists spreading and feeding of the filler material, leading to the production of completely filled joints.

Table 13.1 Composition of silver solders

British Standard 1845. Type	Composition percentage				Approximate melting range (°C)
	Silver min. max.	Copper min. max.	Zinc min. max.	Cadmium min. max.	
3	49 to 51	14 to 16	15 to 17	18 to 20	620–640
4	60 to 62	27·5 to 29·5	9 to 11	–	690–735
5	42 to 44	36 to 38	18·5 to 20·5	–	700–775

Note: Type 4 possesses a high conductivity and is, therefore, very suitable for making electrical joints. It is the most expensive because of its high silver content.
Type 3 is extremely fluid at brazing temperatures which makes it ideal when brazing dissimilar metals. A *low melting point alloy*.
Type 5 is a general purpose silver solder which can be employed at much higher brazing temperatures.

The effectiveness of capillary attraction is governed by the maintenance of appropriate joint clearances. The mating surfaces should be parallel. There should be no break in the uniformity of clearance. If a break occurs due to a widening or closing, then capillary flow will stop in that vicinity and may not go beyond it.

Metals that can be joined by brazing

The following common metals and their alloys may be joined by the process of brazing:
1 copper and copper-based alloys;
2 mild steel, carbon steel and alloy steels;
3 stainless steels and stainless irons;
4 malleable and wrought iron;
5 nickel-base alloys;
6 aluminium and certain aluminium alloys.

Metals and alloys of a dissimilar nature can also be brazed together, for example; copper to brass; copper to steel; brass to steel; cast iron to mild steel; mild steel to stainless steel.

Hard solders

For most metals the brazing alloys used are normally based on *copper–zinc alloys* and are dissimilar in composition to the parent metals to which they are applied. Copper is commonly used as a brazing material for the flux-free brazing of mild steel in reducing-atmosphere furnaces.

Brazing alloys may be classified into three main types:
1 silver-bearing brazing alloys or silver solders;
2 brazing alloys containing phosphorus;
3 brazing brasses or spelters.

Silver solders These are more expensive than the normal brazing alloys because they contain a high percentage of silver, but they offer the advantages of producing very strong and ductile joints at much lower temperatures. Silver solders are very free-flowing at brazing temperatures. Their tensile strength is in the region of 500 MN/m², and because of the low brazing temperatures required have very little heat-effect upon the properties of the parent metals.

By using silver solders it is possible to increase the speed of brazing and to eliminate or to limit 'finishing' operations. One of its main applications is for delicate work in which small neat joints are essential. Table 13.1 gives the compositions of three silver solders together with their melting ranges.

Brazing alloys containing phosphorus Filler materials which contain phosphorus are usually referred to as self-fluxing brazing alloys. These alloys contain silver, phosphorus and copper or, copper and phosphorus, the former possessing a lower melting range. The outstanding feature of these alloys is their ability to braze copper in air without the use of a flux.

These brazing alloys find their greatest application in resistance brazing operations, in refrigerator manufacture, electrical assemblies (electric motor armatures), for brazing seams and fittings in domestic copper hot water cylinders, and in plumbing. Table 13.2 gives the composition and melting ranges of two common brazing alloys containing phosphorus.

Brazing brasses The oldest and best known method of brazing involves the

Table 13.2 Composition of brazing alloys containing phosphorus

British standard 1845 Type	Composition percentage			Approximate melting range (°C)
	Silver min. max.	Phosphorus min. max.	Copper	
6	13 to 15	4 to 6	Balance	625–780
7	–	7 to 7·5	Balance	705–800

Table 13.3 Composition of brazing spelters

British standard 1845 Type	Compositon percentage		Approximate melting range (°C)
	Copper min. max.	Zinc	
8	49 to 51	Balance	860–870
9	53 to 55	Balance	870–880
10	59 to 61	Balance	885–890

Note: This group of copper alloys tends to lose zinc by vapourisation and oxidation when the parent metal is heated above 400°C. This loss of zinc produces relatively higher tensile strength. The brazing alloys containing a high percentage of zinc, therefore, produce joints of the lowest strength.
Type 8 is used for medium strength joints, whilst the strongest joints can be produced by using type 10.

use of brazing brasses or brazing spelters, using *borax* as a flux.

These alloys melt at much higher temperatures than the silver solders and the phosphorus-containing brazing alloys, but produce sound joints having tensile strengths between 400 MN/m² and 480 MN/m². The composition and melting ranges of three common brazing spelters are shown in Table 13.3; increasing the zinc content decreases the melting range. This makes it possible to make a joint in 60/40 brass using a 50/50 brass as the brazing alloy. Converseiy, it is important that a brass

to be joined by brazing should have a high copper content compared with the brazing alloy used.

Fluxes

The need for a suitable flux to remove the oxide coating of the metals being joined, to wet their surfaces and to prevent re-oxidation during brazing has already been introduced on p. 261.

When using brazing brass spelters borax is used as a flux. The borax powder is mixed into a paste with cold water and applied liberally to the joint faces. As the temperature of the joint is

raised, the borax melts and reacts chemically with the oxide film to clean and wet the joint ready for the application of the brass spelter.

Borax-type fluxes are not suitable for use with silver solders which have low melting temperatures. These fluxes are not sufficiently fluid for silver soldering temperatures below 760 °C. Potassium fluoroborate can be used as a suitable flux, it is very active and completely molten at 580 °C.

An efficient flux should melt at a temperature at least 50 °C lower than the melting point of the brazing material and retain its activity at a temperature at least 50 °C above the melting temperature of the brazing alloy being used. Because of this factor it is advisable to use the proprietary fluxes which are available on the market.

Flame or torch brazing

Flame brazing may be used to fabricate almost any assembly, and is particularly useful where the joint area is small in relation to the bulk of the assembly. The gas torch is the most common method of heating. The brazing spelter may be applied in the following two ways.
1 The granulated spelter is mixed with borax paste. As heat is applied from the torch and the joint brought uniformly up to brazing temperature the spelter melts. Borax is usually sprinkled on the joint which is tapped with an iron spatula in order to assist the flow of the molten spelter throughout the joint.
2 In a wire or strip form. The end of the spelter is heated and dipped into the

263

flux which adheres to it. When the joint has been brought up to temperature the fluxed end of the filler metal is applied and flows into the joint.

A heating flame is produced by a suitably designed torch supplied with an oxygen/fuel gas or an air/fuel gas mixture, and the filler metal is fused by the heat conducted from the hot component parts, never by the flame itself.

A wide variety of gas mixtures are available for torch brazing and the most useful of these, in approximate order of decreasing heating power are: oxy-acetylene; oxy-hydrogen; oxy-propane; oxy-coal gas; compressed air–coal gas (or propane, methane, etc.); air-propane, air-butane, air-methane.

Of these the two mixtures most commonly used are oxy-acetylene and compressed air-propane gas. A wide range of heat control is obtained with the use of oxy-acetylene torches. These torches have been developed to a high degree of perfection and, if properly used, offer the most flexible and versatile method of torch heating.

Some aspects of torch brazing are illustrated in Fig. 13.1.

Types of brazed joint

There are basically two types of joints used in brazing operations. They are the *lap* and *butt* joints, and these are illustrated in Fig. 13.2. There are, however, many combinations and variations of these joints designed to

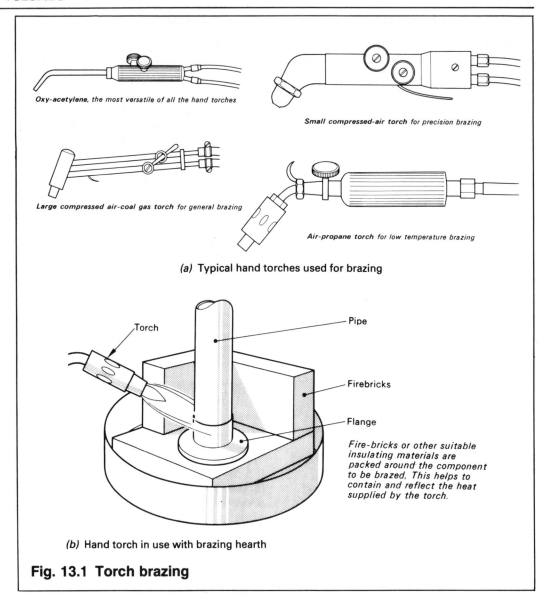

Oxy-acetylene, the most versatile of all the hand torches

Small compressed-air torch for precision brazing

Large compressed air-coal gas torch for general brazing

Air-propane torch for low temperature brazing

(a) Typical hand torches used for brazing

Torch

Pipe

Firebricks

Flange

Fire-bricks or other suitable insulating materials are packed around the component to be brazed. This helps to contain and reflect the heat supplied by the torch.

(b) Hand torch in use with brazing hearth

Fig. 13.1 Torch brazing

meet the requirements of specific conditions.

Lap joints are recommended wherever possible because they are the strongest. An overlap greater than three times the thickness of the thinnest member is the general rule for maximum joint efficiency. Lap joints have the disadvantage of increasing the metal thickness at the joint.

Butt joints should only be used where service requirements are not severe and where strength is relatively unimportant. They are limited in joint area to the cross-sectional area of the mating surface.

Scarf joints are a variation of the butt joint and are used to increase the cross-sectional area and provide a larger surface for the brazing filler metal. Scarf joints are more costly to produce, more difficult to hold in alignment, but have the advantage of no increased thickness at the joint. For maximum joint efficiency the joint area obtained should be over three times the normal cross-sectional area.

The factors affecting the strength of hard-soldered joints are the same as those which apply to soft-soldering, but since the mechanical strength of the brazing alloys used is very much greater than that of soft solders, the overall strength of the joint is higher.

Braze (bronze) welding

Like brazing processes, braze welding is used to join either similar or dissimilar metals by using a filler material of

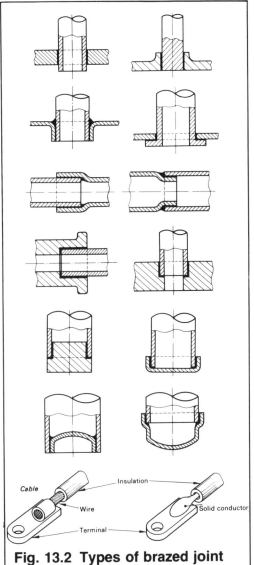

Fig. 13.2 Types of brazed joint

lower melting point than either of the components to be joined. In the brazing process the parts to be joined are tightly fitted together, so that the filler alloy flows through the joint by capillary attraction. If the parts are not closely fitted, so that a relatively large quantity of filler alloy is used, the process is called braze welding.

Braze welding has been termed for many years bronze welding. This was because the process resembled welding and originally, the filler material used was a copper/phosphorus/tin alloy, in other words a *bronze*. However, the term bronze welding is now a misnomer because the filler materials currently used are basically a 60/40 ratio copper/zinc alloy (brass) which may incorporate small amounts of silicon, manganese and/or nickel depending upon the application. Thus in general terms modern filler alloys used for braze welding are brasses. A list of commonly used filler materials are given in Table 13.4.

Basic principles of braze welding

In braze welding, as distinct from fusion welding, the melting point of the filler material is lower than that of the materials to be joined. This means that the process requires a lower temperature than fusion welding, and troubles such as distortion and oxidation of the parent metal, which are generally associated with fusion welding, are reduced considerably.

One important general principle relating to the preparation of joints is

Table 13.4 Composition of copper alloy filler rods for braze welding

British standard 1453 Type	Composition percentage						Melting point °C
	Copper min. max.	Zinc min. max.	Silicon min. max.	Tin max.	Manganese min. max.	Nickel min. max.	
C2	57 to 63	36 to 42	0·2 to 0·5	0·5	———	———	875
C4	57 to 63	36 to 42	0·15 to 0·3	0·5	0·05 to 0·25	———	895
C5	45 to 53	34 to 42	0·15 to 0·5	0·5	– 0·5	8 to 11	910
C6	41 to 45	37 to 41	0·2 to 0·5	1·0	– 0·2	14 to 16	

Note: Type C2 is termed a SILICON-BRONZE filler rod and is specially recommended for the braze welding of BRASS and COPPER sheet and tubes as are used for sanitary and hot water installations. It is also suitable for the braze welding of MILD STEEL and GALVANISED STEEL.
Type C4 is termed a MANGANESE-BRONZE filler rod, it has a higher melting point and is especially suitable for braze welding CAST or MALLEABLE IRON, and also for building up worn parts such as gear teeth.
Types C5 and C6 are NICKEL-BRONZE rods which are recommended for braze welding STEEL or MALLEABLE IRON where the **highest mechanical strength** is required. These are the high melting point welding rods and have a valued application in the reclaiming and building up of wearing surfaces.

that the workpiece must be thoroughly clean and that scale, oil, grease, paint or stains must be removed before attempting the braze welding operation.

The main advantage of braze welding over fusion welding is that the parent metal is only 'tinned' and never melted.

Fluxes of the borax type should be used. A paste or a powdered flux wetted to make a paste can be more thoroughly and evenly distributed than a flux in powder form.

Braze welding utilises the concentrated heat of the oxy-acetylene flame. By careful control of the torch this heat can be localised to bring any area of the joint up to braze welding temperature, and enable perfect control of the molten filler metal to be achieved, without capillary attraction.

The leftward method of welding is employed, the torch nozzle should be about two sizes smaller than for butt welds on metals of the same thickness, and the flame condition should be slightly oxidising. Figure 13.3 illustrates the angles of rod and welding torch for the braze welding of cast iron.

The following metals may be joined by braze welding: copper; mild steel; galvanised mild steel; malleable iron; cast iron; a combination of any two of the above.

Full fusion welding

Fusion welding, as the name implies, is a thermal joining process in which the parent metal to be joined is melted and caused to fuse together with or without the use of filler metal.

The principle of fusion welding is illustrated by two typical joint arrangements, one requiring a separate filler metal, the other self-supplying, in Fig. 13.4.

The two basic types of welding are commonly referred to as *gas welding* and *arc welding* which will now be compared.

Oxy-acetylene welding   In general, all fusion welding processes involve a high temperature heat source, especially when joining high-melting-temperature materials. The oxy-acetylene flame provides the heat required to melt most of the metals and alloys in commercial use.

Other oxy-fuel gas mixtures can be used, but the vast majority of gas-welding processes employ acetylene as the fuel gas. This is becaue acetylene is the most economical gas to use in conjunction with relatively pure oxygen supplied from high-pressure cylinders, to give a flame with a

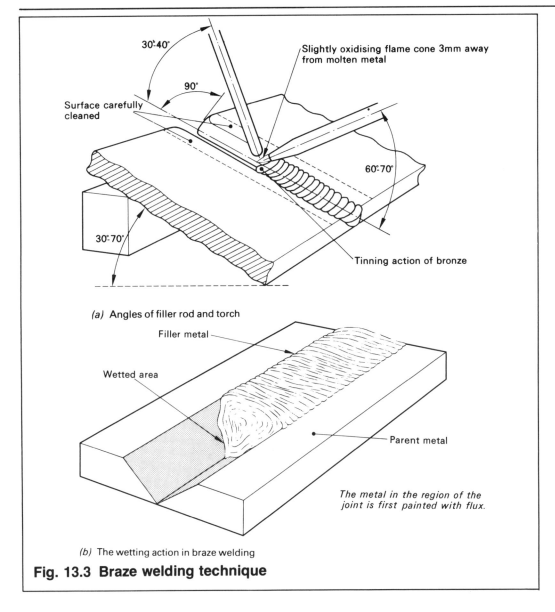

30°-40°

Slightly oxidising flame cone 3mm away
from molten metal

90°

Surface carefully
cleaned

60°-70°

30°-70°

Tinning action of bronze

(a) Angles of filler rod and torch

Filler metal

Wetted area

Parent metal

*The metal in the region of the
joint is first painted with flux.*

(b) The wetting action in braze welding

Fig. 13.3 Braze welding technique

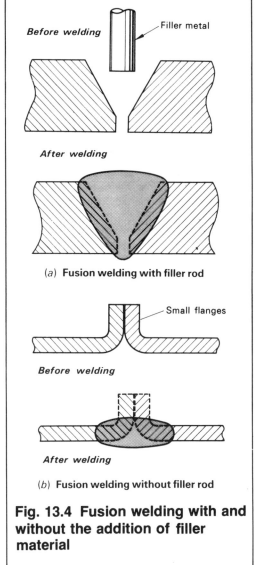

Before welding   Filler metal

After welding

(a) **Fusion welding with filler rod**

Small flanges

Before welding

After welding

(b) **Fusion welding without filler rod**

Fig. 13.4 Fusion welding with and without the addition of filler material

267

maximum temperature of 3200 °C.

Metallic arc welding   By contrast the heat required for welding in arc-welding processes is not obtained by the combustion of a fuel gas with oxygen.

Basically manual metallic arc welding is a process where the energy required for melting the parent metal is obtained from an electrical source, such as a transformer or a generator or a transformer–rectifier.

An *electric arc* is simply a prolonged spark between two terminals of an electric circuit. The terminals used in arc welding are the workpiece and the electrode.

The arc is extremely hot (approximate average temperature in the region of 6000 °C). This very high temperature, being concentrated in a relatively small area, is sufficient to melt instantly the surface of the workpiece and the end of a metal electrode. In metallic arc welding the electrode not only provides a means of melting the surface of the workpiece, but actually provides metal to fill the joint. Figure 13.5 illustrates the basic differences between the oxy-acetylene and manual metallic arc welding processes.

Oxy-acetylene welding (equipment)

Figure 13.6(a) shows the basic equipment for oxy-acetylene (gas) welding, whilst Fig. 13.6(b) shows the differences between oxygen and acetylene cylinders.

Oxygen   This is supplied to the welding

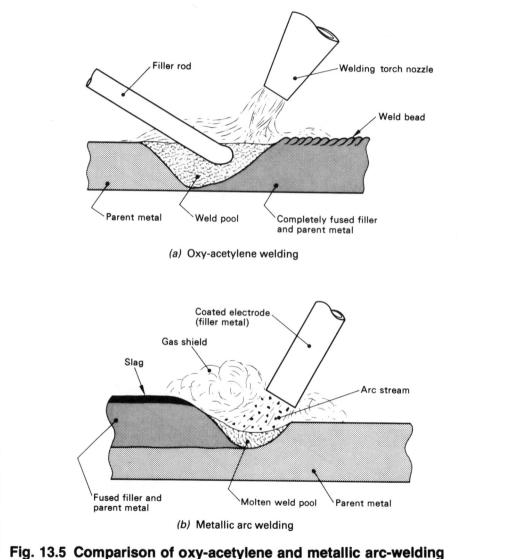

(a) Oxy-acetylene welding

(b) Metallic arc welding

Fig. 13.5 Comparison of oxy-acetylene and metallic arc-welding

torch from a solid drawn steel cylinder where it is contained in compressed form.

The valve outlet on an oxygen cylinder has a right-hand screw thread.
Acetylene For high-pressure welding acetylene is supplied in a solid drawn cylinder as shown in Fig. 13.6(b). High-pressure acetylene is not stable and for this reason it is dissolved in acetone which has the ability to absorb a large volume of the gas and release it as the pressure falls.

Because of the danger of explosions, compressed acetylene is kept in a steel cylinder filled with a porous substance. The construction of the cylinder, its filling and testing, are all strictly controlled by the manufacturers in the interests of safety. The pores in the filling material divide the space into a large number of very small compartments which are completely filled with dissolved acetylene. These small compartments prevent the sudden decomposition of the acetylene throughout the mass, should it be started by local heating or other causes.

The valve outlet on acetylene cylinders is fitted with a left-hand screw thread. Automatic pressure regulators are fitted to oxygen and acetylene cylinders to reduce the pressure and control the flow of the welding gases. Examples are shown in Fig. 13.7. They are fitted with two pressure gauges: one to indicate the gas pressure in the cylinder, and the other to indicate the reduced outlet pressure.

The welding gases at reduced

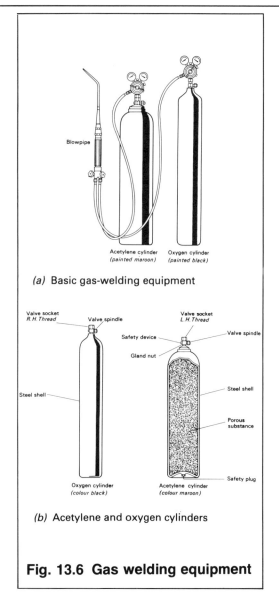

(a) Basic gas-welding equipment

(b) Acetylene and oxygen cylinders

Fig. 13.6 Gas welding equipment

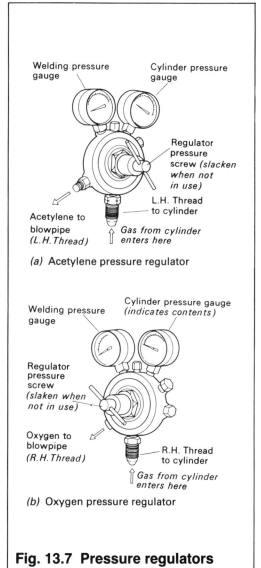

(a) Acetylene pressure regulator

(b) Oxygen pressure regulator

Fig. 13.7 Pressure regulators

pressure are fed through suitable hoses to a *welding torch*. This is a specially designed piece of equipment used for mixing and controlling the flow of gases to the *welding nozzle* or *tip*. The torch provides a means of holding and directing the welding nozzle. Figure 13.8 shows a typical gas welding torch.

The fuel-gas hose fitting on all welding torches has a left-hand thread, making it possible only to screw on the left-hand grooved nuts used on fuel-gas hose. The other fitting, used for oxygen, has a right-hand thread.

There are two *control valves*, usually positioned at the rear end of the torch. After passing the valves, the gases flow through metal tubes inside the handle and are brought together by the *gas mixer* at the front end.

The nozzle is shown as a simple tube tapered down at the outlet end to produce a suitable welding cone. The welding nozzle or tip is that portion of the torch through which the gases pass prior to their ignition and combustion. A welding nozzle enables the operator to guide the flame and direct it with the maximum ease and efficiency. Nozzles are made from a non-ferrous metal such as copper or a copper alloy. These materials possess a high thermal conductivity and their use greatly reduces the danger of burning the nozzle at high temperatures.

Care and maintenance of nozzles
Since nozzles are made from materials which are relatively soft, care must be taken to guard them against damage. The following precautions are advised.

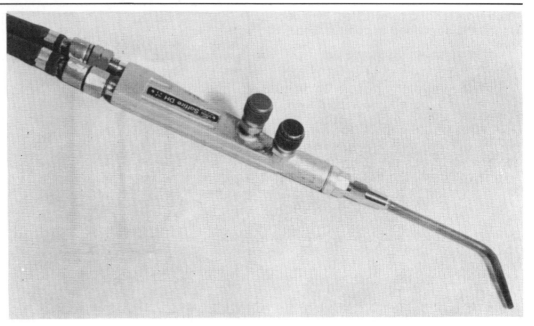

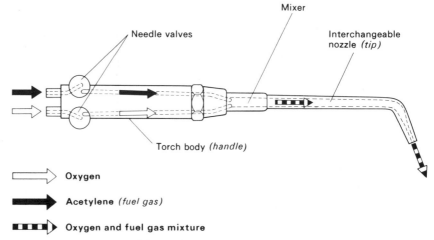

Fig. 13.8 High-pressure welding torch

1 Make sure that the nozzle seat and threads are absolutely free from foreign matter in order to prevent any scoring when tightening on assembly.

2 Nozzles should only be cleaned with tip cleaners which are specially designed for this purpose. A special nozzle cleaning compound is available for dirty nozzles. The correct strength of cleaning solution is obtained by using approximately 50 grammes of compound to 1 litre of water. Dirty nozzles should be immersed in this solution for a period of at least 2 hours.

3 Nozzles should never be used for moving or holding the work.

Oxy-acetylene welding (techniques)

The correct type of flame is essential for the production of satisfactory welds, and the characteristics of the three flames are shown in Fig. 13.9.

Neutral flame   For most applications the neutral flame condition is used as shown in Fig. 13.9(a). This is produced when approximately equal volumes of oxygen and acetylene are mixed in the welding torch.

It is termed neutral because it effects no chemical change on molten metal and, therefore, will not oxidise or carburise the metal.

It is easily recognised by its characteristic, clearly-defined white inner cone at the tip of the torch nozzle.

Correct adjustment is indicated by a slight white flicker (feather) on the end of this cone resulting from a slight

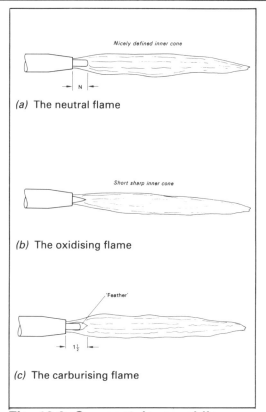

(a) The neutral flame

(b) The oxidising flame

(c) The carburising flame

Fig. 13.9 Oxy-acetylene welding flame conditions

excess of acetylene. When setting this condition, it is best to have a slightly reducing flame.

The neutral flame setting is most commonly used for the welding of mild steel, stainless steels, cast iron and copper.

Oxidising flame   When an oxidising flame is required, as shown in Fig. 13.9(b), the flame is first set to the neutral condition and the acetylene supply is slightly reduced by the control valve on the welding torch.

This flame can be easily recognised by the inner cone of the flame which is shorter and more pointed than that of the neutral flame.

The oxidising flame is undesirable in most cases as it oxidises the molten metal, although this can be an advantage with some brasses and bronzes. The oxidising flame gives the highest possible temperature providing the oxygen/acetylene ratio does not exceed 1·5:1.

Reducing flame   When a reducing flame is required, as shown in Fig. 13.9(c), the flame is first set to the neutral condition and the acetylene supply is slightly increased by the control valve on the welding torch.

This flame is recognised by the feather of incandescent carbon particles between the inner cone and outer envelope.

The reducing flame is used for carburising (surface hardening) and for the flame brazing of aluminium.

Leftward welding

In this method of gas welding the flame is directed away from the finished weld, i.e. towards the unwelded part of the joint. Filler rod, when used, is directed towards the welded part of the joint.

Although this technique is termed leftward welding, it is not confined to right-hand operators. Normally, with right-handed persons, the welding torch is held in the right hand and welding proceeds from right to left, i.e. leftwards. With a left-handed operator the torch is held in the left hand and welding proceeds from left to right.

Leftward welding is used on normal low-carbon steels for the following purposes.

1 Flanged-edge welds for thicknesses less than 20 s.w.g. These welds are made without the addition of filler rod.
2 Square-butt welds on unbevelled steel plates up to 3·2 mm thickness.
3 Vee-butt welds on bevelled steel plates over 3·2 mm and up to 5 mm thickness.

The leftward method of welding is not considered to be economical for thicknesses above 5 mm for reasons which will be explained later.

The angles of the torch and filler rod are clearly illustrated in Fig. 13.10.

Flanged-edge weld   No filler rod is required. The flame should be manipulated with a steady semi-circular sideways movement and progressively forwards only as fast as the edges of the sheet metal are melted. The tip of the flame cone must be kept about 3 mm from the weld pool (Fig. 13.10(a))

Square-butt weld   As the filler rod is melted it should be fed forward to build up the molten pool of weld metal and then retracted slightly. The flame is guided progressively forwards with small sideways movements as fast as the plate edges are melted (Fig. 13.10(b)).

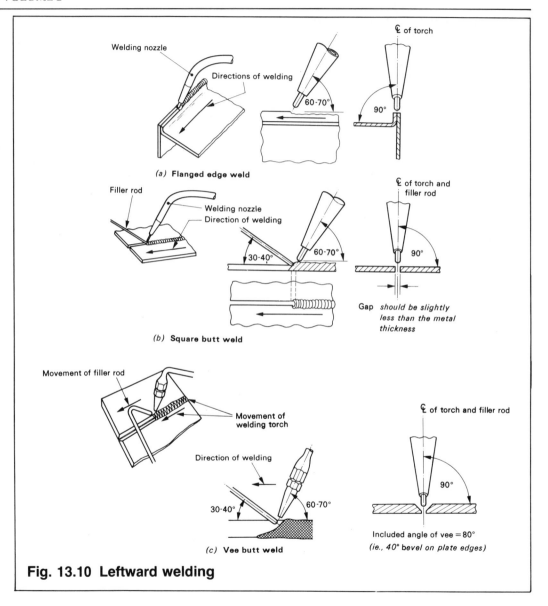

(a) **Flanged edge weld**

(b) **Square butt weld**

Gap *should be slightly less than the metal thickness*

(c) **Vee butt weld**

Included angle of vee = 80°
(ie., 40° bevel on plate edges)

Fig. 13.10 Leftward welding

A pear-shaped melted area (often referred to as an 'onion') should be maintained ahead of the weld pool. Care must be exercised to ensure uniform melting of both plate edges.

Vee-butt weld   The tip of the flame cone should never touch the weld metal or the filler rod. As the filler rod is melted it should be fed forward into the molten weld pool in order to build it up. The rod is then retracted slightly to enable the heat to fuse the bottom edges of the vee. This ensures full penetration of the weld to the bottom of the plate edges (Fig. 13.10(c)).

The side-to-side movement of the welding torch should only be sufficient to melt the sides of the vee.

The weld deposit is built up as the torch and filler rod move progressively forwards filling the vee to a level slightly higher than the edges of the plate.

Rightward welding

With this technique the weld is commenced at the left-hand end of the joint and the welding torch moved towards the right – in the opposite direction to the leftward technique. The torch flame in this case is directed towards the metal being deposited, unlike the leftward method in which the flame is directed away from the deposited metal.

Rightward welding should be used for steel plates which exceed 5 mm thickness as follows.

1 Square-butt welds on unbevelled steel plates between 5 and 8·2 mm thickness (inclusive).

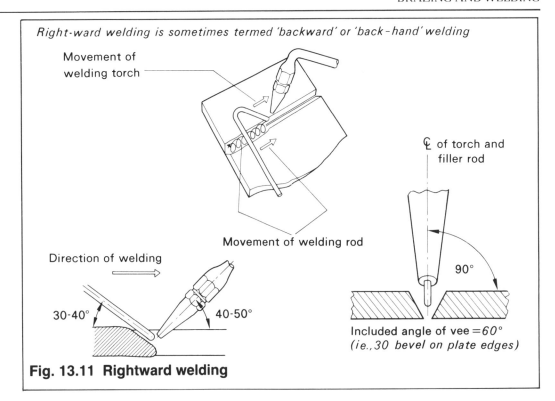

Right-ward welding is sometimes termed 'backward' or 'back-hand' welding

Movement of welding torch

Movement of welding rod

Direction of welding

30-40°   40-50°

℄ of torch and filler rod

90°

Included angle of vee = 60° (ie., 30 bevel on plate edges)

Fig. 13.11 Rightward welding

2 Vee-butt welds on bevelled steel plates over 8·2 mm thickness. The angles of the torch and filler rod shown in Fig. 13.11.

It is important that the flame cone is always kept just clear of the filler rod and the deposited weld metal.

The welding torch is moved steadily to the right along the joint. By comparison with leftward welding (Fig. 13.10(c)), it will be noticed that the cone of the flame is deeper in the vee.

The filler rod is given an elliptical looping movement as it travels progressively to the right. The filler rod and torch must be maintained in the same vertical plane as the weld, otherwise unequal fusion of the two sides of the weld will result. When a weld is completed, examination of the back should show an *underbead* which should be perfectly straight and uniform. The quality of the weld can be judged by the appearance of this underbead. The advantages of rightward welding can be summarised as follows.

1 No bevel is necessary for plates up to 8·2 mm thickness. This saves the cost of preparation and reduces the filler rod consumption.

2 When bevelling of the plate edges becomes necessary the included angle of the vee need only be 60°, which needs less filler rod than would be required to fill the 80° vee preparation for leftward welding.

3 Larger welding nozzles must be used which results in higher welding speeds. With the use of more powerful nozzles the force of the flame holds back the molten metal in the weld pool and allows more metal to be deposited so that welds in plates up to 10 mm thickness can be completed in one pass.

4 The operator's view of the weld pool and the sides and bottom of the vee is unobstructed, enabling him to control the molten metal. This ensures that full fusion of the plate edges, particularly of the bottom edges, is always maintained, and results in an adequate and continuous bead of penetration.

5 The quality and appearance of the weld is better than that obtained with the leftward technique. This is due, to a large extent, to the fact that the deposited metal is protected by the envelope of the flame which retards the rate of cooling.

6 Compared with leftward welding, the smaller total volume of deposited metal with rightward welding reduces shrinkage and distortion. By adopting the rightward technique, the heat of the flame is localised in the joint and is not allowed to spread across the plate. The blowpipe movement associated with leftward welding causes a greater spread of heat. The amount of distortion depends on the amount of heat put in, therefore it is important that this heat be confined as far as possible to the weld-seam itself.

7 The cost of rightward welding is lower than the leftward technique despite the use of more powerful welding nozzles. The greatest economy is in the consumption of filler rods owing to the smaller amount of metal deposited with the rightward technique.

Metallic-arc welding (principles)

The arc is produced by a low-voltage, high-amperage electric current jumping an air gap between the electrode and the joint to be welded. The heat of the electric arc is concentrated on the edges of two pieces of metal to be joined. This causes the metal edges to melt. While these edges are still molten additional molten metal, transferred across the arc from a suitable electrode, is added. This molten mass of metal cools and solidifies into one solid piece.

As soon as the arc is struck, the tip of the electrode begins to melt, thus increasing the gap between electrode and work. Therefore, it is necessary to cultivate a continuous downward movement with the electrode holder in order to maintain a constant arc length of 3 mm during the welding operation. The electrode is moved at a uniform rate along the joint to be welded, melting the metal as it moves.

The greatest bulk of electrodes used with manual arc welding are coated electrodes. A coated electrode consists mainly of a core wire of closely controlled composition having a concentric covering of flux and/or other material, which will melt uniformly with the core wire forming a partly vaporised and partly molten screen around the arc stream. This shield protects the arc from contamination by atmospheric gases.

The liquid slag produced performs three important functions.

1 Protects the solidifying weld metal from any further contamination from the atmosphere.

2 Prevents rapid cooling of the weld metal.

3 Controls the contour of the completed weld.

The function of an electrode is more than simply to carry the current to the arc. The core wire melts in the arc and tiny globules of molten metal shoot across the arc into the molten pool (arc crater in parent metal) during welding. These tiny globules are explosively forced through the arc stream. They are not transferred across the arc by the force of gravity, otherwise it would not be possible to use the manual arc-welding process for overhead welding.

The chemical coating surrounding the core wire melts or burns in the arc. It melts at a slightly higher temperature than the metal core and, therefore, extends a little beyond the core and directs the arc. This extension also prevents sideways arcing when welding in deep grooves.

The *arc stream* and other basic features of manual gas shielded metal-arc welding are illustrated in Fig. 13.12.

The coating on electrodes has several functions some of which are listed.

1 To facilitate striking the arc and to enable it to burn stably.

2 Serves as an insulator for the core wire.

3 It provides a flux for the molten pool, which picks up impurities and forms a protective slag which is easily removed.

4 It stabilises and directs the arc and the globules of molten core metal as shown in Fig. 13.12.

5 It provides a protective non-oxidising or reducing gas shield (smoke-like gas) around the arc to keep oxygen and nitrogen in the air away from the molten metal.

6 It increases the rate of melting (i.e. metal deposition) and so speeds up the welding operation.

7 It enables the use of alternating current.

8 Additions to the coating can be made (during manufacture) which will replace any alloying constituents of the core wire or the parent metal which are likely to be lost during the welding process.

9 It gives good penetration.

10 It increases or decreases the fluidity of the slag for special purposes. It can, for example, reduce the fluidity of electrodes used for overhead welding.

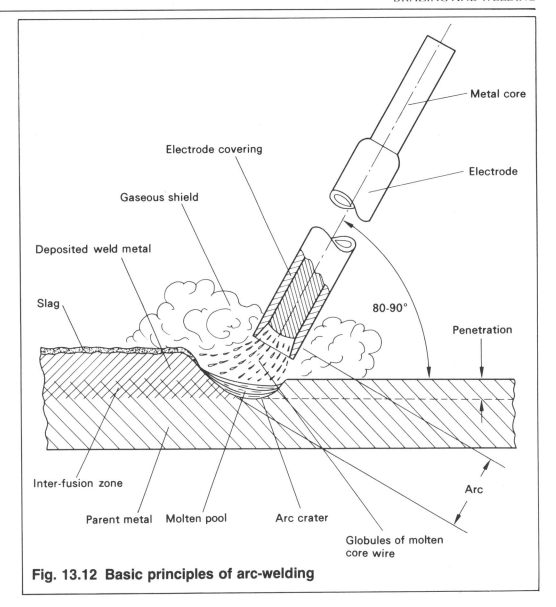

Fig. 13.12 Basic principles of arc-welding

Metal core

Electrode covering

Electrode

Gaseous shield

80-90°

Deposited weld metal

Penetration

Slag

Inter-fusion zone

Parent metal

Molten pool

Arc crater

Globules of molten core wire

Arc

Safety

Gas welding Cylinders for compressed gases are not themselves dangerous. They must comply with rigid government standards and should be regularly inspected and tested.

The fact that gas cylinders are a familiar sight in factories or on sites where welding and cutting is carried out is often the reason why ordinary safeguards are neglected.

For general identification purposes, narrow cylinders contain gases at *high pressure* whilst broad cylinders are used for *low pressure* gases.

A great deal of information is available, usually in the form of safety booklets issued by manufacturers, on the use, handling and storage of gas cylinders. A few of the many safety precautions will now be considered.
1 Cylinders must be protected from mechanical damage during storage, transportation and use. Acetylene cylinders must always be kept upright.
2 Cylinders must be kept cool. On no account should the welding flame, or any other naked light, be allowed to play on the cylinders or regulators. They must also be shielded from direct sunlight, wet or frost on an open site.
3 Cylinders must always be stored in well-ventilated surroundings to prevent the build-up of pockets of explosive mixtures of gases should any leaks occur. Do not smoke in a gas bottle store.
4 Correct automatic pressure regulators must be fitted to all cylinders prior to use. The cylinder valve must always be closed when the cylinder is not in use or whilst changing cylinders or equipment.
5 Keep cylinders free from contamination. Oils and greases ignite violently in the presence of oxygen. Similarly do not wear greasy clothes in the presence of compressed gases.

Explosions can occur in the regulators on oxygen cylinders as a result of dust, grit, oil or grease getting into the socket of the cylinder. Dust (especially coal dust) is highly flammable. The outlet sockets of cylinder valves should be examined for cleanliness before fitting regulators otherwise, if not removed, foreign matter will be projected on to the regulator valve seating when the cylinder valve is opened. The outlet socket can usually be cleaned by turning on the cylinder valve for a brief moment and closing it soundly.

It is extremely dangerous to search for gas leaks with a naked flame. Oxygen is odourless and, whilst it does not burn, it readily supports and speeds up combustion.

Acetylene has an unmistakable smell, rather like garlic, and can be instantly ignited by a spark or even a piece of red-hot metal.

Before leak testing, it is considered good practice to pressurise the system, and the procedure is as follows.
1 Open the control valves on the torch.
2 Release the pressure-adjusting control on the regulators.
3 Open the cylinder valves to turn on the gas.
4 Set the working pressures by adjusting the regulator control.
5 Having established the correct pressure for each gas, close the control valves on the torch.
6 Brush soapy water over every joint and round every valve – bubbles will appear wherever there is a leak.

Explosions can occur when acetylene gas is present in air in any proportions between 2 and 82 per cent. This gas is also liable to explode when under unduly high pressure even in the absence of air, therefore, **the working pressure of acetylene should not exceed 0·62 bars**.

When using gas-welding processes the first essential requirements are:
1 Ensure that there is adequate and proper ventilation.
2 Examine the equipment and see that it is free from leaks.

Explosions in the equipment itself may be caused by *flash-back*. Flash-backs occur because of faulty equipment or incorrect usage. Approximately 80 per cent of these occur when lighting welding or cutting torches, the other 20 per cent when they are in use. As long as the flow of gas equals the burning speed a stable flame will be maintained at the torch nozzle, otherwise mixed gases will arise in one of the hoses, resulting in a flash-back.

Flash-backs may also occur in the following circumstances.
1 By dipping the nozzle-tip into the molten weld pool.
2 By putting the nozzle-tip against the work and stopping the flow.

3 By allowing mud, paint or scale to cause a stoppage at the nozzle.

In every case the obstruction will cause the oxygen to flow back into the acetylene supply pipe and communicate ignition back towards the cylinder or source.

Because of this danger it is *essential* to use a *back-flash arrestor* as well as hose-protectors or non-return valves which prevent the reversal of the flow of gas.

Copper tube or fittings made of copper must never be used with acetylene, and alloys used in the construction of pipes, valves or fittings should not contain more than 70 per cent of copper – the only exception is the welding or cutting nozzle. This is because copper, when exposed to the action of acetylene, forms a highly explosive compound called copper acetylide which is readily detonated by heat or friction.

Electric-arc welding   This equipment is designed to change the high-voltage alternating current mains supply into a safe, low-voltage, heavy-current supply suitable for arc welding. Figure 13.13 shows examples of some typical arc welding sets.

It will be seen that the output can have an alternating current wave form or a direct current wave form. For safety the output voltage is limited between 50 and 100 V; however, the output current may be as high as 500 A. A welding set is basically a transformer to break down the high mains voltage and a tapped choke to control the current flow to suit

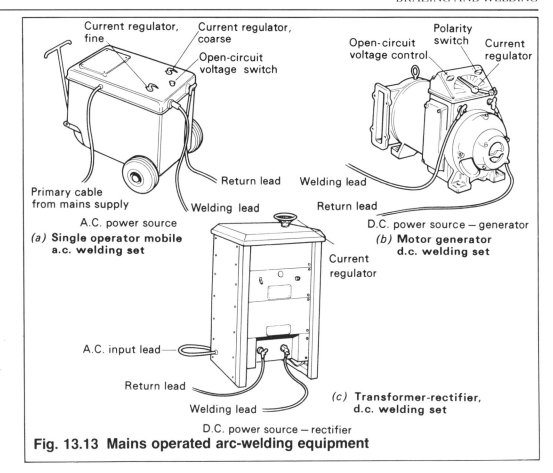

(a) **Single operator mobile a.c. welding set**
A.C. power source

(b) **Motor generator d.c. welding set**
D.C. power source – generator

(c) **Transformer-rectifier, d.c. welding set**
D.C. power source – rectifier

Fig. 13.13 Mains operated arc-welding equipment

the gauge of electrode used.

The hazards that may arise from mains operated welding equipment are set out in Table 13.5. To understand these more fully, constant reference should be made to Fig. 13.14 which shows a schematic diagram of a typical manual, metallic-arc welding circuit. It

will be seen that the circuit conveniently divides into two parts.

1 The primary (high voltage) circuit which should be installed and maintained by a skilled electrician.

2 The secondary (low voltage) external welding circuit which is normally set up by the welder to suit the job in hand.

Table 13.5 Arc-Welding hazards

Circuit – high voltage – Primary

Fault:	Hazard
1. Damaged insulation	Fire – loss of life and damage to property
	Shock – severe burns and loss of life
2. Oversize fuses	Overheating – damage to equipment and fire
3. Lack of adequate earthing	Shock – if fault develops – severe burns and loss of life

Circuit – low voltage – Secondary (very heavy current)

Fault:	Hazard:
1. Lack of welding earth	Shock – if a fault develops – severe burns and loss of life
2. Welding cable – damaged insulation	Local arcing between cable and any adjacent metalwork at earth potential causing Fire
3. Welding cable – inadequate capacity	Overheating leading to damaged insulation and Fire
4. Inadequate connections	Overheating – severe burns – Fire
5. Inadequate return path	Current leakage through surrounding metalwork – overheating – Fire

To eliminate these hazards as far as possible, the following precautions should be taken. These are only the basic precautions and a check should always be made as to whether equipment and working conditions require special, additional precautions.

1 Make sure that the equipment is fed from a switch-fuse so that it can be isolated from the mains supply. Easy access to this switch must be provided at all times.

2 Make sure that the trailing primary cable is armoured against mechanical damage as well as being heavily insulated against the high supply voltage (415 V).

3 Make sure that all cable insulation is undamaged and all terminations are secure and undamaged. If in doubt do not operate your equipment until it has been checked by a skilled electrician.

4 Make sure that all the equipment is adequately earthed with conductors capable of carrying the heavy currents used in welding.

5 Make sure the current regulator has an 'off' position so that in the event of an accident the welding current can be stopped without having to follow the primary cable back to the isolating switch.

6 Make sure that the 'external welding circuit' is adequate for the heavy currents it has to carry.

Personal protection Garments made of wool are generally considered not to be readily flammable. However, a high percentage of outer clothing, normally worn by workers, is usually made from flammable materials. Cuffs on overalls, or turn-ups on trousers are potential fire traps; hot slag, sparks and globules of hot metal can so easily lodge in them.

The protective clothing worn will depend upon the nature of the work, and the following suggestions are offered as a general guide.

1 Asbestos or leather gloves should be worn for all cutting operations which involve the handling of hot metal.

2 Safety boots should be worn to protect the feet from hot slag and, in particular, from falling off-cuts.

3 The wearing of asbestos spats is strongly advised for most cutting operations.

4 The wearing of a leather apron will help to prevent sparks and hot metal globules reaching and burning the sensitive parts of the operator's body. Many welders have experienced the folly of working with their shirts open to the waist, thus presenting a ready-made receptacle for sparks and hot metal spatters.

5 Goggles are essential and must be worn to protect the eyes from heat and glare, and from flying particles of hot metal and slag. Goggles used for

welding and cutting must be fitted with approved filter lenses. Figure 13.15 shows suitable protective clothing for gas welding.

Gas welding goggles are no protection against the *ultra-violet radiation* of the electric arc.

For all arc-welding operations it is essential to protect the welder's head from radiation, spatter and hot slag, and for this purpose either a helmet or a hand shield must be worn.

An arc welder's *hand shield* protects one hand as well as the face. It is fitted with a handle which is made of material which insulates against heat and electricity. The handle may either be fixed inside the shield to protect the hand from the heat and rays of the arc, or fixed outside and provided with an effective guard for the same purpose.

Welder's *head shields* are usually fitted with an adjustable band to fit the wearer's head. This band and the means of adjustment should be thoroughly insulated from the wearer's head, the insulation being non-absorbent as a precaution against dampness, such as perspiration, which tends to make it conductive. Head shields are designed to pivot so as to provide two definitely located positions.
1 Lowered in front of the face – the welding position – for protection.
2 Raised in a horizontal position to enable the welder to see when not striking the arc.

Some welders prefer to use a hand shield, rather than a head shield because it is the less tiring protection to

use. However, head shields provide better protection and allow the welder the free use of both hands.

Screens must also be provided to protect persons working nearby from radiation of the electric arc. Exposure to the radiation can cause blindness. Figs 13.16 and 13.17 show suitable protective clothing for electric arc welding.

Fire hazards

The following important precautions should be rigidly observed.
1 Do not position gas cylinders and hoses where sparks or slag can fall on them.
2 Wooden floors should be kept thoroughly wetted with water, or completely covered, for example, with sand.
3 Wooden structures should be adequately protected by sheet metal or asbestos.
4 All combustible material should be removed to a safe position, or if this is not possible, it should be properly protected against flying sparks; it must be realised that sparks from cutting can travel up to 9 metres along a floor.
5 Suitable safety measures must be taken in the case of cracks or openings in walls or floors.
6 **Keep fire-fighting equipment ready to hand**. A responsible person should keep the site under observation for at least half an hour after the completion of the work in order to watch for and deal with any outbreak of fire. There is always the danger of material smouldering for hours before a fire breaks out.

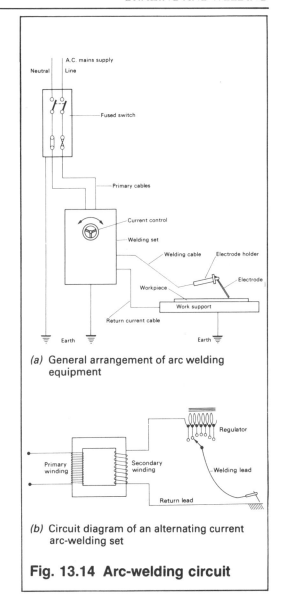

(a) General arrangement of arc welding equipment

(b) Circuit diagram of an alternating current arc-welding set

Fig. 13.14 Arc-welding circuit

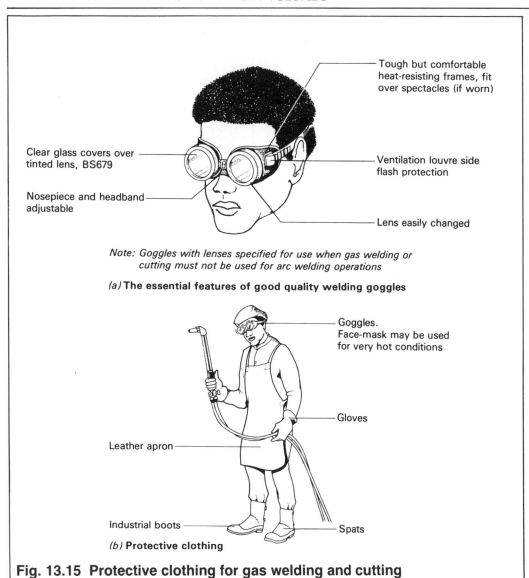

Tough but comfortable heat-resisting frames, fit over spectacles (if worn)

Clear glass covers over tinted lens, BS679

Ventilation louvre side flash protection

Nosepiece and headband adjustable

Lens easily changed

Note: Goggles with lenses specified for use when gas welding or cutting must not be used for arc welding operations

(a) The essential features of good quality welding goggles

Goggles.
Face-mask may be used for very hot conditions

Gloves

Leather apron

Industrial boots

Spats

(b) Protective clothing

Fig. 13.15 Protective clothing for gas welding and cutting

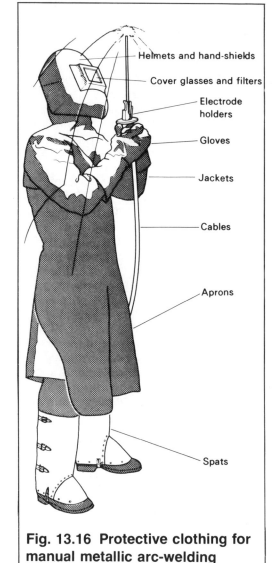

Helmets and hand-shields

Cover glasses and filters

Electrode holders

Gloves

Jackets

Cables

Aprons

Spats

Fig. 13.16 Protective clothing for manual metallic arc-welding

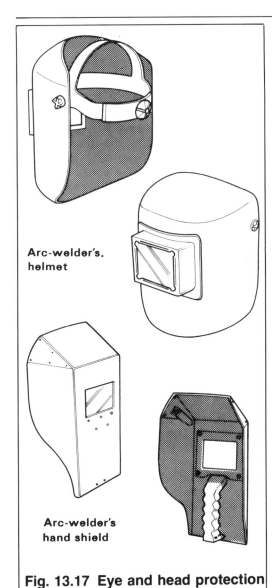

Arc-welder's.
helmet

Arc-welder's
hand shield

Fig. 13.17 Eye and head protection

Exercises

1. Describe what is meant by 'hard' soldering and the precautions that need to be taken to ensure a sound joint.
   State a suitable solder alloy and flux.
2. Brazing is the oldest hard soldering process and gets its name from the spelter used. Give a suitable brazing spelter composition and explain how the composition changes during the brazing process.
3. (a) Describe the essential differences between brazing and braze (bronze) welding.
   (b) With the aid of sketches describe the following types of brazed joints.
      (i) Lap joints
      (ii) Butt joints
      (iii) Scarf joints
4. Describe what is meant by full fusion welding and name the two most commonly used processes.
5. Sketch a set of gas welding equipment and name the various items. Describe the safety precautions that should be used when storing and using bottled gases. How can the cylinders be identified?
6. Describe with the aid of sketches what is meant by:
   (i) oxidising flame,
   (ii) neutral flame,
   (iii) reducing flame,
   (iv) leftward welding,
   (v) rightward welding.
7. (a) List the advantages and limitations of:
      (i) leftward welding,
      (ii) rightward welding.
   (b) With the aid of sketches describe the following welded joints.
      (i) Flanged edge weld
      (ii) Vee butt weld
      (iii) Fillet weld
8. (a) Sketch a set of metallic-arc welding equipment and name the various items.
   (b) Describe the safety precautions that should be used when electric arc welding in order to avoid electrocution, burns, and eye injury.
9. With the aid of a sketch show the principle of arc welding. Describe the purpose of the flux coating that surrounds the electrode.
10. (a) Describe the fire precautions that should be taken when welding.
    (b) Describe the protective clothing that should be worn when gas welding.
    (c) Describe the protective clothing that should be worn when arc welding.

Glossary

anvil Any solid support for a work piece.

arbour A tapered spindle for attaching a drill chuck to the machine spindle. A spindle that carries milling cutters and attaches them to the machine spindle.

bevel lead The sharp taper on the end of a reamer.

bezel The knurled ring surrounding a dial test indicator by which the scale may be rotated for setting purposes.

block A metal block fitted with a scriber for marking lines parallel to a surface.

brazing Hard soldering, using a brass alloy; higher temperatures required but greater strength.

bush A hollow cylinder in which a shaft or drill rotates. A guide for a drill.

cam A mechanisation for converting rotary movement into linear movement. The action is not reversible.

centrescope An optical device for positioning a drill over the scribed centre lines of a hole.

chamfer A 45° taper cut on the edge of the work piece to remove the sharp corners.

chatter Vibration of the cutting tool and work.

chuck A device for holding drills on a drilling machine. Work-holding device on a lathe.

circompresser A device for raising the pressure of air, gases, etc.

clearance The difference in size between a shaft and bearing to allow freedom of movement (freedom to rotate and/or slide).

clinometer A device for setting machine tables and work to specified angles. It contains an adjustable spirit level.

concentric Diameters having a common axis.

datum A common basis for measurement, point, line or surface.

deviation The displacement of the tolerence zone from the basic size as shown below.

dig-in The sudden and uncontrolled penetration of the workpiece by the cutting tool resulting from unstable cutting conditions.

eccentric Diameters having displaced areas

effluent Waste fluids

entectic An alloy of two or more metals whose composition results in the lowest melting point for that alloy.

fiducial indicator The indicator on a measuring device that shows constant measuring pressure is being used.

filler rod Additional metal in the form of a wire or rod that is added to a welded joint.

finish The roughness of a machined surface.

flash {
gutter A groove in a drop forging die to accept the surplus metal (flush)
land A narrow connecting passage between the die cavity and the flash gutter to limit the flow of metal.
line A line left round the forging after the flash has been clipped from it.
}

flash-back When the flame of a gas welding torch gets out of control and travels back up the hose to the cylinder.

fuller Forging tool for lengthening and thinning (drawing down) work pieces.

gear train A series of gears meshing one with next used to transmit motion between two parallel shafts.

gib head A key with a raised head by which it may be extracted.

headstock The assembly on the left hand end of a lathe (viewed from the operation position) that contains the gear base and spindle.

hypo Alloys in which the alloying element(s) are less than the entectic composition.

hyper-entectoid Alloys in which the alloying element(s) exceed the entectic composition.

indexing Rotation of a component through a specified angle whilst machining.

jig Work holding device that also guides the drill.

keyway A groove into which a key may be fitted when coupling wheels to shaft.

land A narrow band of metal immediately behind the cutting edge of a milling cutter tooth. Often left to indicate that the cutter has not been ground undersize. It also stabilises the cutting action.

lead screw A coarse pitch used to convert rotary motion into linear motion to move a machine element, eg. movement of a milling machine table.

lever and scroll system A lever and coarse pitch screw mechanisation that converts linear motion into rotary motion and magnifies it at the same time.

lug A projection from the rear of the casing of a dial test indicator by which it is attached to a support.

malleable Capable of being hammered to shape (material property).

morse taper shank A drill or reamer shank (the part by which it is held) that has been ground to the dimensions of the morse taper system.

NOT GO Those parts of a **elements** gauge which come **GO** into contact with the work piece and determine whether it is over or under size, or the correct size.

oilstone A block of fine abrasive used for sharpening fine edge tools. Oil is applied to its surface before use.

peening To close a sheet metal joint by hammering.

pitch The distance between similar points on adjacent screw threads measured parallel to the axis.

plunger An extension of the rack in some types of dial gauge. It protrudes from the sleeve and moves up and down when pressed.

prussian blue A ready made mixture of blue die and grease used to find 'high spots' on mating components.

rack and pinion A mechanisation for converting linear motion into rotary motion. The rack is a 'linear gear' and engages an ordinary spur gear.

reamer – rose A reamer is a device **– fluted** for improving the accuracy and finish of previously drilled holes. Rose action reamers cut on the ends and sides of the flute, flute action reamers cut on the tip only.

scribing point The point of any marking out instrument.

set over Lateral displacement of the tailstack.

sight glasses Glass insert in a gear box casting through which the oil level may be seen.

slideway A ground surface on a machine tool along which some other part of the mechanism slides

slip gauges Hardened blocks of steel ground very accurately to size and used as standards of measurement.

solder A low melting point tin/lead alloy used for soldering.

spelter A high zinc content brass used for hard soldering (brazing)

spigot Sleeve that guides the plung of a dial test indicator also used as an alternative mounting.

spline A raised projection on a shaft by which movement is transmitted. There are usually many splines equally spaced

round the shaft. They allow axial movement whilst providing a solid rotary drive.

steady An additional support for the work piece on a lathe to help resist the cutting forces.

sticky pin A pin attached to a cutter by putty or plasticine to aid setting up.

stylus A 'finger' that contracts the surface of the work piece in some types of sensitive measuring instruments.

swage Forging tool for converting square sections to circular.

tailstock The assembly on the right hand end of a lathe (viewed from the operating position) used to support long work pieces.

taper lead The more gradual taper just behind the bevel lead on a hand reamer.

thimble The rotating element of a micrometer caliper.

to radius To remove the sharp corner between adjacent faces of a component and replace it with a curve.

tolerance The arithmetical difference between the upper and lower limits of size of a dimension.

trammel A device for marking out large circles.

tup The hammer of a drap forging machine.

vee-block Hardened metal blocks with a vee section groove used to hold cylindrical work.

wander Deviation of a cutter from its true path.

workpiece Any piece of material that is to be worked upon.

zeroed A dial test indicator that has been set to zero reading by rotation of its scale.

Index

ATTACK
OF THE JAGUAR

Other titles in this series:

The Scorpion Secret

ATTACK
OF THE JAGUAR

M. A. Harvey

Chrysalis Children's Books

First published in the UK in 2003 by
Chrysalis Children's Books
an imprint of Chrysalis Books Group Plc,
The Chrysalis Building,
Bramley Road,
London W10 6SP

Text © M. A. Harvey 2002
Illustrations by Garry Walton

The right of M. A. Harvey to be identified
as the author of this work has been asserted.

ISBN 1 84458 000 8

British Library Cataloguing in Publication Data
for this book is available from the British Library.

Printed and bound in Great Britain by
Mackays of Chatham Ltd, Chatham, Kent

10 9 8 7 6 5 4 3 2 1

CONTENTS

A message from

XTREME ADVENTURE INC

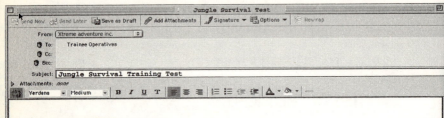

Jungle Survival Test

Send Now | Send Later | Save as Draft | Add Attachments | Signature ▾ | Options ▾ | Rewrap

From: Xtreme adventure inc. ⬦
To: Trainee Operatives
Cc:
Bcc:
Subject: **Jungle Survival Training Test**
Attachments: *none*

Verdana ▾ Medium ▾ | **B** *I* <u>U</u> T | ≡ ≡ ≡ | ≣ ≣ ≣ ≣ | A ▾ ▾ | —

XTREME ADVENTURE INC.
confirms you are authorised to read this top secret
transmission.

To: Trainee operative.
Re: Jungle survival training test.

XTREME ADVENTURE INC. is an organisation dedicated to
protecting the planet and those who inhabit it. Our operatives are
an elite squad who have proved their bravery, survival skills and
brainpower. They can survive in the most dangerous, hostile
places on Earth, and we call on them for rescue missions so
tough that all others would fail.

Do you have what it takes to join us? We shall see.

This training manual contains an adventure story.
Imagine you find yourself abandoned in the South American
rainforest, far, far from modern civilisation and in the greatest
danger from your enemies. All that and more happened to
teenager Simon Jones.
This is his story. We shall call it...

ATTACK OF THE JAGUAR

WILL YOU MAKE THE GRADE?

In each chapter of this story there are quizzes for you to complete. They will test your brainpower and observation skills.

As you read through, keep a note of your answers to the puzzles and quizzes we have set for you.

Then check your credit score at the back of this book to see if you are capable of joining **XTREME ADVENTURE INC**.

Finally, turn to page 126 to try for a place in our ELITE SQUAD.

WARNING

Trainees who look at the answers first fail automatically as this shows lack of discipline and inability to follow instructions. These are serious flaws for XTREME ADVENTURE operatives.

Good luck to all trainees.
Chief of Field Operations

The Nightmare Begins

Simon sat listening to the rain. It pattered softly on the roof, dribbling down the spines of the thick sword-shaped leaves he and his parents had so carefully gathered and woven through a criss-cross of branches to protect them as they lay in their hammocks. The rain ran off the leaf points and fell in mini-waterfalls on to the ground around their open-sided shelter.

Simon was expecting the rain and found it comforting. It fell every evening just before darkness engulfed the Amazon jungle that stretched for thousands of kilometres around their makeshift camp. He smiled to himself, remembering how thrilled he had been when his parents had confirmed that, at 16, he was old enough to come with them on their latest Amazon plant-hunting expedition. And not just to a comfortable tourist lodge but on camping treks deep into the world's biggest rainforest.

Since he had arrived he had experienced a thousand new sights, sounds and smells. He had got used to the fuggy permanently warm rainforest air, which was damp and humid like a bathroom after a hot shower. He had got used to sleeping in a hammock slung between trees and he had even learnt to look forward to camp food cooked over a freshly made fire.

He had learnt that he could cope with most things, but he never quite got used to the way that darkness came to the rainforest so suddenly every night, not at all like the way it crept slowly over things back home. You had to be ready for this dark, with all your equipment safely stowed out of the rain and the reach of thieving wild monkeys. By the time darkness fell at about 6pm you had to be out of your damp day clothes and changed into your spare set. Most importantly, you had to smear every

piece of exposed skin with the strongest mosquito repellent ever devised, and ideally get into your hammock under your mosquito net before you got bitten by the clouds of insects that came out at dusk to feed on your blood.

"Are your toes inside?" his mum always joked before they fell asleep. In some areas vampire bats cruised the forest, looking for mammals with warm blood to suck. It was said they sometimes feasted on human toes left carelessly poking out of sleeping bags. Simon knew this was very rare but the daily joke did serve to remind him that there were dangers to be wary of. He'd seen poisonous snakes, stinging ants and biting spiders since he'd been on the trip. Luckily, he was certain that with his parents' long jungle experience and survival knowledge the family could stay out of trouble, and that's why he was feeling cosy and protected, even with no walls round the camp and the darkness swirling around.

In amongst the towering jungle trees there was another difference from the darkness back home: the rainforest night certainly wasn't silent. Right now Simon could hear chirrups, screeches, clickings...A lot of animals came out at night, some to hunt. Simon wriggled deeper into his hammock at the thought. Only today his dad had pointed out some marks on a tree trunk.

"See those scratches on the bark? A jaguar did that," he had explained. Simon had looked wildly round in panic, knowing full well that a jaguar was a pretty big cat easily capable of killing a human.

His dad had reassured him: "Don't worry. A jaguar won't attack a human unless it's threatened. It won't look for trouble. Besides, I've been keeping an eye out for fresh pawprints and droppings, and I haven't seen any. The jaguar who made these marks isn't close." He added, "Local people think that jaguars are shamans, you know; half-human, half-animal, with mystical powers; a sort of guardian spirit of the jungle. This place has many legends: jungle spirits, monsters, a lost city of gold..."

"I like the sound of that one. Lead me to it!" Simon had replied. His dad had laughed.

"Many people have tried and failed to find *that* legend, and sometimes died looking," he explained. "The mythical golden city is called El Dorado. If it does exist it could be anywhere in this vast jungle. Let's stick to finding plants!"

Simon settled in his hammock. He would have liked to have dreamt of golden cities, but instead another dream slipped softly into his mind like a snake. In this unexpected dreamworld he saw the glowing eyes of a mighty cat. Its mouth was open, showing impossibly long fangs. It reminded him of some long-extinct sabre-toothed tiger, though he knew it was a jaguar.

It was crouching high on a branch as a thunderstorm rolled around. Suddenly lightning struck down through the leaves; the jaguar roared and its branch burst into flames. The roar sounded like a warning.

Simon woke with a jolt. The rain had stopped. He could hear his father gently snoring in the next hammock. He turned restlessly and slept again, this time heavily and dreamlessly.

When he woke natural light was seeping through the jungle canopy above. A fire was lit, but his parents' hammocks were empty.

"Oops. Slept in late," Simon thought guiltily, and struggled out of his hammock. The camp was empty. His mum and dad must have gone to collect firewood or water, or left for an early morning flower hunt.

"Mum! Dad!" he called repeatedly, looking round the camp clearing. Suddenly he felt fear. He noticed signs of a struggle. How could he not have heard? Where were his parents? Simon tried to control his breathing, to fight off the panic attack overwhelming him. Imagine how he felt, suddenly alone in the dark heart of the Amazon...

How did Simon know there had been a struggle on the edge of the camp clearing? Take a look at the scenes before and after the event. How many clues can you spot that show a struggle took place?

OPERATIVE FIELD TEST 1

FILE NO. MB1JAGU100 GW200

ADVENTURE INC.

XTREME ADVENTURE QUIZ 1

1. The Amazon area is in:

a) North America
b) South America
c) Africa

2. The Amazon is the world's second largest:

a) Mountain
b) Live Volcano
c) River

3. The Amazon area is:

a) A huge desert
b) A huge tropical rainforest
c) A huge canyon

4. Virtually every day in the Amazon it:

a) Snows
b) Hails
c) Rains

5. What must you have over you at night in the Amazon?

a) Mosquito net
b) Electric light
c) Portable fan heater

6. The climate in the Amazon is:

a) Usually icy
b) Always warm
c) Cold in winter, warm in summer

Trail to the Treetops

As Simon distractedly picked up his father's battered hat possibilities crowded into his mind. He knew he had to concentrate.

"Be logical. Think it through," he urged himself. Were his parents playing some kind of joke on him? Unlikely. It would be a pretty sick joke. Had they been attacked by an animal? Negative. There was no blood and there hadn't been enough noise to wake him up. That left one other strong possibility, an attack by humans. "Why would anyone do that? I've no idea but one thing's for certain. I'd better get out of here in case they come back for me," Simon reasoned.

He stood still for a moment, staring at the hat

as if it were a precious object, and silently making the most serious promise so far in his young life, "I will never, never give up until I rescue my family and get them to safety."

Logical thinking done. Good. Some kind of plan in place. Good. Now it was time for action. Quickly he found his rucksack and chose the equipment he thought he would need for a prolonged jungle trek. It wasn't easy; he didn't have all that much room in his rucksack. As he hunted around he found that all the communication radios had been taken, so there was no way of calling for long-distance help. With relief he discovered a compass and working GPS handset. "At least I can pinpoint my own position. That must to be worth something," he muttered.

As he bent over to pack his kit he had a peculiar feeling that he was being watched. He stood up straight, snapped his head round and met the gaze of a small Amazon monkey perched on a branch.

"OK, partner. So you want in on this mission, do you? Do you think you're tough enough?" he spoke to the monkey because it was comforting to talk to someone...something. It lifted his spirits and made him feel less alone.

He slung his rucksack on his back and then he examined the scene around him. There were a few well-worn trails around the camp clearing, used by his parents in the course of their work.

"Do you know the story of Hansel and Gretel?" Simon spoke in the direction of the monkey, which cocked its head and stared at him suspiciously. "My mum used to read it to me," Simon continued. "Hansel and Gretel were taken into a forest and abandoned by a wicked relative, but on the way they dropped a trail of breadcrumbs so they could find their way back home. It was a dumb idea; birds ate the breadcrumbs. But mum and dad have been flicking bits and pieces out of their pockets as they were taken away and they've left clues much better than breadcrumbs."

One of the clues told him exactly what he needed to know. It showed him the trail the kidnappers had taken. He took out his compass and checked the direction he was going to follow.

Simon followed the trail, keeping an eye out for items his parents had dropped, feeling a surge of hope and connection with them. His dad had dropped some of the coins he always had in his pockets. His mum had left a silk hankie that still smelt of her perfume. But after a while the clue trail ended, to his huge disappointment. Perhaps the captors had stopped his parents from reaching into their pockets, or maybe they had simply run out of stuff to drop. They must have hated the thought of littering the trail; they were so tidy, so careful to preserve the rainforest as it should be.

Simon's anger rose. "Who forced them to break their own rules like this?" he muttered. He tried hard to channel the anger to make himself feel more determined. "Survival is partly a state of mind," he said out loud. He'd once heard some hero say that in a movie. This time the danger was for real but he reckoned the advice still held good. "Keep in control, Simon," he advised himself, and he was quickly rewarded by a piece of luck.

He reached the "lookout tree", as he and his

parents usually called it when they used it for their work. Its massive roots flared out like giant limbs and it was hung with thick rope lianas, like giant hair strands. On a previous plant-hunting expedition it had been fitted with a system of scaffolds and rope ladders to enable people to climb up through the tree layers and get a view of the rainforest around. Simon stowed his rucksack at the tree base, slung his binoculars and compass around his neck and began climbing.

At first it was the smell he noticed, or rather the way it changed. At the bottom of the tree he could smell the familiar scent of rotting leaves that covered the rainforest ground; but the air gradually grew fresher as he went higher. The tree was enormous, at least 25m tall, like a multistorey building with as many different floors and residents. He disturbed a tiny tree frog on a leaf, no bigger than his thumb; a parrot screeched with outrage at being so rudely disturbed and a lizard scuttled away into a hole. He knew there were thousands of tree insects he couldn't even see, plus birds, butterflies, even a slow-moving

sloth, perhaps. "But hopefully not a tree snake," he muttered.

He climbed on up as high as he could go. From here he saw trees stretching into the distance like hundreds of giant green broccoli tops. Here and there extra-tall "emergent" trees grew and towered over the others.

He looked through his binoculars, to try to pick out any detail, some campfire smoke, perhaps. There was nothing, only green foliage. Then he pointed his binoculars further away. The trail he had followed so far led towards a river, a small tributary of the Amazon, and it could be seen glittering through the trees in the distance, in a northwards direction, according to his compass. "Could they be heading for the river?" he wondered. It would be the quickest way out of the area if they had boats...

Suddenly his eyes caught movement, a shadow sliding across the treetops. With a massive wingspan like that it had to be a harpy eagle. Simon jerked his head up. There it was, the world's biggest eagle. As it swooped nearer he focused on its feet, the size of human hands and armed with seriously sharp talons. It must have seen a tree monkey, ideal for its dinner. A horrible thought crossed Simon's mind. "What if it thinks I'm a monkey?" If so, he knew he was in for a nasty encounter. Should he slip down the rope? A swift movement might attract the eagle more. Should he scream? He'd sound just like a monkey then. There was no choice. He closed his eyes and covered his head with an arm, braced for the hit.

Ages seemed to pass before he heard a terror-filled scream, not his own. It came from a nearby branch. He opened his eyes and saw the harpy eagle sink its talons into a helpless spider monkey and carry it off effortlessly. He let out a long breath he hadn't even realised he was holding. "I've been in this tree long enough," he decided "That harpy might come back for seconds."

He climbed back down, as quickly as he could manage without putting himself in danger. This time the giant butterflies and beautiful bromeliad plants nestling in the branches failed to catch his attention. The harpy eagle incident had pumped him full of adrenalin and he was using the feeling to urge himself onwards, to push back the fear inside him.

"OK, Simon. This jungle is not going to beat you on the first day," he muttered to himself as he hoisted his rucksack once again. He checked his compass. "North to the river," he shouted out loud, as if he was commanding an army. He didn't want to admit that he had never felt so alone.

XTREME ADVENTURE QUIZ 2

1 Choose between:
a) Mobile phone
b) Wellington boots
c) Compass

2 Choose between:
a) Swimming kit
b) Packets of food
c) Deodorant stick

3 Choose between:
a) Hairbrush
b) Spare set of clothes
c) Game Boy

4 Choose between:
a) Pillow
b) Penknife
c) Dressing gown

29

5 Choose between:
a) Diving mask
b) Pair of sandals
c) Medical kit

6 Choose between:
a) Credit card
b) Guidebook
c) Insect repellent

7 Choose between:
a) Water bottle
b) Alarm clock
c) Ball of string

8 Choose between:
a) Camera
b) Sweater
c) Torch

A Thief in the Night

"Don't grab on to branches, Simon. They could be thorny."

"Time to rest now, Simon. Don't forget to drink some water." Simon knew the rules of rainforest trekking. Still, he'd never done it alone before, and he found that occasionally repeating them out loud helped his state of mind. It somehow made him feel as if his parents were there with him, talking. If only they were.

Once or twice he found hopeful signs he was on the right route. He came across a big spider web, the kind woven by a colony of spiders. Instead of stretching across the tree trunks like a net, it hung down in tatters. Humans could have broken it, perhaps, and that was confirmed when he spotted a cigarette butt nearby.

Although thick jungle plants didn't grow under the dense trees there were still plenty of roots to trip over and soggy leaves to slide on. That, plus the heat and humidity, made him tire quickly. He felt almost grateful when he glanced at his watch and found it was nearly 4pm. He slid off his rucksack, reciting the most important trek rule of all. "Never trek in the dark!"

His words died away.

No one answered.

"Rules are rules," he continued. In fact, at the moment those "rules" felt like the only thin thread connecting him to the human world. Most rainforest animals came out as the day ebbed away and there was plenty of noise around, birds twittering or screeching, frogs calling, yet having no human contact left Simon feeling isolated and on edge.

"Snap to it, Simon. Don't get down," he muttered. "OK, let's start home-making. It'll take two hours, and then it'll be dark."

There were a couple of branches ideally placed for Simon's hammock but before he tied it he checked for insect or spider colonies.

"Nothing worse than stirring up an ants' nest, except perhaps for a big hairy spider plopping on to me from above. Yeugh!" he grinned to himself. He also checked to see if there was any fruit up above him. He remembered his mum telling him how a friend had once been badly injured by a falling coconut and had to be airlifted to hospital, fighting for his life. You never forgot that kind of true-life story.

He set about finding firewood and soon had a coffee and some canned food on the go. "Check the GPS," he muttered and clocked his current position in relation to base camp, where his parents had been snatched. "If I run out of food or water I can get back there," he thought, but later, as he lay in darkness, doubts began to arrive big-time.

"Maybe I should go back tomorrow morning. What would mum and dad want me to do? Stay put? Well, probably not go far from base, anyway. OK, but I'd rather be with them and captured than on my own worrying...and anyway, I'm not lost yet. I know I'm travelling due north now, and I can still get back to base camp with the GPS...so I needn't give up the search, not yet. I'll keep going one more day, try to make it to the river..."

He tried to breath deeply, a relaxation technique Mum once showed him from her yoga class. It might have worked if a deer hadn't suddenly barked nearby and made him jump out of his skin. It was a bad start to a long night, and a lot more mysterious snuffling and grunting as various animal visitors passed by. Simon knew he wasn't in any real danger but, all the same, sleeplessness was no fun.

Dawn broke to the strangest alarm he'd ever heard, a scary roar like some horror-movie monster. A group of howler monkeys had set up residence in trees nearby and now they were making their bizarre mega-loud calls.

"Wouldn't it be something to roll out of bed, shuffle on some slippers and sit eating chocolate cereal in front of the TV," Simon thought, but he knew that life in the Amazon took a lot more work and effort than that. First he had to bang his shoes to dislodge any creepy-crawlies that might have moved in during the night (and probably slept better than him). Yesterday's still-dampish clothes had to go back on and the fire had to be rebuilt before he could enjoy a cup of coffee and a bowl of oatmeal (OK it wasn't chocolate cereal, but it wasn't bad once you got used to it).

"Right. Pack up. Get going. One more day's search and, if I don't find Mum and Dad, then I'll trek back towards base camp," Simon said out loud. A sign of madness, perhaps? No, just a way to get through the situation, he reassured himself. "OK, let's see. Torch. Water bottle. GPS handset...Where did I put that last night?"

The GPS handset was nowhere to be found, and nor was the compass. Simon tried to think back to last night. He'd set up camp. He'd checked his position; then...Damn. He'd left the compass and the GPS handset lying out on a log. He hadn't packed it away, a big mistake, and now he was going to pay the price. Round here there were plenty of curious thieves: the monkeys. Had they taken his stuff? He guessed so, but he'd never find out for sure and had no chance of getting it back. "Yeah, well, the GPS needs batteries and I've got them!" he shouted up into the treetops. It was a useless gesture but it made him feel better.

"Now it's crunch time," he admitted quietly. Because he'd checked the compass yesterday he knew from the spot where he was sitting which way was north and which was south. North was by the biggest tree over to his right. But once he got away from the familiar surroundings he would have no accurate way of finding true north or south.

He sat thinking, and the seriousness of the situation seemed to focus his mind. There was no point in panicking, only in being logical..."I can't navigate by the sun...I can't even see it from under these trees...So I have to find another method...I have to make a compass!" He cried out as the idea flashed into his mind. He jumped up and searched feverishly in his pack. He took out a mini sewing kit and extracted a needle from inside it. Then he poured a little water into a plastic cup and floated a small thin leaf blade on the surface.

"I haven't done this since Mr Knott's science class in school," he chuckled to himself. He rubbed along the needle several times with his Mum's silk hankie, always rubbing in the same direction, to magnetise it, then he gently placed it on the leaf blade in the water. It immediately spun round in the water.

"Yes! My very own mini magnet! Thank you, Mr Knott!" Simon shouted delightedly.

But which end of the needle was north? The eye of the needle pointed to the big tree... The eye showed north! If Simon did the same trick regularly as he trekked along he should be able to keep himself roughly on a northern course.

The morning's trek didn't seem so hard because Simon was buoyed up by his compass success. Every now and again he repeated it to check his route direction, before carefully drinking the water from the cup. Then he got his second big surprise of the day when he came out of the trees on to some kind of a rough vehicle track.

He walked along it for a little way, looking down. There was no mistaking the clues it offered him. He could see that a vehicle had driven in both directions along the track, and had done so very recently.

"I'd bet my compass needle that my parents were unwilling passengers," he murmured. He dropped his rucksack on to the ground and sat down on it to think about his next move.

OPERATIVE FIELD TEST 3

he Amazon rainforest is
home to many extraordinary
creatures. The more you know
about them, the less
dangerous a visit will be.
Test your knowledge with
this animal quiz. Note your
answers and check them when
you finish the story.

ADVENTURE INC.

XTREME ADVENTURE QUIZ 3

1 Which creature hangs upside down in a rainforest tree?

a) Sloth
b) Parrot

2 Which creature drinks blood from mammals?

a) Hummingbird
b) Vampire bat

3 What is the pattern on a jaguar's fur?

a) Stripes
b) Spots

41

4 An electric eel can generate a big electric shock to:

a) Stun prey
b) Light its way at night

5 The giant harpy eagle eats:

a) Monkeys
b) Fruit

6 What is a group of monkeys called?

a) A troupe
b) A pride

Caught!

Simon tried to think through what to do next. Which way had the vehicle gone with his parents inside? There had to be a way to find out. He wandered along the middle of the road a little way, distracted by the problem. Then he bent down to study the tyre prints closely, and that was the moment when he felt a sting on the back of his neck. As he fell unconscious the last thing he saw was a pair of black eyes in a flaming red face.

Much later, maybe days later, he woke up. He tried to turn but couldn't because his hands and feet were tightly tied. His prison was some kind of large hut made from stakes and woven leaves. It was dusty; he sneezed and the noise made a small child jump up from somewhere behind him and scutter away crying. He lay back, his head throbbing. "I've failed," he thought miserably. "How did I think I'd ever succeed, a dumb city boy like me?"

The child must have alerted other people. Now two men came into the hut. They were Amazon Indians, naked except for thin thongs around their waists and strings of beads around their necks. One of them had red paint on his face like a mask stretched across his eyes. He spoke, first in a local dialect to his colleague, then in Spanish to Simon.

"Do you understand me?" he asked.

"Yes. I speak a little Portuguese," Simon replied, with an effort. His throat felt terrible, as if it had been burnt on the inside. The man muttered to his friend, who left and quickly returned with a bowl of liquid. He knelt and helped Simon swallow the sweet fruit juice. It made Simon's throat feel easier.

"Why am I tied?" he asked in halting Portuguese. He had learnt some at school but now he was struggling to put together the phrases.

"We have tied you because you are a thief," the man replied.

"You are wrong," Simon stuttered. "I am Simon Jones. My parents study plants. They help look after the rainforest. They work in a camp near here." The man with the red face looked at him keenly.

"My parents were taken. Did you snatch them? I want to see them," Simon demanded. The Indians said nothing; they left the hut and Simon could hear voices outside having a discussion. Then the red-painted man returned with a knife. Simon shut his eyes. The man came close. Simon could smell his body sweat.

"If this is the end, make it fast, please," Simon muttered in English, but instead of killing him the man cut his bonds.

"Come," he said and helped Simon to get up. He led him gently out of the hut.

Outside, the light glared fiercely into Simon's aching eyes. The Indians had cut a clearing from the forest for their settlement and a few small crop fields. The long hut where they had tethered Simon was their main living quarters, shared by everyone. But there were a few

home-made hammocks outside, and in the centre of the clearing there was a fire.

As Simon walked into view children pointed at him and their mothers snatched them up, evidently thinking he was a threat. Simon's rescuer said something and motioned him towards the fire, where several men were sitting. The eldest-looking one was chewing, nuts or leaves probably. He turned and spat on the ground before nodding to the red-painted man, who spoke to Simon again.

"I am Kaipo. I speak some Spanish and Portuguese because I have travelled away from here many times to trade our goods with others, and to try to get governments to protect our lands. This is Maco, our head man. I will explain his words to you."

The old man, Maco, motioned for Simon to sit and conversation between the Indians ensued. Then Kaipo turned to Simon. "We are sorry we hurt you. We know your parents. They are good people, but we have also seen strangers come to our forest to steal. We thought you were one of them." A wave of relief washed over Simon. He knew that many tribes of

Amazon Indians had had a terrible time from strangers, illegal loggers and miners invading their land, spreading disease and even murdering them. But his parents had always respected them, asked permission to come on their land and left them in peace.

Kaipo continued. "Your parents helped us once. They rescued one of our children when she went into the rainforest and was bitten by a snake."

"My parents have been taken. Can you help?" Simon pleaded.

The old head man, Maco, nodded and drew Simon's attention. He laid a selection of paper scraps out on the floor and pointed, as Kaipo translated what he said:

"A truck came by on the road the strangers made. Someone threw these out of the window. One of us picked up the pieces." Simon stared at the crumpled paper scraps, then stretched out a hand and rearranged them. There were words written on them. As he spoke them out loud, wonderingly, the Indians glanced at each other. They understood something of what he had said.

Maco spoke, his voice fast and urgent.

"Have I upset him?" Simon asked worriedly.

Kaipo put a reassuring hand on his shoulder and guided him from the fire. "Maco is not angry. He says that we will help you," Kaipo explained. "We will talk it over and make a plan tonight, but first we must hunt. Do you want to come?" He picked up a thick tube, a blowpipe that was leaning against the hut. Then he slung a quiver over his back.

"Are your arrows dipped in poison?" Simon asked.

"Yes," Kaipo confirmed. "These hunting arrows have deadly poison on them from the skin of a frog. We darted you with a weaker one dipped in plant poison. We can make many mixtures that do different things."

Simon rubbed his neck at the unpleasant memory. He still felt quite tired and washed-out from the poison effects.

"You stay here," Kaipo smiled, then set off with the other men into the rainforest, leaving Simon surrounded by staring, laughing children and their mothers, who seemed calmer about him now. They motioned for him to sit.

Soon Simon had been draped with necklaces made from red and black plant seeds, and his face had been carefully painted red. In return he had spilled out the contents of his rucksack and every new object filled the kids with delight. They took him by the hand and pulled him to the places where they stored their own special treasures: fine bead necklaces, beautiful tropical bird feathers threaded into headdresses, even a kind of flute carved from a hollow animal bone. One small girl proudly showed him her best possession, a silver dollar coin. He couldn't understand her, nor she him, but he could tell she was trying to explain something so he made a mental note to ask Kaipo to translate.

He was feeling relaxed with these gentle people when Kaipo returned.

"You look good," he grinned.

"I feel much better," Simon agreed. When he quizzed Kaipo about the little girl and her silver dollar the Indian nodded knowingly. "Your father gave that to her, to help her forget the pain of the snake bite."

To Simon's surprise he felt hot tears prick his

eyes. "Dad and his coins. He loves collecting them," he murmured. "I want him back. I want Mum back. Who has taken them, Kaipo?" he raised his voice, angry at the kidnappers and angry at himself for crying.

"You will learn the truth soon," Kaipo replied. "Come, sit by the fire."

OPERATIVE FIELD TEST 4

XTREME ADVENTURE QUIZ 4

1 Which option would be best?

a) Find a river and follow it downstream
b) Find a river and follow it upstream

2 Which option would be best?

a) Travel by night
b) Travel by day

3 Which option would be best?

a) Drink lots of water
b) Drink as little water as possible

4 Which option would be best?

a) Sleep on the ground
b) Sleep in a hammock

5 Which option would be best?

a) Eat only cooked food
b) Eat only raw food

6 Which option would be best?

a) Cover up your skin with clothing
b) Wear as little as possible, to stay cool

7 Which option would be best?

a) Only drink water purified with tablets
b) Only drink water fresh from a stream

A Helping Hand

The fire was built afresh and the whole of the tribe sat around the clearing as evening came. Simon was given an important place next to Maco. "There is going to be a meal first, in honour of your visit," Kaipo explained. "Then we will talk."

"Great," Simon replied but inwardly panicked about what he would be expected to eat. He didn't want to offend anyone by refusing something.

"Oh well, do what the locals do. It's their party," he thought. That's what his parents would say, he knew.

He was given honey and some kind of fruit; Kaipo called it "guanabana". It looked like a grapefruit covered in blunt spikes. Then he was handed a haunch of roast monkey. "It could have been something worse," he decided. "I hope it was the monkey that stole my GPS." Finally he was handed a milky mushy drink that he had seen before. It was called "masato", and was drunk all over the Amazon region. It was made from a plant called manioc, mixed with water and spit, and it was slightly alcoholic. "I wish I didn't know about the spit, but here goes," Simon muttered under his breath and gulped some of it down as best he could.

Finally he was given a handful of little crunchy roasted balls. "Beetle babies," Kaipo explained, laughing. For insect grubs, Simon had to admit they made a pretty good snack, and the whole meal had been free since it all came from the rainforest. It was impressive how well the Indians knew the jungle and how to live in it.

After the meal Maco called to the tallest Indian in the group, who stood up and spoke. Kaipo summarised: "This man is our best tracker. He went out today and followed the path of the truck that carried your parents away. He came to the place where their

captors were resting and eating on their journey. He crept close and stole a paper from a pile of their clothing. From a distance he saw your parents and he says they looked as if they were OK, but they were tied up."

The tall tracker handed Simon a paper, a map with a very clear X marked on it.

Simon smoothed it out on his knee and after studying it for a while he pointed out some map features to Kaipo. "This long double line is a river, with rapids and a waterfall marked on it. These pale areas along the edge of the river are beaches or mudflats on the riverbank. The lines around the river are called contours. They show the shape of the landscape. These round ones show a hill..."

Kaipo clapped him on the back, looking pleased with himself. He announced something to the others, then explained to Simon: "I know where this X is. Tomorrow I will show you."

"It could be the place where my parents are being held captive," Simon replied eagerly. "But I still don't understand who has kidnapped them."

"It was the strangers we spoke of. I am sure

of it," Kaipo explained. "They came here and made the road for their trucks, so they can come in and out of the forest. If they see us they shoot their guns, so we hide and watch them. We have seen them steal animals from the forest, not a fair share for eating, but to cage them," he continued. "This is wrong, very wrong. The animals they take are rare. We also believe that every animal has a powerful spirit. The spirits will grow greatly troubled if they are caged. It would be bad for the forest."

When Kaipo had finished, Maco began gabbling angrily, stabbing his finger into the air like a spear. "Maco says the strangers will be punished by the Caipora," Kaipo translated.

"The Caipora...Is that the jungle spirit, the one with the strange feet?" Simon asked. His mother had told him lots of Amazon tales and legends, and he remembered hearing this one.

"The Caipora is a gentle spirit, a creature whose feet are turned from back to front, like this..." Kaipo mimed with his hand. "He cares for the animals in the forest and heals them when they are wounded. If a hunter kills too many animals then the Caipora will punish him."

"Here's hoping," Simon muttered. "I'll bet my parents stumbled on these people at their work. That must have made them a threat."

Kaipo nodded in agreement. "Your parents would have been angry to see what the strangers did," he added. "They are our friends. We won't abandon them." As the kind Indians talked and ate around him Simon felt hope for the first time. He knew that giving up, on himself and on his parents, would be the worst thing to do. Tied up in the hut he'd very nearly reached that point. But now his confidence was going back up again. He was sure he knew where his parents were, and he wasn't alone any more. Who knows, the Caipora might be looking after him, too. He slept deeply and dreamlessly that night.

The next morning he was woken by the children, who were giggling.

"Glad I'm so entertaining," he remarked, as he struggled out of his own hammock with its built-in mosquito net.

Kaipo arrived, smiling. "They think you look like a giant beetle grub hiding in your strange bag," he explained. "Come on, I want to show you something." He took Simon through the forest until they reached a small river tributary, one of many that threaded through the vast rainforest to the mighty Amazon River itself.

"Follow me," Kaipo said, and shinned up on to a rock by the riverbank to get a good view of the surroundings. He made climbing look very easy. For Simon it was tougher, and he needed Kaipo's helping hand.

"If there was an Olympic rock-climbing event you'd win the medal!" Simon remarked.

"I climb well, yes, because I have done it for a long time. And you read maps well, because you are experienced with them. We are a team. It's good that we work together," Kaipo grinned.

"Yeah, it's good," Simon agreed, and inwardly felt really pleased. He did have his uses, after all! He unfolded the map and compared it with the landscape ahead.

"Can you spot the place where the X marks?" Kaipo said.

"Over there," Simon replied, pointing.

Kaipo looked serious. "We must tell Maco," he murmured. He took Simon quickly back to the

Indian settlement and spoke to Maco, who frowned hard and then spoke. It sounded as if he had come to a decision and was announcing it to everyone.

"The X on the map shows a place we call the Lair of the Jaguar. It is a place we avoid because it is full of spirits, and the strongest spirit of all is the jaguar. He is the guardian of the forest, and the lair is the heart of his kingdom," Kaipo said quietly. "We stay away from this place, not wishing to anger him."

"But I must go there!" Simon cried. "It has to be the key to this kidnapping!"

Kaipo agreed: "It has been decided that we must go there, too, to free the stolen animals from their cages. We risk the jaguar spirit's angry temper, but we hope he will be pleased that we save his creatures."

"And my parents. Will you help me free them, too?" Simon pleaded.

"Yes, my brave friend. We will give you a helping hand," Kaipo nodded, and turned to pick up his spear. "We must prepare for fighting."

"Perhaps," Simon murmured. "But let's hope there is another way."

"It will be as the jaguar spirit wishes," Kaipo replied.

The people of the rainforest have their own unique way of life. The more you understand, the better you will get along with them. Test your knowledge in this true/false quiz. Keep a note of your answers and check your score when you have finished the story.

XTREME ADVENTURE QUIZ 5

1 Rainforest people often decorate their faces and bodies.

a) True
b) False

2 Rainforest people never wear jewellery.
a) True
b) False

3 Rainforest people live in treehouses.

a) True
b) False

65

4 Rainforest people use poisoned arrows to hunt.

a) True
b) False

5 Rainforest people buy most of their food from shops.

a) True
b) False

6 Rainforest people usually wear trainers.

a) True
b) False

7 Rainforest people believe in rainforest spirits.

a) True
b) False

Dangerous waters

"We will go by boat," Kaipo explained. "It will be quicker than travelling over land."

Simon agreed. His mind felt sharp now, and ready for action.

"It will be easier to escape afterwards by water, too," he replied. "I don't know what shape my parents will be in. They might not be able to get very far on foot."

Kaipo reassured him. "If your parents cannot walk, we will carry them to the boat. We are strong."

Simon grinned. He was glad to have found such great allies. "OK, let's get going," he said, feeling full of energy.

"Wait a minute," Kaipo said. "Your face is very

white apart from the red the children painted on your cheeks. You will be too easy to spot as you creep along. Here, let me rub this on." He smudged over Simon's skin with a piece of burnt wood, to darken his features as forest camouflage.

A small party returned to the river: Kaipo, Simon and two other young Indian men, the fastest and bravest of the tribe.

"Four is enough. The fewer feet we have, the less noise we will make," Kaipo remarked.

"A crack patrol," Simon smiled. "I like it."

The boat they were to travel in was a local canoe cut from a tree. It was light and manoeuvrable, but at first making headway was hard work because they had to paddle against the current. When they reached rapids they beached the canoe and carried it along the shore between them before launching it once again on the other side.

The river was murky, filled with muddy sediment washed from the land. On the riverbank mudflats they saw caiman sunbathing. Caiman are smaller cousins of the African crocodile but capable of being just as dangerous. When they heard the canoe one or two slipped into the water, disturbed by the splashes.

Eventually Kaipo steered the boat into a pool area darkened by overhanging branches.

"Are there piranha here?" Simon asked nervously. "Anaconda? Stingrays? Electric eels, perhaps?" He knew all the scariest creatures, remembering them from rainforest books he'd read as a kid.

Kaipo smiled and shook his head. "Most piranhas don't eat meat, Simon. But if there were some of the meat-eating kind, and if you were cut and bleeding...Well, they might take a bite, I suppose. Stingrays sleep in the mud, so you would have to step on one to get an injury from their poisoned sting. Electric eels? They are not common here. But the anaconda, the great river snake, is a different matter. He sleeps..."

Kaipo suddenly stopped talking. The others pulled in their paddles, and the boat began to drift.

"What is it?" Simon asked, then fell silent at a signal from Kaipo.

"There are people coming, along the riverbank," Kaipo whispered. Simon strained to hear. No, nothing. Wait a minute. Yes, there was some rustling of branches. He could hear it now.

Kaipo glanced around "Quick! Into the water!" he whispered urgently. "Go!" He pushed Simon, clearly expecting him to climb over the side of the boat. Simon hesitated.

"GO!" Kaipo whispered again, shoving harder. Simon went over with a splash surely loud enough to alert everyone nearby. He gulped a breath and submerged himself, shutting his eyes but treading water as gently as he could to stop himself sinking.

When he risked putting his head up to take another breath he saw that the Indians had swung the canoe round to block any view of him from the bank. They were also making exaggerated splashes with their paddles, mimicking the sound he'd made when he'd gone in. With luck, whoever had arrived would think the Indians were harmlessly rowing along on a fishing trip.

The water surrounding Simon was brackish,

and he suspected it might be crawling with bacteria. He was relieved when he felt a hand reach down and yank him upwards. "OK, come out now," Kaipo whispered and helped pull him onboard. "Lie down in the canoe." He motioned. "They have gone, but we should take no chances."

"Who were they?" Simon asked.

"The strangers, out hunting," Kaipo explained. "We should retreat a little and shelter somewhere safe for a while. We will pretend to fish, I think."

They moored the boat in a shady side stream. One of the Indians took out a rod made from a bamboo pole, as if he was on an innocent expedition to catch some dinner.

"Simon, you must take off your clothes," Kaipo said.

"Yeah, they're soaking. I've brought a spare set in my bag," Simon replied.

"I am thinking of the leeches," Kaipo remarked.

"Oh..." Simon shuddered. Sure enough, there were now several fat black leeches anchored to his skin, busy sucking his blood. "Yeeugh!" he cried, and felt physically sick.

"Sit still. It will be OK," Kaipo reassured him. "You must take off a leech properly or you will get an infected wound. Look for the small end of the leech. Then push it sideways with your fingernail...Like this. Flick it. See? Then flick the fat end. There...It's gone."

Simon got the hang of it, though he was left with lots of small wounds where the leeches had fixed on to him. He put on his dry clothing and tried to calm down.

"Better leeches than the old anaconda," Kaipo grinned, and Simon's calm instantly disappeared.

"Look, over there," Kaipo pointed to a soft mud bank. There was a long track in the mud. "The anaconda snake just made that track when he dragged his body into the water," Kaipo remarked nonchalantly. "He has lived here for as long as I can remember."

"Why didn't you tell me? The heaviest snake in the world was nearby! It could have crushed me to death in its coils!" Simon blurted out.

"Trust me, Simon," Kaipo chuckled. "I saw the old snake basking on the riverbank. There was a fat bulge inside his skin so I knew he had just eaten something, maybe a deer, and he wouldn't want you. Not today, anyway. By the way, your face is now streaky black and red," Kaipo chuckled. "You look twice as scary, like a bad spirit."

"Well, I'll fit right in at the Lair of the Jaguar," Simon smiled ruefully.

When they judged the coast was clear they floated the canoe back into the pool and along another sideshoot of the river. They moored it so it was well hidden under an overhanging tree, and they stepped out on land. Kaipo pointed to a thin trail leading from the water's edge into the foliage. "We will take this route to the Lair of the Jaguar. It is used by the jaguar himself when he needs to drink from the river. He has many secret ways."

The track led up a hillside, dense with jungle. Trees had once been cut down here, and that had allowed other plants to grow. Once or twice they passed large stones overgrown with moss and choking vines. Simon paused and brushed his hand across one of them, revealing a carving of a face. One of the Indians muttered darkly, and waved a feather pulled from his necklace, as if he was warding off a curse.

"This looks like Inca work," Simon whispered, amazed. It was as if his history lessons were suddenly springing to life around him. The Inca civilisation had once flourished, he'd learnt, but it was destroyed by Spanish and Portuguese invaders. The last survivors were said to have fled into the rainforest to build hidden cities. Could this be one of them? It was certainly an ideal place for a hideout and, legendary city or not, right now Simon just wanted to find his parents and get away.

Kaipo signalled for the group to stop. There were voices in the distance. The four of them crept closer, up a ridge, and from a hidden vantage point behind a ruined wall they witnessed an extraordinary scene.

It looked as if there had definitely been a city here once, or at least some kind of town. Ruined stone buildings were dotted among the foliage, some choked by vines, one or two recently cleared and renovated. In one area there was a modern aviary, recently constructed. Inside they could see the distinctive plumage of several blue macaws. Found only in the rainforest, these are amongst the rarest birds in the world. Another cage contained small monkeys, probably tamarinds and marmosets. All of them were endangered species supposed to be protected from poachers by international law, but unfortunately Simon knew they would all fetch a high price in the illegal animals trade. A truck was parked near the aviary and a few guards stood round. He didn't like what he saw. They were obviously heavily armed.

"Don't think negatively," Simon reminded himself, willing away his fear and instead focusing on a building in the centre of the area. It was the only one with a doorway that was being guarded. "I think I've found my parents," he thought, and gestured silently towards the guards. Kaipo nodded as Simon pointed to other important details he'd noticed. There were tripwires set up on pathways plus security cameras, the kind that fed a picture back to a guard looking at screens, maybe in one of the renovated buildings. It seemed the smugglers had taken no chances with security; but Simon noticed a slip-up. There was one unguarded path, narrow and neglected, with no cameras pointing towards it and no tripwires.

They were in luck.

OPERATIVE FIELD TEST 6

ADVENTURE INC.

rect medical knowledge could
ve someone's life in a
ainforest emergency. Find out
how you would cope in this quiz.
Keep a note of your answers to
check when you finish the story.

XTREME ADVENTURE QUIZ 6

1 A snake's poison is called:

a) Venom
b) Serum

2 What is the best way to remove a leech?

a) Pull hard in the middle
b) Flick the ends

3 Before you go to the rainforest, which is most important?

a) Getting jabs against disease
b) Getting your head shaved

FILE NO. MB1JAGU100 GW2003

4 Piranha fish are attracted by:

a) Perfume
b) Blood

5 What creature can pass on malaria?

a) A mosquito
b) An ant

6 Which Amazon creature is capable of biting a human?

a) Hummingbird
b) Tarantula spider

7 Which is more important for your health in the jungle?

a) Eating salt regularly
b) Eating sugar regularly

Going In

Kaipo pointed to his eyes. "We watch," he was silently suggesting, and Simon agreed. They needed to check out the place carefully, note the position and behaviour of the guards, bide their time and make their plan.

They stood motionless for what seemed like ages. Simon slipped up only once, when he sneezed, but he gave Kaipo lots of warning and Kaipo made a bird call, as perfect as the real thing, to cover up the noise of the sneeze. After a while Simon suggested, with a motion of his arm, that they retreat back towards the boat so they could speak quietly together.

"I wish I had my blowpipe," Kaipo said. "Maybe we should go back and get some."

"We'd never get close enough to use them without giving ourselves away," Simon disagreed. "Our knives will be enough, I think. I have come up with something that just might work. The two guards on the main building look like Amazon Indians. Am I right?" he asked.

"They are from another tribe," Kaipo hissed, disgusted. "They must be making money from these people. They should be ashamed."

"Well, it could help us," Simon replied, and they were soon huddling together working out their next move.

It was already about 5pm by the time they returned up the jaguar's trail. Evening light was illuminating the ancient Inca ruins that littered the jungle, throwing several carvings of jaguar faces into relief. It was stunningly beautiful, Simon thought, yet terrifying at the same time. The jungle was alive with birds and frogs calling and chirruping their evening messages. Mosquitoes were coming out, too. Simon hoped his mosquito repellent had stood up to his dunking in the river. He hadn't had time to reapply it.

Once they reached the ridge the scene was

just as they anticipated. Most of the guards were sitting around a fire near their own shelter away from the prison building. They were eating. And they were drinking, too, with luck something strong that would slow them down later. They'd left the two Indian guards still stationed at the front doorway.

Simon and the others circled round the area until they reached the unguarded path. They crept along it, keeping to its shadowy sides. Simon was amazed how the Indians in front of him moved so smoothly on their bare feet that they seemed to blend perfectly into the foliage, as if they were part of the forest itself. Beside them he felt clumsy in his boots. "I hope I don't give everyone away," he thought, and tried as hard as he could to follow their lead.

The prison came into view. The guards were lolling around, bored. All the better. Kaipo signalled to the other Indians to be prepared. He gestured towards the animal cages, and the Indians showed they were holding their knives. Then he nodded to Simon and cupped his hands to his mouth.

The scream that followed was the most

unearthly thing that Simon had ever heard, guaranteed to send anyone unprepared jumping clean out of their skin. A stranger to the jungle might have taken it for a dying monkey being attacked by a predator, but it was truly terrifying to the Indian guards who had grown up with the story of the vengeful forest spirit Caipora, the very name that Kaipo was screaming out.

"CAIPORA!"

The two guards didn't stop to think of any other possibilities. They dropped their guns and fled. Now there was a window of opportunity, just a few minutes, until the rest of the guards would be alerted. Kaipo's two Indian colleagues sprinted towards the animal cages to prize them open with their knives.

Simon bounded towards the prison doorway, covered by Kaipo holding his knife in readiness for any unwelcome visitor.

"I just hope they're in there," Simon prayed. "Mum? Dad?" he whispered.

Inside it was gloomy, damp and stinking. At first he couldn't make anything out. Then he saw two shapes hunched in a corner.

"Simon?" one of the shapes spoke and he realised it was his mum. "Simon, is that you? Have you been captured?"

"No. I've come to get you out," Simon whispered. "Can you walk?"

"Son! You came! We knew you would," his Dad spoke this time. "But we can't walk. Our hands and feet are tied up."

Simon realised with a sickening jolt that he had forgotten his own knife. He couldn't simply slice through the rope. What a mistake! Precious seconds were already slipping away. He heard parrots screeching outside. Kaipo's friends had succeeded in opening the animal cages and the captives were escaping noisily. The guards might come running at any moment.

Simon helped his parents to stand. "I am going to get you out of here," he promised.

"Can you untie us?" Dad replied.

"OK, but we don't have much time..." Simon warned. "Think, Simon, think!" he urged himself. He looked at the bonds on his parents' hands. If he could untie one person, they could help him untie the second one.

The knots were roughly tied. The captors hadn't done a very thorough job because they were armed with guns, and didn't think the couple had any chance of escaping.

Simon assessed the knots, then pulled at one of the rope ends. To his great joy it unravelled like magic.

Which knot will
untie most easily
if Simon pulls at
one end?

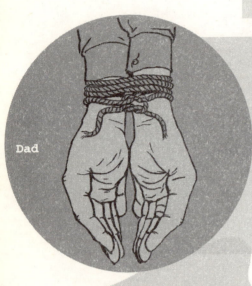

Dad

Reefknot

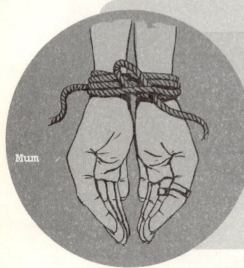

Mum

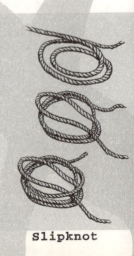

Slipknot

OPERATIVE FIELD TEST 7

What actions would help you
if you were being tied up by
a captor? Three of these tips
are real, and the rest are
false. Can you choose the
three correct actions?

XTREME ADVENTURE QUIZ 7

1 As rope is being tied round your chest
take a deep breath and puff out your chest.

2 If you are being tied around the ankles,
keep them apart by pushing your toes
together.

3 As your hands are being tied, push your
wrists apart.

4 As your ankles are being tied keep them tightly together.

5 As your hands are being tied, cross over your wrists.

6 As rope is being tied round your chest, breathe in as much as you can.

7 As your hands are being tied, hold them tightly together.

Spirit of the Forest

Simon could never quite explain just how he managed to get his parents out of that awful prison so fast, though he suspected it was a mixture of extreme effort and sheer determination on the part of everyone that saw them through in the end.

When they reached the doorway there were still no guards to be seen. The Indians had fled in terror and the others hadn't registered anything unusual about the animal noises that had been heard when the cages were opened. There were noises like that all the time in the rainforest at sunset. Most importantly, it seemed that nobody was looking at the security camera images...Not yet.

When Kaipo saw Simon emerge, he immediately ran over, knife in hand. "He is my friend! I'll explain later," Simon reassured his terrified-looking parents. Kaipo quickly used the knife to cut their remaining bonds.

"We have to run. Mum, Dad, can you manage it?" Simon asked anxiously.

Suddenly a shout signalled that at last an alarm had been raised. Someone had gone back to the security building and seen something on the camera screens.

Mayhem broke out in the camp. Guards grabbed their guns. Some ran over to the prison, where they found that the captives had disappeared. The guards regrouped.

"Which way did the prisoners go?" they demanded of the security man.

"That way. No, that way...And that way. All over the place!" he cried, unable to make sense of the camera shots on his screens.

"Spread out," someone ordered. "Get them back. Kill them if you have to. They could threaten the whole operation."

Meanwhile the Indians had fanned out. Kaipo and his friends had taken different tracks away from the camp, leaving Simon to guide his parents to the boat. Kaipo was going to double back to join them if he could. The others were going to melt into the forest and mislead the guards with a selection of tricks: thrown voices and dummy crashes in the undergrowth to send them the wrong way. As darkness fell, they hoped the search would soon have to be abandoned as hopeless.

"Are you OK? Can you make it?" Simon whispered. His parents were stumbling along the narrow trail, finding it hard to stand upright after being tied up for so long.

"Yes, yes. You've come this far. We're not going to let you down," his Mum insisted. "Lead the way!"

They moved as fast as they could back towards the boat, though Simon's dad was hobbling and gritting his teeth with pain.

"Aargh!" He suddenly clutched his ankle.

"Dad!" Simon and his mum swung round.

"Go on, go on! I'm right behind you," his dad cried, and then they saw his eyes widen in astonishment. His gaze was directed behind them on the trail.

They both turned back and saw what he was looking at. Their way was blocked by a jaguar. It stood across the path, almost close enough for them to reach out and touch. In the quickly falling dusk it looked surprisingly long and bulky, but enough light still reached through the leaves to illuminate its huge gold eyes. Its coat was subtly marked and stunningly beautiful. No wonder Inca kings and warriors of the past had worn its pelt so proudly, hoping to take on some of its strength and overpowering majesty. Simon remembered seeing pictures of Inca kings standing on their altars, the spotted fur on their backs as they were about to sacrifice human victims...

"Yaguara," Kaipo's voice whispered from behind them. He was using the Indian word. Simon wished he didn't know it meant "kills with one leap", or that the giant cat's teeth were capable of biting through a skull. It might well be feeling cornered. It could possibly have young cubs nearby to protect. If so, they were in deep trouble because in either circumstance it would attack.

Nobody spoke, and they all chose instinctively

to stay frozen to the spot, even though a guard might come running up behind them any minute, brandishing a loaded gun.

The jaguar seemed to look directly at Simon, staring unblinkingly, its eyes glowing with a natural power.

Simon felt that somehow there was communication between them, that there was a question being asked of him, even though the jaguar made no sound.

"Please, let us go," he thought, silently but pleadingly. For a moment he got the overwhelmingly strong feeling that the jaguar was looking inside him, searching into his very heart and laying bare all his motives, his reasons for living. Then it turned slowly, as if satisfied, and padded silently away into the night.

"The spirit of the forest is pleased with our work," Kaipo breathed, unable to disguise the husky note of relief mixed with fear in his voice. "The jaguar will allow us to go."

He stepped forward and put an arm round Simon's dad to support him. Simon did the same with his mum.

"The boat isn't far. Can you make it?" he asked anxiously.

"With you, yes," Mum smiled.

XTREME ADVENTURE QUIZ 8

1 Wear light-coloured clothing to blend in with the jungle background.

2 Don't step on fallen branches in case you make too much noise.

3 Move swiftly.

FILE NO. MB1JAGU100 GW2003

4 Make your approach at midday, when the guards are likely to be having lunch.

5 Wear dark-coloured clothing to blend in with the jungle background.

6 Move slowly.

7 Step on fallen branches to help keep your feet off the ground, making less noise.

Final Evidence

Simon helped Kaipo paddle the canoe away from the Lair of the Jaguar, and while they did so he explained to his parents where he and Kaipo had come from. "We are not going back to the settlement, though," he told them. "Guards may come to find us there. We will be going another way. What I really want is to get you to safety, and a comfortable hotel room, but I'm afraid that'll have to wait."

"I'm enjoying the ride!" his dad replied.

Simon felt inwardly pleased that his parents seemed so positive. It was going to make the next few days easier.

It was now dark but a trickle of moonlight fell on the river water, giving them just enough guidance to manoeuvre the canoe. It was easier this time, because they were going with the current.

When they reached a shady side channel they beached the canoe and helped Simon's parents into the forest. "We're not going far," Simon assured them, which was just as well because it was very tough to walk in the dark, even with the aid of a small torch from Simon's bag. Roots and rotting leaves made the journey tricky.

"Wait! I think I can hear someone," his mum hissed suddenly.

"Yes, you are right. You have good hearing. But don't worry; they are friends," Kaipo grinned.

They reached a clearing, where the other Indians from their party were already waiting. They had easily confused the guards back at the Lair of the Jaguar and then slipped away through the rainforest to the pre-arranged rendezvous. They'd already been busy. Hammocks were set up and a small fire was going. Something from the forest was being cooked in its ashes.

"We will have to lie low here for a few days," Simon explained to his parents. "We're guessing the smugglers' next move will be to check the Indian settlement. They won't find out anything, you can be sure of that, but they'll probably go back and search through our old camp, too. We have to stay hidden for a while. Kaipo will bring us food and water. We can have a fire at night, not in daylight, though, in case our enemies spot the smoke."

"Your planning sounds perfect," Simon's dad grinned. "To say I'm impressed is a big understatement!"

Simon hugged his parents. It was so good to see them again, and to know that he had kept part of his promise to himself.
He'd rescued them; now all he had to do was get them to safety.

"You're looking good, Simon. That's very scary warpaint. I like the streaks," his mum joked. "So tell us, what happened to the guards outside our prison?" she continued, puzzled. "We heard some kind of scream."

Simon chuckled. "Your guards were local people and when they heard Kaipo's bloodcurdling scream they thought the Caipora spirit had arrived to punish them for helping the animal smugglers," he explained. "They decided not to wait around to meet him."

While Simon and his mum tended to his dad's ankle, cut by the ropes that had bound it, his dad explained what had happened on the morning of their capture.

"We had a suspicion about what was going on; we'd seen the smugglers in the forest the day before but we didn't mention it to you because we weren't sure what to think, and we didn't want to spoil your first trip."

He smiled ruefully.

"We thought the smugglers hadn't spotted us watching, but we were wrong. They came for us early the next morning. They crept close to the shelter and one of them cut the screen. We heard something and got up, trying not to wake you in case it was just some animal snuffling round. As soon as we went outside they grabbed us."

"While I just slept on and didn't hear a thing," Simon added, ashamed.

"I'm glad you did. You were our only chance,

Simon! We quickly realised the smugglers didn't know you were there, so we kept quiet and let them take us," his mum explained. "We knew we could count on you to get help."

"You did?" Simon replied. "Hmm. After you were gone I made some bad mistakes, you know. There were times when I pretty much lost confidence in myself," he admitted, and told them about his lonely forest trek, the loss of his GPS and his capture. "I know I was in physical danger but by far the worst part was lying in the hammock, full of self-doubt," he recalled.

"Everyone loses confidence sometimes," his dad reassured him. "The point is, you battled on, got yourself back on track. Now that is impressive."

"Thanks, Dad, but I guess we've some way to go yet before this business is finished," Simon continued. "We have to stop this animal trade."

"Agreed," Dad said. "But this is a big smuggling operation. We can't end it on our own. We're going to have to get help."

"And we're going to need some sort of proof of our story, right?" Simon suggested.

"Hmm," Dad seemed less sure about that.

"This might help," Simon replied. He took out a document wallet from inside his shirt. "The guards left it at the prison entrance when they ran. Look, it's marked 'top secret'. As soon as I saw that I grabbed it."

"Simon, you are one quick-thinking operator!" his dad gasped, amazed.

Inside the wallet there was a small book with a code written in it, along with a print-out of a coded message.

"OK, let's work this out. The first one to crack it gets first go with the mosquito spray," Mum suggested.

Once they translated the code they knew they had the vital proof they needed to make the case against the smugglers.

For the next few days Simon and his parents stayed put while his mum and dad rested and grew stronger. Kaipo and his friends brought them daily food and news. The smugglers had visited the Indian settlement and were apparently convinced the Indians knew nothing.

"Maco was very good," Kaipo laughed. "He told them their camp was cursed by the jaguar, and they looked quite terrified after he'd finished shouting."

As the days and nights slipped by, Simon began to feel as if the three of them were in a cosy, safe room cradled by the rainforest around them. He and his parents talked and talked, of Kaipo and the rainforest, of the jaguar and the mysterious ruins. Yet he knew they couldn't hide for much longer and he watched his parents' health anxiously.

"We have to get out of here, Dad. Is your ankle up to it?" he asked eventually.

"Yes, it's fine, but I'd hop on one leg if I had to, to stop those smugglers," his dad replied. "I'm ready to roll," his mum agreed.

Early next morning they spoke to Kaipo. "It is time for us to go, but we'll be back with help," Simon explained.

"I know. I trust you. We're a team, remember?" Kaipo replied and bounded off into the forest. Later he returned and led them back to the water's edge, where a well-stocked canoe was waiting. They stepped on board, and with his help they let the stream take them towards the wide waters of its mother river,

the Amazon itself.

Eventually they reached a larger riverside settlement, where they said goodbye to Kaipo.

"See you later," Simon shouted.

"See you later," Kaipo agreed. "I'll be waiting for you." A few days later a river plane took them out of the rainforest and they made it back home.

It was time to call Xtreme Adventure Inc.

ADVENTURE INC.

od XTREME ADVENTURE operative
st have a sharp memory. Find
t how much you remember from
he story you have just read.
Keep a note of your answers and
check them in the final section.

XTREME ADVENTURE QUIZ 9

1 What was the name of the head man of Kaipo's tribe?

2 Which way did Simon's compass needle always point?

3 How many Amazon Indians went with Simon on the boat trip to the Lair of the Jaguar?

111

4 What kind of animal stole Simon's compass and GPS handset?

5 What were the criminals smuggling out of the rainforest?

6 What kind of boat did the Amazon Indians use on the river?

Well done. You have almost finished your training. Read the Mission Report to find out how the adventure ends...

XTREME ADVENTURE INC.

ATTACK OF THE JAGUAR:
MISSION REPORT

TOP SECRET

AUTHORISED AGENTS ONLY

MISSION REPORT:

Simon Jones and his parents returned
home with a powerful case, backed up with
decoded evidence, against the smuggling
operation they had uncovered.
XTREME ADVENTURE INC. were contacted
for our world expertise in rainforest
operations and survival. .

A message from

Situation judged URGENT.

Action taken:

The evidence was reviewed and surveillance agents put in place. The smugglers had proceeded, judging their captives to be dead or lost in the rainforest. They continued to capture animals and went ahead with a planned airlift of creatures. At this point XTREME ADVENTURE INC. went in.

RESULT:

All smugglers captured and turned over to the authorities. All smuggling equipment destroyed. All animals released.

Follow-up work:

Smugglers' business contacts found and charged. All previously kidnapped animals traced to owners and recovered.

115

SPECIAL EXTRA REPORT

Lost city:

A survey has been completed by our archaeology operatives. They confirm it is an Inca site, previously unrecorded. It contains certain rare Inca treasures related to a jaguar cult.

Recommended action:

To keep location secret to preserve the rainforest environment and ecology. Monitor the area regularly to ensure it remains undisturbed.

AGENT REPORT: SIMON JONES

Simon Jones was recommended as ideal material for XTREME ADVENTURE INC. training. He showed ingenuity, bravery, sharp thinking and the ability to overcome difficulties, not least his own doubts. He showed sensitivity to others, and good language skills.

Mistakes made: Did not pack equipment up at night. Forgot knife at crucial moment.

Recommendation: During training concentrate on equipment-handling.

Update: Following training S. Jones has become an outstanding operative.

Location: Worldwide capabilities.

Codename: Jaguar.

Alias: Plant scientist.

117

AGENT REPORT: KAIPO

Kaipo was recommended as ideal material for XTREME ADVENTURE INC. training. He showed outstanding knowledge of the rainforest. He was calm under pressure, quick-thinking and has exceptional language skills. He has useful expertise in plant and animal poisons.

Mistakes made: Attacked and subdued the wrong target.

Recommendation: During training concentrate on surveillance skills.

Update: Following training, Kaipo is an excellent operative in the field.

Location speciality: South America.

Codename: Caipora.

Alias: Amazon Indian trader.

YOUR AGENT REPORT

Did you pass the tests as well as Simon and
Kaipo? Score your answers to the puzzles and
quizzes. Then take the ultimate **ELITE SQUAD**
Amazon test before you finish.

<u>Operative Field Test 1</u> (page 16)

Score 1 per clue.
* A can has fallen. * There is a broken stick.
* There is a broken leaf on the far right. * The hat is on the ground. *The screen has been damaged.

Quiz 1 Score 1 for each correct answer.

1 b) South America **2** c) River **3** b) A huge tropical rainforest **4** c) Rains **5** a) Mosquito net **6** b) Always warm

<u>Operative Field Test 2</u> (page 28)

Score 2 for the correct answer.
Simon should take the path to the north-east. His mother's handkerchief is the furthest object dropped, and is some way along this path.

Quiz 2 Score 1 for each correct answer.

1 c) Compass. It will help you navigate. A mobile phone won't work. Wellington boots will be uncomfortable and damp.
2 b) Packets of food will help keep you alive. Swimming kit and deodorant stick are unnecessary.
3 b) A spare set of clothes. Your clothes will get damp every day in the humid heat. A

hairbrush and Game Boy are unnecessary.
4 b) A penknife may be useful for many things.
A dressing gown and pillow are luxuries.
5 c) A medical kit is vital. Sandals will be
useless. The water is too muddy for a diving
mask.
6 c) Insect repellent is vital. A guidebook is a
luxury. A credit card is useless in the jungle.
7 a) A water bottle is vital. An alarm clock is
unnecessary. A ball of string would be useful,
but not as vital as a water bottle.
8 c) A torch would be useful at night. A
sweater would be useless. A camera would
be a luxury.

Operative Field Test 3 (page 40)

Score 1 for each clue.

* There are identically patterned tyre tracks
going both ways. * There is an oil leak, which
would have been washed away unless it was
recent. * There are splashes from a puddle
still on the leaves.

Quiz 3 Score 1 for each correct
answer.
1 a) Sloth **2** b) Vampire bat **3** b) Spots
4 a) Stun prey **5** a) Monkeys **6** a) Troupe

Operative Field Test 4 (page 52)

Score 4 for the message.
THE LAIR OF THE JAGUAR

Quiz 4 Score 1 for each correct answer.
1 a) Go downstream. You are more likely to reach a bigger river and so find people. **2** b) Travel by day. Travelling by night is dangerous. **3** a) Drink lots of water. You will lose lots by sweating every day. **4** b) Sleep in a hammock safe from creepy-crawlies and damp. **5** a) Eat cooked food. Raw food could be covered in germs. **6** a) Cover up so you get fewer scratches and bites. **7** a) Drink purified water to avoid disease.

Operative Field Test 5 (page 64)

Score 2 for the location.
The X is up a stream that is opposite the left-hand hill topped with an old ruin.

QUIZ 5 Score 1 for each correct answer.
1 a) True. They make body paint from plants.
2 b) False. They make their own jewellery.
3 b) False. They live in communal huts.
4 a) True. They dip arrows in poison.
5 b) False. They gather food from the forest.
6 b) False. They go barefoot.
7 a) True. They believe in forest spirits.

Operative Field Test 6 (page 78)

Score 2 for the correct path.
Path **d** is unguarded, with no cameras
or tripwires.

QUIZ 6 Score 1 for each correct
answer.
1 a) Venom **2** b) Flick the ends **3** a) Jabs are
vital to acquire disease immunity **4** b) Blood
5 a) Mosquito **6** b) Tarantula spider **7** a) Eating
salt regularly is vital, as you lose lots by sweating
in a hot climate. Without enough, you would
become seriously ill.

Operative Field Test 7 (page 88)

Score 2 for the correct answer.
Mum's knot would untie the most easily.

QUIZ 7 Score 1 for each correct
answer.
1 Breathe out.
2 Push your ankles apart.
3 Push your wrists apart.
These techniques would give you extra room
when you relaxed after being tied, making it
easier to slip out of the rope.

Operative Field Test 8 (page 98)

Score 3 for the correct answer.
Route C is correct because it shows the print of footwear, not worn by any of the Indians. **Route A** was taken by one of the Indians, who dropped a feather. **Route B** was taken by an Indian, who left a bare footprint. **Route D** was taken by an Indian who left an arrow behind.

QUIZ 8 Score 1 for each correct answer.

2 Don't stand on fallen branches. They may be rotten and so break noisily.
5 Wear dark-coloured clothes to blend in with jungle shadows.
6 Move slowly. You will make less noise.

Operative Field Test 9 (page 110)

Score 4 for correct message.
The message reads: CONFIRM ANIMALS TO BE FLOWN OUT ON LAST DAY OF NEXT MONTH

QUIZ 9 Score 1 for each correct answer.
1 Maco **2** Compass needles point north **3** Simon had three companions **4** A monkey stole Simon's stuff **5** The criminals were smuggling rare animals **6** A canoe

A message from

XTREME ADVENTURE INC.

Total up your score from a possible 80

Score of 1-30

You need to brush up your skills. Better luck next time.

Score of 31-50

You nearly qualified, but not quite. Try another XTREME ADVENTURE.

Score of 51-80

You are definitely good enough to join XTREME ADVENTURE INC. Well done!

Welcome to:
XTREME ADVENTURE INC

Now you are ready to take:
THE ELITE SQUAD
AMAZON TEST

Somewhere in the pictures of this book we have hidden the following animals. Find them all to join our ELITE SQUAD, used for top missions.

Two Monkeys
One Tree Snake
Three Bats
Two Ants
Two River Dolphins
One Hummingbird
Three Frogs
One Mantis
One Sloth
One Macaw
One Ground Snake
One Butterfly
One Spider
A mystery pair of shining eyes

Good luck, and we'll see you on the next adventure...

A holiday in Egypt suddenly becomes dangerous for Tom and his big stepbrother Zak. What is the secret of the Scorpion? Who abandoned them in the sweltering desert? What exactly is hiding inside the Scorpion Tomb? Join in the action and check out your own survival skills in the next exciting XTREME ADVENTURE INC. title:

The Scorpion Secret

Spondon Springfield Primary School
West Road, Spondon,
Derby   DE2 7AB.
Headteacher: R. J. C. Wardle
Tel: Derby 673846